Red Hat® Linux® 7
fast&easy™

Send Us Your Comments

To comment on this book or any other Prima Tech title, visit our reader response page on the Web at **www.prima-tech.com/comments**.

How to Order

For information on quantity discounts, contact the publisher: Prima Publishing, P.O. Box 1260BK, Rocklin, CA 95677-1260; (916)787-7000. On your letterhead, include information concerning the intended use of the books and the number of books you wish to purchase.

Red Hat® Linux® 7
fast&easy™

Brian Proffitt

PRIMA TECH

A DIVISION OF PRIMA PUBLISHING

©2000 by Prima Publishing. All rights reserved. No part of this book may be reproduced or transmitted in any form or by any means, electronic or mechanical, including photocopying, recording, or by any information storage or retrieval system without written permission from Prima Publishing, except for the inclusion of brief quotations in a review.

A Division of Prima Publishing

Prima Publishing and colophon are registered trademarks of Prima Communications, Inc. PRIMA TECH and Fast & Easy are trademarks of Prima Communications, Inc., Roseville, California 95661.

Publisher: Stacy L. Hiquet
Marketing Manager: Judi Taylor
Associate Marketing Manager: Heather Buzzingham
Managing Editor: Sandy Doell
Acquisitions Editor: Kim Spilker
Cover Design: Prima Design Team
Project Management: Echelon Editorial & Production Services
Project Editor: Joell Smith
Technical Reviewer: Laine V. Campbell
Copy Editor: Karen Oliver
Interior Layout: Regina Rexrode
Indexer: Grant Munroe
Proofreader: C. Michael Woodward

Important: Prima Publishing cannot provide software support. Please contact the appropriate software manufacturer's technical support line or Web site for assistance.

Prima Publishing and the author have attempted throughout this book to distinguish proprietary trademarks from descriptive terms by following the capitalization style used by the manufacturer.

Information contained in this book has been obtained by Prima Publishing from sources believed to be reliable. However, because of the possibility of human or mechanical error by our sources, Prima Publishing, or others, the Publisher does not guarantee the accuracy, adequacy, or completeness of any information and is not responsible for any errors or omissions or the results obtained from use of such information. Readers should be particularly aware of the fact that the Internet is an ever-changing entity. Some facts may have changed since this book went to press.

ISBN: 0-7615-2679-x
Library of Congress Catalog Card Number: 00-108121
Printed in the United States of America

00 01 02 03 04 DD 10 9 8 7 6 5 4 3 2

"The most incomprehensible thing about the universe is that it is comprehensible."

-A. Einstein

Acknowledgments

It has been just about a year since I started writing about Linux full-time, and boy have I learned a lot! Mostly I learned how much I *didn't* know when I started!

This just emphasizes the amount of team effort that goes into these books. Without my editors, friends, and family, you would not be holding this book in your hands, and I would like to thank them all profusely, even the editor I recruited in the YMCA swimming pool.

As always, my family gets big thanks while I huddled away in the inner sanctum taking screenshots until the wee hours of the morning discoursing on all things Linux when I came out of my hidey-hole for food.

I hope you like what you have in your hands. Thanks for checking it out!

About the Author

Brian Proffitt lives and works deep in the booming metropolis known as Indianapolis, where three times a year race fans swoop in and drive like maniacs—in RVs, no less. Otherwise, a nice place to live. When he's not writing, Brian loves being a dad and husband.

In his very limited spare time, Brian does some swooping of his own as a soloing student pilot, trying to get his private pilot's license before it starts snowing. Which in Indiana means October.

Contents at a Glance

Introduction xvii

PART I
GETTING STARTED WITH LINUX 1

Chapter 1	Discovering Linux 3
Chapter 2	Working with Program Windows 27
Chapter 3	Moving around Your Desktop 41
Chapter 4	Customizing the Screen Display 53
Chapter 5	Managing Your Destktop 75

PART II
USING THE FILE SYSTEM 93

Chapter 6	Exploring the File System 95
Chapter 7	Organizing the File System 113
Chapter 8	Managing in a Multi-User Environment 129
Chapter 9	Maintaining Your Linux 149

PART III
MAKING LINUX WORK FOR YOU 171

Chapter 10	Working with Files. 173
Chapter 11	Working in the Console. 183
Chapter 12	Getting Organized Using Linux. 195
Chapter 13	Printing Files 217
Chapter 14	Sounding Off with Your Computer 225

PART IV
TUNING UP YOUR LINUX 243

Chapter 15	Adding Applications to Your Linux 245
Chapter 16	Getting On the Internet 255
Chapter 17	Surfing the Web. 263

PART V
APPENDIX 243

| Appendix A | Installing Linux. . . . . 285 |

Glossary. 301

Index 309

Contents

Introduction xvii

PART I
GETTING STARTED WITH LINUX 1

Chapter 1   Discovering Linux 3
Starting Linux for the First Time 4
    Starting X Window 4
    Creating a New User 6
Exploring Gnome 9
    Understanding Desktop Elements 9
    Starting Programs from the Main Menu Button 11
    Using Buttons, Menus, and Dialog Boxes 11
Exploring KDE 15
    Understanding Desktop Elements 15
    Starting Programs from the Application Starter 17
Getting Help 18
    Getting Help on the Desktop 18
    Finding Help Files in Applications 23

Chapter 2   Working with Program Windows. 27
Opening Program Windows 28
    Displaying a Program Window 28
    Making Windows Animate When Opened 30

	Resizing a Window 32
	Using the Maximize Button 32
	Using the Mouse 33
	Shading and Iconifying Windows 35
	Moving a Window around the Screen 38
	Closing a Program Window 39

Chapter 3 Moving around Your Desktop 41

Working with Multiple Windows 42
    Finding a Few Applications to Open 42
    Cleaning Up Your Desktop with Shading 44
Creating Virtual Desktop Areas 46
    Understanding the Gnome Pager 46
    Making Workspaces and Virtual Desktops 48
Working with Virtual Desktops and Workspaces 49
    Pushing Windows off a Desktop 49
    Moving Between Workspaces 51
    Searching for Lost Applications 52

Chapter 4 Customizing the Screen Display 53

Changing the Desktop Background 54
    Using a Solid Color Background 54
    Creating a Gradient Background 57
    Selecting a Wallpaper 60
Setting Up a Screen Saver 64
Working with Themes 66
    Selecting a Window Theme 67
    Choosing an Interface Theme 68
Changing the Screen Resolution 68

Chapter 5 Managing Your Desktop 75

Working with Applets on the Gnome Panel 76
    Entertaining from the Gnome Panel 76
    Playing Your CDs 77

CONTENTS

  Moving Applets around on the Gnome Panel 79
  Removing Applets from the Gnome Panel 80
 Using Application Launchers 80
  Adding a Launcher to the Gnome Panel 80
  Changing the Launcher Icon 82
  Deleting Launchers 84
 Adding Drawers to the Gnome Panel 85
  Creating the Drawer 85
  Filling up the Drawer 87
  Creating a Drawer from the Main Menu 89
 Changing Launcher and Drawer Icon Backgrounds 90
 Part I Review Questions 92

PART II
USING THE FILE SYSTEM 93

Chapter 6   **Exploring the File System** 95
 Opening the File System 96
  Looking at File Manager 96
  Understanding the Linux File System 98
 Browsing the File System 100
 Selecting Files 103
  Using the Mouse 104
  Using Selection Criteria 106
 Sorting the File List 107
  Reordering the File List 107
  Filtering the File List 109

Chapter 7   **Organizing the Filing System.** 113
 Creating Directories 114
 Copying and Moving Files 116
  Using Drag and Drop 116
  Using a Control Menu 118
 Renaming Files 122
 Removing Files and Directories 123

CONTENTS

Deleting Files 123
Working with Confirmation Dialog Boxes 123
Finding Files in Your Home Directory 125
Working with Files on Your Desktop 126
    Moving a File to the Desktop 127
    Opening a File 127

Chapter 8   **Managing in a Multi-User Environment 129**
Working with User Accounts 130
    Creating a New User Account 130
    Editing a User Account 133
Allowing Users to Change Their Password 140
Forming Groups 142
    Creating a Group 143
    Assigning Users to a Group 144
Sharing Files with a Group 146
    Setting File Permissions 146

Chapter 9   **Maintaining Your Linux 149**
Finding System Information 150
Mounting a Floppy Disk Drive 153
    Creating a Linux Floppy Drive 153
    Creating a DOS Floppy Drive 157
    Mounting the Floppy Drive in the User Account .. 162
    Browsing the Floppy Drive 164
Preparing a Boot Disk 165
Checking for Available Disk Space 166
Resetting the Clock 167
Part II Review Questions 169

PART III
MAKING LINUX WORK FOR YOU 171

Chapter 10	Working with Files 173
	Creating a New File 174
	Working with Text 176
	Selecting Text 176
	Copying and Deleting Text 177
	Saving a File 179
	Closing a File 181
	Opening an Existing File 182

Chapter 11	Working in the Console 183
	Entering Console Mode 184
	Managing Directories 185
	Changing Directories 185
	Making Directories 189
	Removing Directories 190
	Managing Files 190
	Copying Files 190
	Moving Files 192
	Renaming Files 193
	Deleting Files 193

Chapter 12	Getting Organized Using Linux 195
	Adding It up with the Calculator 196
	Turning on the Calculator 196
	Performing Simple Math Calculations 197
	Keeping Track of Important Dates 200
	Starting the Calendar 200
	Changing the Time View 201
	Adding an Appointment 202
	Maintaining an Address Book 207
	Opening the Address Book 207
	Adding an Address 208

	Updating Address Information 211
	Sorting Addresses 212
	Adding Column Headings 213
Chapter 13	**Printing Files** **217**
	Configuring a Local Printer 218
	Setting Up the Printer 218
	Testing the Printer 222
	Printing Files 223
Chapter 14	**Sounding Off with Your Computer** **225**
	Configuring Your Sound Card 226
	Setting System Sounds 231
	Changing the Keyboard Bell 231
	Changing Sound Events 233
	Tuning Up with the CD Player 236
	Starting the CD Player 236
	Playing Music CDs 237
	Keeping a Play List for Your Favorite CDs 239
	Part III Review Questions 241

PART IV
TUNING UP YOUR LINUX 243

Chapter 15	**Adding Applications to Your Linux** **245**
	Starting the Gnome RPM 246
	Verifying Installed Packages 247
	Installing a Package 249
	Installing from the PowerTools CD 250
	Installing from Third-Party RPMs 251
Chapter 16	**Getting On the Internet** **255**
	Creating the Connection 256
	Setting Up a PPP Connection 256
	Connecting to Your ISP 260

Chapter 17 Surfing the Web 263

Using the Netscape Navigator Web Browser 264
    Accessing Web Pages 264
    Changing Your Home Page 267
    Keeping a List of Often Visited Web Sites 268
Setting Up E-mail and News Accounts 272
Managing E-mail 276
    Receiving Messages 276
    Sending Messages 278
Lurking through the Newsgroups 279
    Subscribing to Newsgroups 279
    Reading Newsgroup Messages 281
Part VI Review Questions 282

PART V APPENDIX 283

Appendix A Installing Linux 285

Understanding Your Installation Options 286
Getting Ready 287
Determining Your System Devices 288
Loading the Linux Operating System 291

Glossary 301
Index 309

Introduction

This *Fast & Easy* series guide from Prima Tech will help you to quickly gain an understanding of the Red Hat Linux 7 operating system and use it to your best advantage. You'll learn about Gnome and KDE, the graphical user interfaces that make it easy for you to configure your computer and use the Linux features and programs. The built-in desktop tools and applications work together with standard conventions to allow applications to cooperate with each other.

This book will help you quickly install Red Hat Linux 7 and navigate your way through the maze of tasks associated with learning a new operating system and show you how to make Red Hat Linux 7 a friendly and exciting new addition to your computing world. In an easy step-by-step fashion, this *Fast & Easy* guide will get you up and running with Red Hat Linux 7 in no time.

Who Should Read This Book?

As you thumb through this book, you'll find that it is filled with easy-to-follow directions and illustrations that show you what you'll see on your screen as you progress through the directions. This book is the perfect tool for those who are familiar with other computer operating systems and want to get up to speed with Red Hat Linux 7 and the Gnome graphical user interface, which is the primary interface used in this book. You may need to read all of the individual chapters in a particular section of the book to master its subject matter, or you may only need to read certain chapters to fill any gaps in your existing knowledge. This book is structured to support the method that suits you best.

It should be noted that while this book does examine some of the functionality of the Linux command line, it does concentrate mostly on the graphic interface aspects of Red Hat Linux 7. Readers who might want more in-depth on the command-line interface may wish to read another book in the Prima Linux Series.

Red Hat Linux 7 Fast & Easy also makes a great reference tool. As you work with Red Hat Linux and learn new things, you may sometimes need a quick reminder about how to perform a specific task. You can easily and quickly refer to those things in this book.

Helpful Hints to Increase Your Skills

Included in this book are additional elements that will provide you with more information on how to work with Red Hat Linux 7 and the graphical user interface without encumbering your progress:

- Tips offer shortcuts for various Linux and Gnome features, to make your job a little easier.
- Notes offer additional information about a feature or advice on how to use the feature.

The appendix shows you how to install Red Hat Linux 7 on a PC in step-by step fashion!

Have fun with this *Fast & Easy* guide. It's the quickest and simplest way to get started with the Linux operating system.

PART I

Getting Started with Linux

Chapter 1
  Discovering Linux. 3

Chapter 2
  Working with Program Windows 27

Chapter 3
  Moving around Your Desktop 41

Chapter 4
  Customizing the Screen Display 53

Chapter 5
  Managing Your Desktop 75

1
Discovering Linux

Congratulations! You've decided to take the plunge and give Linux a try. Some things that will make your life a lot easier are the Gnome and KDE user interfaces. These interfaces, also known as desktop environments, make it easier for you to become familiar with this new operating system. Gnome and KDE use graphical elements such as icons and menus to open applications, perform tasks, and navigate around the screen. Before you begin, take the time to create a user account. Then you can explore Gnome or KDE. In this chapter, you'll learn how to:

- Start the Linux operating system and Gnome or KDE
- Create a user account for your daily Linux activities
- Use the different Gnome and KDE screen elements
- Find additional help
- Exit Linux

Starting Linux for the First Time

When you installed Linux on your computer (if you haven't yet installed Linux, see the appendix in the back of this book), the installation creates at least one password. Anyone with this installation password can log in as the superuser, using **root** as the user ID, and have access to the entire operating system. Using the root account all of the time is dangerous, because it is too easy for root to make major changes to your system. If the root user makes a mistake, it could be costly. The person in charge of the computer should set up a user account for each person who will be using the system. Then, each user can use Linux according to their personal preferences without upsetting the important Linux system files.

Starting X Window

When you installed Linux, you were given the option to start the X Window graphical interface (also called "X") when your computer reboots. If you selected this option, you'll automatically see the graphical interface on your screen. If you decided not to start X automatically, or if there was a problem during the X configuration process, you'll see the localhost login prompt. This is called the Linux console, and it is your cue that Linux is ready for you to begin.

> **NOTE**
> If X starts, you will see the graphical login on your screen. Skip steps 1 through 3 and begin this task on Step 4.

> **CAUTION**
> If I haven't emphasized this enough, be careful when you are logged into the system as root. The root user account has total access to the entire Linux operating system. You'll have great power, which can be used to create or destroy.

STARTING LINUX FOR THE FIRST TIME 5

```
Red Hat Release 7.0.1 (Winston)
Kernel 2.2.16-8 on an i586

localhost login: root
Password:
```

1. Type root at the localhost login prompt and **press** the **Enter** key. The Password prompt will appear.

2. Type the **password** that you chose during the installation process and **press** the **Enter** key. A message will appear showing when you last logged into your Linux system and the [root@localhost /root]# prompt will display.

```
Red Hat Release 7.0.1 (Winston)
Kernel 2.2.16-8 on an i586

localhost login: root
Password:
Last login: Fri Sep 29 08:23:13 on :0
[root@localhost /root]# startx_
```

3. Type the command **startx**. Then **press** the **Enter key**. The X Window interface will appear on your screen.

4. Type root at the Login prompt and **press** the **Enter key**. The Password prompt will appear.

5. Type the **password** that you chose during installation and **press** the **Enter key**. The X Window interface will appear on your screen.

Creating a New User

This section will show you how to use a terminal window (which emulates this console within X) so that you can create a user account for yourself. We're going to assume, for now, that you selected Gnome as your desktop environment.

STARTING LINUX FOR THE FIRST TIME 7

Creating a user account is done from the root account. You'll only want to use this root account to perform system administration and maintenance. Your regular user account is where you should be working with Gnome, KDE, and other applications.

1. **Click** on the **Gnome Terminal emulation program button** on the Gnome Panel. The Gnome Terminal window will open.

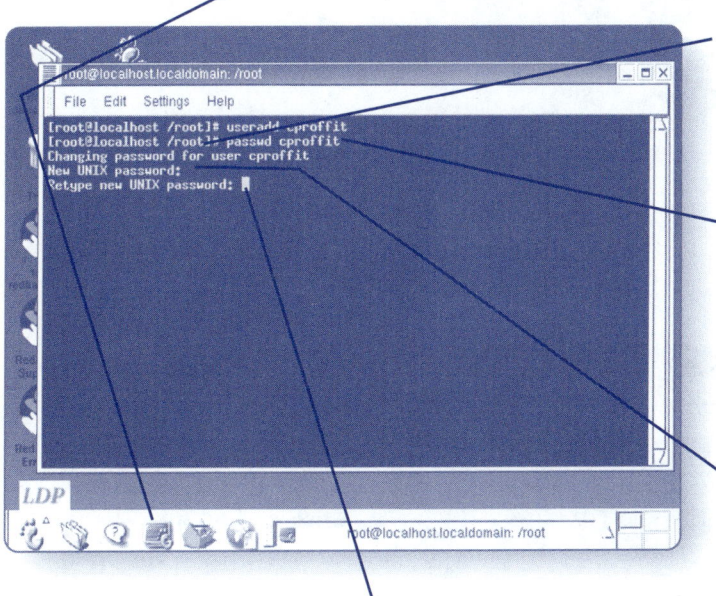

2. **Type** the command **useradd**, a **space**, and a **user name** for yourself. Then **press** the **Enter key**.

3. **Type** the command **passwd**, a **space**, and the **user name** you created in step 2 and then **press** the **Enter key**. The New UNIX password prompt will appear on the next line.

4. **Type** a **password** and **press** the **Enter key**. The Retype new UNIX password prompt will appear.

5. **Retype** the **password** from step 4 and **press** the **Enter key**. You'll be returned to the root prompt. You'll see a note that the password authentication was successful.

> **NOTE**
> Use a password that is not based on any word you might find in a dictionary—they are easy to crack. Red Hat will warn you if your password is too easy to figure out.

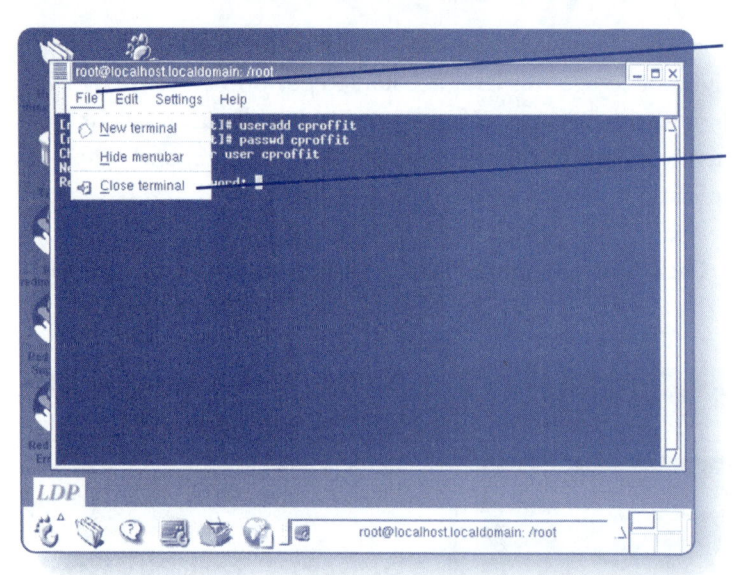

6. Click on **File**. The File menu will appear.

7. Click on **Close terminal**. The Gnome Terminal window will close.

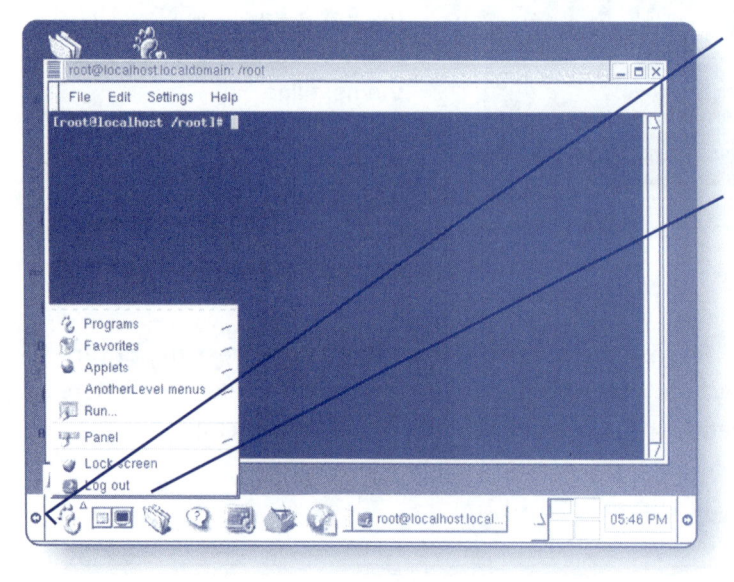

8. Click on the **Main Menu button**. The Main Menu will appear.

9. Click on **Log out**. The Really log out dialog box will open.

10. Click on the **Yes button**. The Gnome desktop environment will close and the graphical login will appear.

11. Type the new **user name** and **password** that you just created. Now you're ready to start Gnome as a regular user.

Exploring Gnome

When Gnome appears on your screen, you'll see some familiar icons and windows from the Windows and Macintosh operating systems, but some things may look different.

Understanding Desktop Elements

Like every graphical interface, Gnome has a ubiquitous set of controls for users to manipulate their work onscreen.

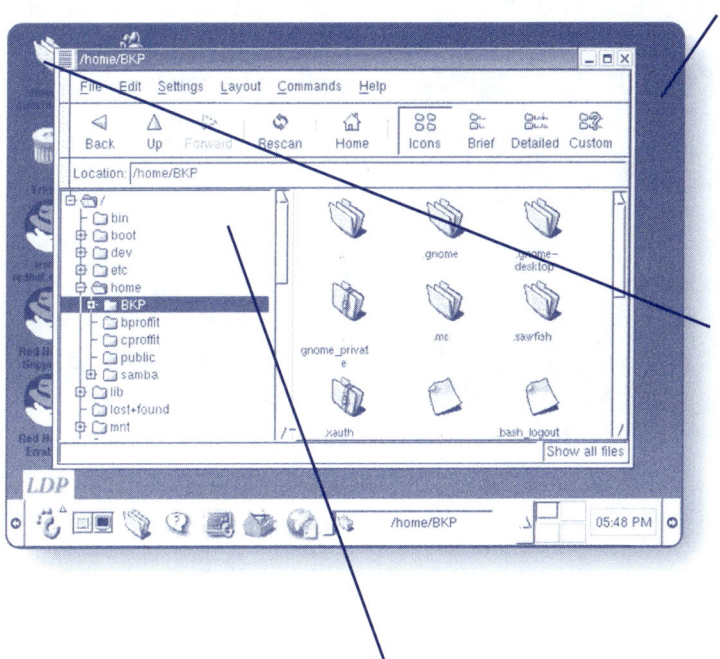

- The desktop is the background for all of the elements you see on your screen. You'll learn how to change the desktop background in Chapter 4, "Customizing the Screen Display".

- Desktop icons are called Launchers. Launchers open applications, files, or directories quickly. You can place icons on your desktop for those programs and files you use frequently. You will learn more about this in Chapter 4.

- Windows are framed areas that contain menus, buttons, and scroll bars. Applications and files appear inside windows. You'll find out how to resize a window in Chapter 2, "Working with Program Windows". Find out how to work with several windows at one time in Chapter 3, "Moving around Your Desktop".

The Gnome Panel resides at the bottom of your screen. The Gnome Panel contains the Main Menu button, a number of panel applets, and the Gnome Pager.

- The Main Menu button opens a menu of all the applications, utilities, and actions you can perform with Gnome. To display the menu, click on the Main Menu button (it's the foot at the far left). To close the menu, click on the Main Menu button a second time or click on an empty area of the desktop.

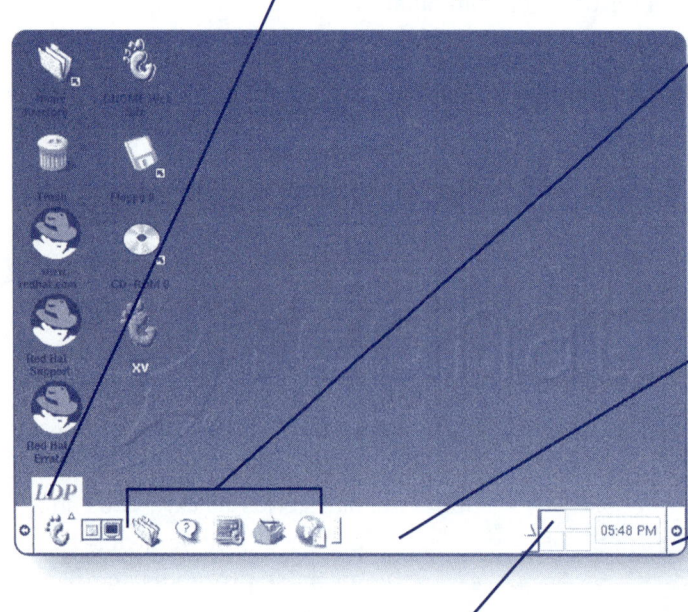

- Panel applets are small programs that can be started easily by clicking on the applet icon. You can add and delete applets from the panel. Learn how to do this in Chapter 4, "Customizing the Screen Display".

- The Pager displays all open tasks or applications currently running on the displayed desktop.

- At each end of the Gnome Panel are the pixmap arrows. These arrows, when clicked, hide and display the Gnome Panel.

- The Desk Guide shows you which applications and files are open on your computer and where they are located on the virtual desktops. You'll learn more about the Gnome Pager and virtual desktops in Chapter 3, "Moving around Your Desktop".

Starting Programs from the Main Menu Button

Now it's time to take a look at some of your software applications and get a quick overview of how to use the common window interface elements. The next few sections will show you how to use the basic elements of a Linux application by using the Gnome Calendar.

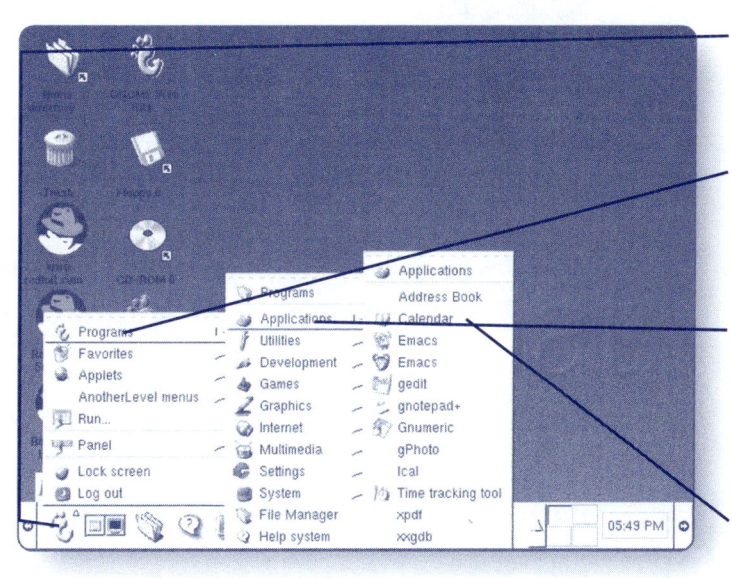

1. Click on the **Main Menu button**. The Main Menu will appear.

2. Move the **mouse pointer** over the Programs menu item. The Programs menu will appear.

3. Move the **mouse pointer** over the Applications menu item. The Applications menu will appear.

4. Click on the **Calendar** option. The application window will open on your screen.

Using Buttons, Menus, and Dialog Boxes

You've successfully opened a Linux application and now you're ready to see how it works. Program windows contain elements such as menus, command buttons, resize buttons, and a host of other elements. Take some time to explore the different menus to see what is available. This section will show you how to use buttons and menus to execute commands.

CHAPTER 1: DISCOVERING LINUX

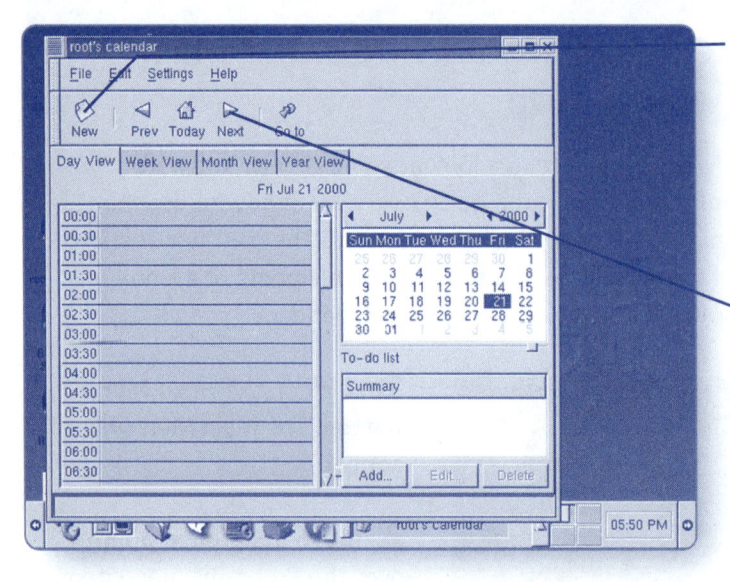

1. Place the **mouse pointer** over a button on the toolbar. The button will be highlighted and a tip will open telling you what function the button performs.

2. Click on a **button**. The command associated with the button will be executed. The command may be executed automatically or a dialog box will open allowing you to make choices about the command you wish to execute.

NOTE
If you've opened a dialog box, click on the Close button. The dialog box will close and any choices you made in the dialog box will be ignored

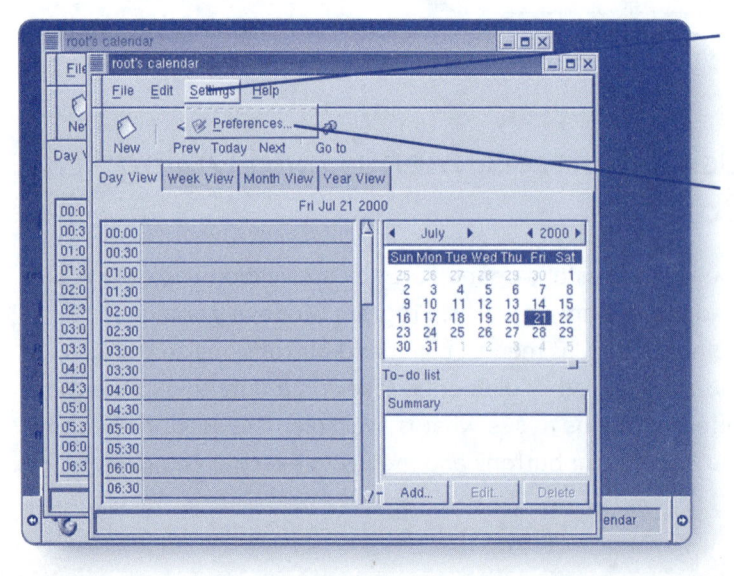

3. Click on a **menu item** to open a menu. A list of menu commands will appear.

4. Click on a **command**. A dialog box will open or a function will be performed.

EXPLORING GNOME   13

Dialog boxes contain buttons that display secondary dialog boxes, buttons that let you select options, lists that let you select a number of predefined options, and tabs that group several dialog boxes into one.

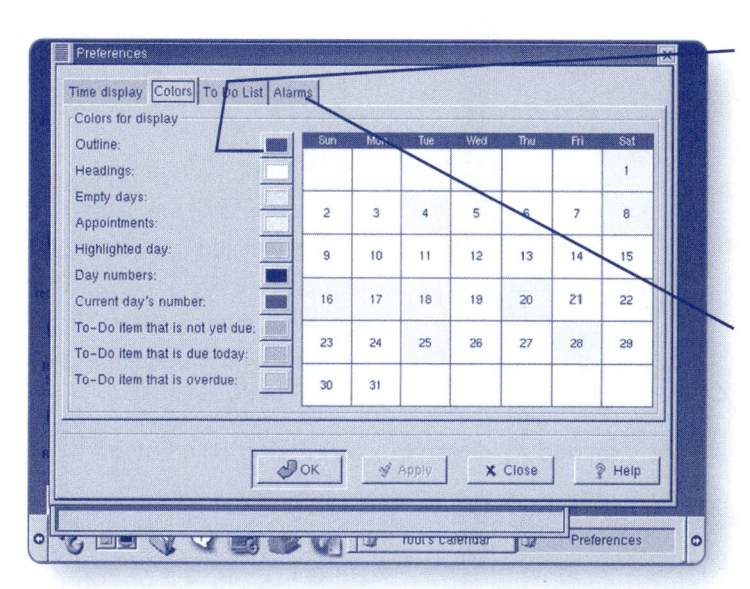

- Open applets from which you can perform a task or make a selection by clicking on the down arrow within the dialog box. The choice you make will appear in the text box next to the down arrow.

- Find more options by clicking on a tab.

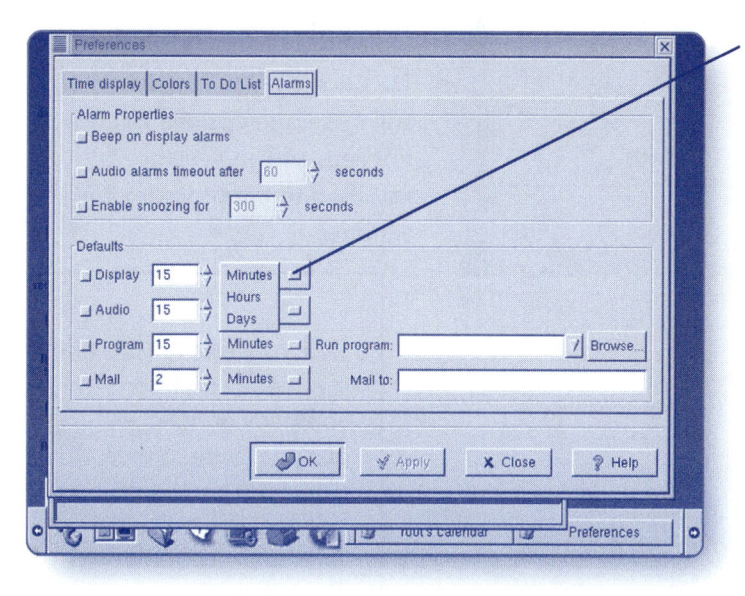

- Open drop-down lists by clicking on the list button to display a list of options, and then click on the option you want. The choice you make will appear in the text box.

14 CHAPTER 1: DISCOVERING LINUX

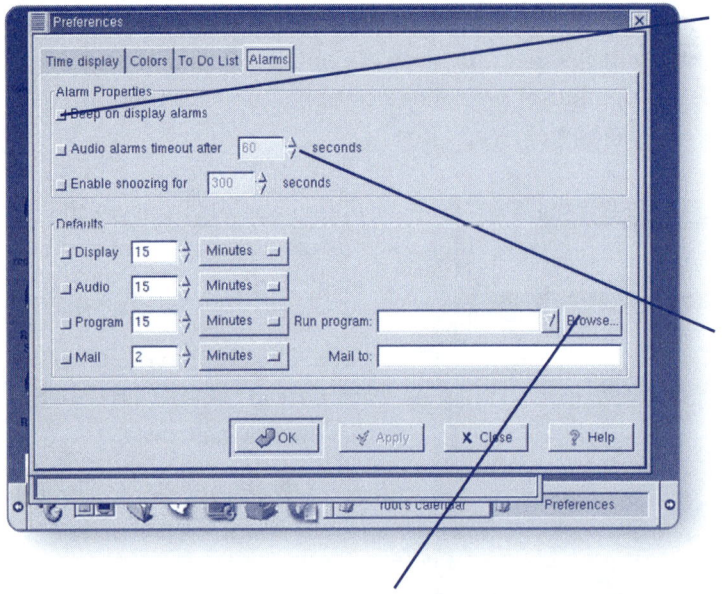

- Turn features on and off by clicking on the selection box next to the feature name. The selection box will become recessed when the feature is turned on. The selection box is raised when the feature is turned off.

- Adjust numbers by clicking on the up and down arrows, which are called spin controls. The up arrow will increase the number in the text box. The down arrow will decrease the number in the text box.

- Access a secondary dialog box by clicking on a button.

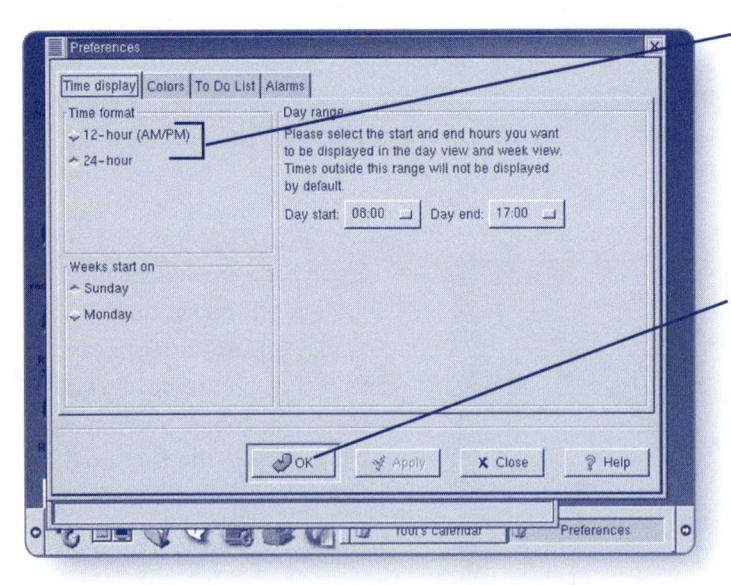

- Select one of a group of options by clicking on the option button. The option button will become recessed when the option is selected. Option buttons that are raised are not selected.

5. Click on **OK**. The dialog box will close, the options will be applied, and you will be returned to the program window.

> **TIP**
> Click on Close or Cancel if you don't wish to apply any of the changes you made to the dialog box or you decide that you no longer want to execute the command.

EXPLORING GNOME 15

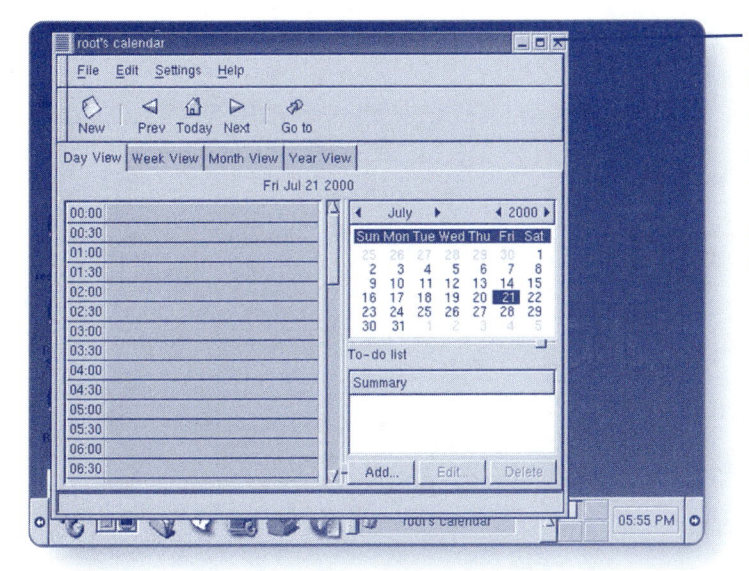

6. Click on the **Kill button** at the top right of the program window when you are finished working with the application. The application will close and you will be returned to the Gnome interface.

NOTE
If a window refuses to close, right-click on the Kill button and a pop-up menu will appear from which you can select Destroy. The Destroy option is the ultimate utility to stop applications that are stuck.

Exploring KDE

KDE (which stands for the K Desktop Environment), is a lot like Gnome, in that it too has menus, dialog boxes, and windows. Red Hat Linux 7 ships with KDE as well as Gnome. There are some subtle differences, mostly in the descriptions of the KDE environment, not in the behavior.

Understanding Desktop Elements

In Gnome, you had a pretty easy time getting around the desktop. You will find a lot of familiar controls in KDE, though they may not have the same names.

CHAPTER 1: DISCOVERING LINUX

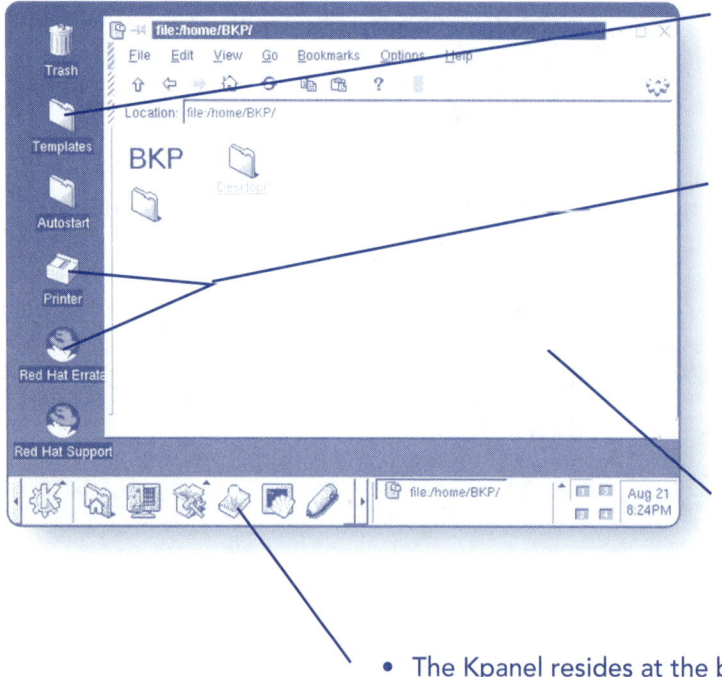

- The desktop is the background for all of the elements you see on your screen.

- Desktop icons are called Nicknames in KDE. As in Gnome, nicknames open applications, files, or directories quickly. You can place icons on your desktop for those programs and files you use frequently.

- Windows are framed areas that contain menus, buttons, and scroll bars, just like other graphic interfaces.

- The Kpanel resides at the bottom of your screen. The Kpanel contains the Application Starter button, a number of panel applets, and the desktop manager.

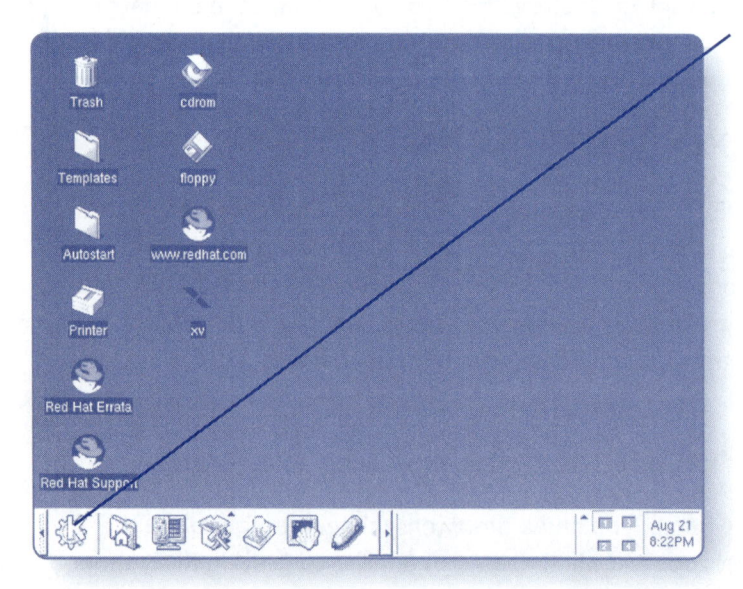

- The Application Starter button opens a menu of all the applications, utilities, and actions you can perform with KDE. To display the menu, click on the Application Starter button. To close the menu, click on the Application Starter button a second time or click on an empty area of the desktop.

EXPLORING KDE   17

- The icon bar contains small programs that can be started easily by clicking on the, er, icon.

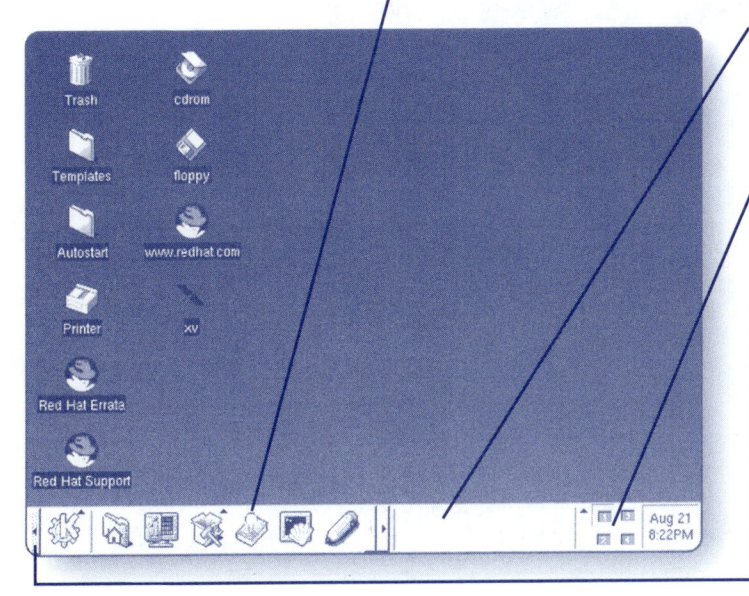

- The Taskbar displays all open tasks or applications currently running on the displayed desktop.

- The Desktop Buttons manage the virtual desktops on your system.

- This textured bar controls the hide and show feature of Kpanel. Click this bar to remove or display the Kpanel on your desktop.

NOTE
Pressing Alt+F1 simultaneously will open the Application Starter menu.

Starting Programs from the Application Starter

When you want to start applications in KDE, you use the Application Starter, what else?

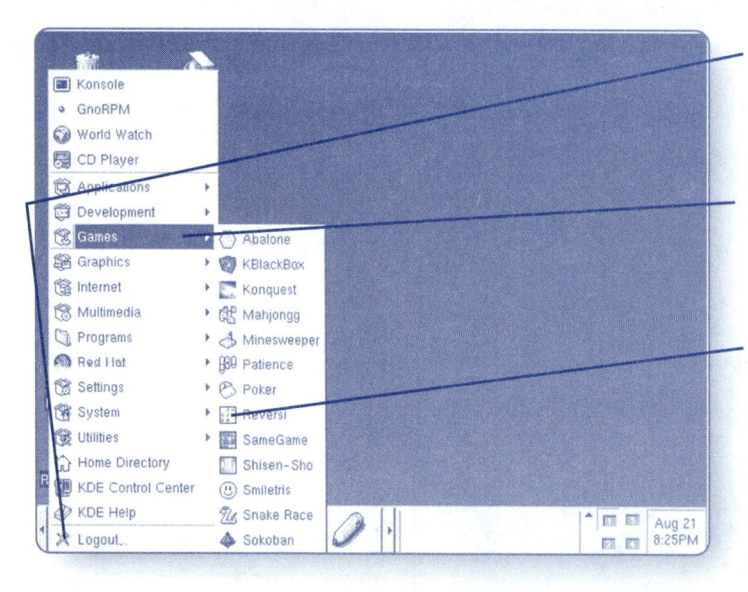

1. **Click** on the **Application Starter Button**. The Application Starter Menu will appear.

2. **Move** the **mouse pointer** over the Games menu item. The Games menu will appear.

3. **Click** on **Reversi**. The Reversi window will open on your screen. Have a little fun!

Getting Help

After reading this book, you'll feel comfortable using Linux with the Gnome and KDE interfaces. But this is just the beginning of your journey, since Gnome or KDE is not the only ways to use Linux. As you get more involved in your new Linux operating system, you'll find new uses for some of the features you've learned about so far and discover new features that you'll want to explore.

When you want to expand your horizons within Linux, the online help system is just the thing to help you on your way. In this section, you'll examine the Gnome Help system.

Getting Help on the Desktop

The Gnome Help Browser is your one-stop place for all the Linux and Gnome help files. This help system does not contain a search feature. You'll need to read through the list of contents and click on the help topic that you want to read. This section will show you how to access and work with the Gnome User's Guide.

Browsing the Help Files

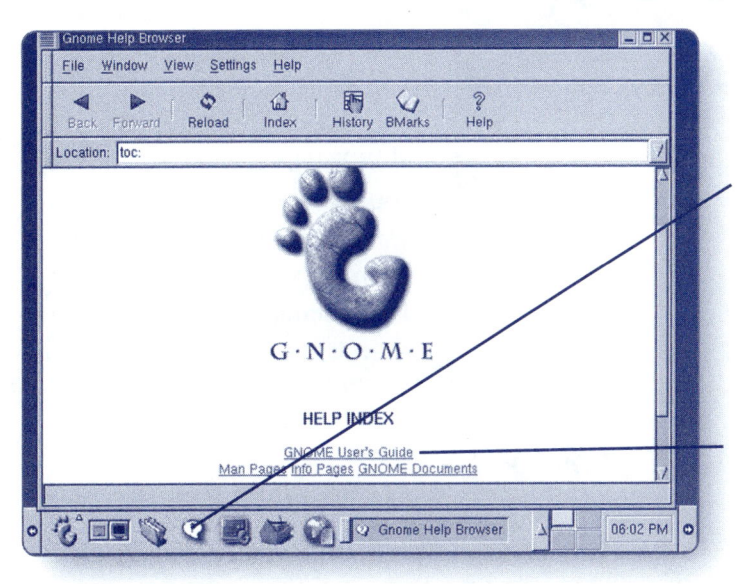

Like reading a book, you can peruse the help files to educate yourself at your own pace.

1. Click on the **Help button** if the Gnome Help Browser is not displayed on your screen. The Gnome Help Browser will appear displaying the Index page.

2. Click on the **Gnome User's Guide link**. The table of contents for the Gnome User's Guide will appear.

NOTE

After you become more familiar with Linux and want to know more about using Linux commands, you may want to check out the Man Pages. The Man Pages are notes written by Linux programmers that tell you how to use all the Linux commands. The Man Pages are the complete documentation package for all Linux distributions, and will be looked in Chapter 11, "Working in the Console".

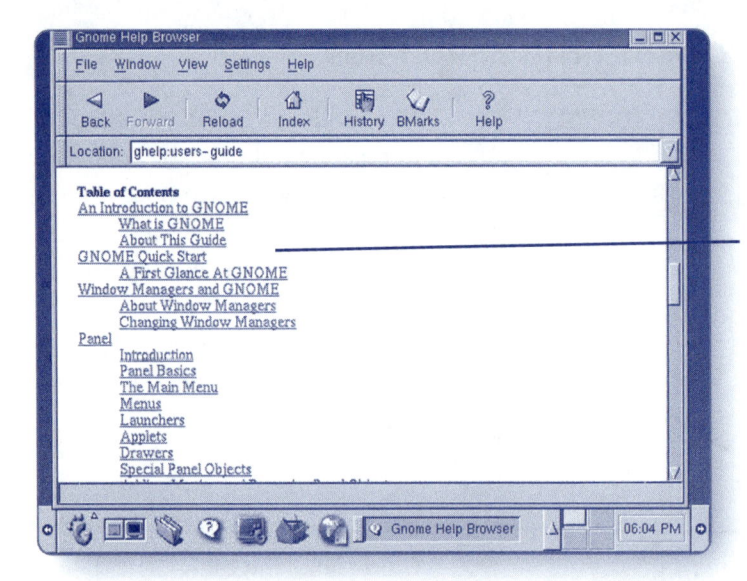

3. Read through the list of **topics** until you find the one that matches the information you need.

4. Click on the **link** for the help topic you want to read. If you want to read the user's guide from start to finish, click on An Introduction to Gnome link. The associated help file will open in the browser.

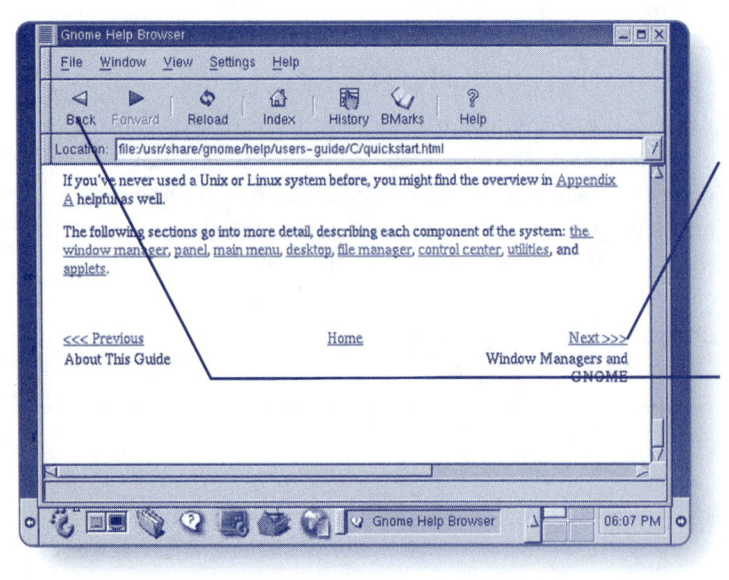

5. Read the **information** on the page.

6. Click on the **Next link** to read the next page from the list of contents. The next page in the user's guide will open in the browser.

7. Click on the **Back button**. The last page that you viewed will open in the browser.

GETTING HELP   21

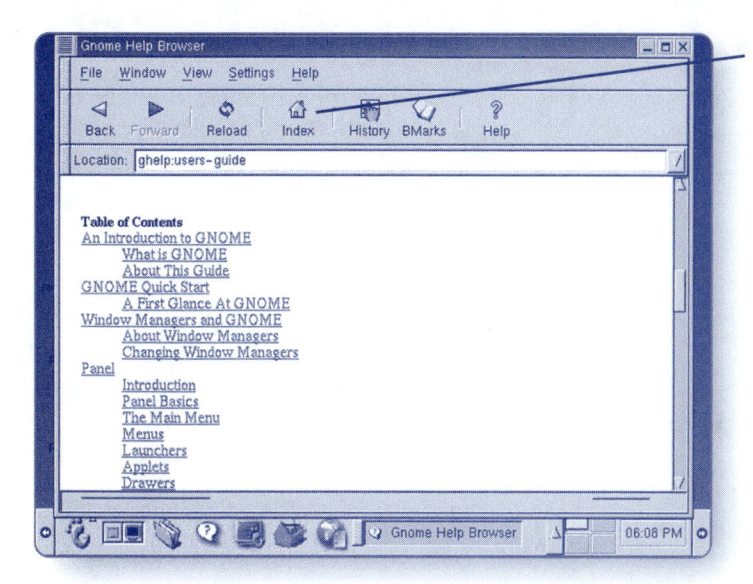

8. Click on the **Index button** to return to the main page of the user's guide. The title page of the Gnome User's Guide will open in the browser.

Setting Bookmarks

When you find a page that contains useful information that you think you'll need again, you can set a bookmark to make it easy to find the information again. Or, if you're reading the user's guide from cover to cover and want to remember where you left off, mark the spot with a bookmark.

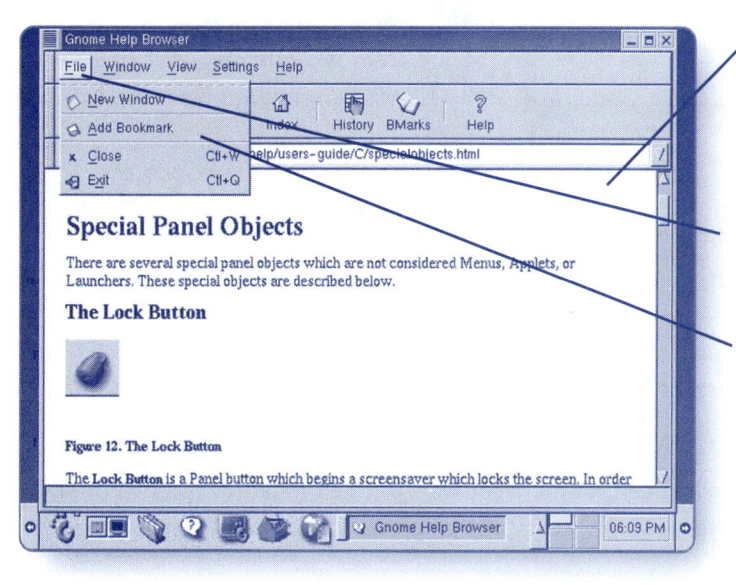

1. Open the **page** to which you want to set a bookmark in the browser window. The page will open in the browser.

2. Click on **File**. The File menu will appear.

3. Click on **Add Bookmark**. A bookmark will be created for you.

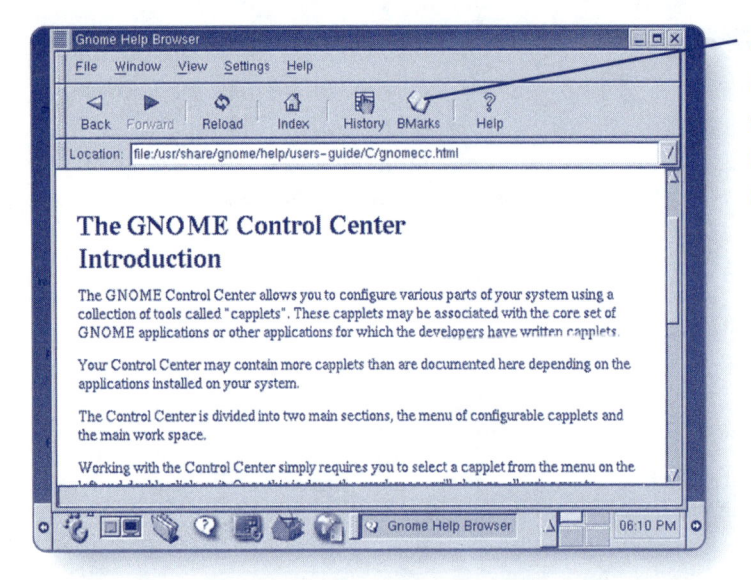

4. Click on the **BMarks button** if you want to display a help topic that you previously bookmarked. The Gnome Help Bookmarks dialog box will open.

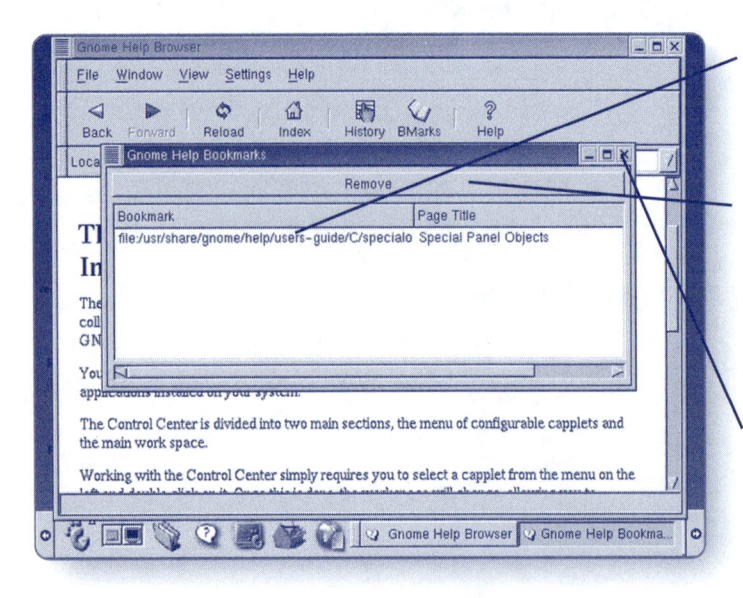

5. Click on the **help topic** that you want to read. The help topic will open in the browser window.

6. To delete a bookmark, **select** the **bookmark** you want to remove and **click** on the **Remove button**. The bookmark will be removed from the list.

7. To close the bookmark window, **click** on the **Kill button**. The dialog box will close.

Finding Previously Viewed Help Files

There may be times when you know you've read a help file but just can't remember where it was located. You can open a history list and see what help topics you viewed and when.

GETTING HELP 23

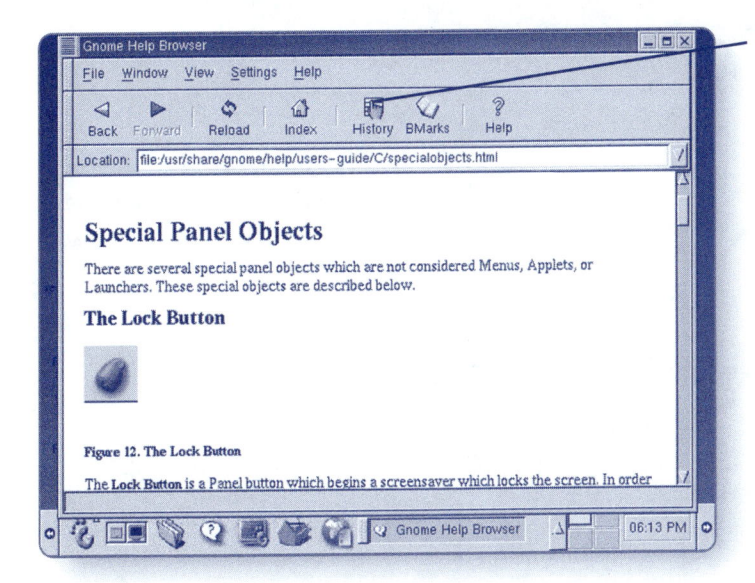

1. Click on the **History button**. The Gnome Help History dialog box will open.

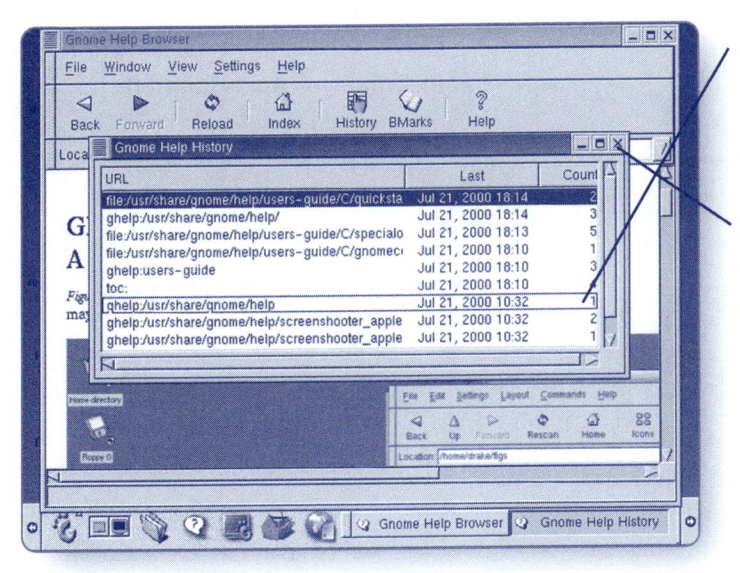

2. Browse through the **list** and **click** on the **help file** that you want to view. The help file will open in the browser window.

3. Click on the **Kill button** when you are finished with the history list. The Gnome Help History dialog box will close.

Finding Help Files in Applications

You can also find help that is specific to the application or window in which you are working. If the application does not have a Help button, you can find help from the Help menu.

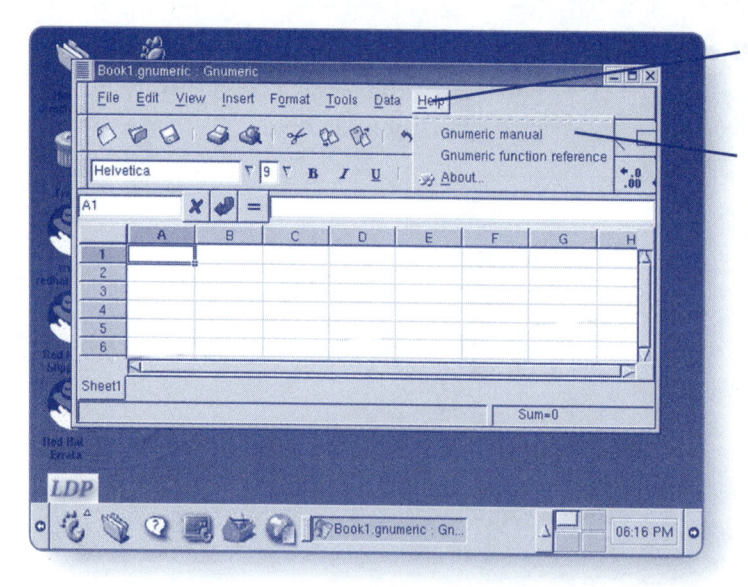

1. **Click** on **Help**. The Help menu will appear.

2. **Click** on the **topic** that you want to read about. A help file will open in a browser window.

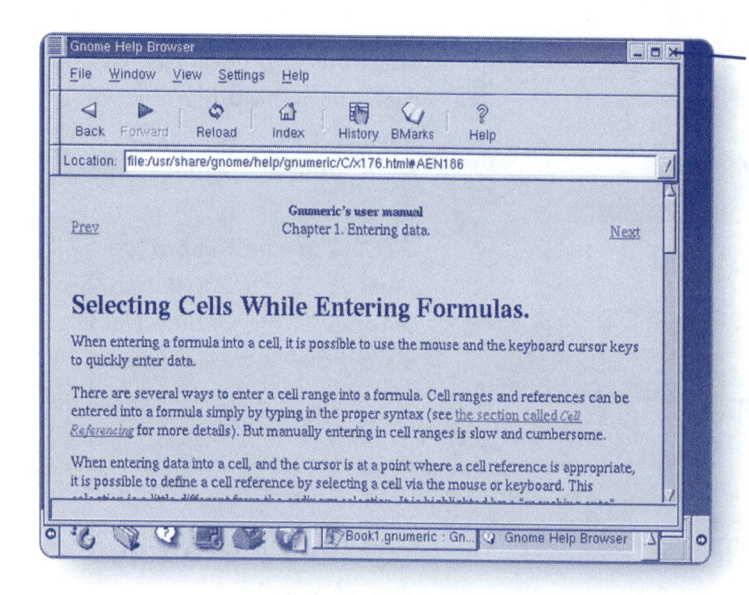

3. **Click** on the **Kill button** when you are finished reading the help file. The browser window will close.

Exiting Linux

When you are finished working with Linux, you'll want to log out of your user account so that others using the same computer will not have access to your user files and directories. You can also make sure that any settings you may have changed will be just the way you left them the next time you log into your user account.

EXITING LINUX

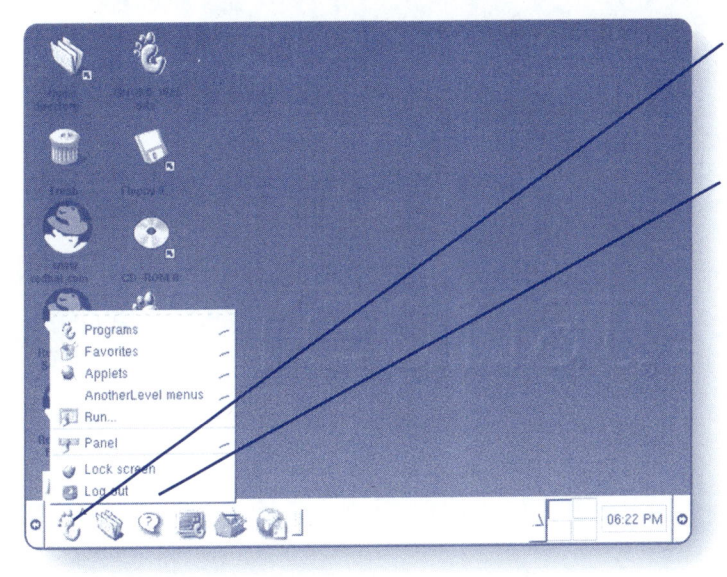

1. Click on the **Main Menu button**. The Main menu will appear.

2. Click on **Log out**. The Really log out? Dialog box will open.

3. Click on the **Logout option button**. The option will be selected.

4. Click on **Yes**. Gnome will close and you will return to the graphical login screen, where you can let another user log in.

NOTE
If you want to turn off your computer, click on the Halt button.

NOTE
If you are logged in as a user other than root, you may be asked for your password one more time before Gnome closes. Type the password in and click OK to continue.

TIP
If you want your screen to appear the same way it looked when you logged out, click on the Save current setup selection box.

2

Working with Program Windows

The screen element that you'll use often in the Linux graphical interfaces is the program window. A window is a boxed area on your screen where you do all your work. From a window, you can work with an application, view your computer's filing system, and perform computer maintenance tasks. You have the option of changing the size and appearance of each window with which you will be working. In addition, there are ways to customize the appearance of a window and how it displays on your screen. In this chapter, you'll learn how to:

- Open a window and change the way it opens on the screen
- Change the size of a window
- Move the window to a different place on the screen
- Minimize and shade a window
- Close a window

Opening Program Windows

When you start an application, a window opens that contains the application and a number of elements that control the window's size. Take some time to learn how to manipulate a single window. It will make it easier for you to work with the application and data inside the window. These skills will also help when you begin working with multiple windows.

Displaying a Program Window

It only takes a few mouse clicks to open a window. In this section, you'll learn to work with windows by opening the Gnumeric spreadsheet.

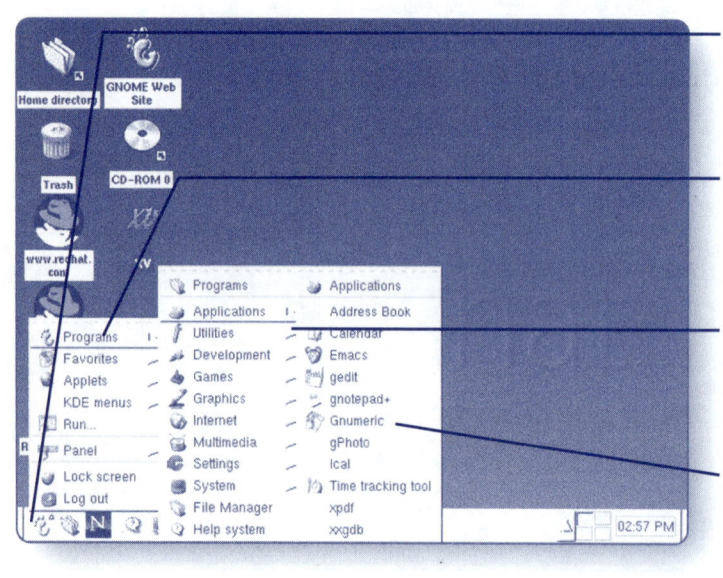

1. Click on the **Main Menu** button. The **Main Menu** will appear.

2. **Move** the mouse **pointer** to Programs. The Programs menu will appear.

3. Move the **mouse pointer** to Applications. The Applications menu will appear.

4. Click on **Gnumeric**. The Gnumeric spreadsheet application will open displaying a blank workspace.

OPENING PROGRAM WINDOWS 29

Most windows share a number of common elements that make it easy for you to move and resize a window.

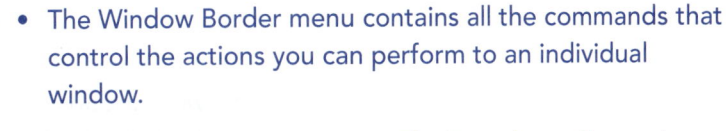

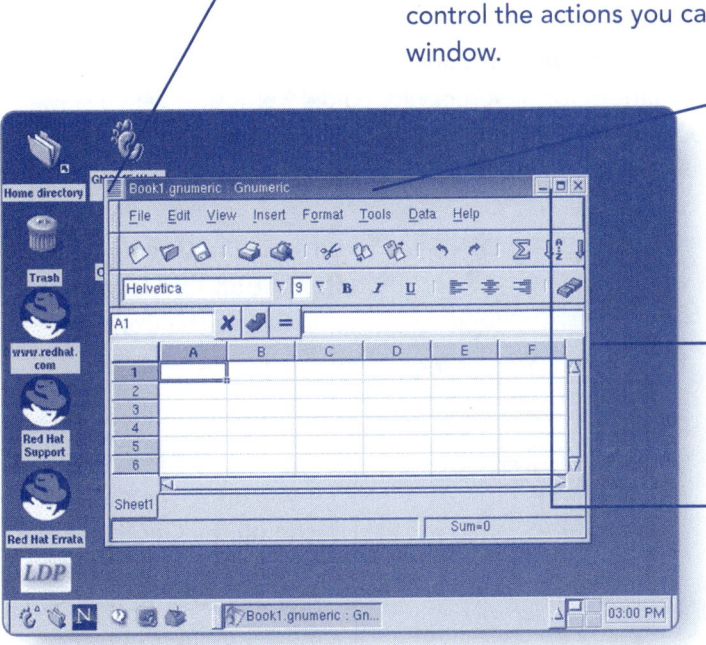

- The Window Border menu contains all the commands that control the actions you can perform to an individual window.

- The Drag bar tells you in which application you are working and also provides the easiest way to move a window around on your screen.

- The window border lies around the outside edge. You can use it to resize the window.

- The Minimize, Maximize, and Kill buttons will turn a window into an icon on the Pager, change the size of the window, and close the window, respectively.

NOTE
You can open an application from a desktop launcher by double-clicking on the icon.

Making Windows Animate When Opened

By default, windows just vanish from the screen when a program or file is executed. If you would like to see the window grow while it opens, try out one of the different sliding methods. If you have an older computer with a slow processor, this feature may cause your system to react even slower.

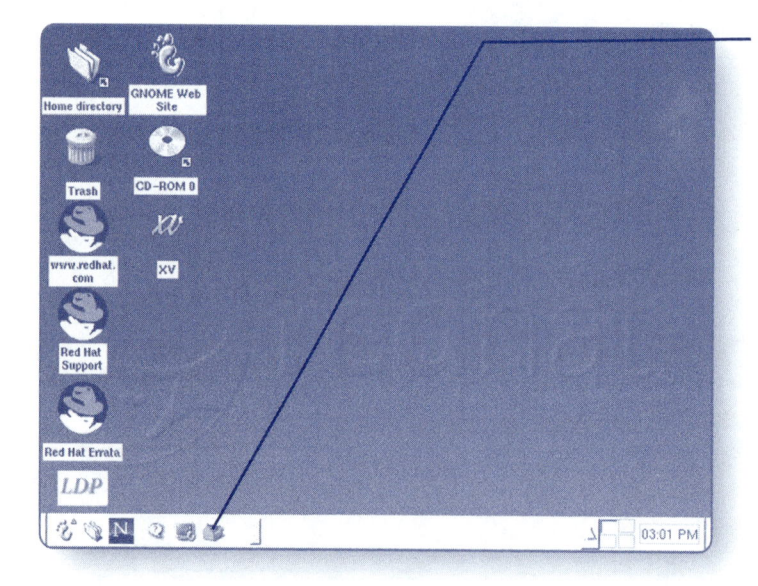

1. Click on the **Gnome Configuration Tool icon** on the Gnome Panel. The Control Center window will open.

> **NOTE**
>
> If you don't see this icon on the Gnome Panel, click on the Main Menu button, move the mouse pointer to Programs, then Settings, then click on Gnome Control Center.

OPENING PROGRAM WINDOWS 31

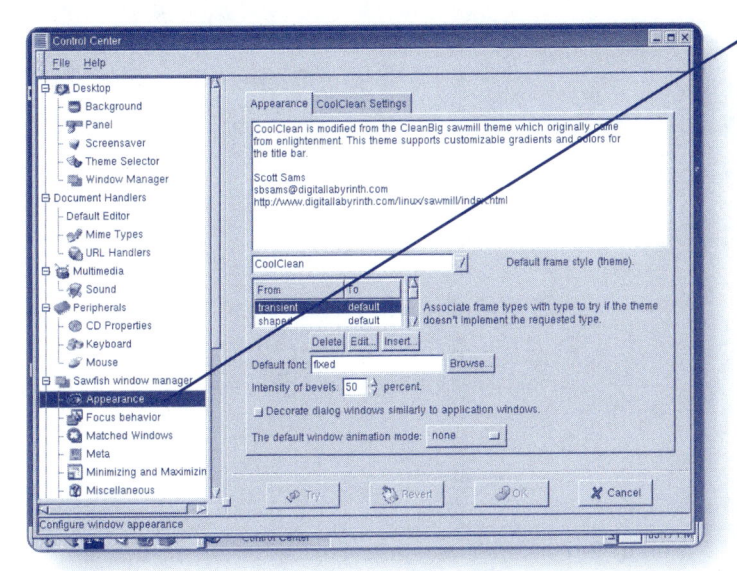

2. Click on **Appearance** under the Sawfish window manager category. The Appearance pane will open.

TIP

To change the size of the two windows in the Control Center, click and hold on the resize handle at the bottom of the bar between the two panes and drag in the direction that you want to resize the panes.

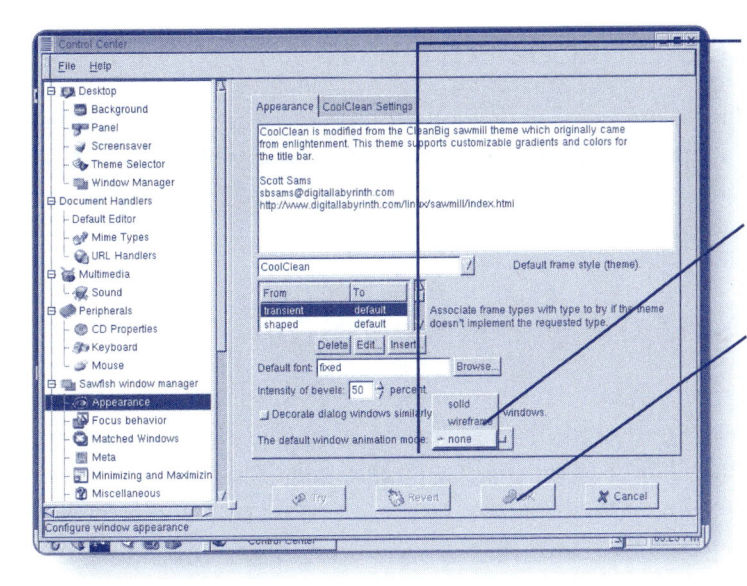

3. Click on the **Default window animation mode** drop-down menu. The animation options will appear.

4. Click on **solid**. The option will be selected.

5. Click on **OK**. Your changes will be applied and the Gnome Control Center pane will open.

TIP

If you want to see your changes in action before you close the Control Center, open a second application. If you don't like the effect, make some changes.

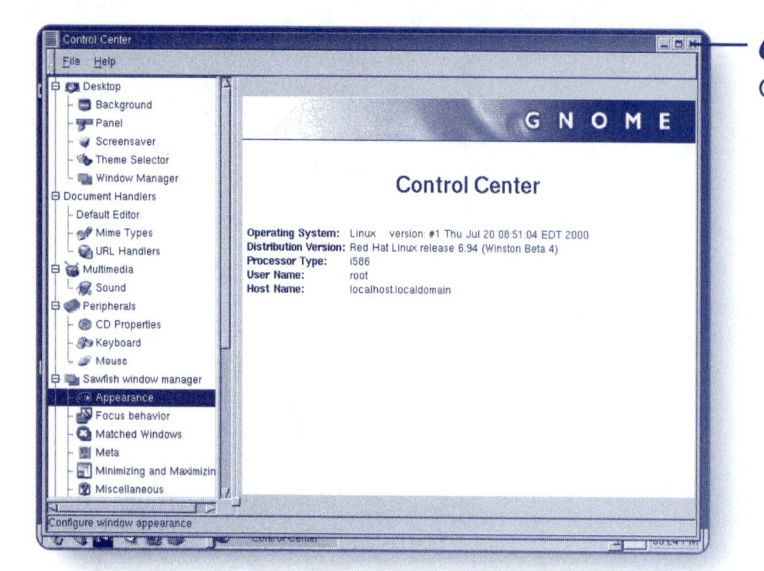

6. Click on the **Kill button**. The Control Center will close.

Resizing a Window

When a program window opens on your screen, it may not be in a size that is adequate for you to do your work. When this is the case, you'll need to resize the window. There are several options.

Using the Maximize Button

The easiest place to change the size of a window is with the Maximize button. The Maximize button is used to change the window from its smaller size so that it fills the screen. When you click on the Maximize button a second time, the window reverts to its original size.

RESIZING A WINDOW 33

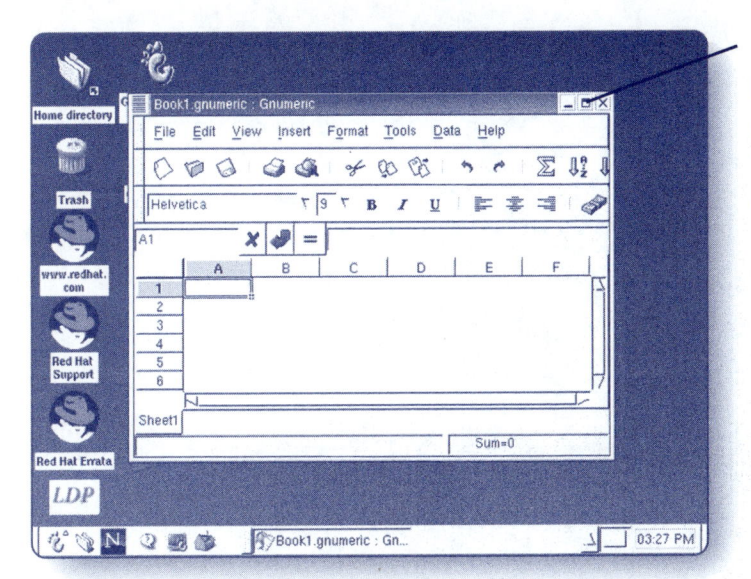

1. Click on the **Maximize button** on a window that is smaller than the screen area. The window will fill the entire screen.

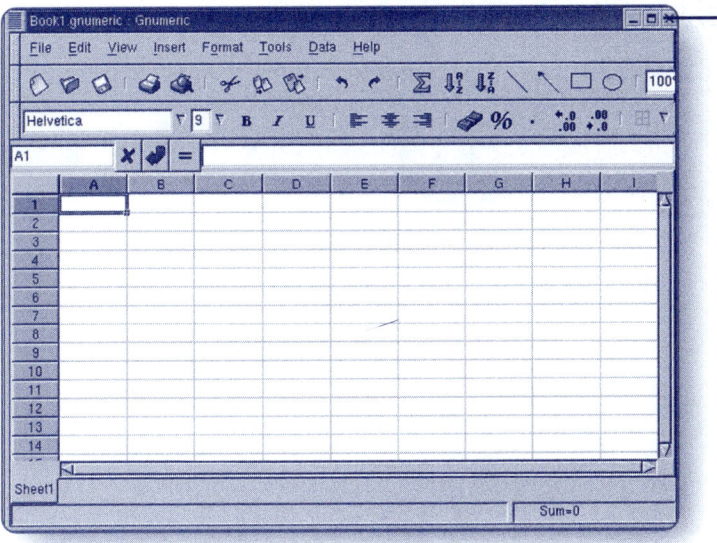

2. Click on the **Maximize button** on a window that fills the entire screen. The window will revert to its smaller, default size.

Using the Mouse

If you want more control over the size of a window, use the mouse. By dragging the window borders, you can create a window that is any size you need.

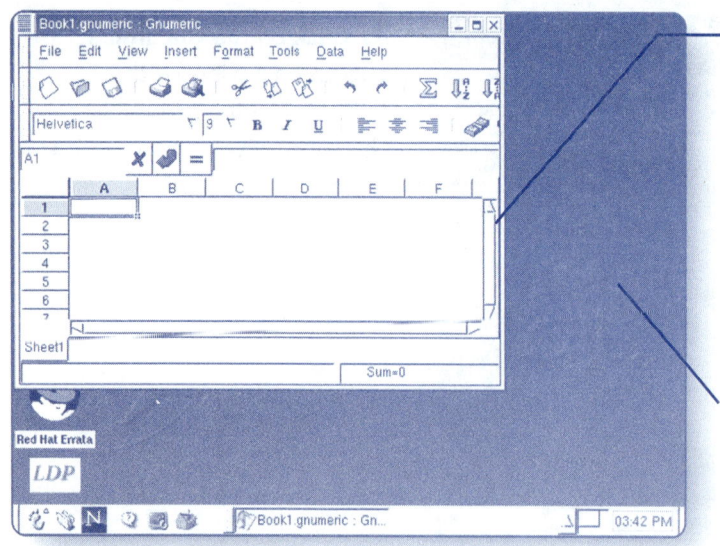

1. **Click** and **drag** either the **left** or **right window border**. Move the mouse pointer toward the window to make the window narrower. Move the mouse pointer away from the window to make the window wider. An outline of the window will appear.

2. **Release** the **mouse button** when the window is the desired size. The window will be resized.

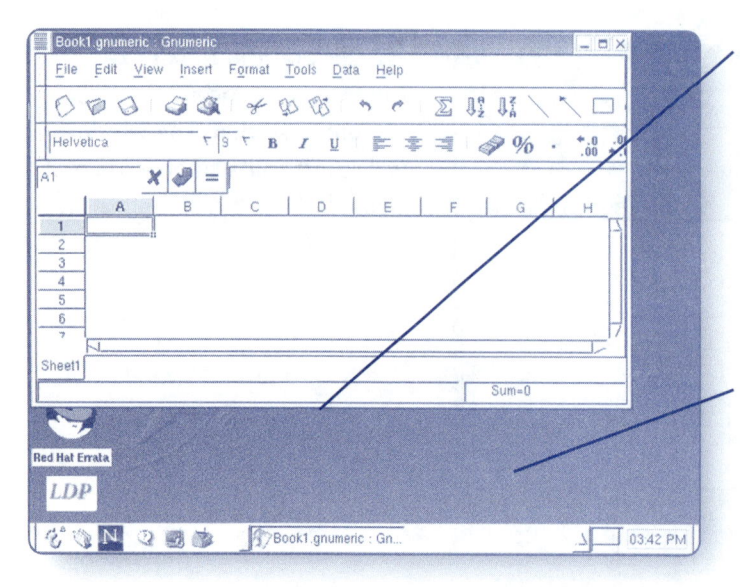

3. **Click** and **drag** the **bottom border**. Move the mouse pointer toward the window to make the window shorter. Move the mouse pointer away from the window to make the window longer. An outline of the window will appear.

4. **Release** the **mouse button** when the window is the desired size. The window will be resized.

SHADING AND ICONIFYING WINDOWS   35

5. Click and **drag** the **bottom right** or **bottom left corner** of the window. Move the mouse pointer away and down from the window to make it wider and longer at the same time. Move the mouse pointer up and toward the window to make it shorter and narrower at the same time. An outline of the window will appear.

6. Release the **mouse button** when the window is the desired size. The window will be resized.

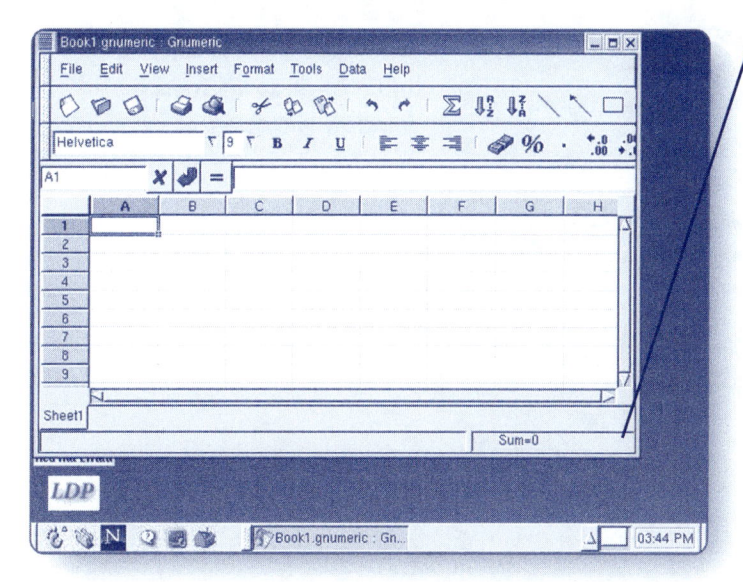

Shading and Iconifying Windows

You can hide a window on the screen without closing the program or window. The first method is called "iconifying" the window and the second is known as "shading."

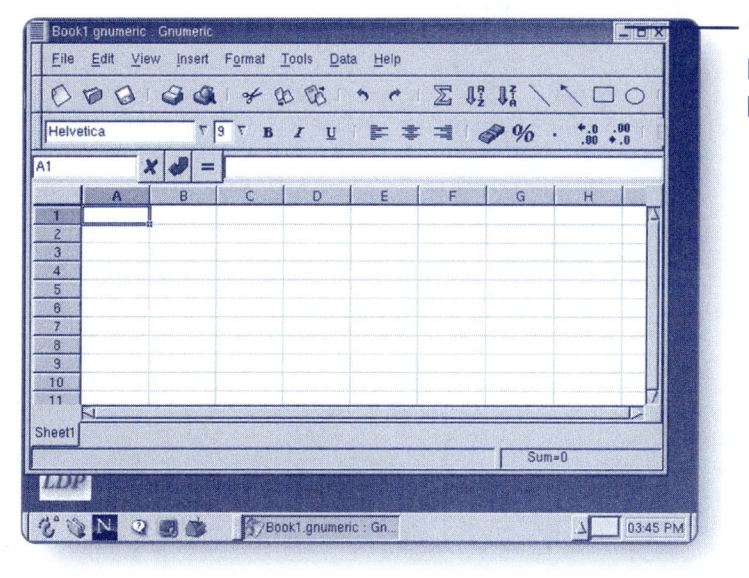

1. Click on the **Minimize button**. The window will become an icon on the Pager.

36 CHAPTER 2: GETTING STARTED WITH LINUX

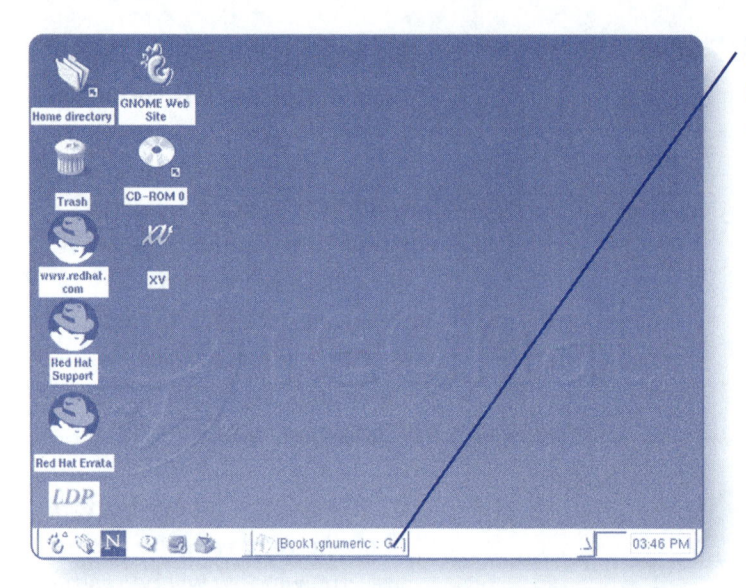

2. Click on the **icon** for the hidden window. The program window will open.

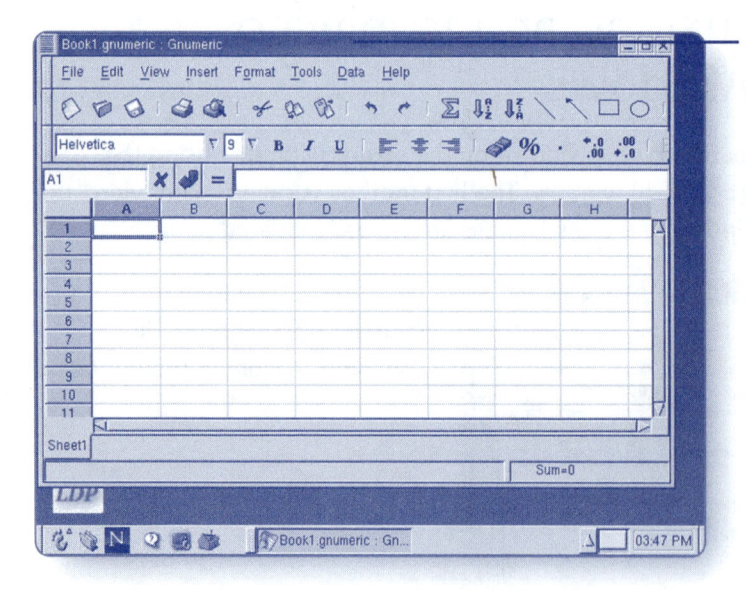

3. Double-click on the **Drag bar** located at the top of the program window. The program window will disappear (or shade) so that only the Drag bar and a border for the window is displayed.

SHADING AND ICONIFYING WINDOWS 37

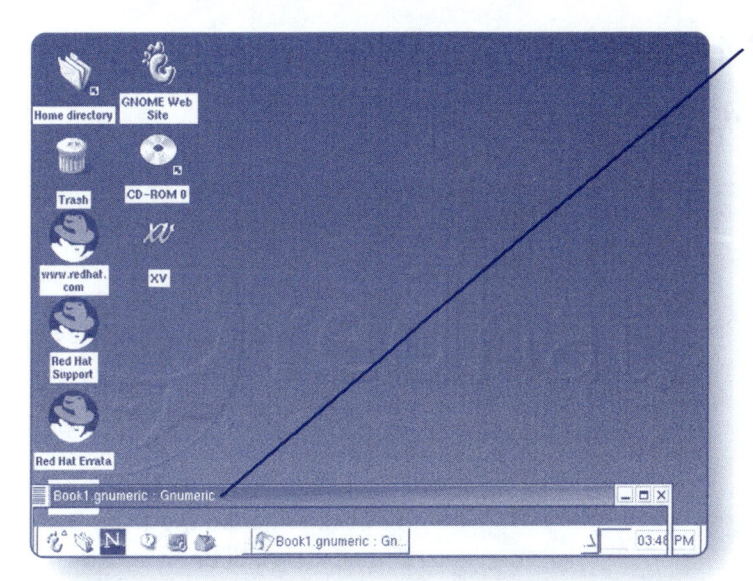

4. Double-click on the **Drag bar**. The window will unshade.

NOTE
You can click and drag the shaded Drag bar to any location on your screen.

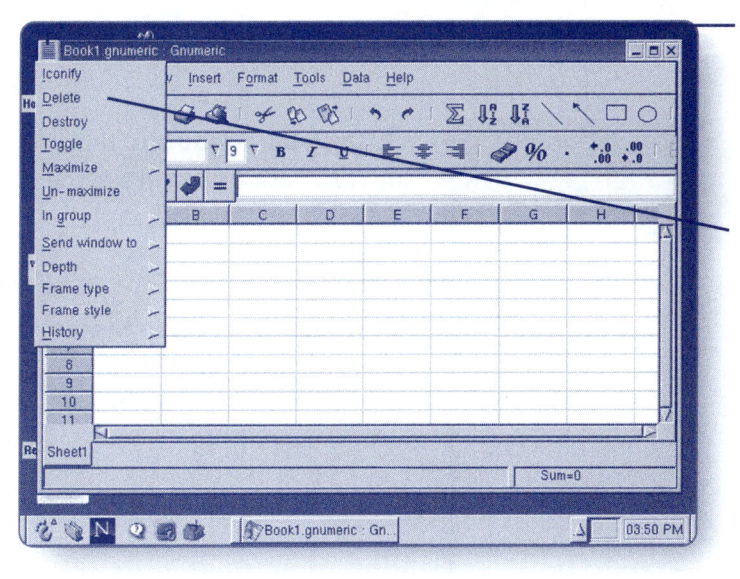

5. Click on the **Windows Options menu** located on the left of the Drag bar. A menu of window functions will appear.

6. Click on **Iconify**. The program window will become an icon on the Pager.

Moving a Window around the Screen

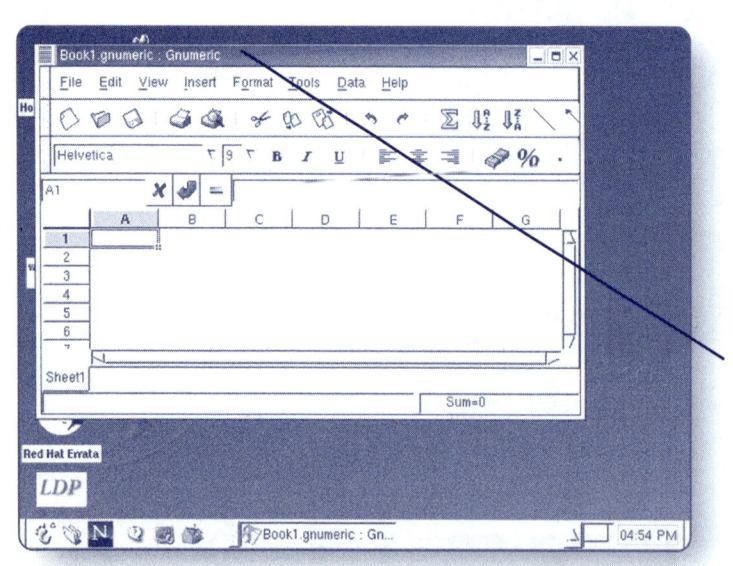

You may want to move a window around on your screen to make room for another program window. Or you may want to move it out of the way so that you can see something (like a program or shortcut icon) on your desktop.

1. Click and **hold** the **Drag bar**. The window will be selected.

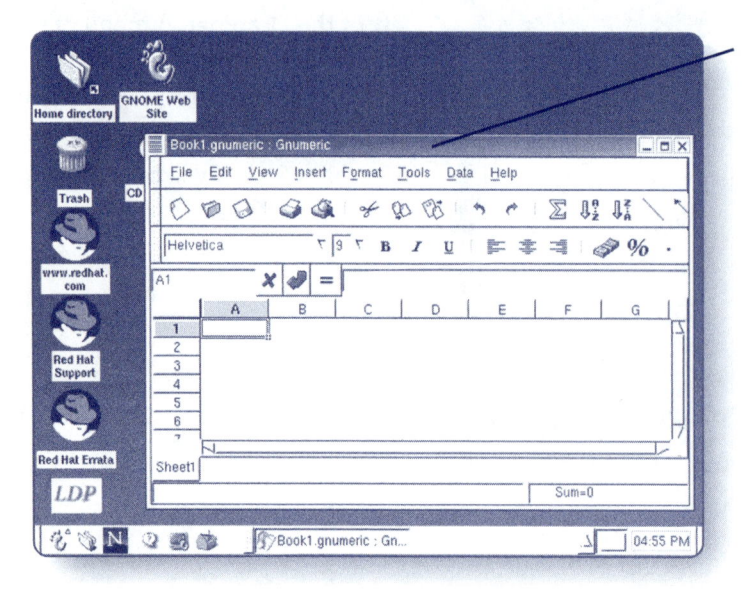

2. Drag the **window** to the desired position. You'll see the outline of the window as it moves.

3. Release the **mouse button** when the window is in the desired position. The window will be moved.

Closing a Program Window

When you are finished looking at a program window, you can close it. If you've been working in the program (which you'll learn about in Chapter 10, "Working with Files"), you'll first need to save your work.

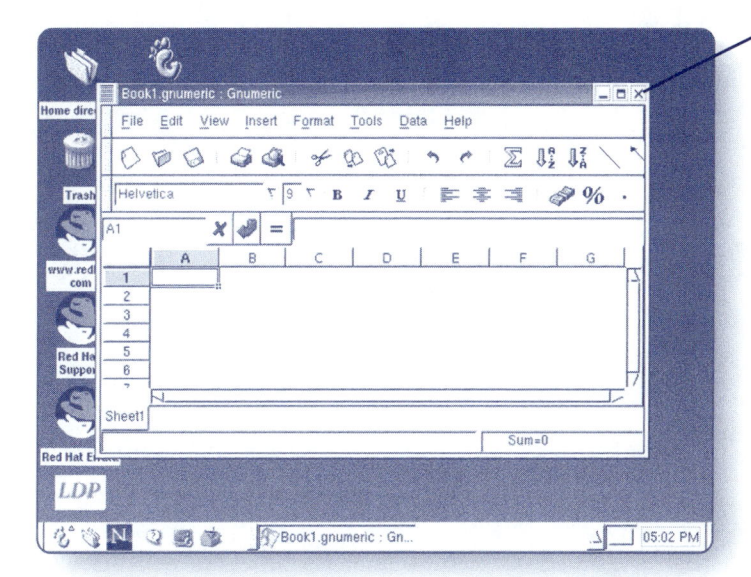

1. Click on the **Kill button** located at the far right of the Drag bar. The program window will close.

NOTE

If the window refuses to close, right-click on the Kill button, which "destroys" the window.

3

Moving around Your Desktop

In the last chapter, you learned how to open a window and move it around on your desktop and you experimented with how to change the appearance and behavior of windows. One Linux strong suit is its multitasking capability. It is easy to work with multiple applications, multiple windows, and even multiple screens. You'll begin by opening and arranging multiple windows on a desktop area and then progress to using multiple desktop areas…which is like having more than one monitor on your desk. In this chapter, you'll learn how to:

- Arrange multiple screens on your desktop
- Move around between desktop areas with the Gnome Desktop Pager
- Change the number of desktop areas available on your desktop

Working with Multiple Windows

It's a simple task to open many applications, but keep in mind your computer's capabilities. It may or may not have enough memory and speed to manage a lot of open windows. (Though you will notice Linux handles things a lot more efficiently than Windows.) Also, too many multiple windows will pile on top of each other, making it hard to find a particular application window.

Finding a Few Applications to Open

One of the exciting features of your Linux system is the ability to multitask. Not only can you work with multiple applications at one time, but you can also group them on different desktop areas. Open a few windows on your desktop and experiment with the examples in this chapter.

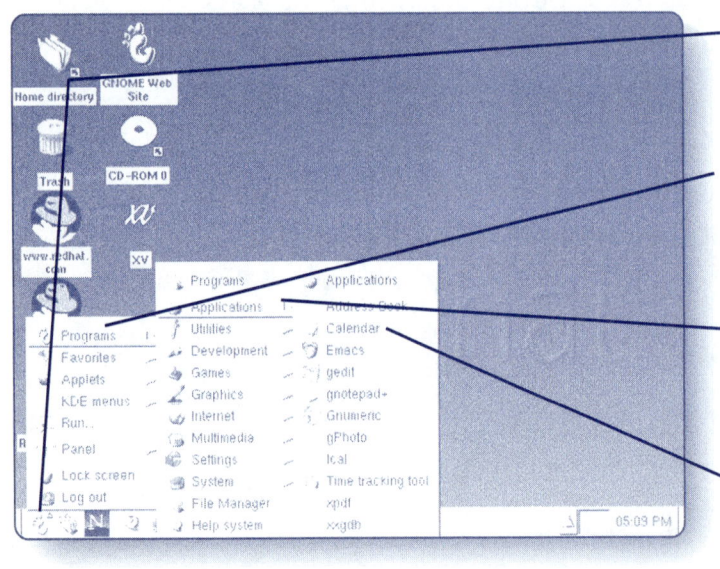

1. Click on the **Main Menu button.** The Main Menu will appear.

2. Move the **mouse pointer** to Programs. The Programs menu will appear.

3. Move the **mouse pointer** to Applications. The Applications menu will appear.

4. Click on an **application**. The program window for the application will open on your desktop area.

WORKING WITH MULTIPLE WINDOWS 43

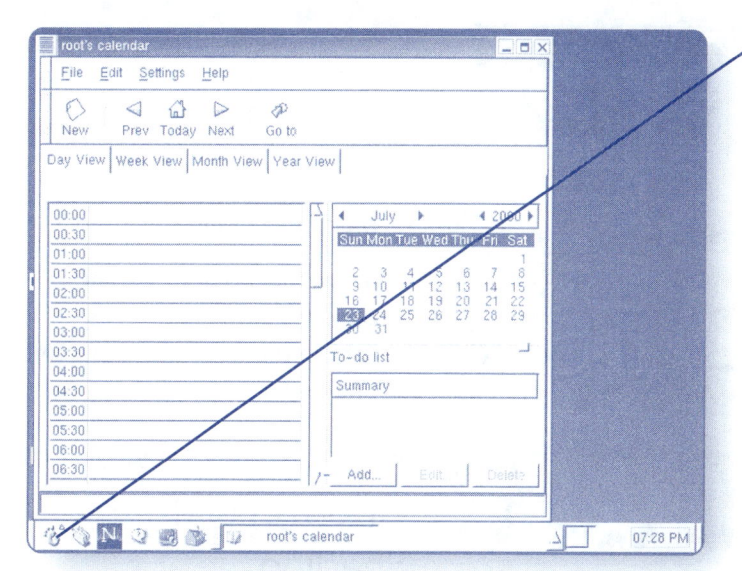

5. Repeat steps **1** through **4** until you have a half dozen open windows on your desktop area. The desktop will probably look cluttered and disorganized.

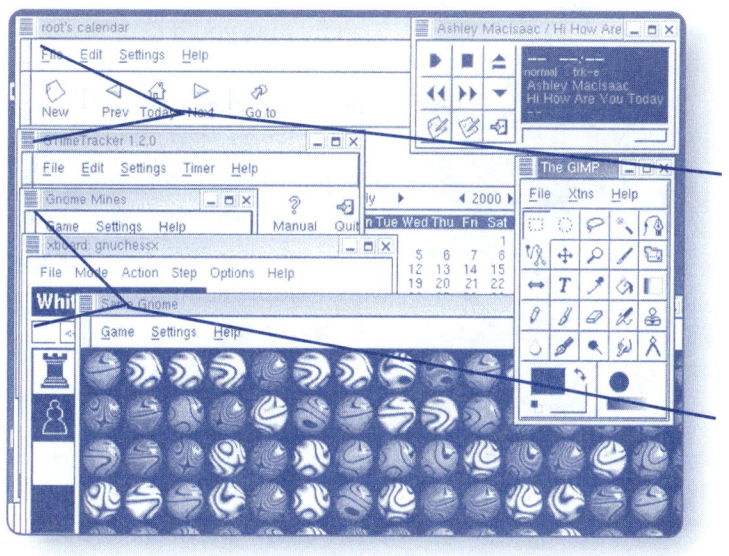

In this example, it may be hard to see, but here are seven open windows.

- The Calendar and the Time Tracking Tool can be found in the Applications menu. These are a couple of the productivity tools that you may find useful.

- You'll find several fun games to help you waste a little time (and practice your mouse skills, of course) in the Games menu.

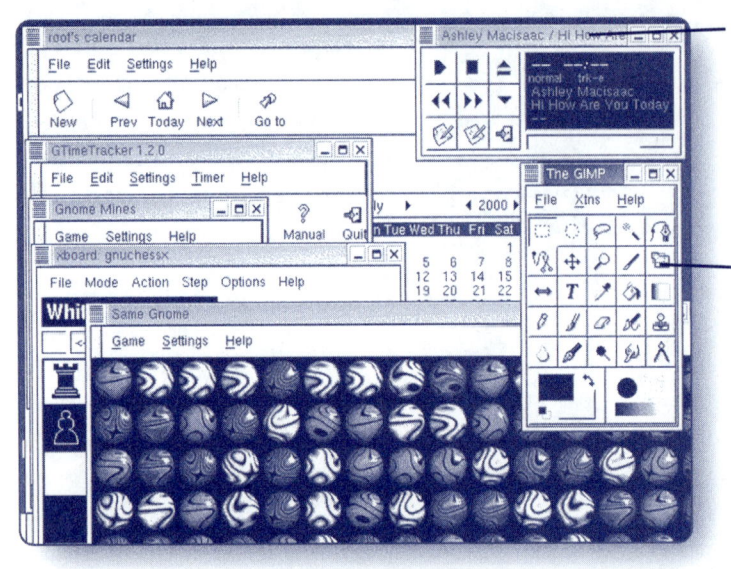

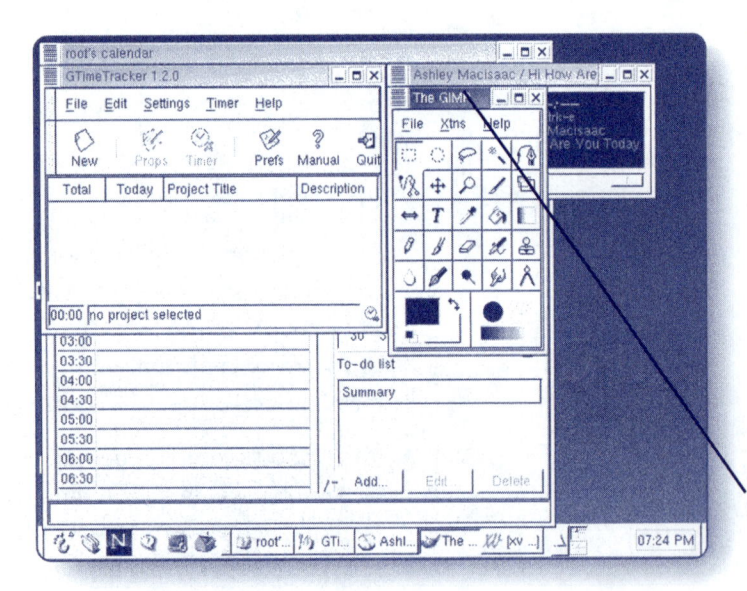

- When only tunes will get you through times of hard work, plug in the CD player and listen to the sound. You'll find the CD player in the Multimedia menu.

- If you feel artistic or want to enhance scanned images, look in the Graphics menu for The Gimp.

Cleaning Up Your Desktop with Shading

The arrangement of so many open windows may be less user-friendly than you'd like. You still have too many application windows to manage them efficiently or quickly find the one you want. Furthermore, your desk is still cluttered. Here's another trick for working with multiple applications and files at one time.

1. Double-click on the **drag bar** of an application window. The window will become shaded by rolling up inside the drag bar.

WORKING WITH MULTIPLE WINDOWS   45

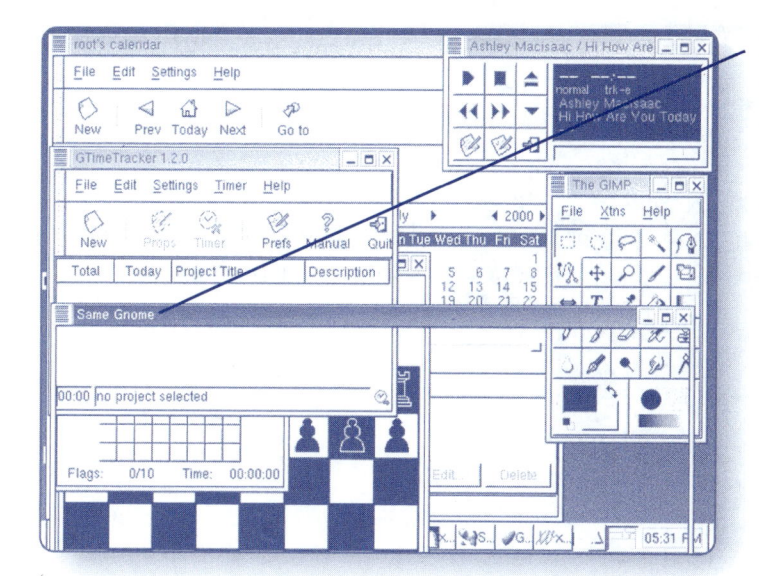

2. Double-click on the **drag bars** of the other open windows on your desktop until all of the windows are shaded. Only the titles of the applications running in the window will show on the drag bar of each window.

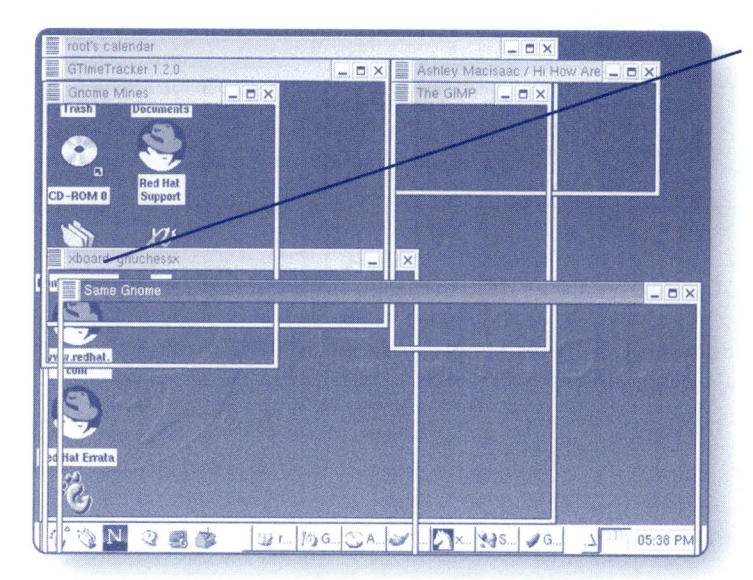

3. Click and **hold** the **drag bar** of the shaded application. The application window is selected.

4. Move the **drag bar** across the Desktop. The shaded window will be moved.

CHAPTER 3: MOVING AROUND YOUR DESKTOP

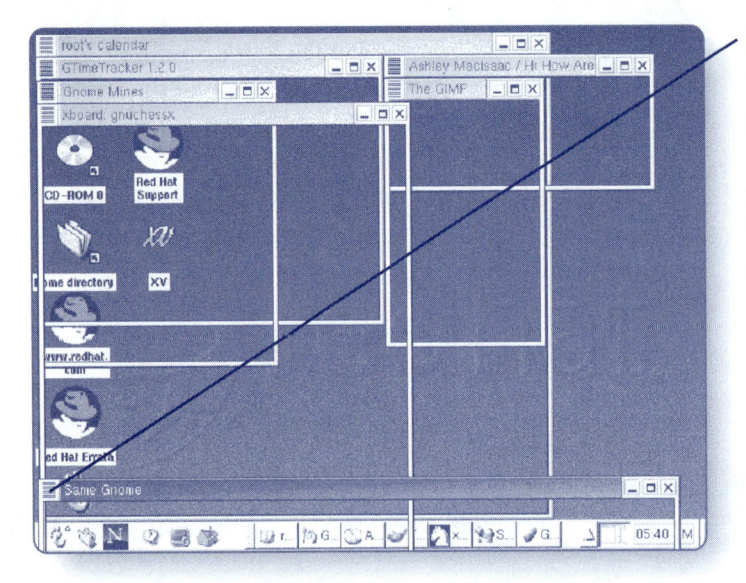

5. Release the **mouse button**. The application window will be placed in the new location.

6. Repeat steps **3** through **5**. The shaded windows on your Desktop will be organized.

> **NOTE**
> This can be a useful way to store windows temporarily when you need space on the desktop to work, but the real solution is to get more desktop areas.

Creating Virtual Desktop Areas

When Red Hat Linux 7 ships, the Gnome desktop environment contains just one virtual desktop, called a workspace. This is a big change from earlier versions, in which the default number of desktops was four. To take advantage of multiple workspaces in Linux 7, you will need to make some new ones!

Understanding the Gnome Pager

The Gnome Pager is an applet that runs inside the Gnome Panel. The Gnome Pager shows all the desktop areas and which applications are on them.

CREATING VIRTUAL DESKTOP AREAS   47

- **The Desk Guide**. This view shows the number of desktop areas (which is like having separate monitor screens) available on the desktop. Each box within the desktop view is a desktop area. The desktop view also shows the arrangement of windows inside the desktop area.

- **The Pager.** The Pager displays all the icons representing open files and applications. If you can't find an application window, look at the icons and click on the one you need. The associated window will come to the front of the screen.

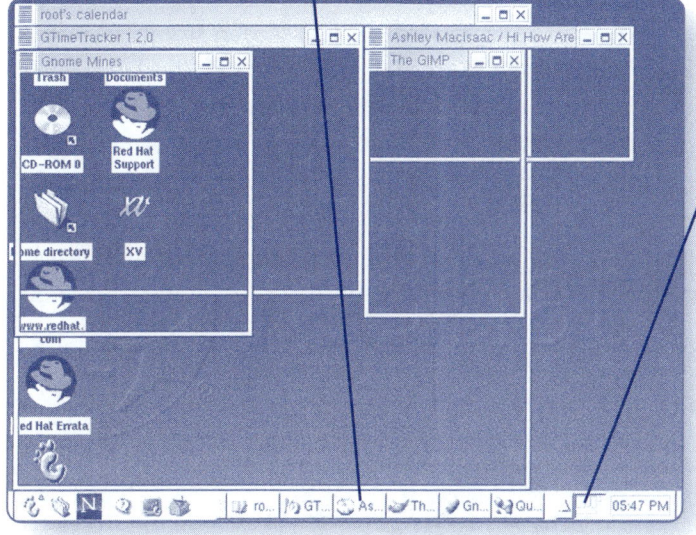

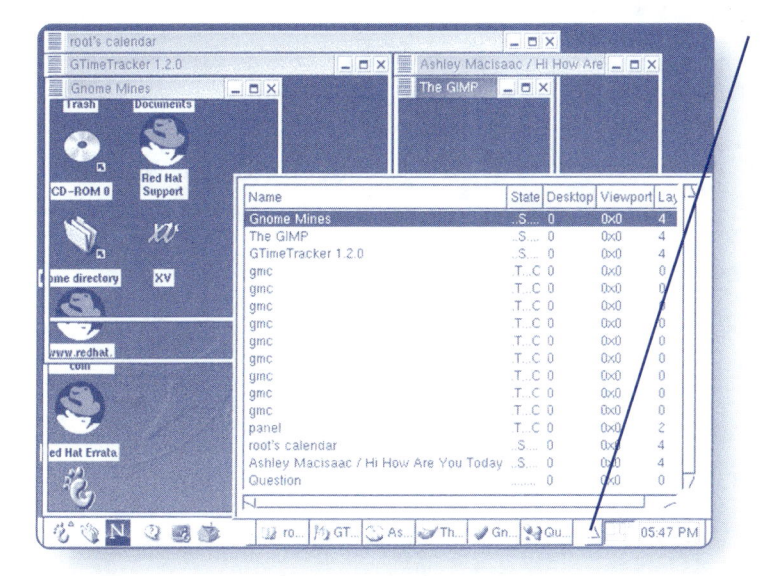

- **Task List.** The task list shows all the open applications. This list comes in handy when working with multiple applications on multiple desktop areas.

Making Workspaces and Virtual Desktops

Linux can use your video hardware to its maximum capabilities, as it can support a virtual screen size much larger than your actual monitor screen's dimensions. This large virtual screen can be divided into separate desktop areas, which are different from the workspaces Gnome can manage. A workspace is similar to the virtual desktop, in that you can move windows from area to area. With workspaces, however, you can't slide windows across areas, you must formally assign them to a workspace. Workspaces also contain desktop areas.

The Gnome Pager on the Panel can navigate from desktop area to desktop area and keep track of your applications.

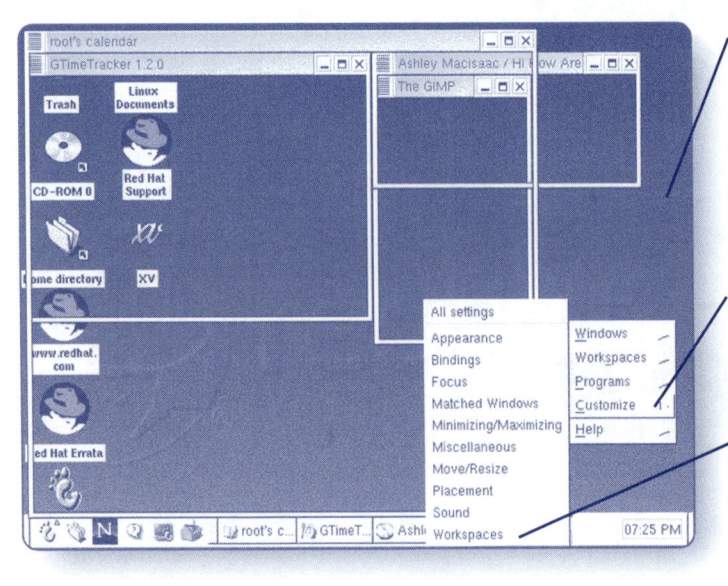

1. Click on **both mouse buttons** (or the center mouse button on a three-button mouse) on an empty area of the Desktop. The Desktop control menu will open.

2. Move the **mouse pointer** to **Customize**. The Customize menu will appear.

3. Click on **Workspaces**. The Sawfish configurator dialog box will open.

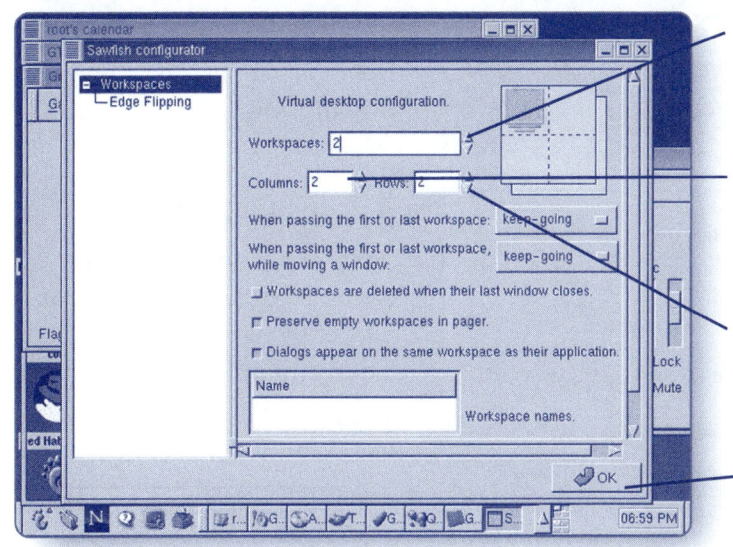

4. Click on the **Workspaces spin control**. The number of Workspaces should equal 2.

5. Click on the **Columns spin control.** The number of columns should equal 2.

6. Click on the **Rows spin control.** The number of rows should equal 2.

7. Click on **OK**. The Sawfish configurator dialog box will close and two workspaces with four virtual desktops each will open in the Desk Guide.

Working with Virtual Desktops and Workspaces

Now that you have made a couple of workspaces and a whole lot of virtual desktops, here's how you can use them to your advantage.

Pushing Windows off a Desktop

Some people deal with cluttered desks by pushing things off, so try to push one of the windows off your desktop. The window will still be available, but it will be on a different desktop area.

CHAPTER 3: MOVING AROUND YOUR DESKTOP

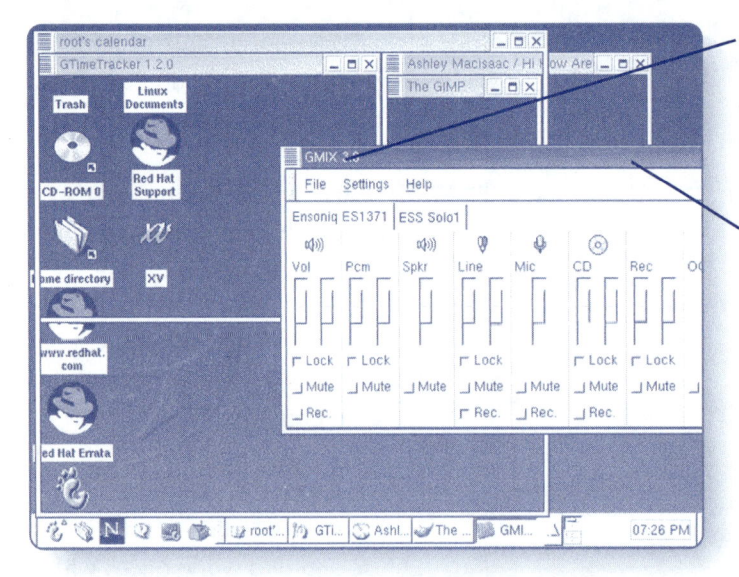

1. Click and **hold** on the **drag bar** of an open window on your desktop. The window will be selected.

2. Drag the **window** to the right. The window will move beyond the desktop area and part of the window will be hidden from sight.

NOTE

If you watch the upper-left desktop area in the upper workspace within the desktop view of the Gnome Pager, you'll see the window move.

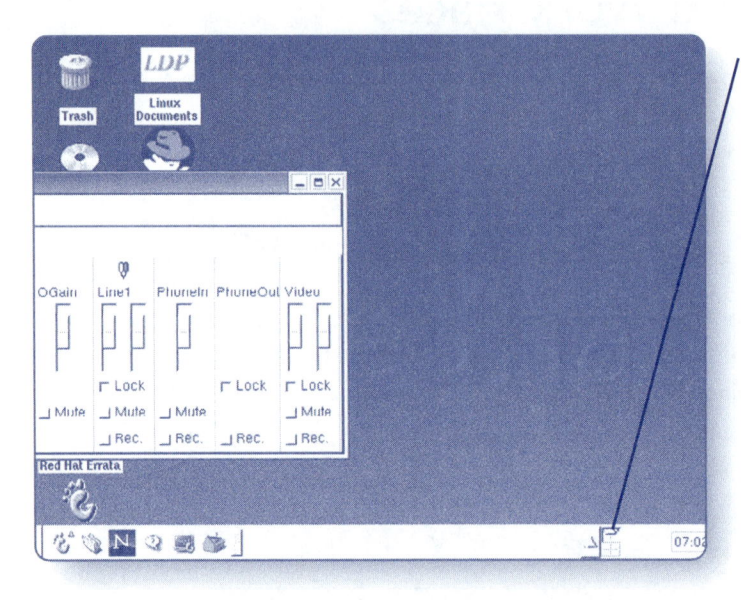

3. Click on the **upper-right desktop area** in the desktop view of the Gnome Pager. Another desktop area will open and you'll see the part of the window that you moved off your original desktop area.

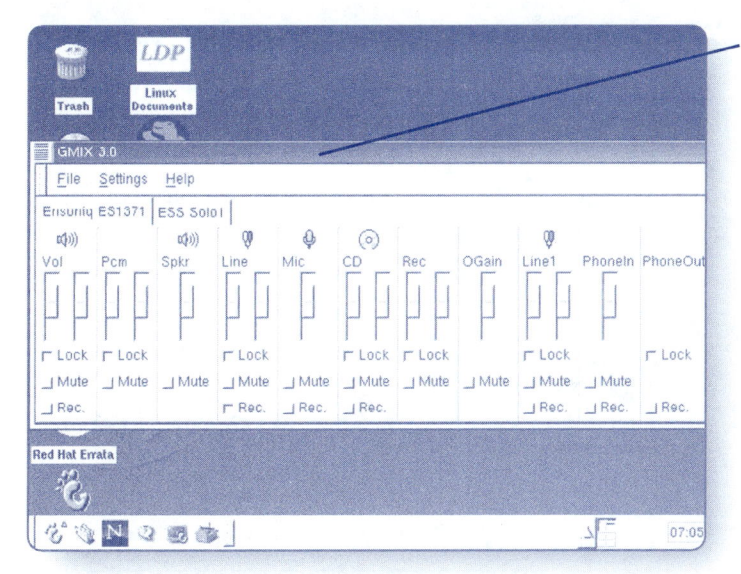

WORKING WITH VIRTUAL DESKTOPS AND WORKSPACES 51

4. Click and **drag** the **application window** so that it is completely displayed in the second desktop area. The window will be open in the second desktop area on your screen.

Moving Between Workspaces

Moving windows between virtual desktops is pretty simple. Luckily, it's just as simple to move between workspaces.

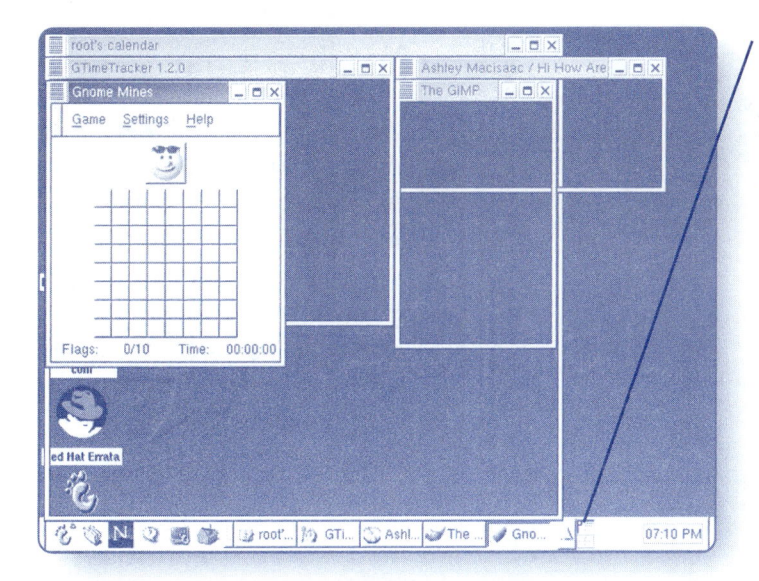

1. Click in the **upper-left desktop area** of Workspace 1 in the Gnome Pager to return to your original desktop. You move to that desktop but the window you dragged into the top-right desktop area will be left behind.

> **NOTE**
> If the application window you lost is located on another desktop area or workspace, you will be switched to that desktop area or workspace.

CHAPTER 3: MOVING AROUND YOUR DESKTOP

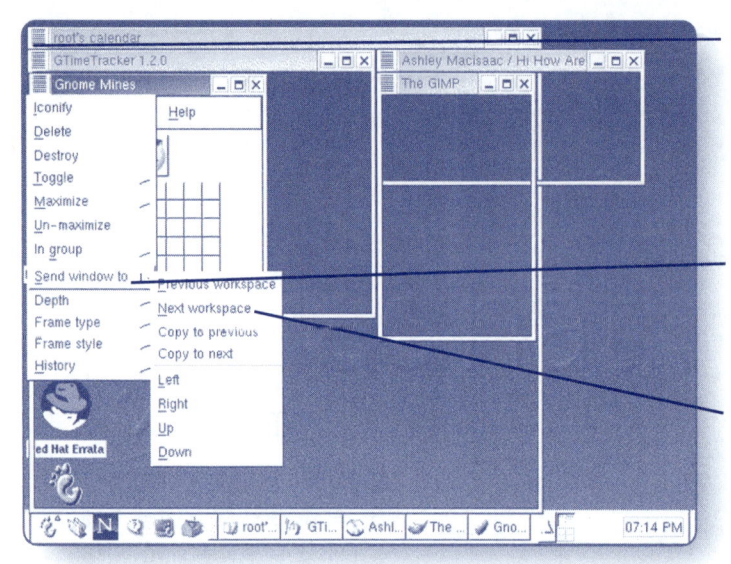

2. Click on the **Window Options menu** of a window that you want to move to a different workspace. The Window Options menu will appear.

3. Move the **mouse pointer to Send Window To**. The Send Window To menu will appear.

4. Click on **Next Workspace**. The window will be moved to the adjacent workspace and the Desktop will display that workspace.

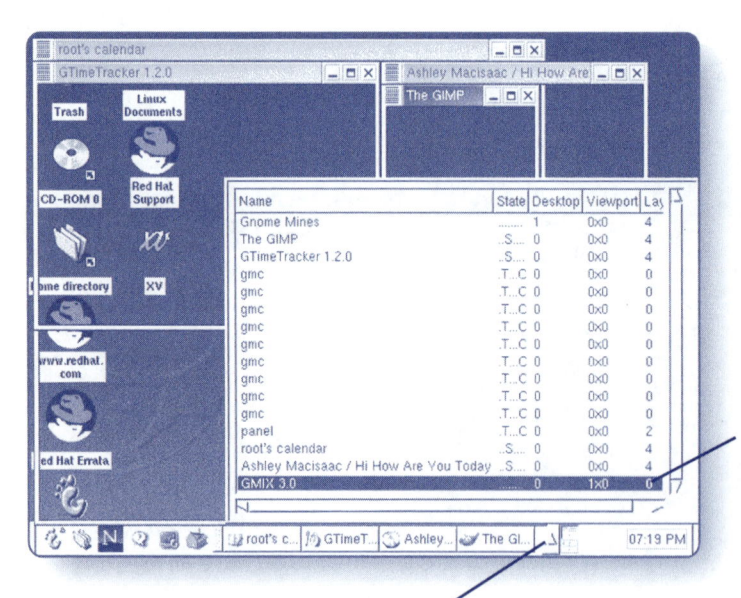

Searching for Lost Applications

You could just start dragging things off your cluttered desktop area onto other desktop areas and workspaces willy-nilly until you get to the bottom, but the Gnome Pager can help you organize this easily.

1. Click on the **Task List button**. A window will open with a list of all the open applications on all the desktop areas.

2. Click on the **listing** for the application window that you are having trouble locating. The application window will be selected and will open at the top of the stack in your desktop area.

4
Customizing the Screen Display

If you want to make your desktop more attractive, there are some cosmetic changes that you can make. For a little variety, change the picture or pattern that you use for a desktop background. To keep your screen from staying in one place for too long when you're not working, use a screen saver. There are many screen savers from which to choose, and you can change settings if you need to slow down the motion. You can also change the appearance of window borders, mouse pointers, and dialog boxes. In this chapter, you'll learn how to:

- Create stylish desktop backgrounds
- Find some fun screen savers
- Use themes to change the look of window borders, mouse pointers, and dialog boxes.

Changing the Desktop Background

Whenever you're not looking at an application window, you'll probably see part of your desktop. You can really have some fun here, or you may opt for a background that makes it easier for you to see other screen elements such as windows and desktop icons. Browse through the selection of solid colors, gradients, and images.

Using a Solid Color Background

A solid color is the easiest background to create and the easiest on your eyes.

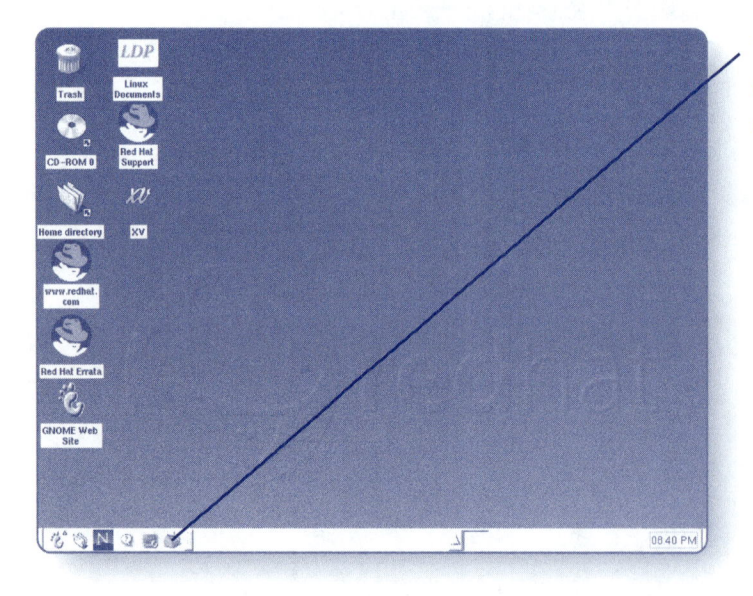

1. Click on the **Gnome Configuration Tool icon**. The Control Center will appear.

CHANGING THE DESKTOP BACKGROUND

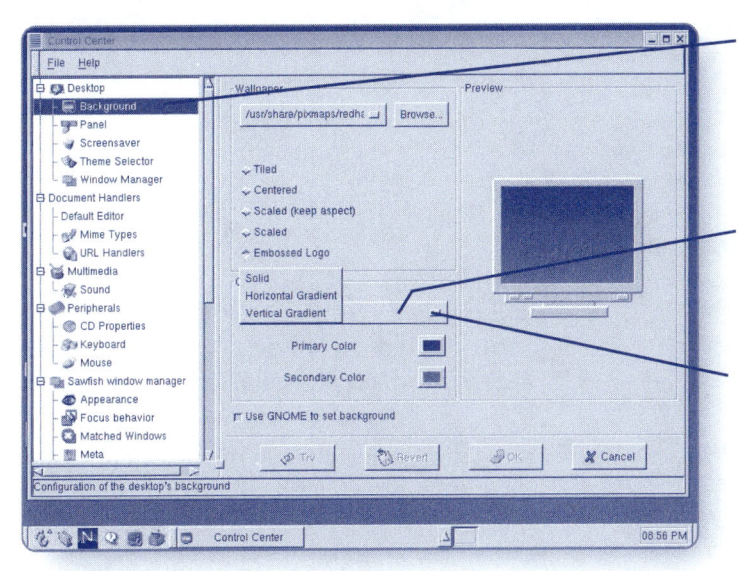

2. Click on the **Background option**. The Background pane will appear on the right side of the Control Center.

3. Click on the **Color drop-down list**. A list of options will be displayed.

4. Click on **Solid**. The option will be selected.

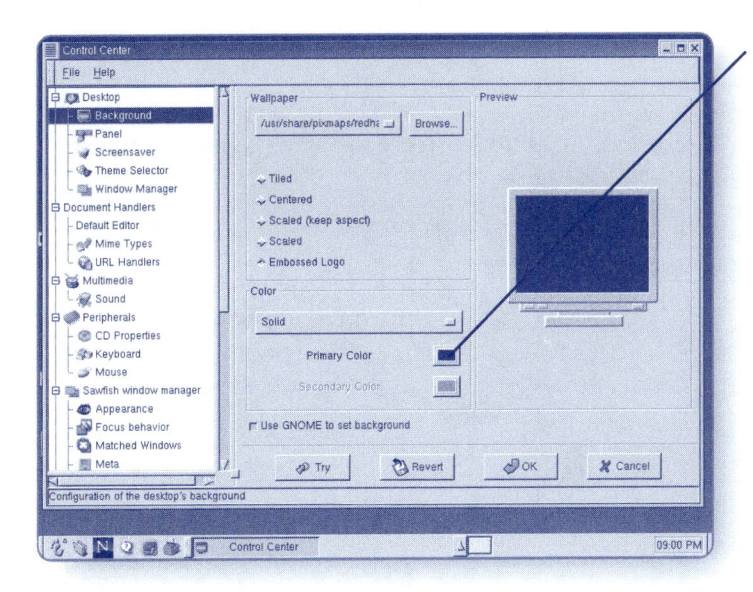

5. Click on the **Primary Color button**. The Pick a color dialog box will open.

CHAPTER 4: CUSTOMIZING THE SCREEN DISPLAY

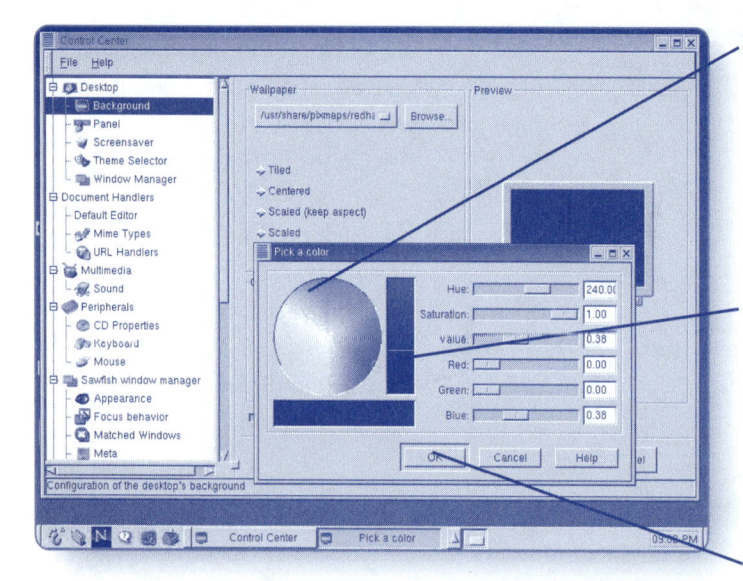

6. Click on a **color** on the color wheel that matches the color you want to use as a background. The color will appear in the bar to the right of the color wheel.

7. Click and **drag** the red **slider line**. Dragging the slider up will make the color lighter. Dragging the slider down will make the color darker. The color balance will change.

8. Click on **OK**. You will be returned to the Control Center and the color you selected will appear in the screen preview at the top of the Background pane.

9. Click on the **Try button**. You'll see your background color appear on the desktop.

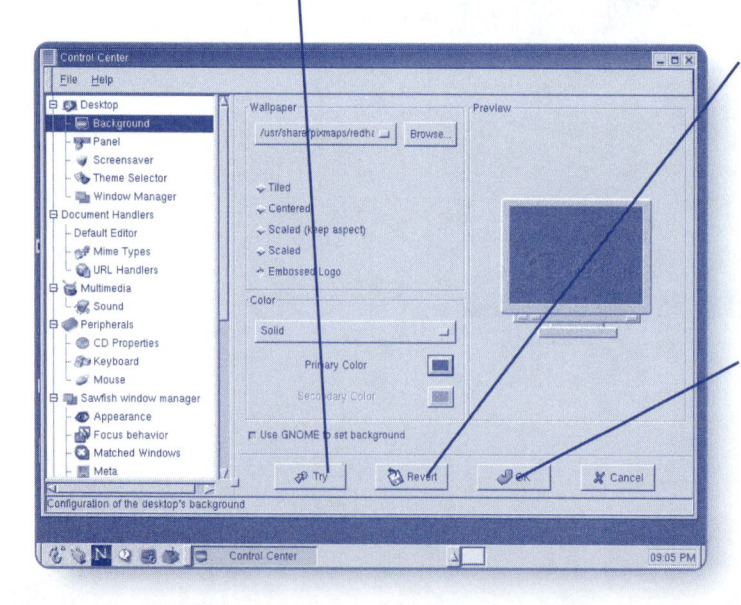

10. Click on the **Revert button** if you don't like the way the color matches the various screen elements. Your desktop background will change back to the original color. You can then try a different color.

11. Click on **OK** when you are satisfied with your color selection. Your changes will be applied and the background pane will disappear.

CHANGING THE DESKTOP BACKGROUND   57

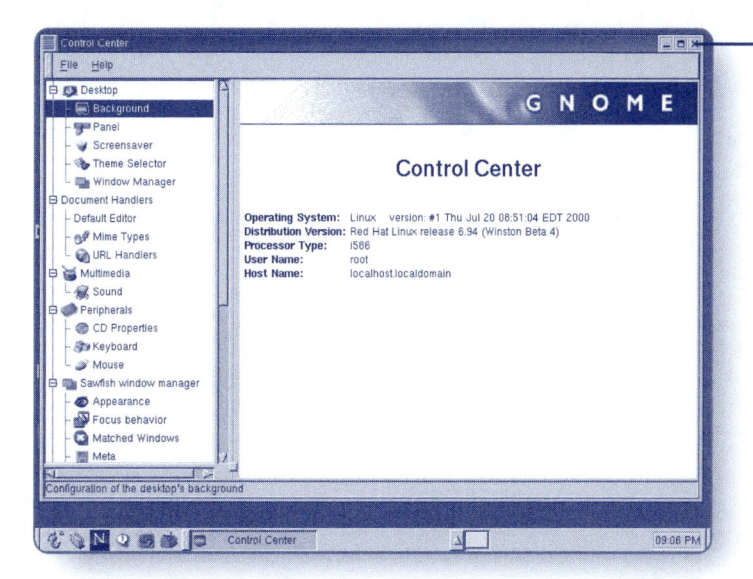

12. Click on the **Kill button**. The Control Center will close.

Creating a Gradient Background

A gradient is a combination of two colors. One color goes from darker to lighter and then blends with the second color, which also changes in brightness. If you're looking for a slightly psychedelic look that's also easy on the eyes, experiment with this background effect.

1. Click on the **Gnome Configuration Tool icon**. The Control Center will open.

2. Click on the **Background option**. The Background pane will appear on the right side of the Control Center.

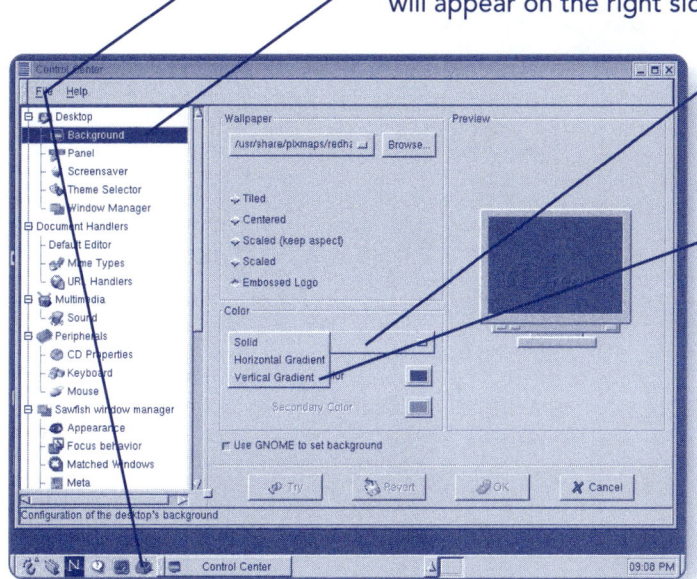

3. Click on the **Color drop-down list**. A list of options will be displayed.

4. Click on **Vertical Gradient**. The option will be selected.

CHAPTER 4: CUSTOMIZING THE SCREEN DISPLAY

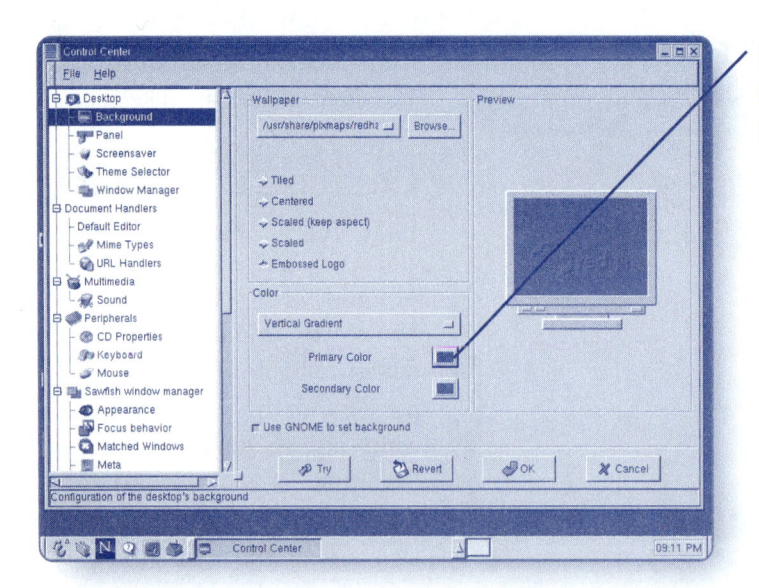

5. Click on the **Primary Color button**. The Pick a color dialog box will open.

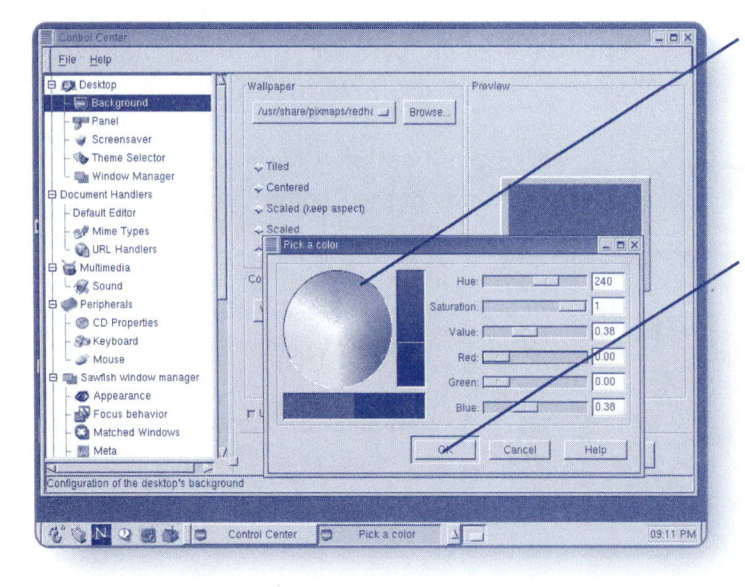

6. Click on a **color** that matches the color you want to use first. The color will appear in the two bars next to the color wheel.

7. Click on **OK**. You will return to the Control Center.

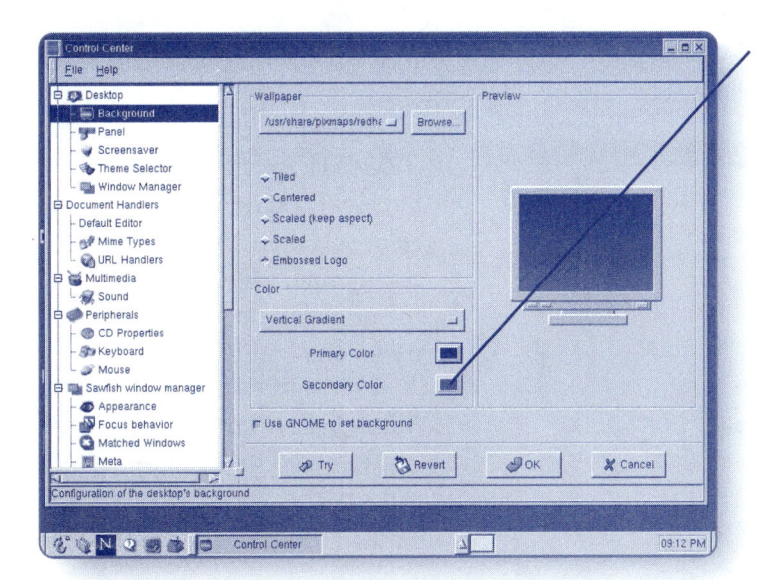

CHANGING THE DESKTOP BACKGROUND   59

8. Click on the **Secondary Color button**. The Pick a color dialog box will open.

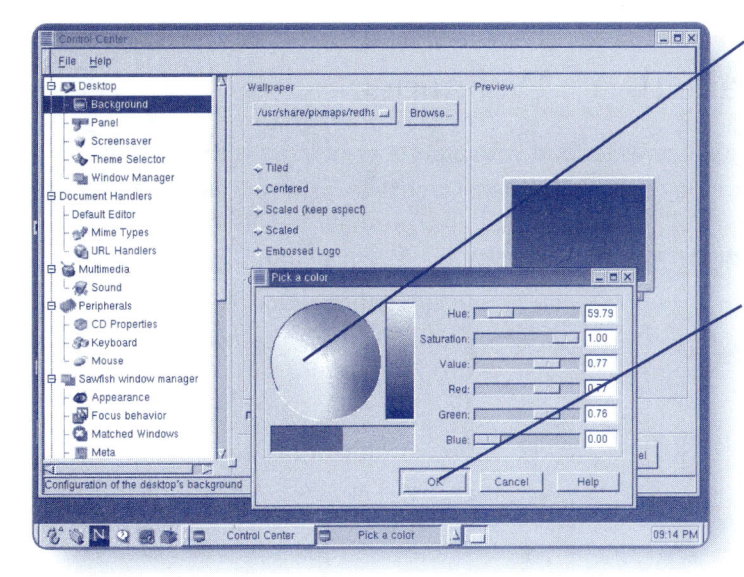

9. Click on a **color** on the color wheel that matches the color you want to use as the second color. The color will appear in the two bars next to the color wheel.

10. Click on **OK**. You will be returned to the Control Center.

CHAPTER 4: CUSTOMIZING THE SCREEN DISPLAY

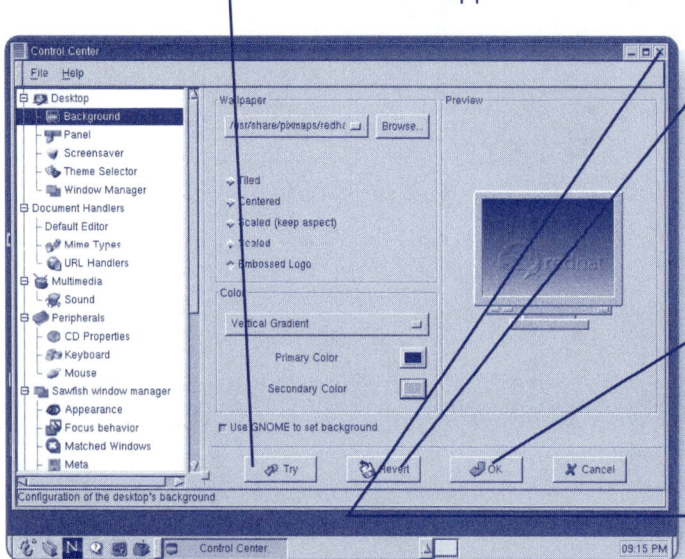

11. **Click** on the **Try button**. You'll see your background color appear on the desktop.

12. **Click** on the **Revert button** if you don't like the color selection. Your desktop background will change back to the original color. You can then try a different color.

13. **Click** on **OK** when you are satisfied with your color selection. Your changes will be applied.

14. **Click** on the **Kill button**. The Control Center will close.

Selecting a Wallpaper

Linux comes loaded with a number of images that you can arrange in various ways to create a desktop wallpaper.

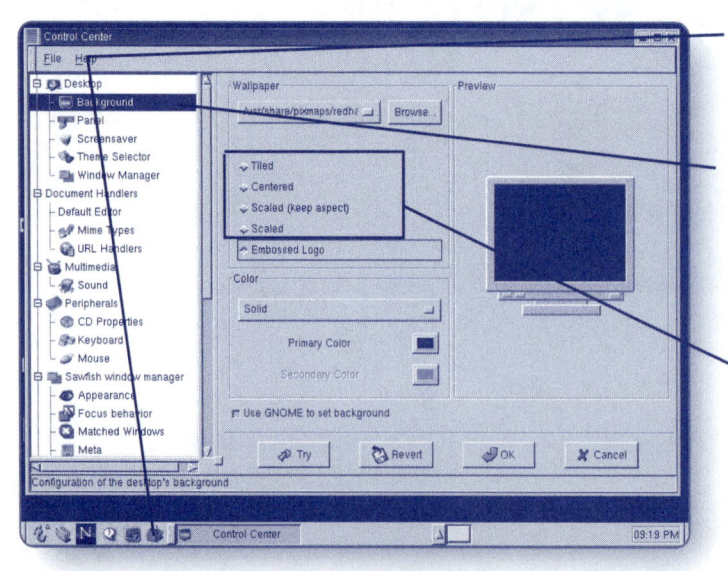

1. **Click** on the **Gnome Configuration Tool icon.** The Control Center will open.

2. **Click** on the **Background option**. The Background pane will appear on the right side of the Control Center.

3. **Click** on a **Wallpaper option button**. The option will be selected.

CHANGING THE DESKTOP BACKGROUND 61

- **Tiled.** This option tiles several copies of the image in rows and columns across the screen.

- **Centered.** This places one copy of the image in the center of the desktop. Any areas that are not used by the image will display the background color used.

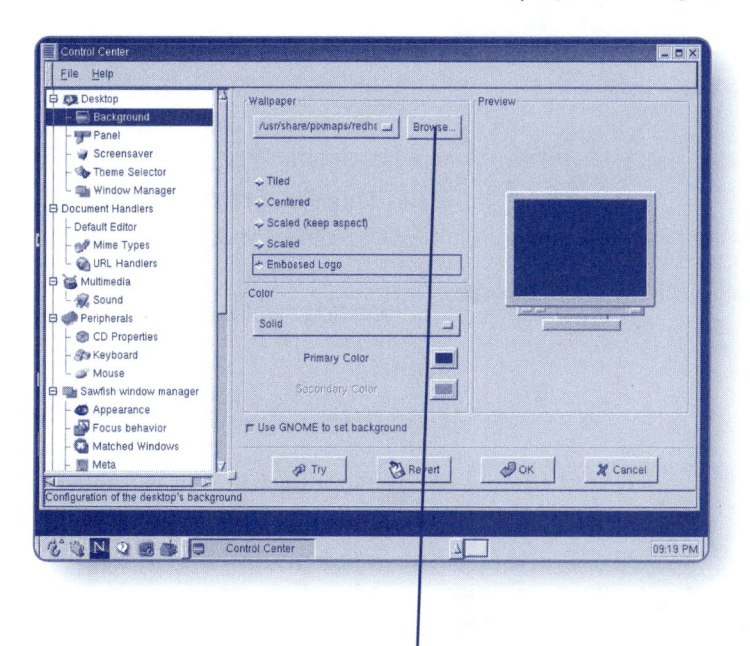

- **Scaled (keep aspect).** This Scaled option stretches the image so that it takes up the majority of the desktop area but still keeps its original height and width proportions.

- **Scaled.** Scaled fills the entire desktop with the image. The image may appear to be distorted.

- **Embossed logo.** This is the default wallpaper option, which displays an attractive, transparent Red Hat logo on the Desktop.

4. Click on the **Browse button**. The Wallpaper Selection dialog box will open.

CHAPTER 4: CUSTOMIZING THE SCREEN DISPLAY

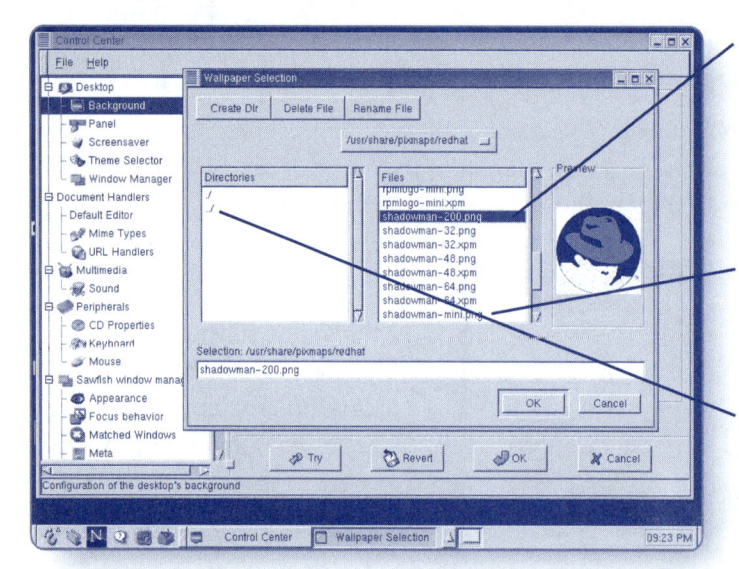

5. Click on a **file**. A preview of the background will appear in the Preview pane and the file name will appear in the Selection text box.

6. Click on **another file** if you didn't like the first selection. The file will be selected.

7. Double-click on **../** to go back to the previous directory. The main list of wallpaper directories will appear.

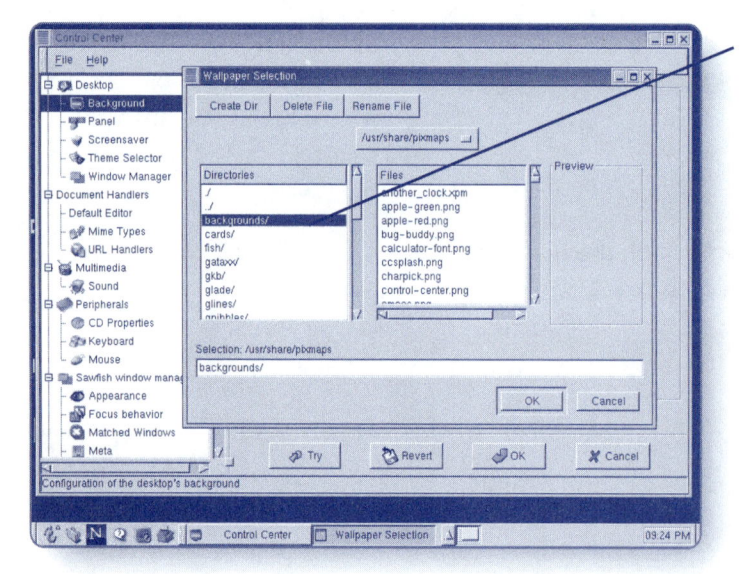

8. Double-click on a **directory** if you want to try another group of wallpapers.

CHANGING THE DESKTOP BACKGROUND 63

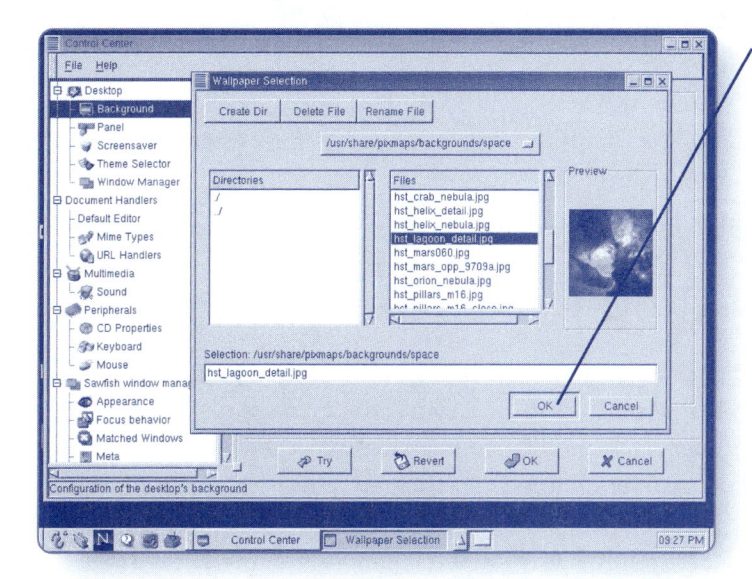

9. Click on **OK** when you have selected a wallpaper that you like. You will return to the Control Center.

10. Click on the **Try button**. You'll see a preview of the wallpaper in the preview screen at the top of the Control Center.

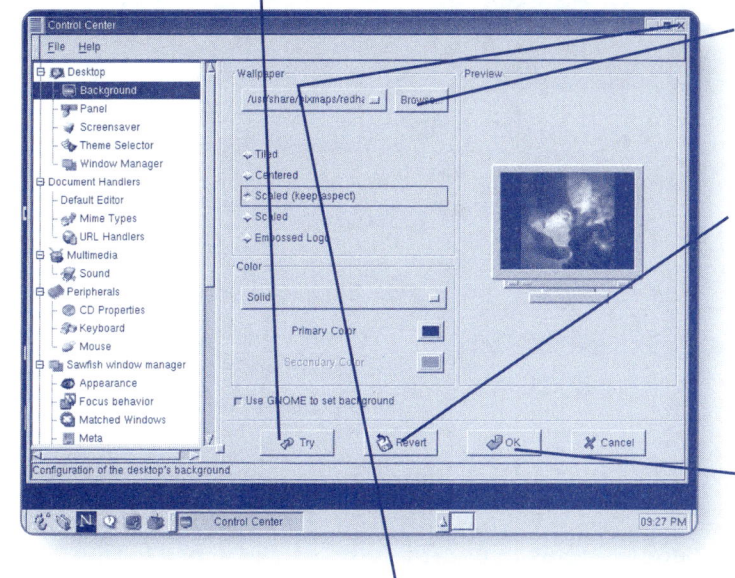

11. Click on the **Browse button** to try out other wallpapers if you are not satisfied.

12. Click on the **Revert button** if you don't like the wallpaper selection. Your desktop background will change back to the original wallpaper. You can then try a different one.

13. Click on **OK**. Your changes will be applied and the Background pane will disappear.

14. Click on the **Kill button**. The Control Center will close.

> **TIP**
> You can use the graphics applications (such as xpaint and The Gimp) that are installed by Linux to create your own wallpaper.

Setting Up a Screen Saver

In the olden days of computers, oh, say, five years ago, it was never a good idea to let a single static image display for a long period of time on your screen. After a while, the image would appear "burned" into the monitor.

Thankfully, this is no longer a technological issue. But screen savers are still around as aesthetic eye-pleasers. Screen savers also allow you to password-protect your desktop so that others can't use the computer while you are away.

1. Click on the **Gnome Configuration Tool icon**. The Control Center will open.

2. Click on **Screensaver**. The Screensaver pane will appear on the right side of the Control Center.

3. Click on a **screen saver**. The screen saver will be selected, and you'll see a preview in the Screen Saver Demo section.

4. Click on the **Settings button** if you would like to change setting such as speed, number of colors used, redraw rate, or number of pictures to use. The settings dialog box for the selected screen saver will open.

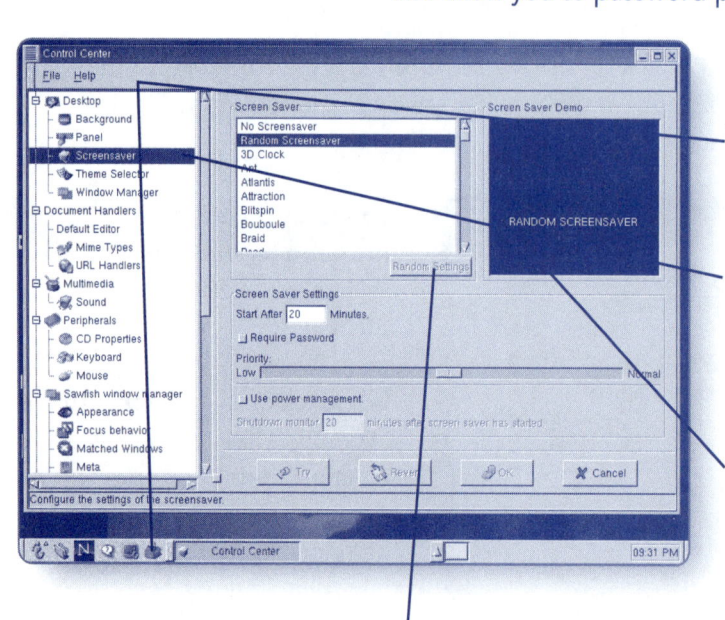

SETTING UP A SCREEN SAVER 65

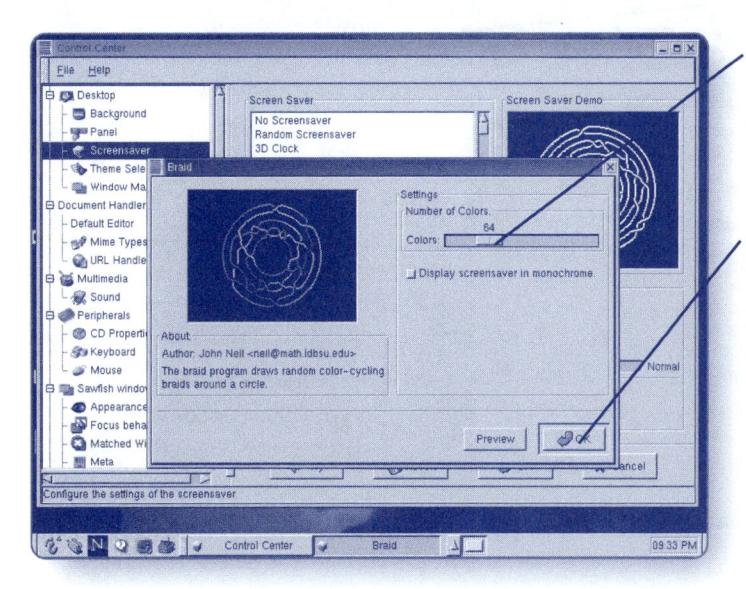

5. Click and **drag** the **sliders** to adjust the various settings for the screen saver. The settings will be changed.

6. Click on **OK**. The screen saver settings will be applied, and you will return to the Control Center.

TIP

You can see the screen saver in action by clicking on the Preview button. To leave the screen saver and return to the Control Center, press the Escape key on your keyboard.

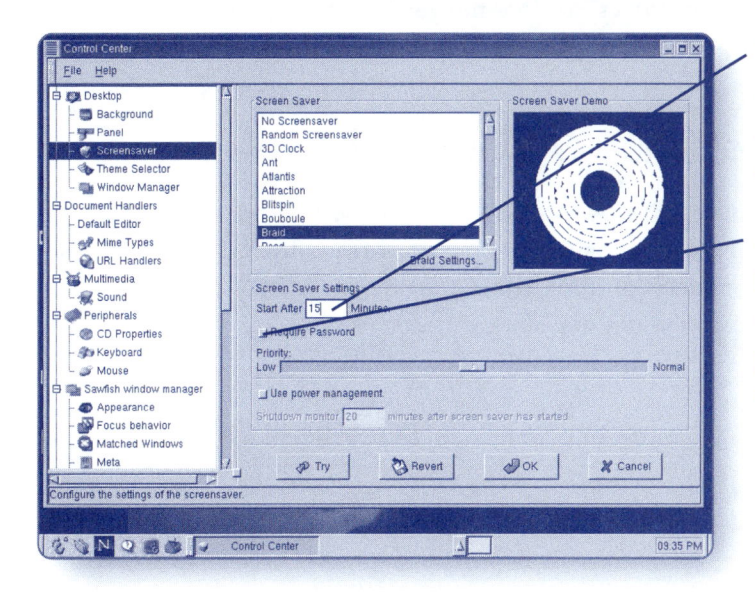

7. Type the **number of minutes** of no activity on your computer after which you would like the screen saver to start.

8. Click on the **Require Password check box** if you want the screen saver password-protected. The option will be selected.

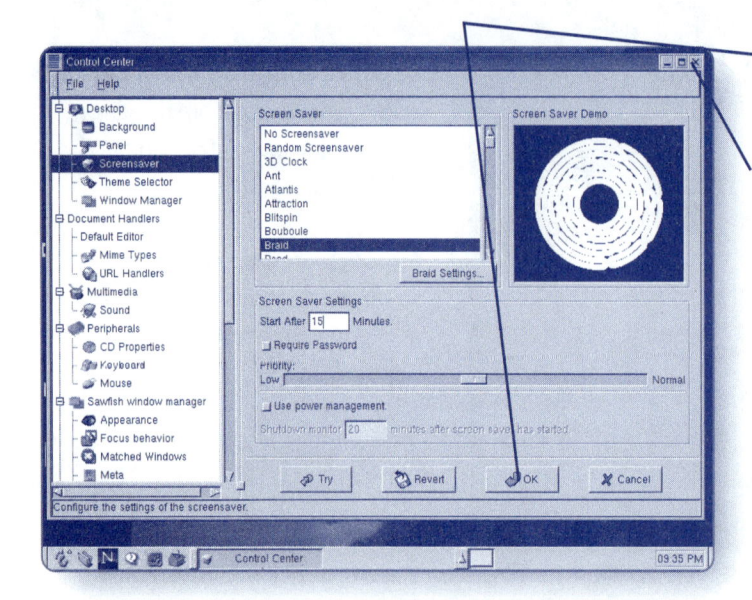

9. **Click** on **OK**. The new screen saver will now be used.

10. **Click** on the **Kill button**. The Control Center will close.

> **NOTE**
>
> Your screen saver uses your user account password.

Working with Themes

There are a number of elements that you see when working with windows and dialog boxes that can be given a different look. If you find the default look difficult to see or too boring for your tastes, explore the various themes. There are a number of themes already included with Red Hat Linux.

Selecting a Window Theme

You can change the look of a window's border and decorations using a number of installed themes in the Sawfish Configuration Tool. These themes do not change anything located inside the window border.

WORKING WITH THEMES

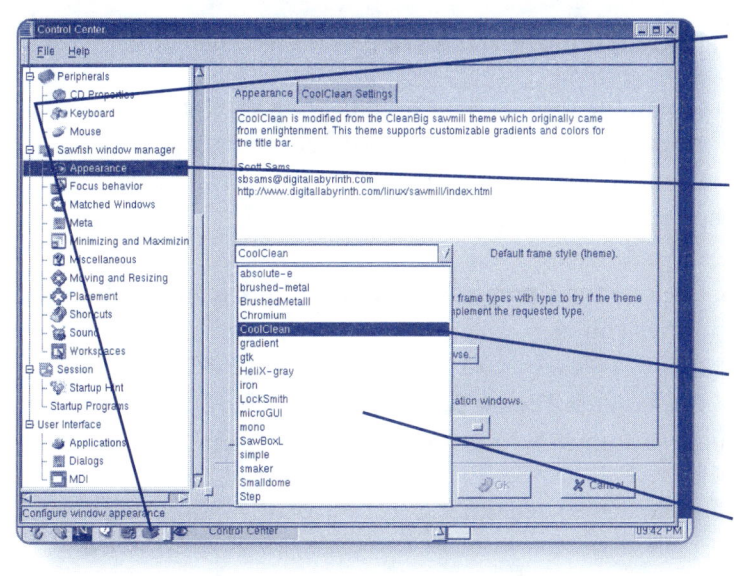

1. Click on the **Gnome Configuration Tool icon**. The Control Center will open.

2. Click on the **Appearance option** under the Sawfish window manager category. The Appearance pane will appear.

3. Click on the **Default frame style drop-down list**. The list of theme options will appear.

4. Click on a **theme**. The theme will be selected.

5. Click on the **Try button**. You'll see your background color appear on the desktop.

6. Click on the **Revert button** if you don't like the color selection. Your desktop background will change back to the original color. You can then try a different color.

7. Click on **OK** when you are satisfied with your color selection. Your changes will be applied.

8. Click on the **Kill button**. The Control Center will close.

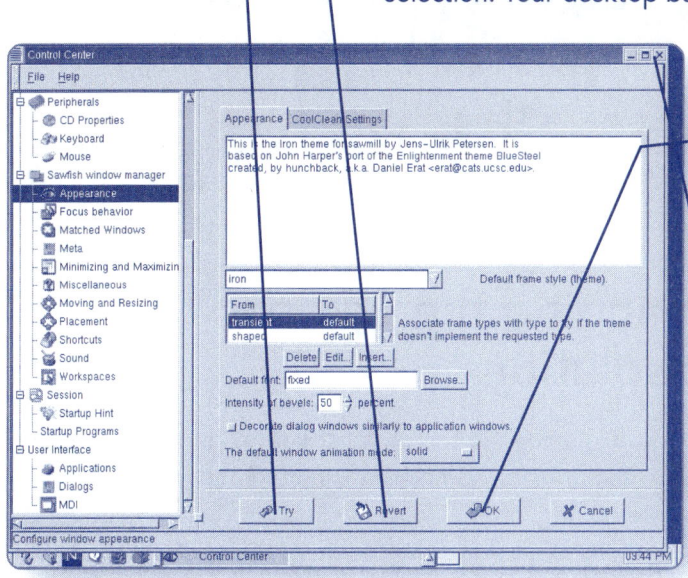

Choosing an Interface Theme

If you find the dialog boxes hard to work with, use one of the interface themes to give the dialog box elements a more familiar feel. Interface themes change the look of scroll bars, check buttons, and radio buttons.

1. **Click** on the **Gnome Configuration Tool icon**. The Control Center will open.

2. **Click** on the **Theme Selector option**. The Theme Selector pane will appear on the right side of the Control Center.

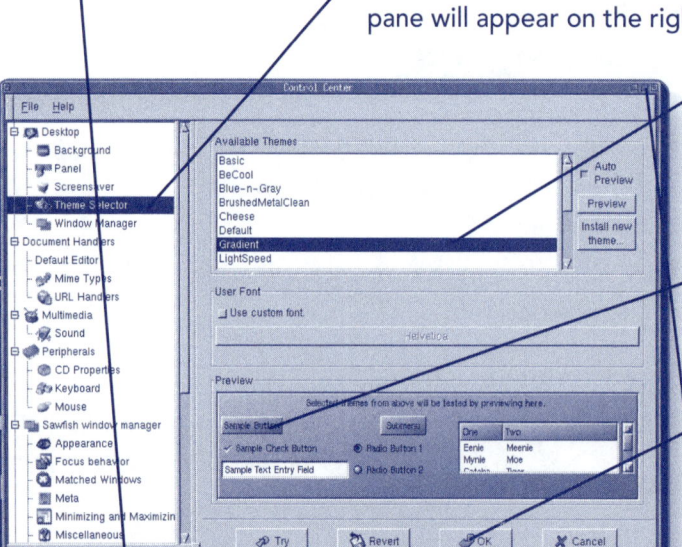

3. **Click** on a **theme**. The theme will be selected and you'll see a preview in the Preview section.

4. **Click** on a **sample** to test how different elements function.

5. **Click** on **OK** when you find a theme that you like. Your changes will be applied.

6. **Click** on the **Kill button**. The Control Center will close.

NOTE
If you don't see the Preview section, click on the Auto Preview button.

Changing the Screen Resolution

I'll let you in on a little secret: for the most part, changing the screen resolution of X Windows is not something you are going to do very often. Once you find a screen resolution you like, you're going to want to keep the desktop there.

CHANGING THE SCREEN RESOLUTION 69

Still, there are exceptions to this rule, like writing a *Fast and Easy* book. Most of the screenshots in this book and 640-pixel by 480-pixel resolution, to make things easier to see. The screens in this chapter, however, were set at 800 × 600. To change the resolution on a monitor to something else, you need to use the Linux console via the terminal emulator. Here, you will launch and use the nifty text-based program Xconfigurator, which is the best tool to switch video resolutions.

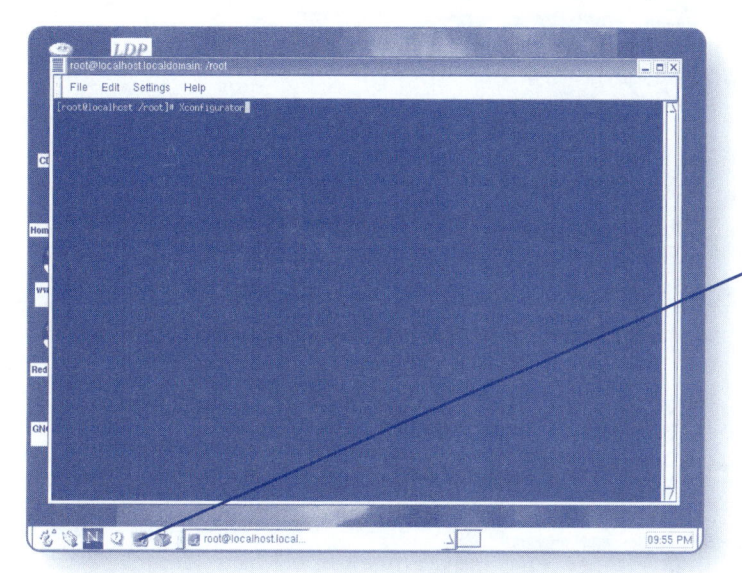

1. Click on the **Terminal emulation program icon**. The Terminal window will open.

2. Type Xconfigurator and **press Enter**. The Xconfigurator application will start within the Terminal window.

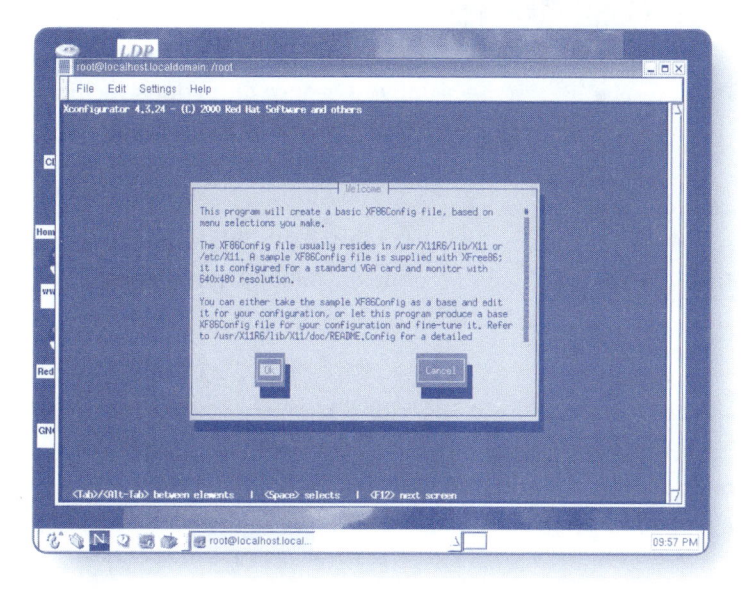

3. Press Enter again. The introductory screen will be replaced by the results of a probe of your PC's video card.

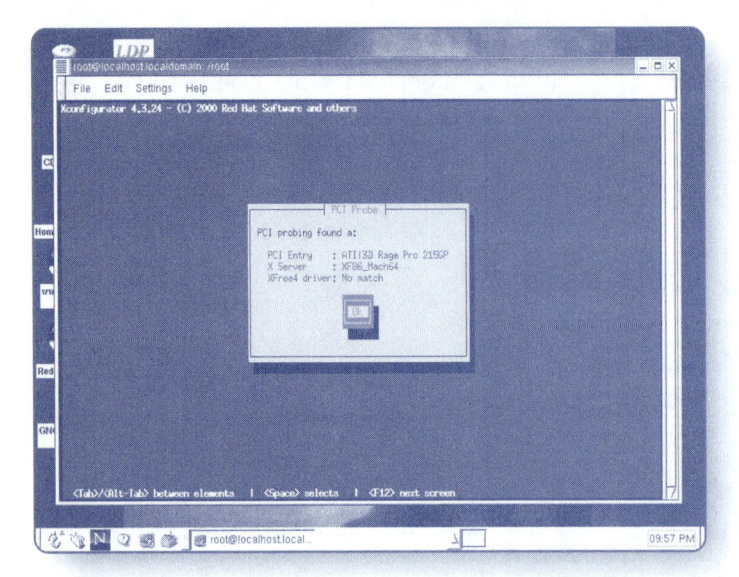

4. Press the **Enter key**. The Monitor Setup screen will replace the probe screen.

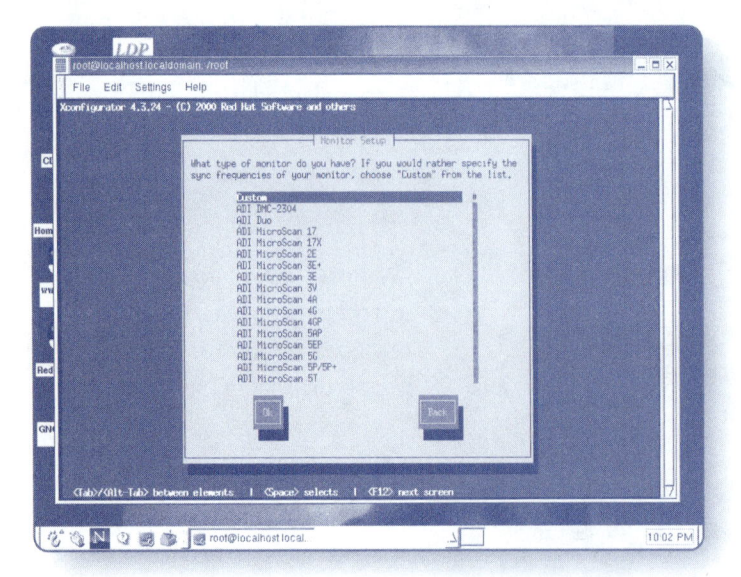

5a. Press the **arrow keys** to select your monitor type. The monitor will be selected.

or

5b. Select the **Custom option** if you cannot find your specific monitor. The option will be selected.

6. Press the **Tab key**. The OK button will be highlighted.

7. Press the **Enter key**. The Video Memory screen (see step 15) will replace the Monitor Setup screen if you specified a monitor or the Custom Monitor Setup screen if you specified the Custom option.

CHANGING THE SCREEN RESOLUTION 71

> **CAUTION**
> Be sure you have selected the exact type of monitor from the list. Many monitors carry similar names, but have vastly different configurations.

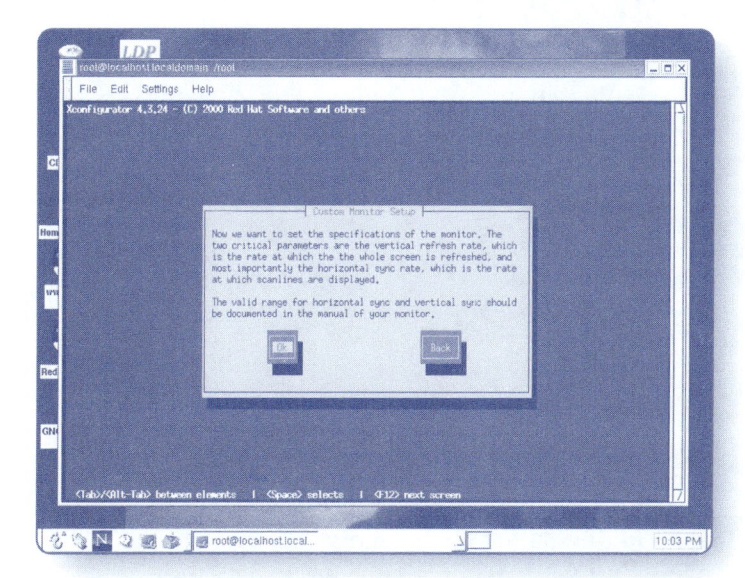

8. Press the **Enter key**. The horizontal sync range screen will replace the Custom Monitor screen.

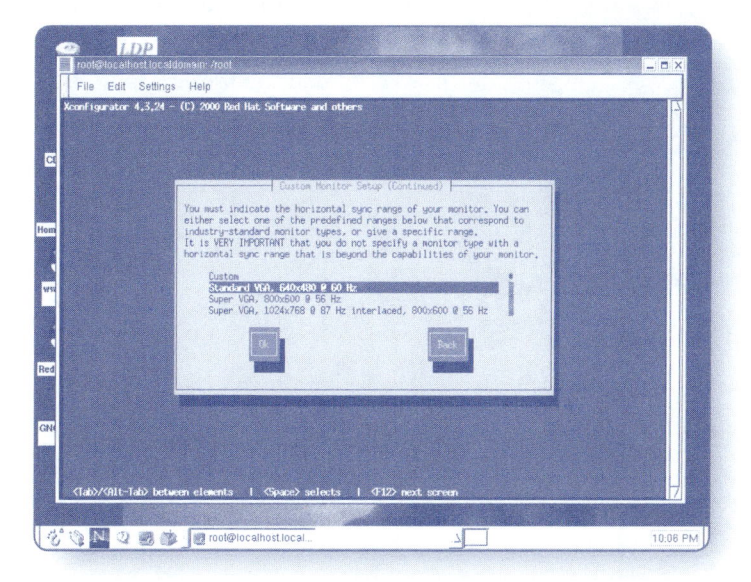

9. Press the **arrow keys** to select your horizontal sync rate. The option will be selected.

10. Press the **Enter key**. The vertical sync range screen will replace the horizontal sync range screen.

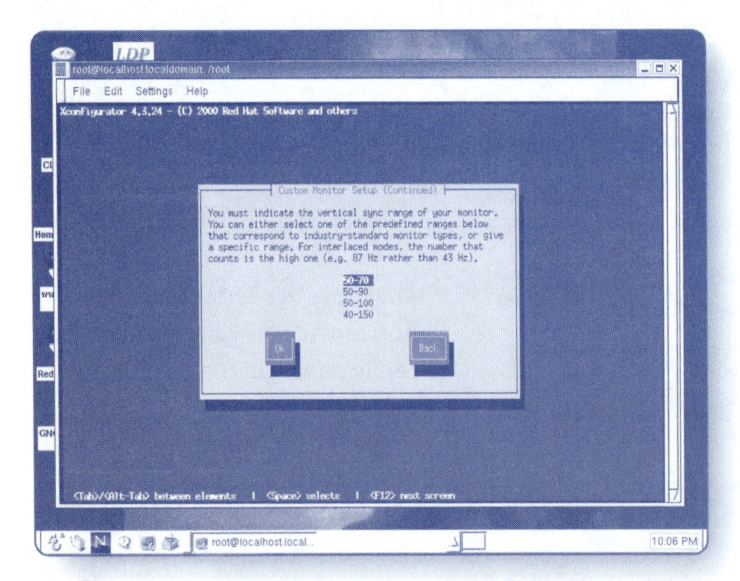

72 CHAPTER 4: CUSTOMIZING THE SCREEN DISPLAY

11. Press the **arrow keys** to select your vertical sync rate. The option will be selected.

12. Press the **Enter key**. The Video Memory screen will replace the vertical sync range screen.

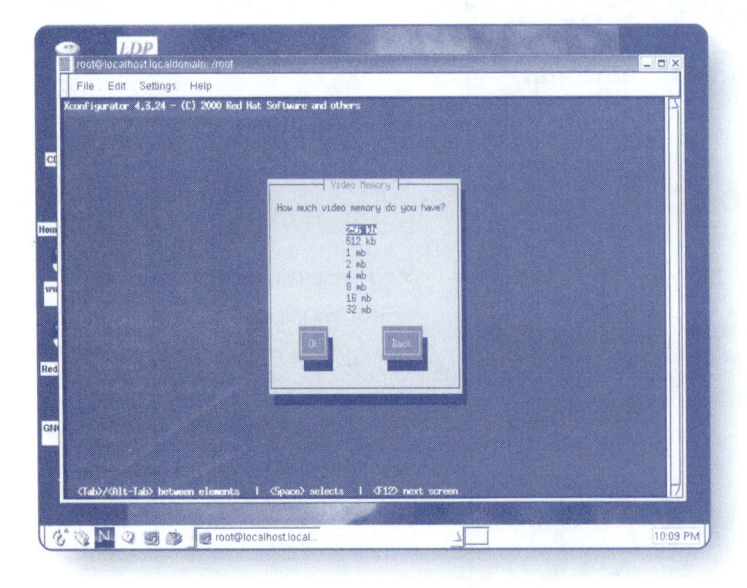

13. Press the **arrow keys** to select the amount of video memory your system has. The option will be selected.

14. Press the **Enter key**. The Clockchip Configuration screen will replace the Video Memory screen.

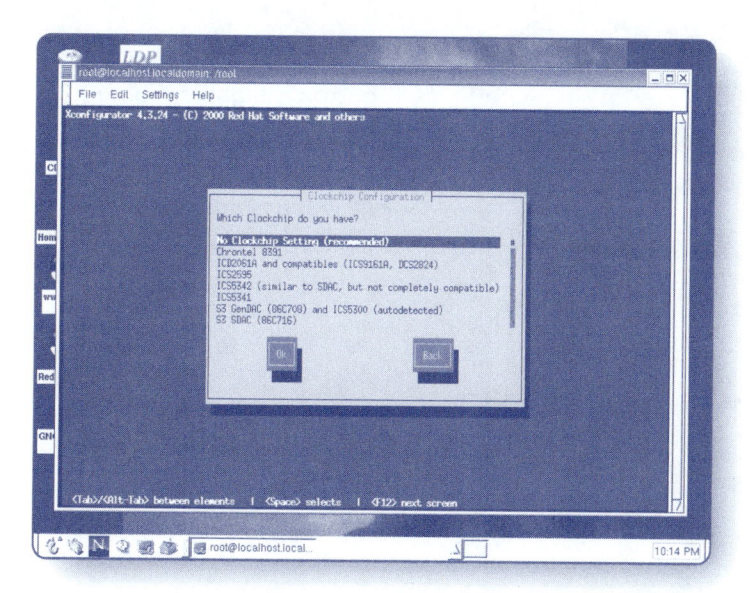

CHANGING THE SCREEN RESOLUTION

15. Press the **arrow keys** to select the appropriate clockchip option. The option will be selected.

16. Press the **Enter key**. The Select Video Modes screen will replace the Clockchip Configuration screen.

TIP
Many newer video cards do not have clockchips, so you will likely select the No Clockchip Setting option.

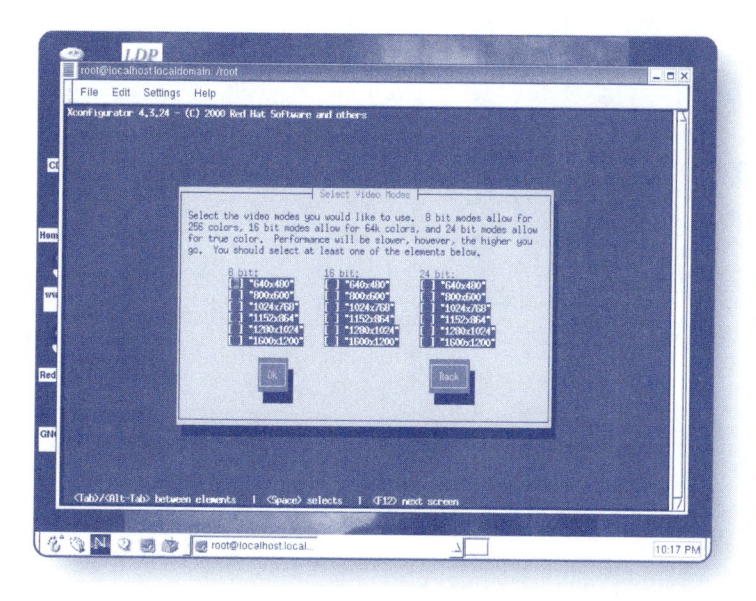

17. Press the **arrow keys** to move up and down the video mode column. The options will be highlighted as you go.

18. Press the **Tab key** to move between columns. The options will be highlighted.

19. Press the **Spacebar** to select the options you want. An asterisk appears next to the selected options.

CHAPTER 4: CUSTOMIZING THE SCREEN DISPLAY

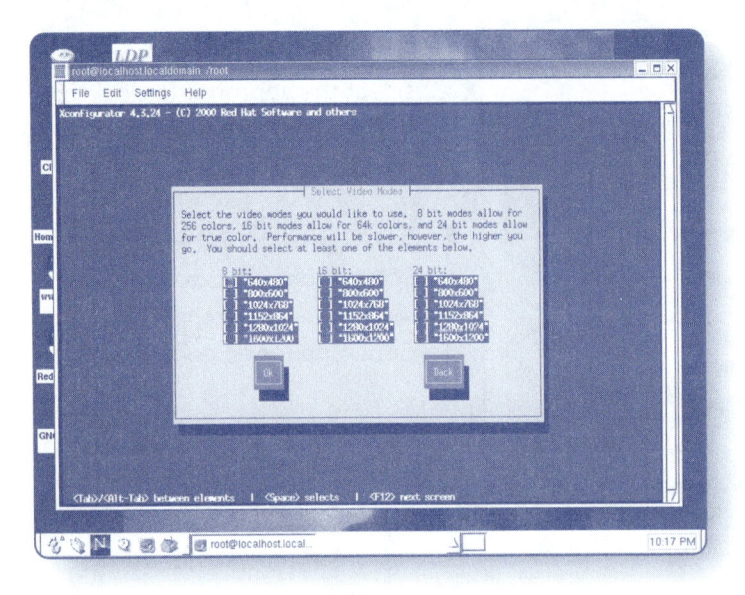

20. **Press** the **Tab key** until the OK button is highlighted.

21. **Press** the **Enter key**. The Select Video Modes screen will be replaced by the Starting X screen.

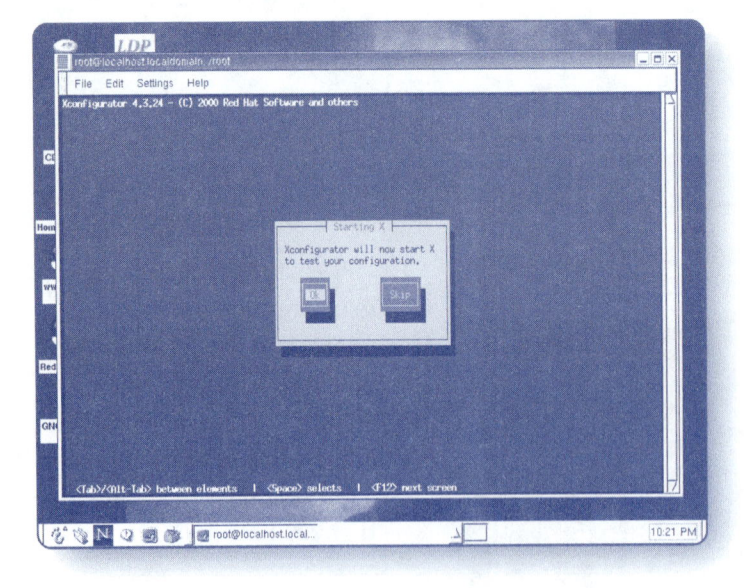

22. **Press** the **Enter key**. The Starting X screen will be replaced by a test of the X Window settings you selected. You will see an interrogative message asking you if you can see that message.

23. **Click** on **Yes**. X will then ask if want to start X automatically when you reboot.

24. **Click** on **Yes**. You will then see a message indicating that your changes are about to be stored.

25. **Click** on **OK**. The test of X will close and the Xconfigurator application will close.

Your changes will take affect upon restarting X.

5

Managing Your Desktop

The Sawmill Window Manager controls the appearance, behavior, background, and user interactions of windows. As you learned earlier, Sawmill makes managing the virtual screens, configuring multiple workspaces, and choosing themes and backgrounds a lot less complex. The Gnome interface adds more control and utilities to help you manage your desktop. Gnome allows you to create handy shortcuts to help you launch applications quicker. Gnome also helps you manage tasks and tools easily. In this chapter, you'll learn how to:

- Place applets on the Gnome Panel
- Use launchers to open applications and files
- Create drawers to store frequently accessed programs

Working with Applets on the Gnome Panel

There are already a number of applets on the Gnome Panel. The Gnome Pager is an applet and so is the clock. These applets are small applications that are available to assist you by performing various tasks or displaying important information. There are several applets from which you can choose. You'll find everything from amusements that provide a visual distraction to utilities for working with your computer's peripherals.

Entertaining from the Gnome Panel

There are a couple of fun games that you can keep permanently open on the Gnome Panel. They're small and unobtrusive, so maybe you won't find them so distracting.

1. Click on the **Main Menu button**. The Main Menu will appear.

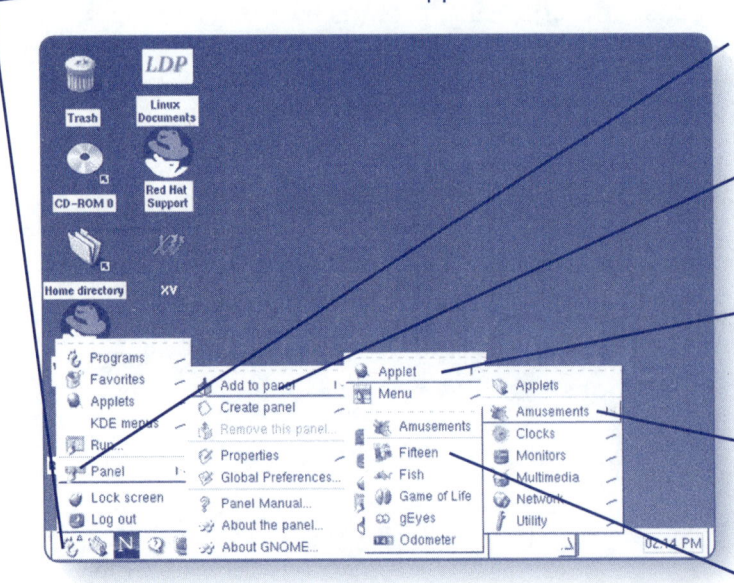

2. Move the **mouse pointer** to Panel. The Panel menu will appear.

3. Move the **mouse pointer** to Add to panel. The Add to panel menu will appear.

4. Move the **mouse pointer** to Applet. The Applet menu will appear.

5. Move the **mouse pointer** to Amusements. The Amusements menu will appear.

6. Click on **Fifteen**. The icon for the Fifteen game will appear on the Gnome Panel.

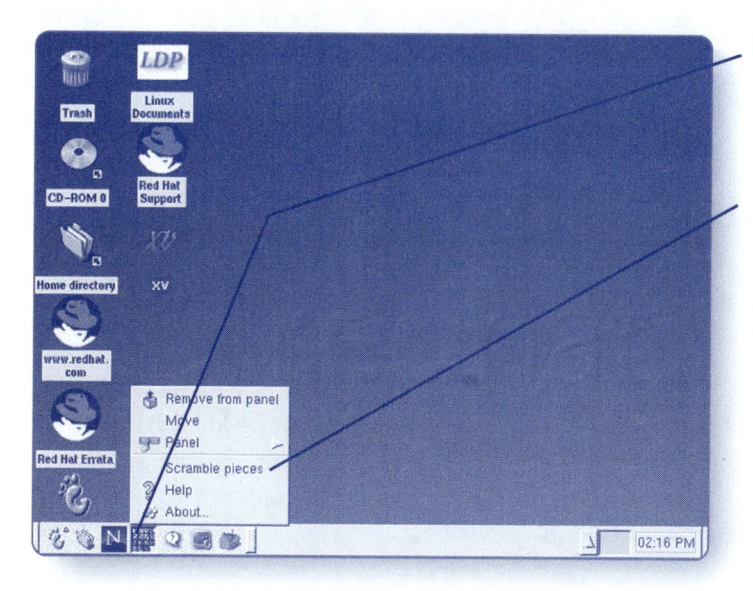

WORKING WITH APPLETS ON THE GNOME PANEL 77

7. Right-click on the **Fifteen icon**. A control menu for Fifteen will appear.

8. Click on **Scramble pieces**. The puzzle pieces will be mixed up and you can try and rearrange the individual squares so that they are in order.

Playing Your CDs

If you like to listen to music while you're working at your computer, keep a CD player on the Gnome Panel.

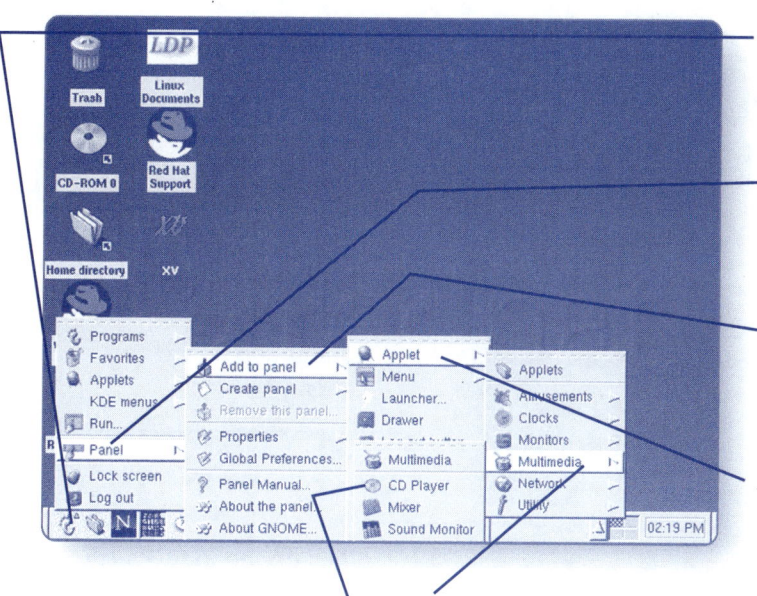

1. Click on the **Main Menu button**. The Main Menu will appear.

2. Move the **mouse pointer** to Panel. The Panel menu will appear.

3. Move the **mouse pointer** to Add to panel. The Add to panel menu will appear.

4. Move the **mouse pointer** to Applet. The Applet menu will appear.

5. Move the **mouse pointer** to Multimedia. The Multimedia menu will appear.

6. Click on **CD Player.** The icon for the CD Player applet will appear on the Gnome Panel.

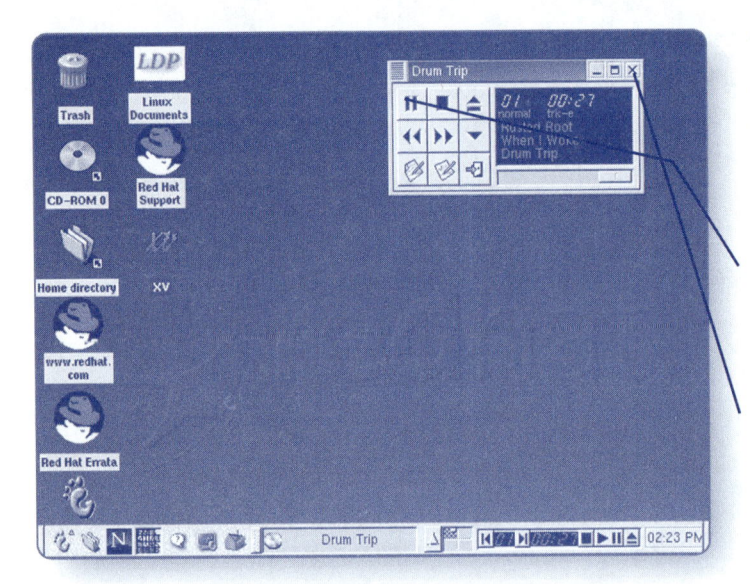

7. Place a music **CD** in your computer's CD-ROM drive. The CD Player application will open and should begin to play the CD immediately.

8. Click on the **Pause button** on the CD Player. The CD should pause playing.

9. Click on the **kill button** on the CD Player application. The application will close.

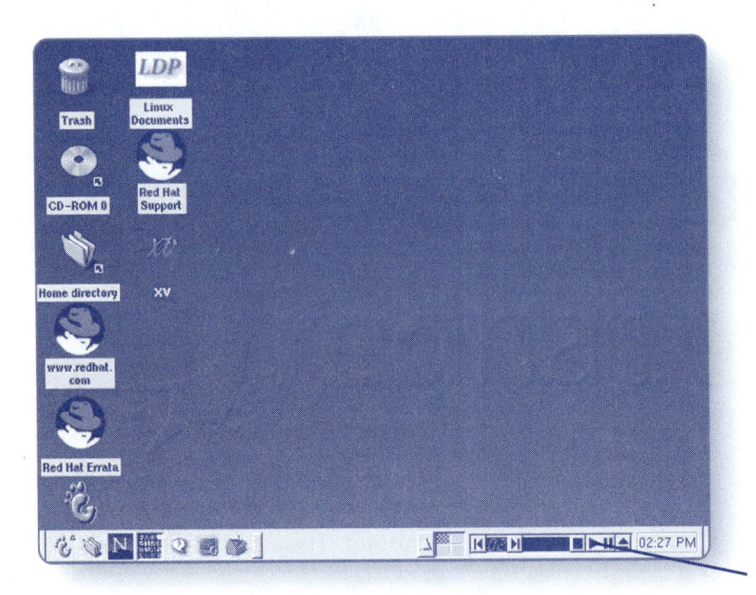

> **TIP**
>
> If you don't hear sound out of your speakers, Linux may need to be configured to use your sound card. See Chapter 14, "Sounding Off with Your Computer," for more information on configuring sound cards.

10. Click on the **Play/Pause button** on the CD Player applet. The CD will continue playing without desktop space being used.

WORKING WITH APPLETS ON THE GNOME PANEL 79

Moving Applets around on the Gnome Panel

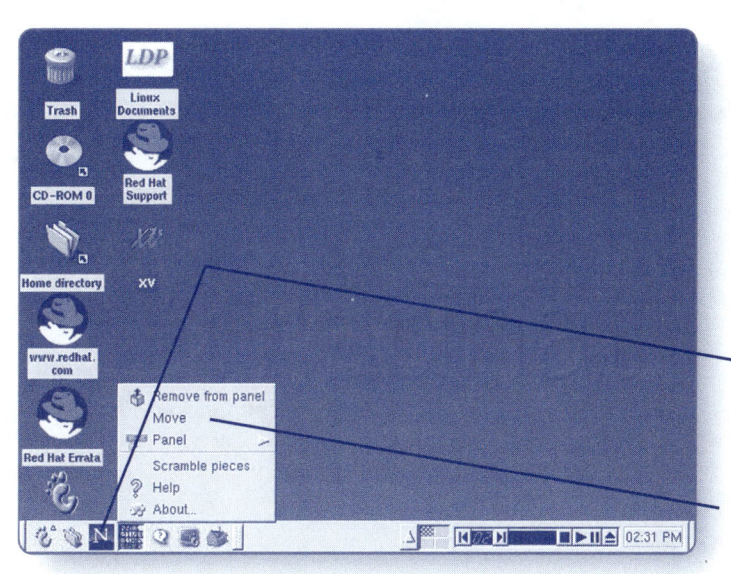

You may not like where the applet was placed on the Gnome Panel by default. You can move any applet to any place on the Gnome Panel.

1. Right-click on the **applet** that you want to move. A menu will appear.

2. Click on **Move**. The applet will become a floating object on the Gnome Panel and the move cursor will appear.

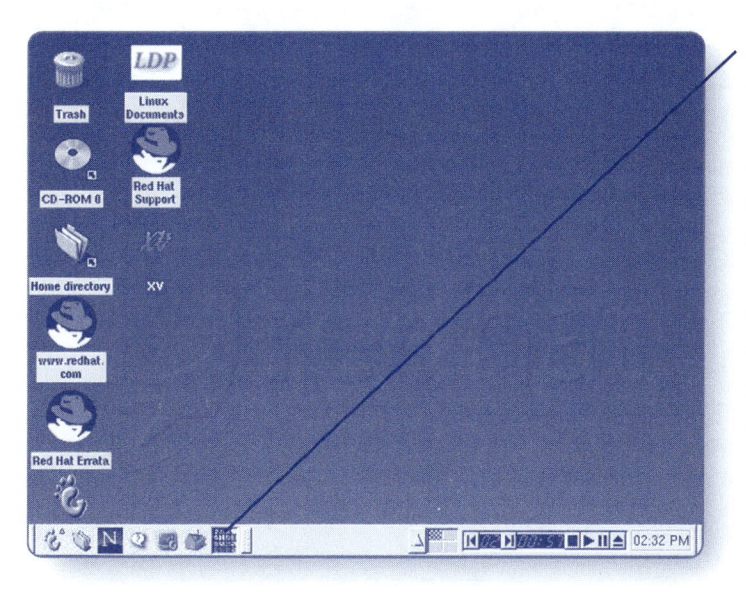

3. Move the **mouse pointer** to the place on the Gnome Panel where you want to move the applet. The move cursor will shift the applet along as you move it.

4. Click the **mouse button** when the applet is in the place where you want it. The applet will be positioned in the new spot.

Removing Applets from the Gnome Panel

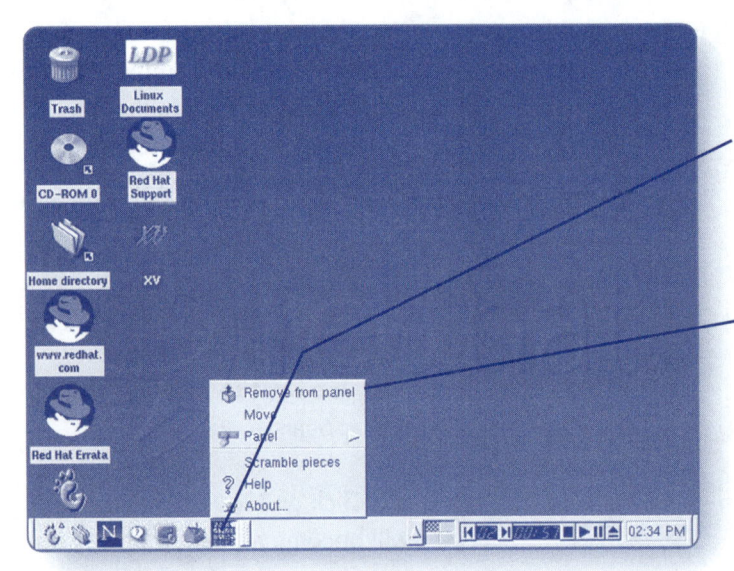

You can also remove applets from the Gnome Panel.

1. Right-click on the **applet** that you want to remove from the Gnome Panel. A menu will appear.

2. Click on **Remove from panel**. The applet will no longer appear on the Gnome Panel.

Using Application Launchers

Application launchers are small icons that you place on the Gnome panel and the Desktop to start an application when you click on them. You can use these launchers to customize the panel and place all the tools and applications you need within easy reach.

Adding a Launcher to the Gnome Panel

If the application or utility that you want to launch from the Panel is listed in the Gnome menu, use this quick method to place a launcher on the Gnome Panel.

USING APPLICATION LAUNCHERS   81

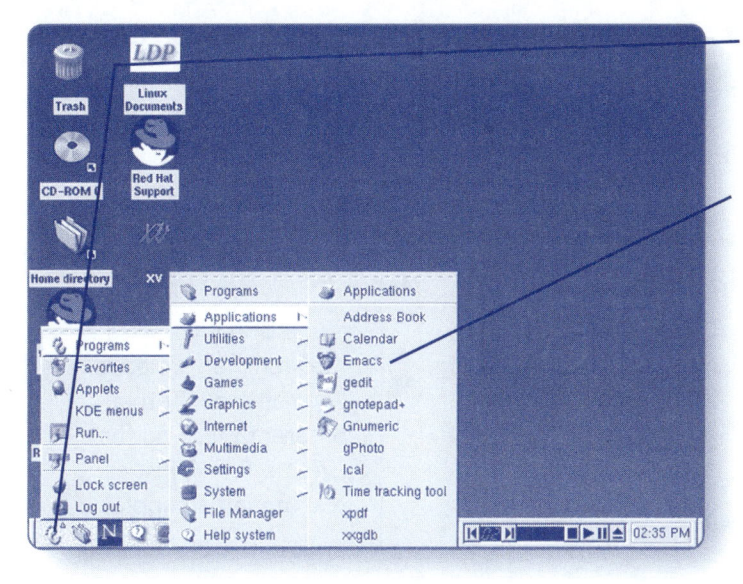

1. Click on the **Main Menu button**. The Main Menu will appear.

2. Display the **menu** that contains the application that you want to place on the Gnome Panel. The menu will appear.

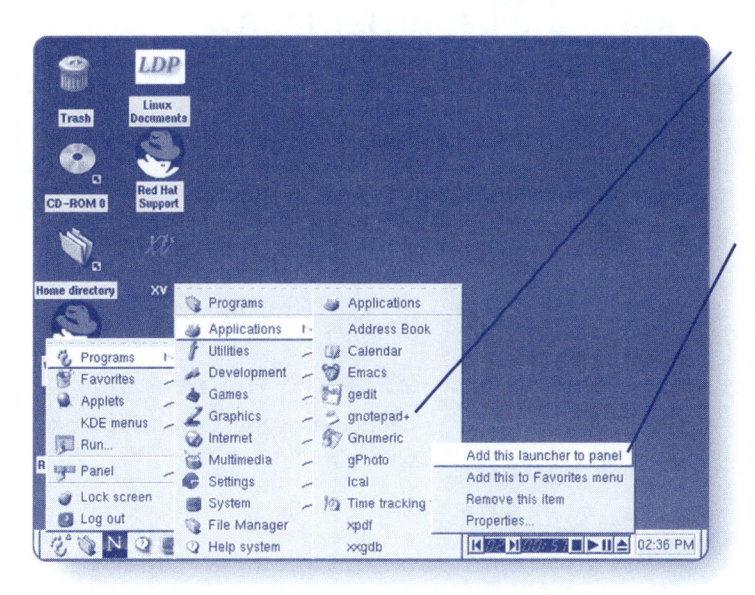

3. Right-click on the **application or utility** you want to launch from the Gnome Panel. A menu will appear.

4. Click on **Add this launcher to panel**. A launcher icon will appear on the panel.

CHAPTER 5: MANAGING YOUR DESKTOP

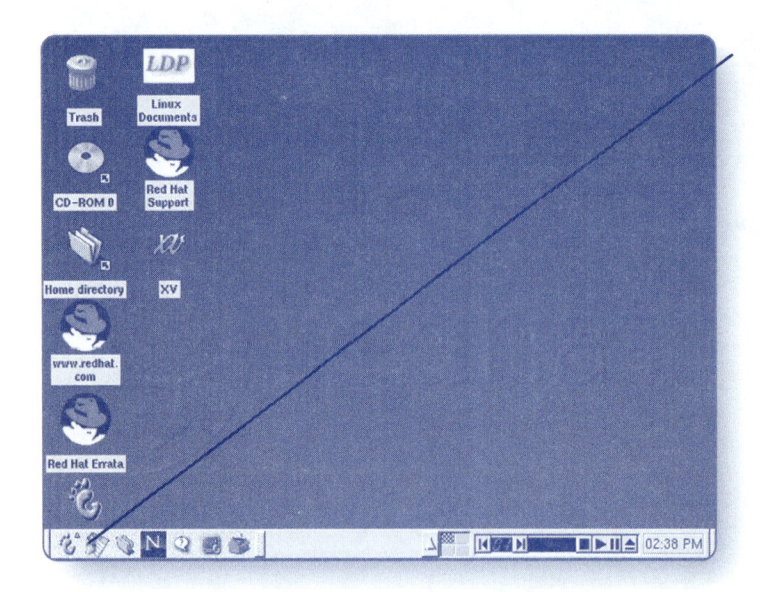

5. Click on the **Panel launcher icon**. The application will start.

> **NOTE**
> If you don't like where the launcher is placed, you can move it to a different place on the Gnome Panel, just as you moved an applet.

Changing the Launcher Icon

Each application has a default launcher icon. If you want something different, there are many different icons from which you can choose.

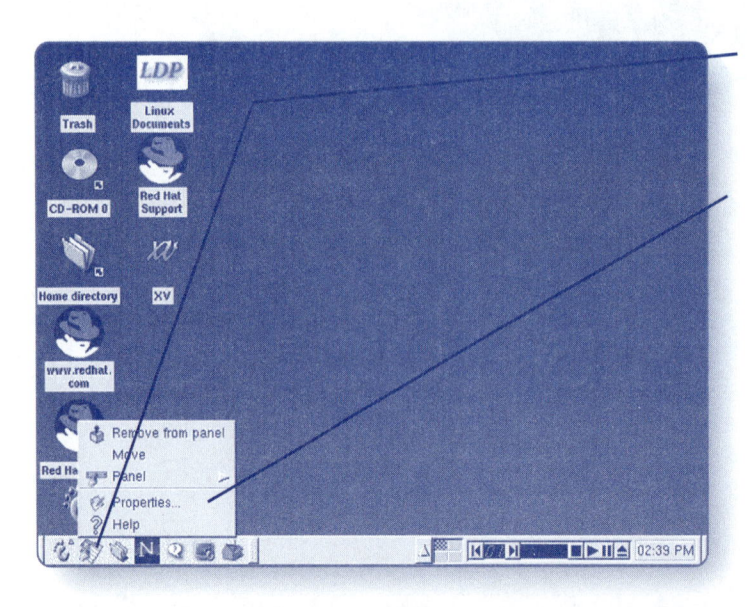

1. Right-click on the **launcher icon** you want to change. A menu will appear.

2. Click on **Properties**. The Launcher properties dialog box will open.

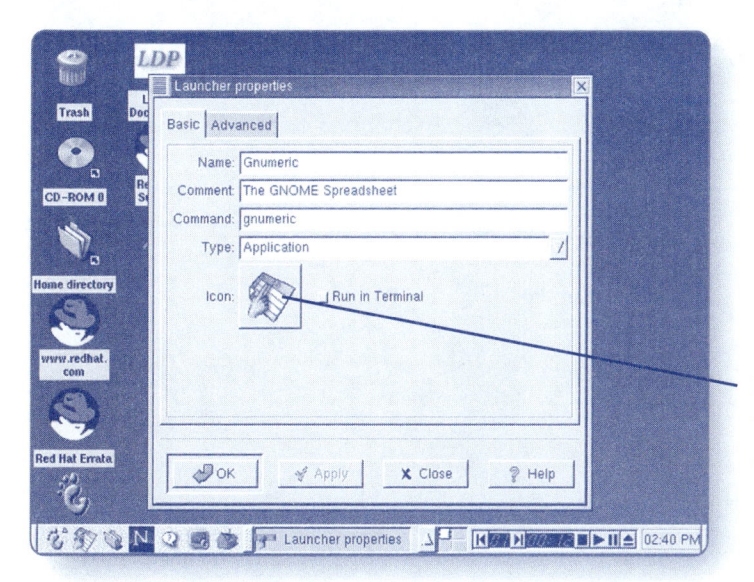

USING APPLICATION LAUNCHERS 83

TIP
To change the tool tip that appears when the mouse is held over the launcher icon, edit the text in the Comment text box.

3. Click on the **Icon button**. The Choose an icon dialog box will open.

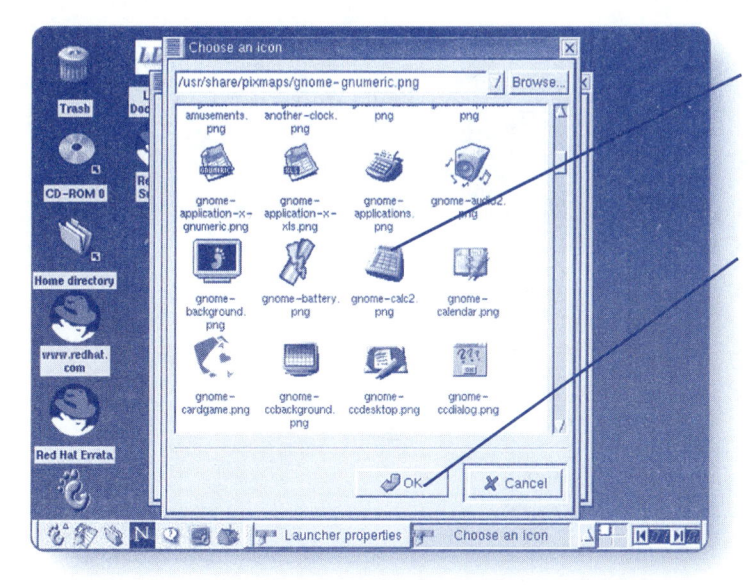

4. Click on the **icon** that you want to use from the list of thumbnails. The icon will be selected.

5. Click on **OK**. You'll return to the Launcher properties dialog box and the icon you selected will appear on the Icon button.

TIP
If you have a picture stored on your computer that you want to use for the icon, click on the Browse button to find it.

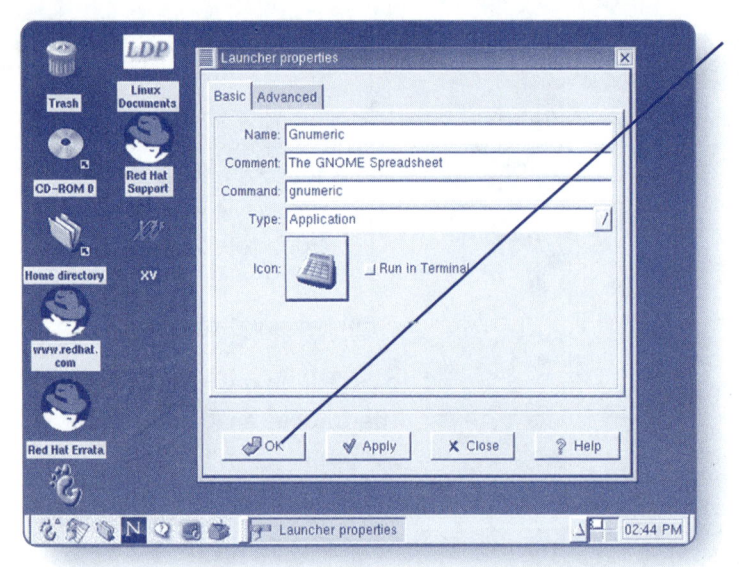

6. Click on **OK**. The picture used for the launcher icon changes on the Gnome Panel.

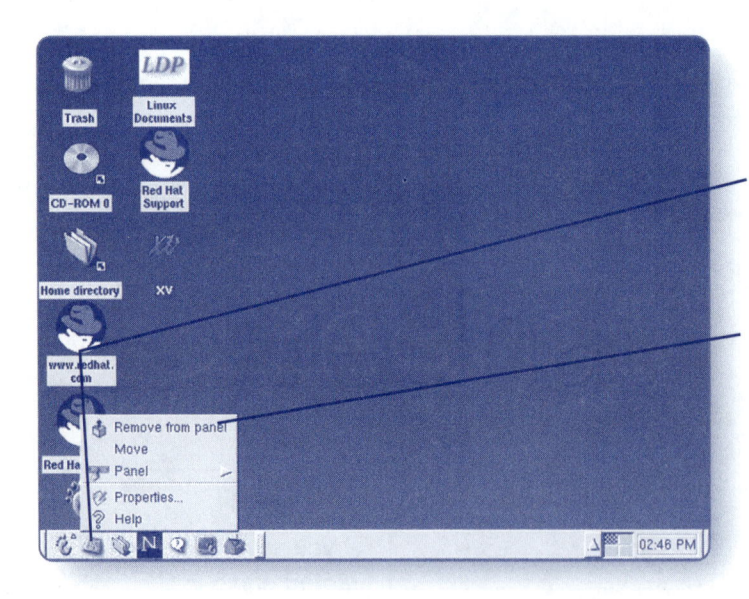

Deleting Launchers

You can delete unused or unnecessary launchers from the Panel with a few mouse clicks.

1. Right-click on the **launcher icon** that you want to delete. A menu will appear.

2. Click on **Remove from panel**. The launcher will disappear from your Gnome Panel.

Adding Drawers to the Gnome Panel

Drawers are small pop-up menus of launcher icons that sit as a button on the Panel. You may use them to keep all the applications associated with a particular job together or you may even select a whole menu of items from the Gnome menus and place it on the Panel as a drawer.

Creating the Drawer

Creating a drawer on the Gnome desktop is a piece of cake!

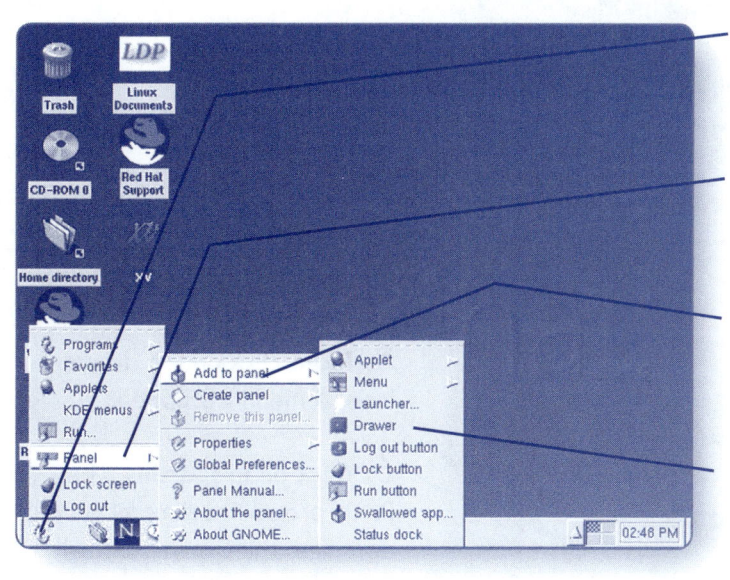

1. Click on the **Main Menu button**. The Main Menu will appear.

2. Move the **mouse pointer** to Panel. The Panel menu will appear.

3. Move the **mouse pointer** to Add to panel. The Add to panel menu will appear.

4. Click on **Drawer**. An empty Drawer will appear.

CHAPTER 5: MANAGING YOUR DESKTOP

NOTE

The drawer is open and empty. To close the drawer, you can either click on the icon on the Gnome Panel or click on the down arrow at the top of the open drawer.

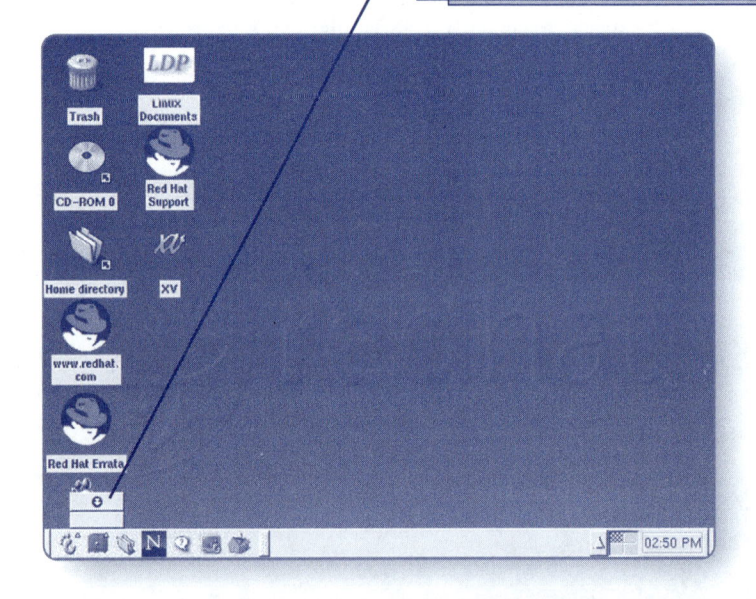

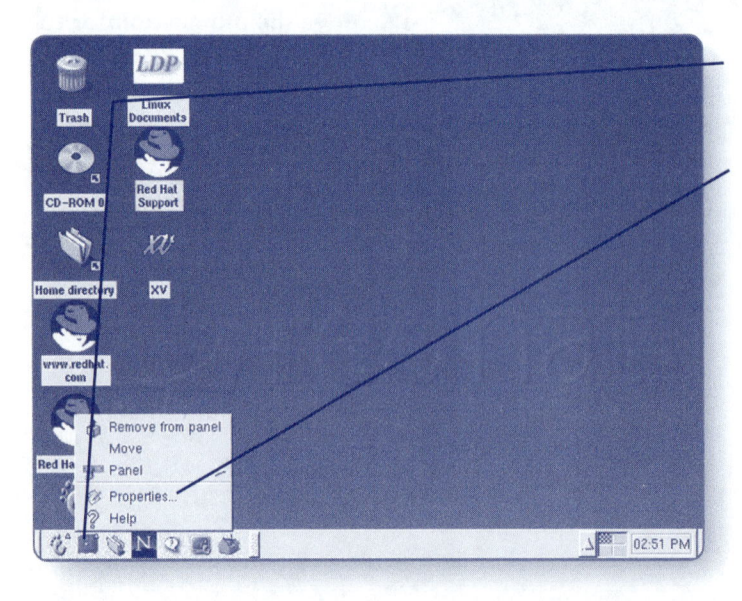

5. Right-click on the **drawer icon**. A menu will appear.

6. Click on **Properties**. The Panel properties dialog box will open and the Drawer tab will be at the top of the stack.

ADDING DRAWERS TO THE GNOME PANEL

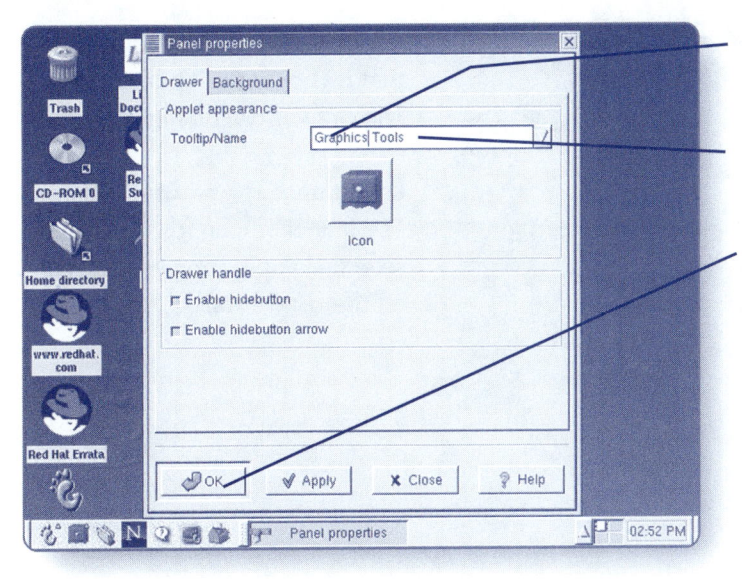

7. Click in the **Tooltip/Name text box**.

8. Type a **name** you want to use to identify the drawer.

9. Click on **OK**. The dialog box will close. When you hold the cursor over the new drawer, the tooltip name appears.

> **NOTE**
> You can move the drawer to any spot on the Gnome Panel.

Filling up the Drawer

Now you'll need to add some things to the new drawer. Before you begin adding items to the drawer, you'll want to make sure the drawer is open.

1. Click on the **Main Menu button**. The main menu will appear.

2. Click on the **menu** that contains the application that you want to add to the drawer. The menu will appear.

3. Click and **hold** on the **application** that you want to add to the drawer. The application will be selected.

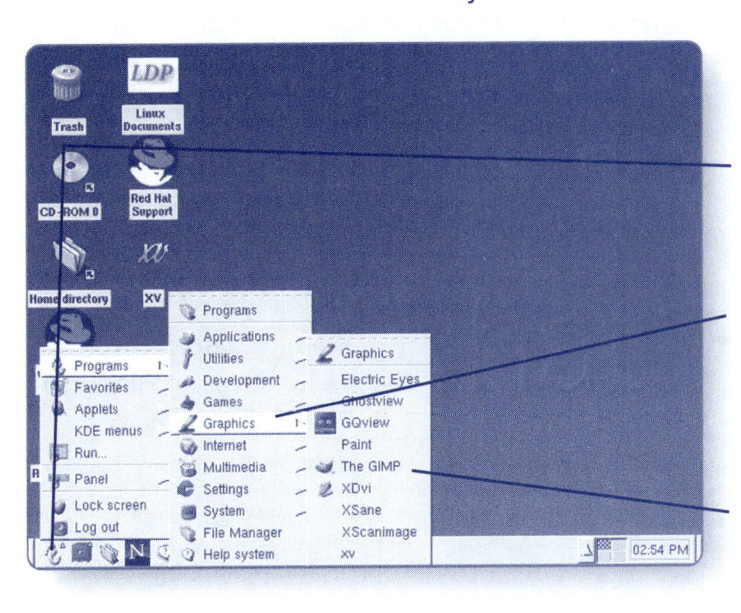

88 CHAPTER 5: MANAGING YOUR DESKTOP

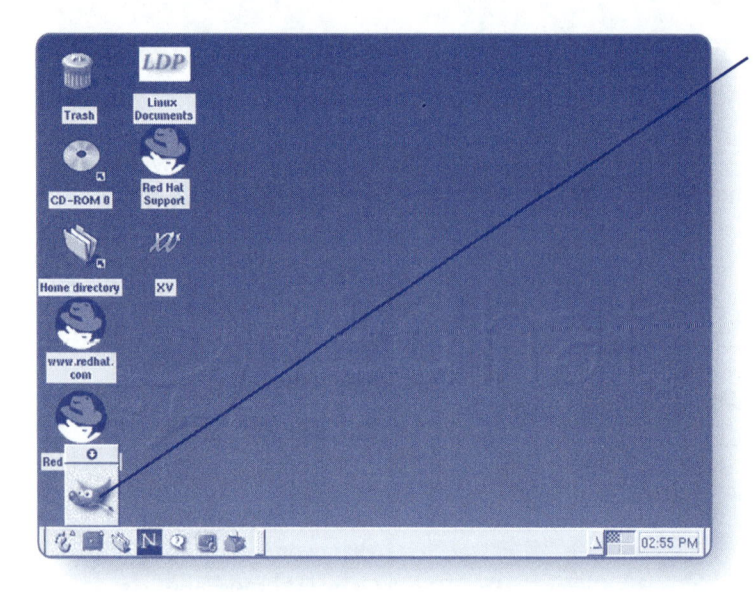

4. Drag the **mouse pointer** so that it is over the open drawer. The drawer will be highlighted.

5. Release the **mouse button**. The launcher icon for the selected application will appear on the drawer tab.

NOTE

If the Main Menu or any of its submenus are covering the drawer tab, you must move the drawer before you can place the application in the drawer.

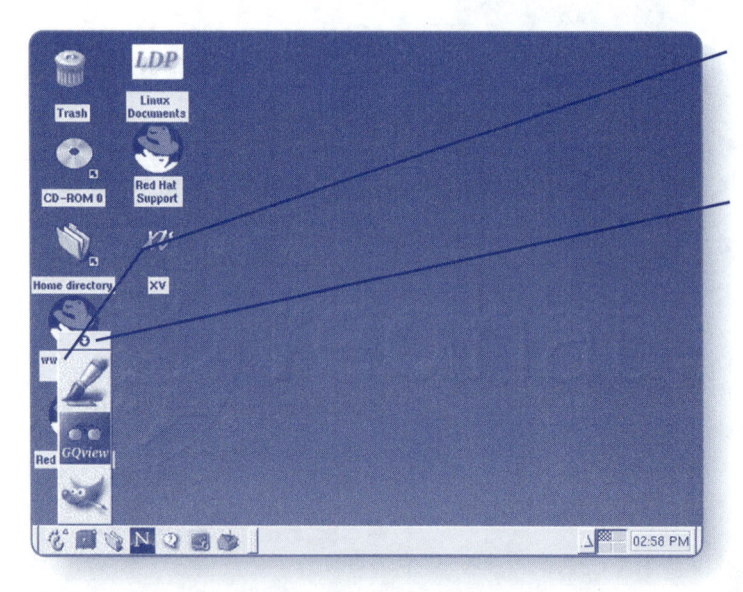

6. Drag more **applications** from the menu to the drawer and watch the icons line up.

7. Click on the **down arrow** on the drawer tab or on the drawer icon. The drawer will close.

ADDING DRAWERS TO THE GNOME PANEL   **89**

Creating a Drawer from the Main Menu

You can make an entire submenu from the Gnome menus into a drawer.

1. Click on the **Main Menu button**. The Main Menu will appear.

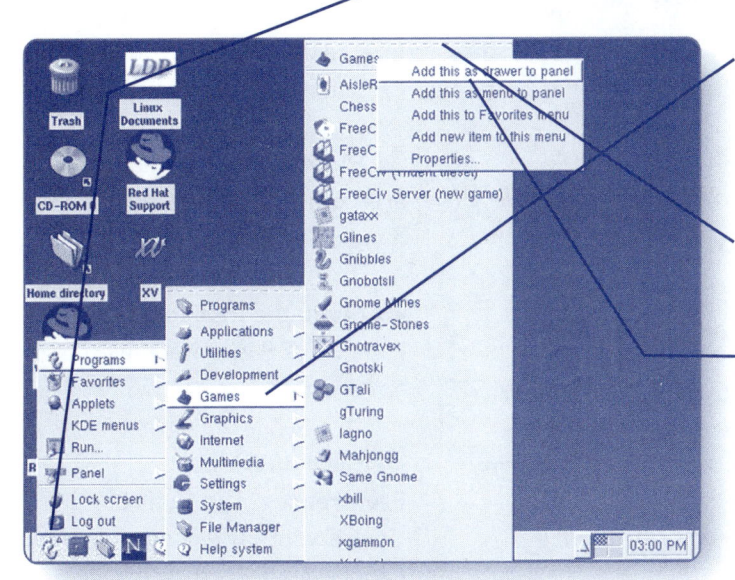

2. Display the **menu** that you want to turn into a drawer on the Gnome Panel. The menu will appear.

3. Right-click on the **menu title bar**. A menu will appear.

4. Click on **Add this as drawer to panel**. The drawer and all of the contents of the menu will be placed on the Gnome Panel.

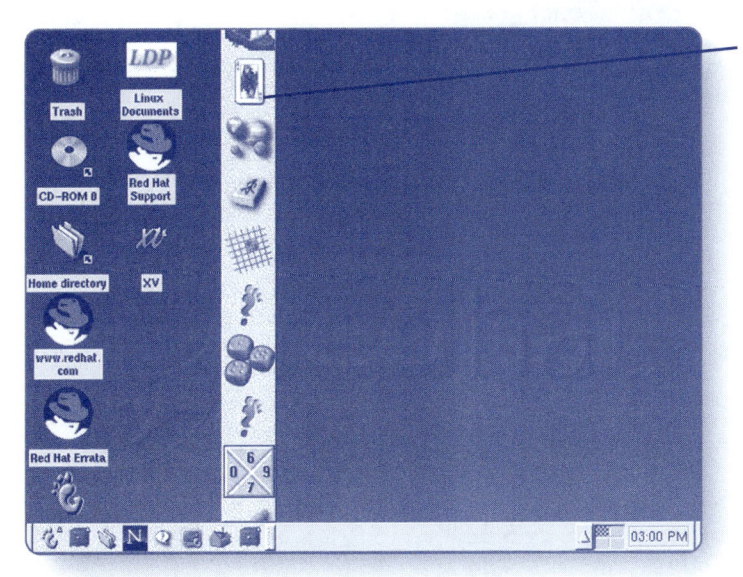

The menu contents will become icons on the drawer tab.

TIP

To delete an item from the drawer, right-click on the icon you want to delete and select Remove from panel from the menu that appears.

Changing Launcher and Drawer Icon Backgrounds

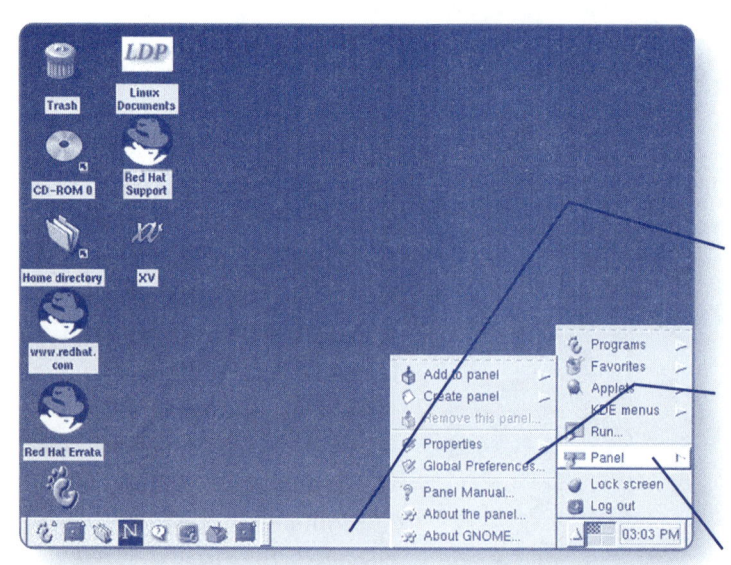

You'll notice that each of the icons on the Gnome Panel contains a picture on top of a gray textured background. You can change this background.

1. Right-click on an **empty area** of the Gnome Panel. A menu will appear.

2. Move the **mouse pointer** to Panel. The Panel menu will appear.

3. Click on **Global Preferences**. The Control Center window will open to the Panel pane.

4. Click on the **Buttons tab**. The tab will come to the top of the stack.

5. Click on the **Normal tile button**. The Browse dialog box will open.

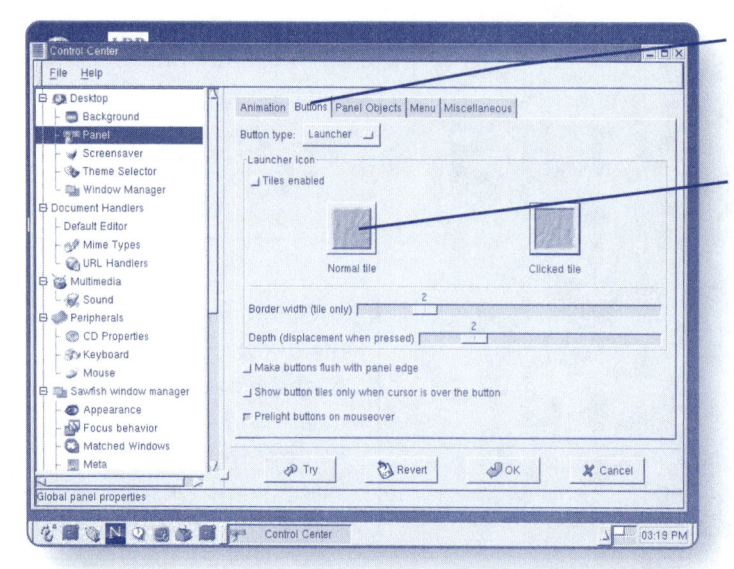

TIP

Try to select an icon with the "up" notation for a normal tile and a "down" notation for a clicked tile.

CHANGING LAUNCHER AND DRAWER ICON BACKGROUNDS

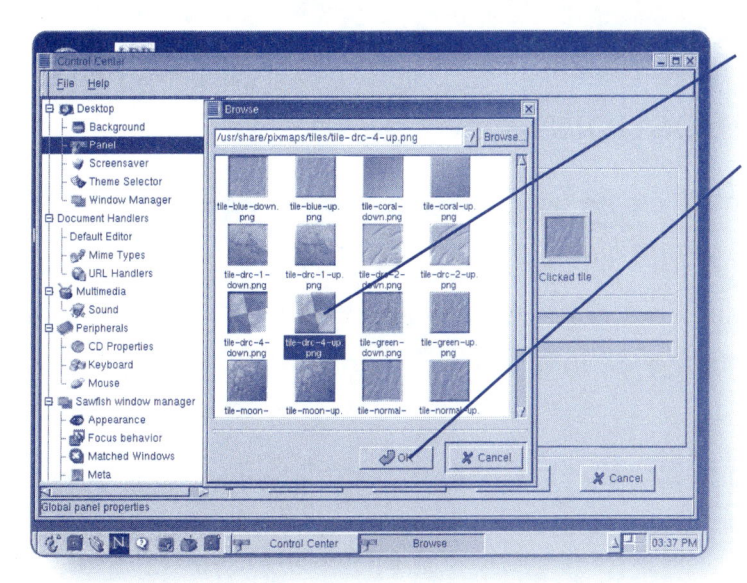

6. Click on a **tile icon** in the list. The tile will be selected.

7. Click on **OK**. You'll be returned to the Control Center and you'll see the tile you just selected in the Normal Tile button.

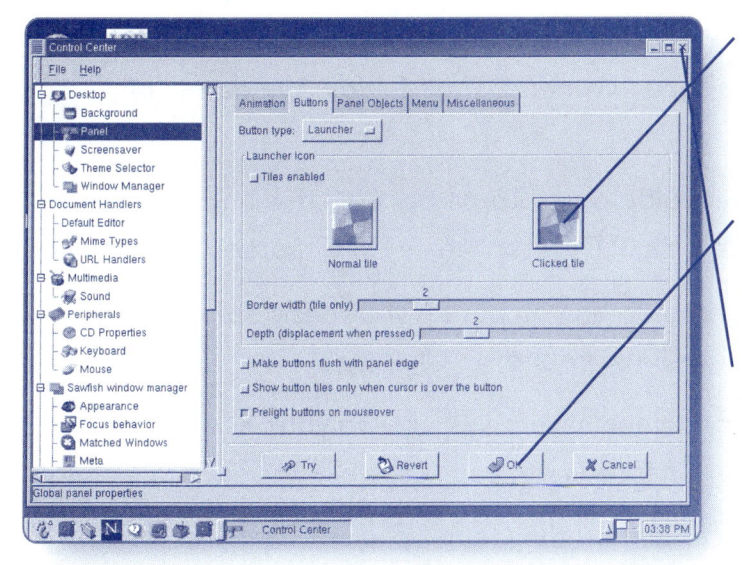

8. Repeat steps 5 through **7** to change the tile for the Clicked Tile button. The tile background will be changed.

9. Click on **OK**. The icon backgrounds will be changed on the Desktop.

10. Click on the **Kill button**. The Control Center will close.

TIP

If you begin to run out of space on the Gnome Panel, you can always add another panel. Right click on an empty area of the Gnome Panel and select Add new panel from the menu that appears.

Part I Review Questions

1. Why is it so important to create user accounts and not work in the root account? *See "Starting Linux for the First Time" in Chapter 1*

2. What are the basic elements of the Gnome and KDE user interfaces? *See "Exploring Gnome" and "Exploring KDE2" in Chapter 1*

3. How do you open an application in Gnome? *See "Opening Program Windows" in Chapter 2*

4. Name two different methods you can use to change the size of a window. *See "Resizing a Window" in Chapter 2*

5. Can Gnome automatically arrange the multiple open windows on your desktop for you? *See "Working with Multiple Windows" in Chapter 3*

6. How do you navigate multiple desktop areas with the Gnome Pager? *See "Creating Virtual Desktop Areas" in Chapter 3*

7. What kinds of backgrounds can you put on your desktop? *See "Changing the Desktop Background" in Chapter 4*

8. Where do you find the screen savers available to you? *See "Setting Up a Screen Saver" in Chapter 4*

9. How do you place an applet on the Gnome Panel? *See "Working with Applets on the Gnome Panel" in Chapter 5*

10. Why would you want to put drawers on the Gnome Panel? *See "Adding Drawers to the Gnome Panel" in Chapter 5*

PART II

Using the File System

Chapter 6
    Exploring the File System **95**

Chapter 7
    Organizing the Filing System **113**

Chapter 8
    Managing in a Multi-User Environment **129**

Chapter 9
    Maintaining Your Linux **149**

6

Exploring the File System

It's time to take a look at one place in the Linux operating system where you'll be spending a lot of time—the file system. You'll be using the Gnome File Manager to create directories and manage files. (You will also be using the KFM application in KDE to accomplish much the same thing.)

The applications also use the file system to save and access files that were created or modified. If you've never used Linux or Unix before, you'll find that the Gnome File Manager uses a filing system that is different from what you may have used with other operating systems. In this chapter, you'll learn how to:

- Identify the basic parts of the file manager
- Navigate the directory structure
- Select files in the directory structure
- Sort through your file list

Opening a File System

Before you start working with applications and creating files, take some time to get familiar with the Linux file system. You'll perform most of your file maintenance tasks from the file manager, which is an easy-to-use graphical filing system.

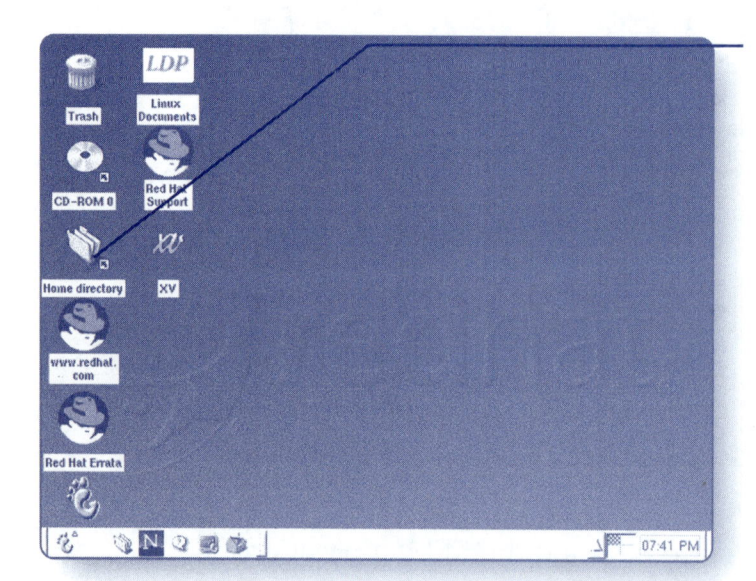

1. Double-click the **Home directory** launcher. The Gnome File Manager will open. When the File Manager opens, your user directory will be selected.

NOTE

If you don't see the Home directory launcher, open the Main Menu button and click on Programs, File Manager.

Looking at File Manager

The Gnome File Manager is the graphical interface where you'll perform all your filing tasks. You may find similarities between this file manager and file managers used with other operating systems.

OPENING THE FILE SYSTEM

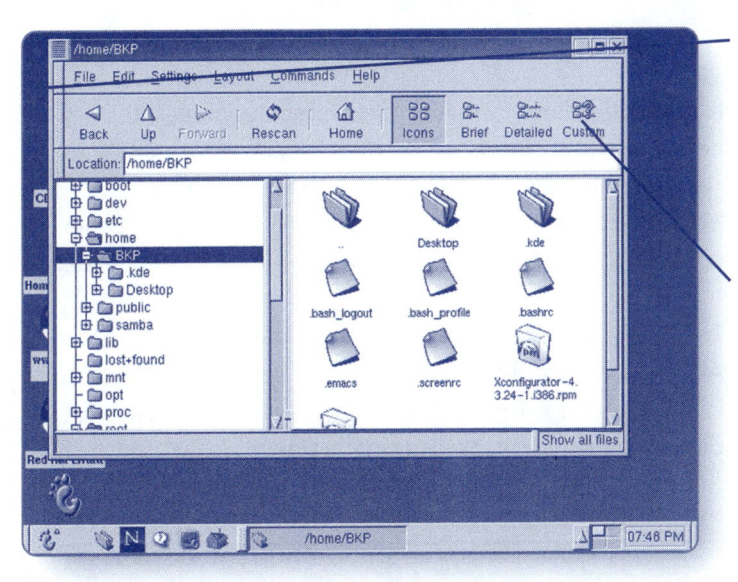

- The menus contain all the commands you can perform with the file manager. You can create directories, delete files, sort files, and view directories.

- The toolbar makes it easy to navigate the file system and change how you view your files and directories.

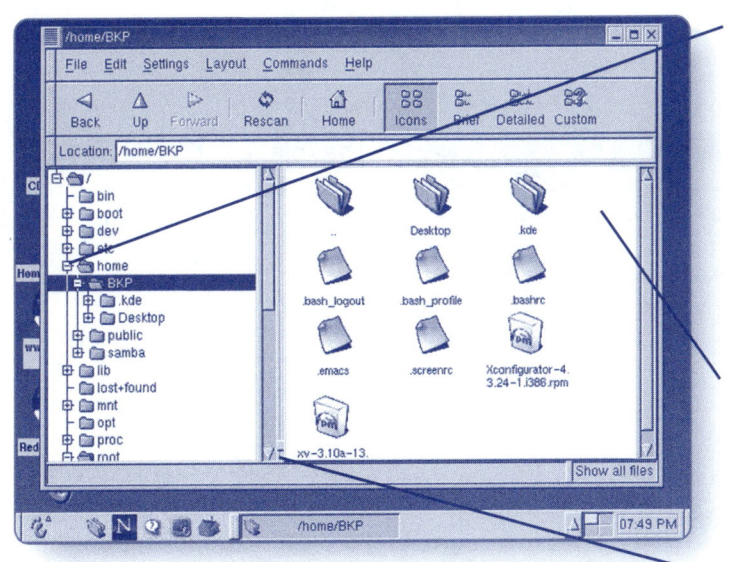

- The tree view is located in the left pane and shows all of the directories on your Linux system. When you open the file manager, your home user directory is selected by default. This is the main directory where you will store your user files and folders.

- The directory view is located in the right pane and shows all the files and subdirectories stored in a directory selected in the tree view.

- You can change the size of the tree view and directory view panes. Click and drag the resize box located at the bottom of the bar between the two panes.

Understanding the Linux File System

Before you dive into the Linux file system, you need to understand the contents of the directory structure that was set up when you installed your Linux. Some of these directories contain information that you'll find useful. Other directories are best if left alone unless you are a Linux expert.

- The / or root directory is the base of the Linux file system. All of the files and directories for the system are contained in this directory. This directory is different from the /root directory the root superuser maintains.

> **TIP**
> Do not store any of your files in the / directory!

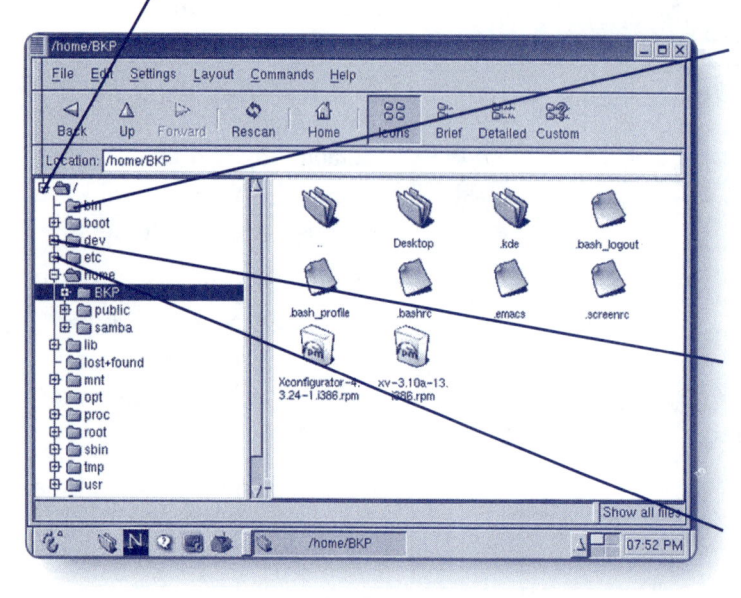

- The /bin directory holds the basic Linux programs and commands. You probably won't need to use this directory. The Gnome interface accesses many of these programs and commands for you.

- The /dev directory is where all of the device files for each hardware component on your computer are stored.

- The /etc directory contains system configuration files and initialization scripts.

OPENING THE FILE SYSTEM

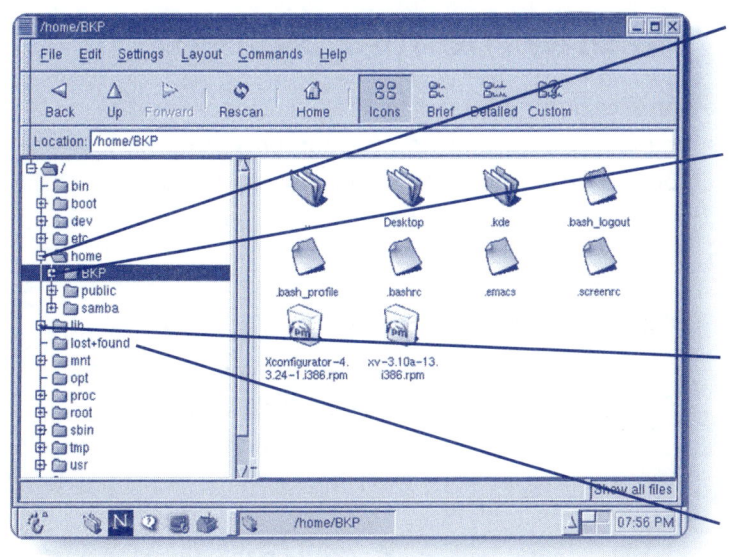

- The /home directory contains directories for all the user accounts on the system.

- Each user has a home directory in which to store personal files. You cannot access another user's files from your user account.

- The /lib directory is where the library files for C and other programming languages are stored.

- If Linux has lost a file, it might be found in the /lost+found directory.

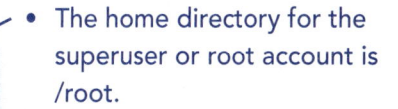

- The home directory for the superuser or root account is /root.

- The /sbin directory contains a number of tools used for system administration.

- The /tmp directory is a place where all users can store files on a temporary basis.

- The /usr directory contains a number of Linux commands and utilities that are not a part of the Linux operating system, documentation files and some utility programs, and the Linux game collection.

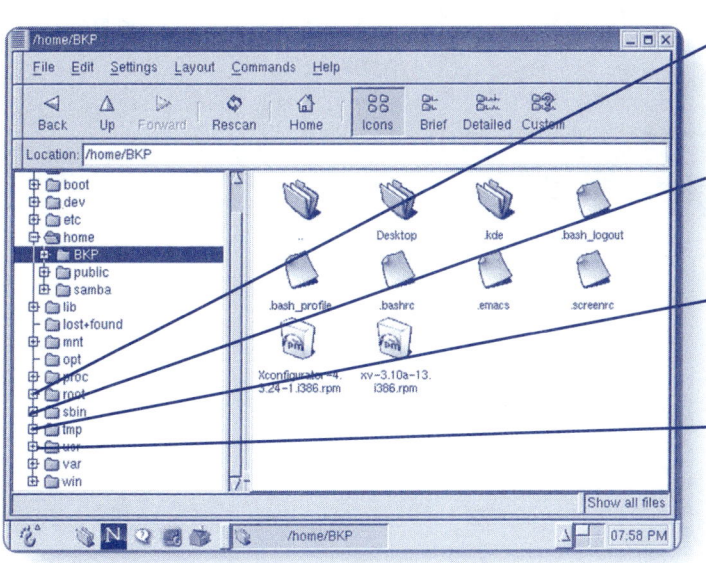

CAUTION

If the system is rebooted, all files in the tmp directory will be lost.

Browsing the File System

The graphical interface used by the file manager makes it easy to move around and view the contents of the various directories. Because you don't have any directories created in your user account, the safest place to play in the file system is the /usr directory.

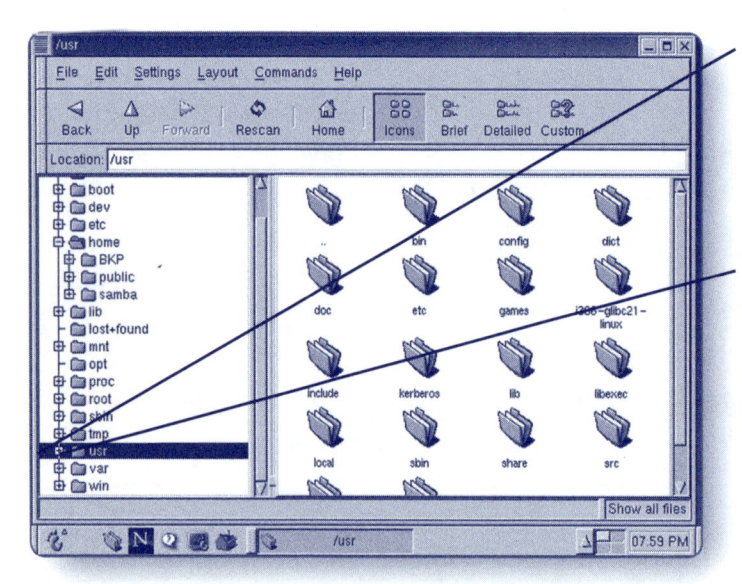

1. Click on the **/usr directory** in the tree view. The list of subdirectories and files contained in the /usr directory will appear in the directory view.

2. Click on the **plus sign** next to the /usr directory. The list of subdirectories will appear under the /usr directory in the tree view.

BROWSING THE FILE SYSTEM   101

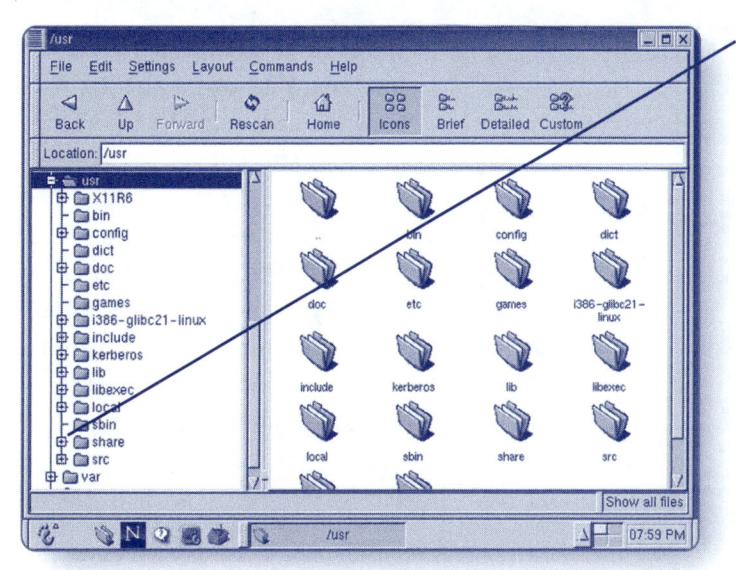

3. Click on the **plus sign** next to the /usr/share directory. The directory in the tree view will expand and the list of directories and files contained in the /usr/share directory will open in the directory view.

NOTE
To move to the directory one level up from the selected directory, click on the Up button on the toolbar.

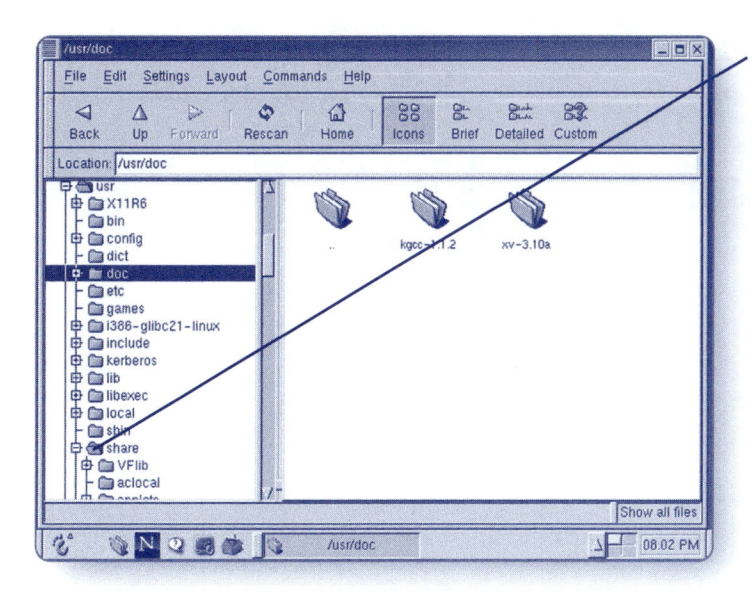

4. Click on the **/usr/share** directory. The list of files contained in the directory will open in the directory view.

NOTE
To go back to the directory you previously viewed, click on the Back button on the toolbar.

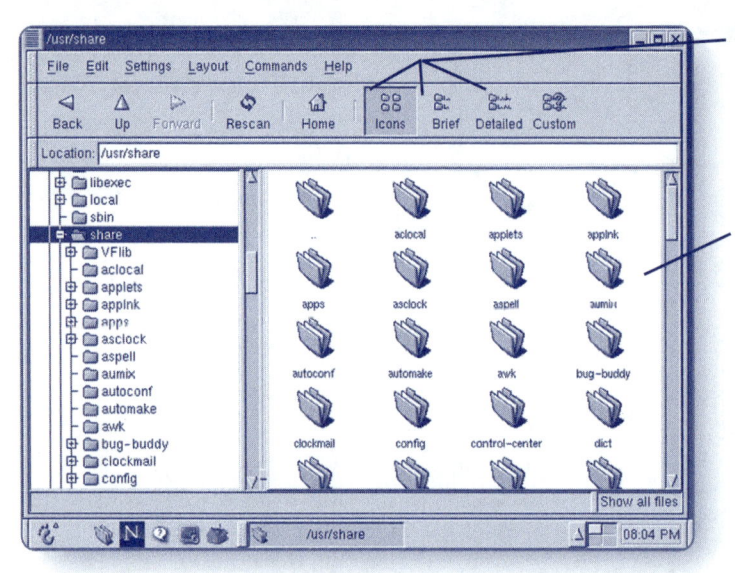

5. Click on each of the **view buttons**. You will be able to view the contents of a directory in three different ways.

- The Icons view shows a picture that represents the file type and the name of the file underneath. This is useful if you're looking for a quick way to determine file types.

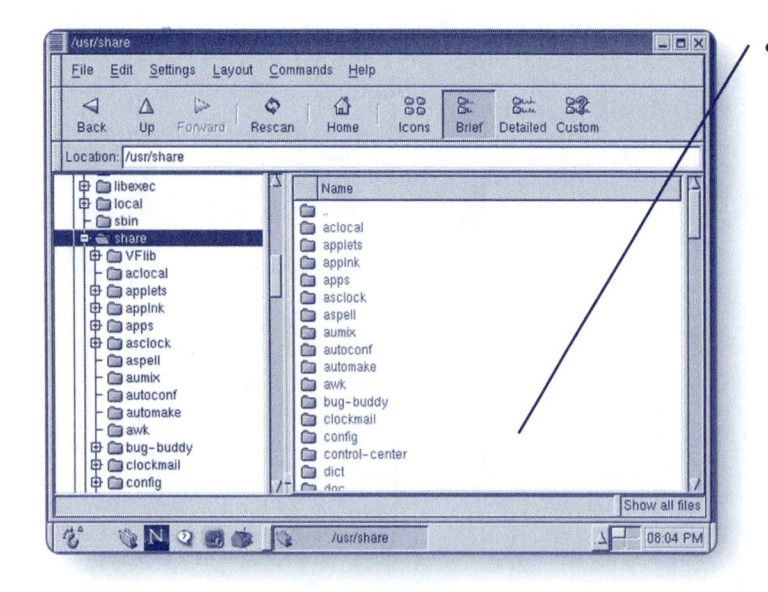

- The Brief view provides a simple list of the files stored in the directory.

BROWSING THE FILE SYSTEM 103

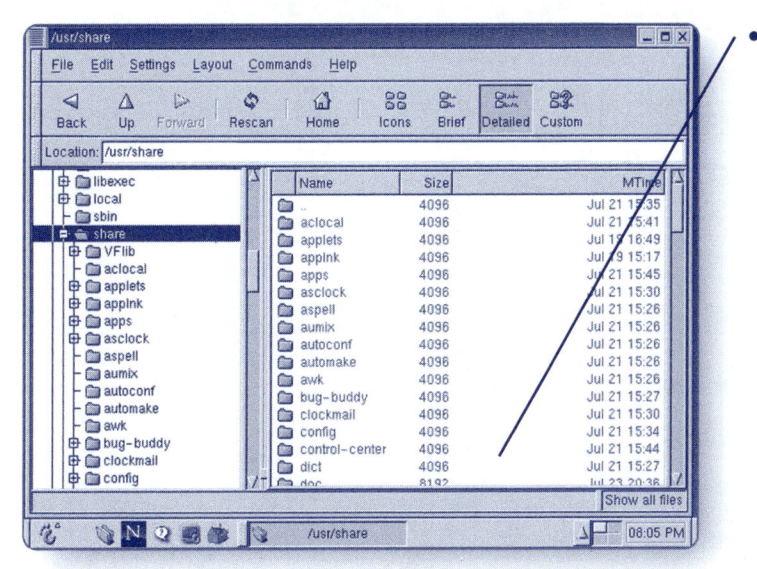

- The Detailed view gives information about the file size and when it was last used. This view allows you to sort the list in a number of ways.

> **TIP**
>
> To change the size of the directory view columns, click and drag the edge of the column heading.

Selecting Files

Before you can perform a task to a file (such as copy or rename), you'll need to select the file in the file manager. You have the choice of selecting files yourself by clicking on the files with the mouse. You can also tell the file manager the types of files you want to select and it will search the directory and select those files for you.

CHAPTER 6: EXPLORING THE FILE SYSTEM

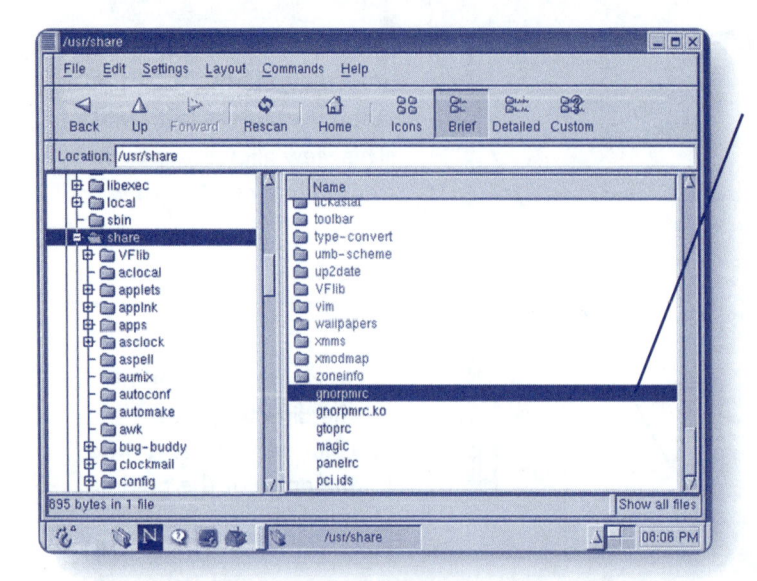

Using the Mouse

- To select a single file, click on the file.

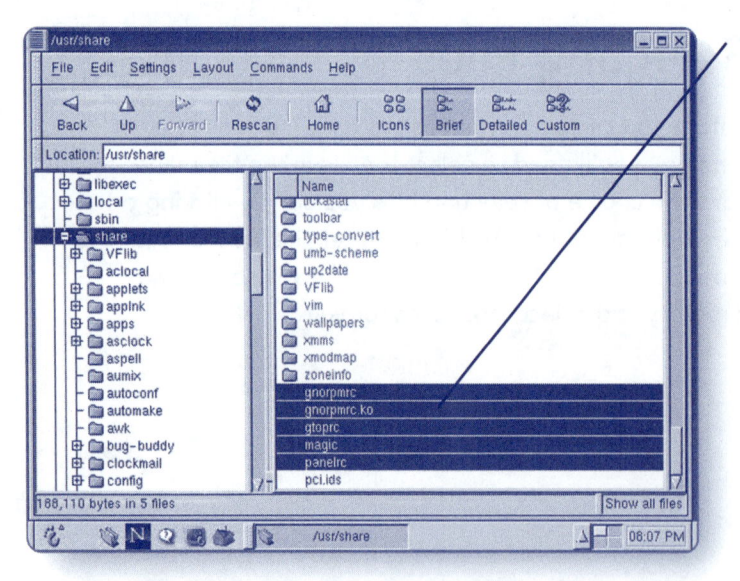

- To select several contiguous files, click on the first file that you want to select, then press the Shift key and click on the last file you want to select.

BROWSING THE FILE SYSTEM

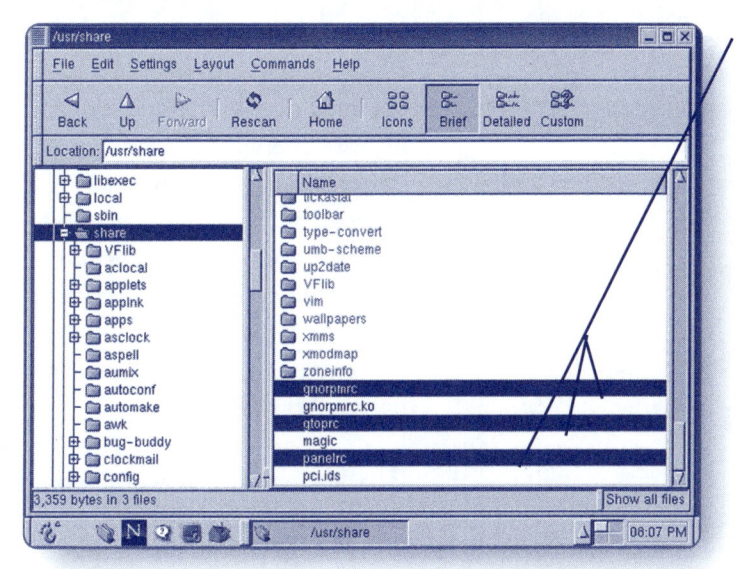

- To select files that are not located next to each other, press and hold the Ctrl key while you click on each file that you want to select.

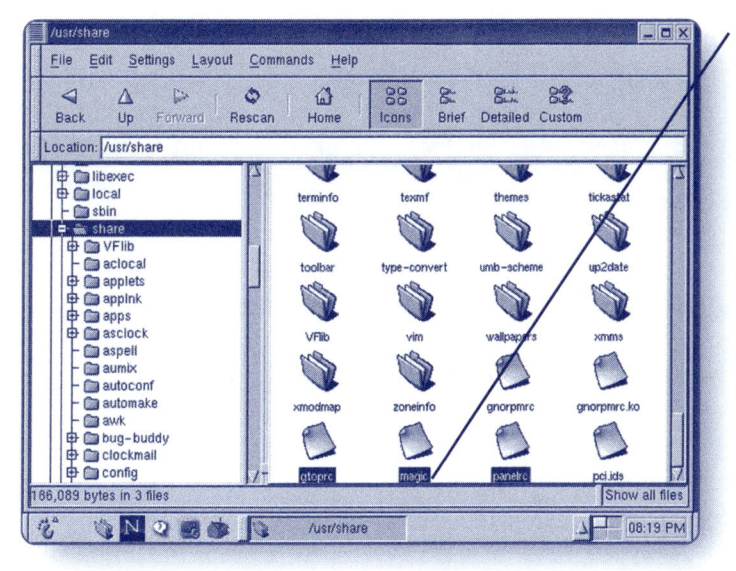

- To select several contiguous files in the Icons view, click and hold the mouse button at the beginning of one file, then drag the mouse to the end of the last file you want to select.

Using Selection Criteria

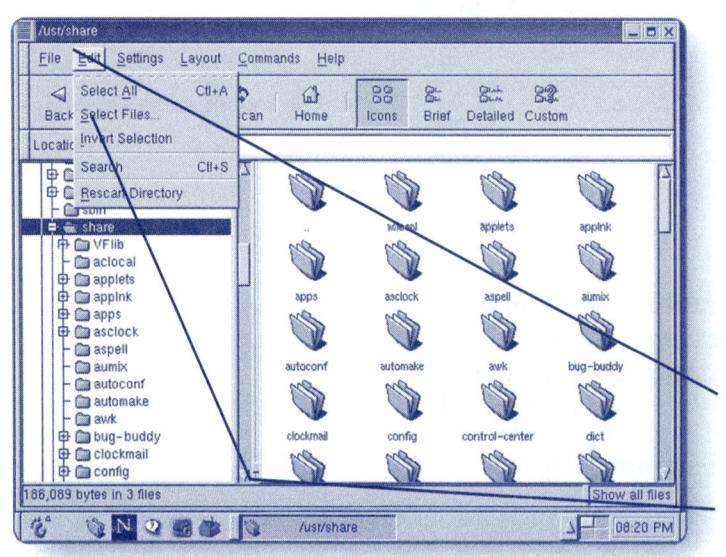

You may decide that you don't want to search through a directory and select files yourself. If the files all contain a common element, such as the same file extension, or the files begin with the same combination of letters, you can use the sort filter.

1. **Click** on **Edit**. The Edit menu will appear.

2. **Click** on **Select Files**. The Select File dialog box will open.

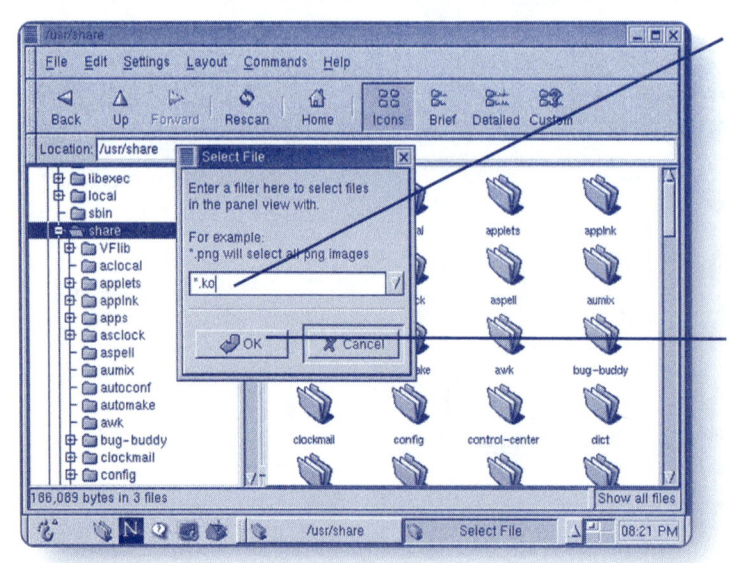

3. **Type** the **criteria** for the files you want to select. For example, if you want to find all files that use the "pcx" file extension, type ***.pcx**. If you want to select files starting with "LX," type **LX***.

4. **Click** on **OK**. The filter will search for those files that match the criteria you typed.

BROWSING THE FILE SYSTEM   107

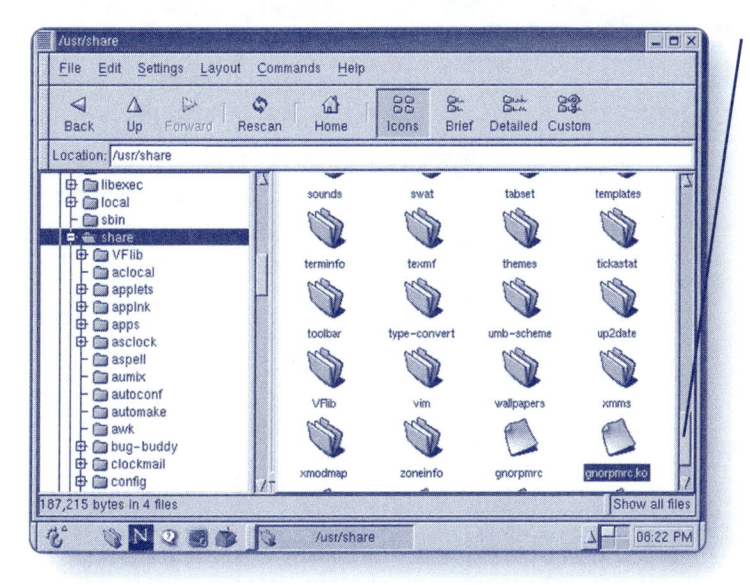

- All the files that matched the criteria will be selected in the file manager window. You may need to scroll down the directory view pane to see highlighted files.

TIP
When you are finished looking through the /usr directory and want to go back to your user account directory, click on the Home button.

Sorting the File List

You can sort the list of files in the detailed view by file name, file size, and date last accessed.

Reordering the File List

The column headings at the top of the directory view allow you to sort your files quickly.

CHAPTER 6: EXPLORING THE FILE SYSTEM

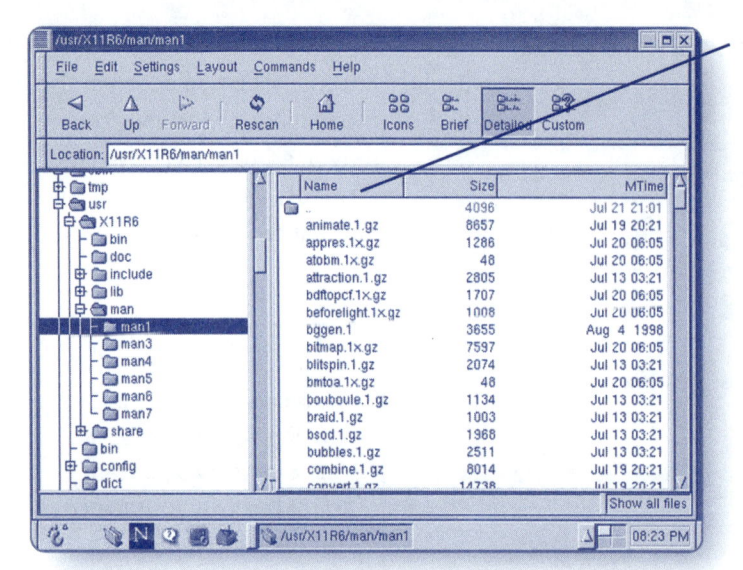

1. Click on the **Name column** heading. The list of files will be sorted by name, with files beginning with Z at the top of the list and those starting with A at the bottom.

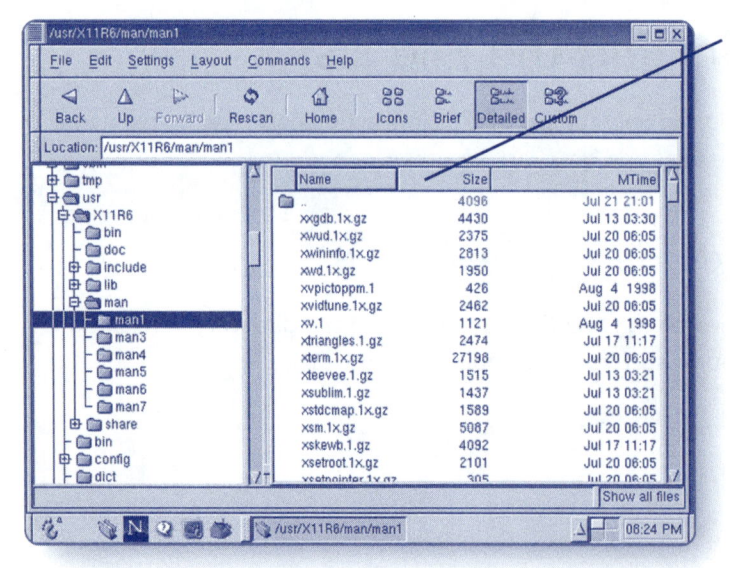

2. Click on the **Size column** heading. The list of files will be sorted by size from the smallest file size down to the largest file size.

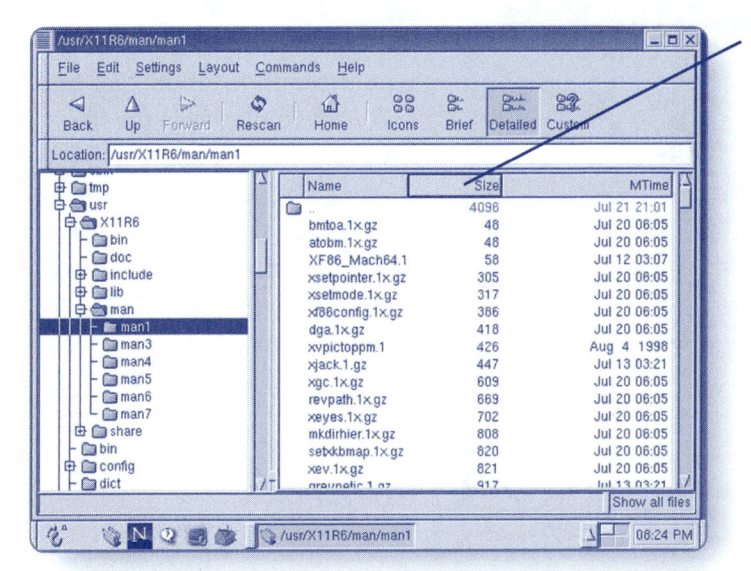

BROWSING THE FILE SYSTEM

3. Click on the **Size column heading** a second time. The list of files will be sorted from the largest file size down to the smallest file size.

> **NOTE**
>
> You can also sort files by the date they were last used by clicking on the MTime column heading.

Filtering the File List

You may decide that you only want to see certain files listed in the directory view. Here's how you can hide those files that you don't need to view.

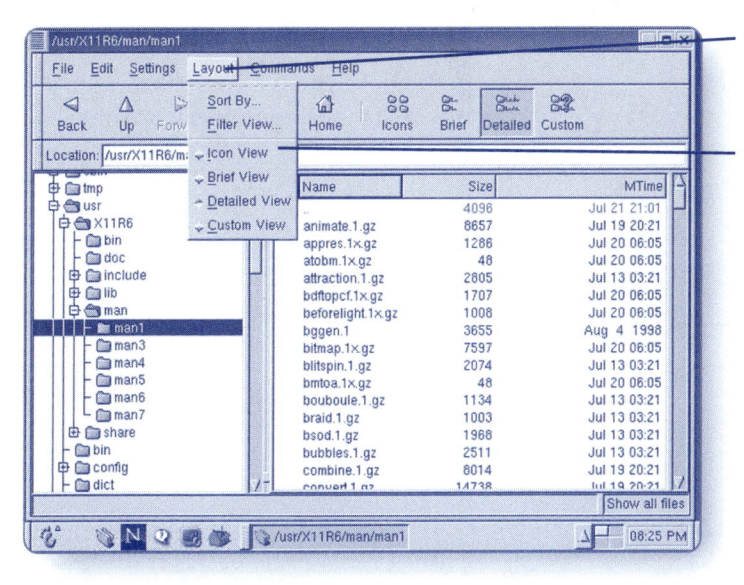

1. Click on **Layout**. The Layout menu will appear.

2. Click on **Filter View**. The Set Filter dialog box will open.

CHAPTER 6: EXPLORING THE FILE SYSTEM

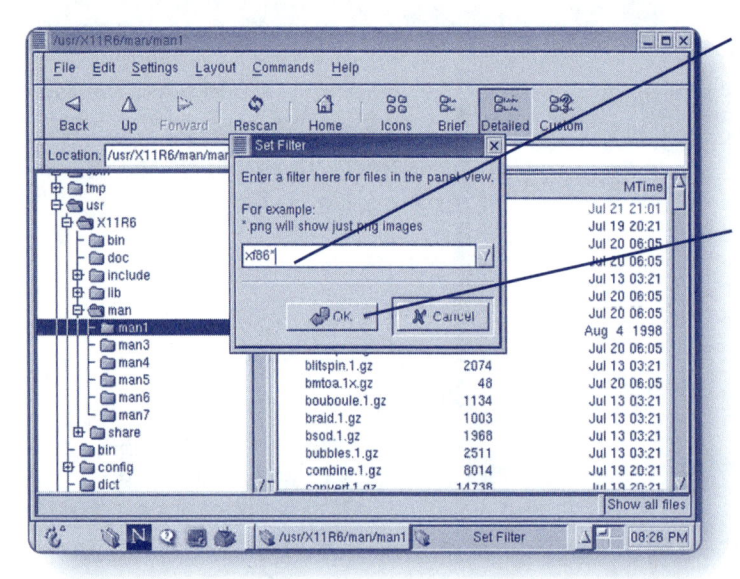

3. Click in the **text box** and type the criteria for the files that you want to display in the file list.

4. Click on **OK**. The filter will search for those files that match the criteria you typed. Only those files that fit the selected criteria will display.

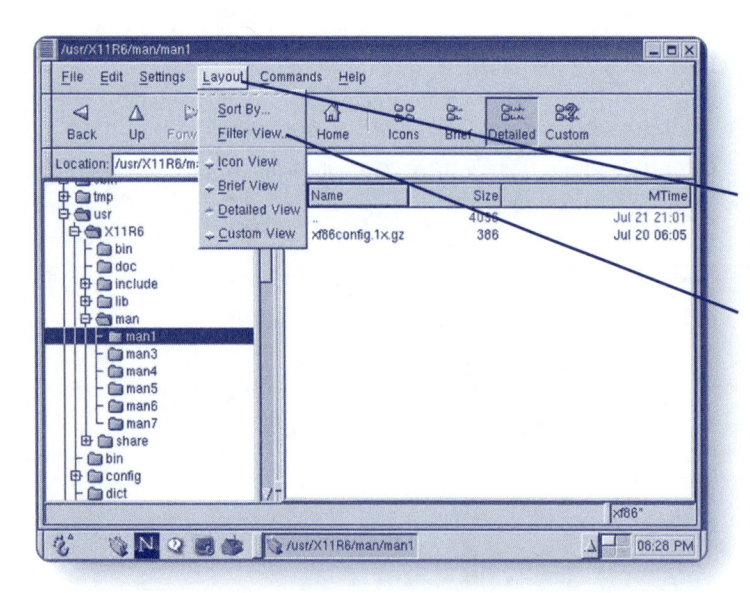

If you filtered a file list and want to see the entire contents, you will need to remove the filter.

5. Click on **Layout**. The Layout menu will appear.

6. Click on **Filter View**. The Set Filter dialog box will open.

BROWSING THE FILE SYSTEM

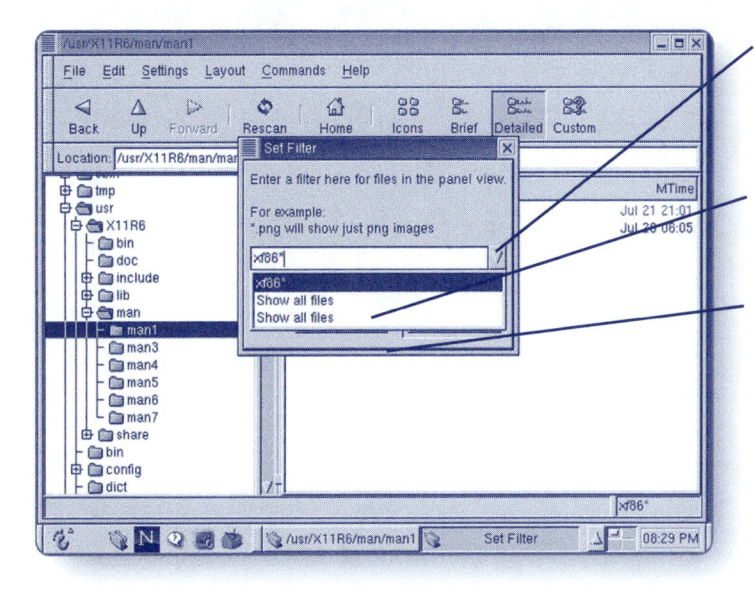

7. Click on the **down arrow** to the left of the text box. A drop-down list will appear.

8. Click on **Show all files**. The option will be selected.

9. Click on **OK**. The entire list of files contained in the directory will open in the directory view.

7

Organizing the File System

Inside your Linux system, you set up a superuser (or root) account during the Linux installation and one or more user accounts along the way. When you log in to your user account and open the file manager, the home directory for your account is already selected. This is the only directory on the Linux system where you have permission to store your files. Once you build a personal filing system, you can begin to move your files around. In this chapter, you'll learn how to:

- Create a new directory
- Move and copy files
- Rename and delete files and directories
- Search for misplaced files in your home directory
- Move frequently used files to your desktop

Creating Directories

When you create a file in an application, you'll need to save it to the Linux file system. You could place all the files in the home directory, but things might get cluttered after a while. The first task is to create a few directories in which to categorize your work. For example, create a folder for each type of document—word processing, spreadsheet, graphics—or for a small business, set up a separate folder for each client or project.

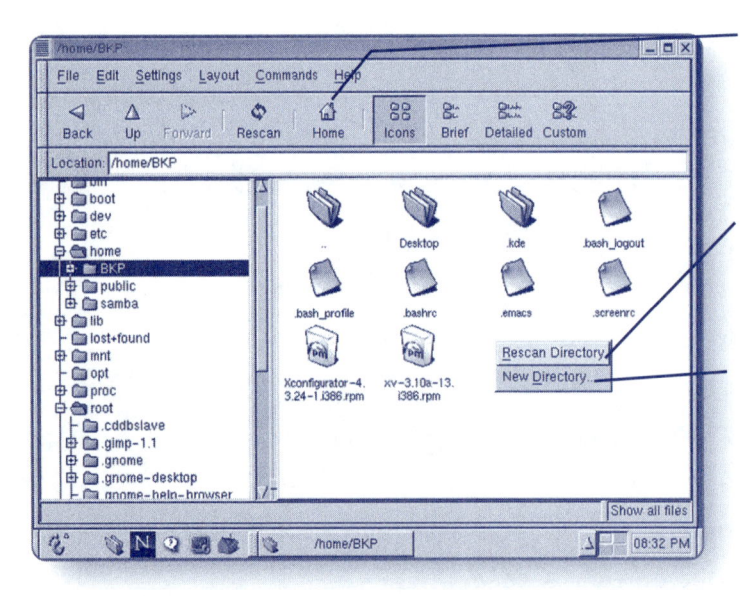

1. Double-click on the **Home button**. The home directory for your user account will be selected in the tree view.

2. Right-click on an **empty area** of the directory view. A menu will appear.

3. Click on **New Directory**. The Create a New Directory dialog box will open.

CREATING DIRECTORIES 115

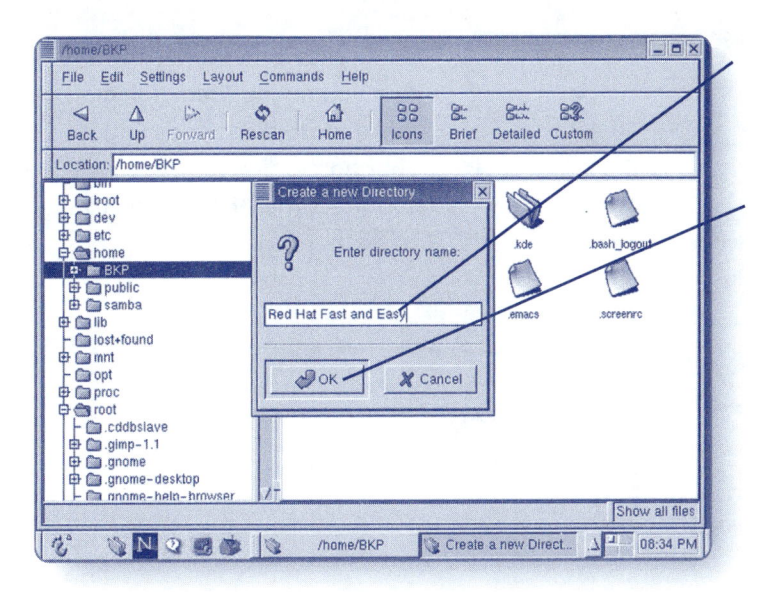

4. Type a **name** for the directory in the Enter directory name text box.

5. Click on **OK**. The new directory will open in the directory view.

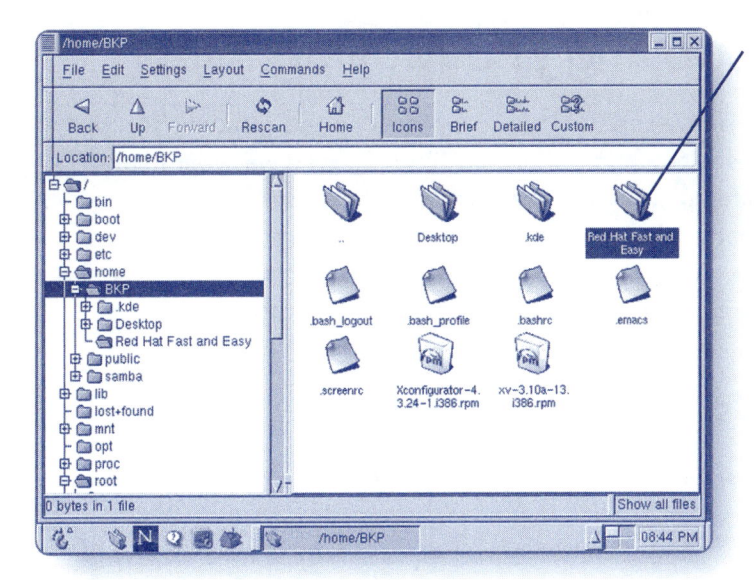

6. Double-click on the new **directory** in the directory view. The folder will be added to your user account in the tree view and the directory view will be empty.

116 CHAPTER 7: ORGANIZING THE FILE SYSTEM

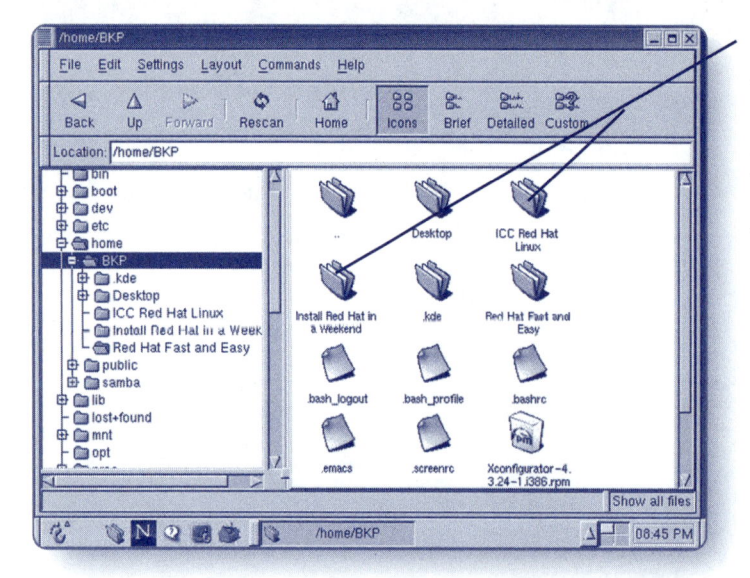

7. Create other **directories** that you might need. You can make more directories under your home directory, or make subdirectories within directories to further organize your files.

Copying and Moving Files

If you've used any Linux applications and created a file, the default location where the file was saved was your home directory. You can copy or move these files into directories that you've created under your home directory. This will make it easier to keep your filing system organized. You'll learn how to create files in Chapter 10, "Working with Files".

Using Drag and Drop

The easiest way to copy and move files is with the mouse.

COPYING AND MOVING FILES 117

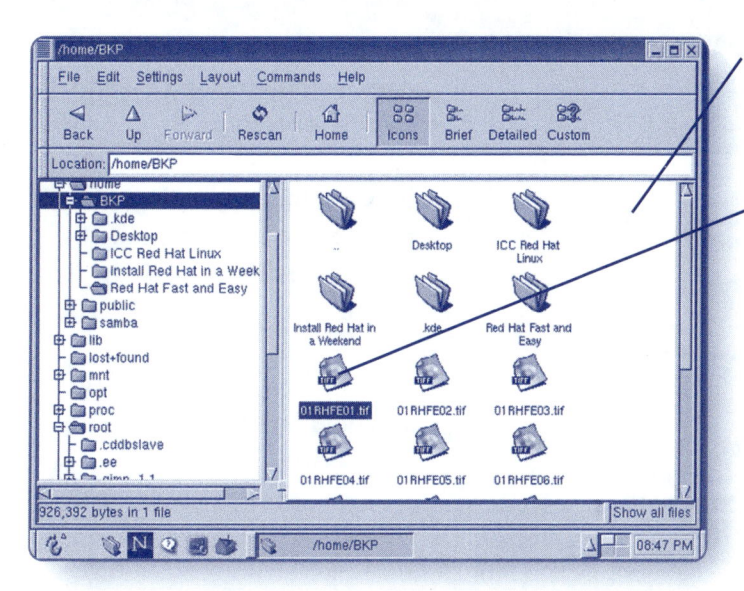

1. Click the **originating** directory in the tree view. It will be displayed.

2. Click and **hold** on the **file** that you want to move. The file will be selected.

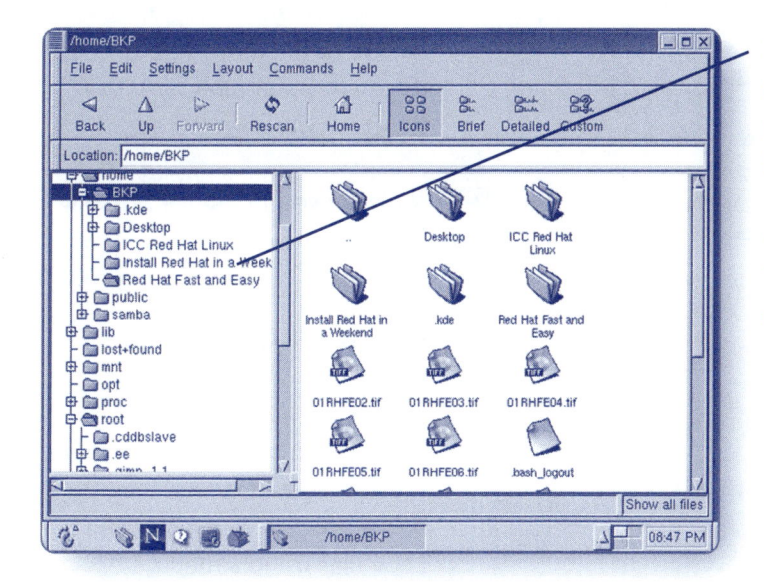

3. Drag the **mouse pointer** to the directory where you want to move the file. The directory will be selected.

4. Release the **mouse button**. The file will be copied to the destination directory.

> **TIP**
>
> You can copy or move multiple files. Select all the files that you want to copy or move, then click and drag one of the files in the group to the destination directory.

CHAPTER 7: ORGANIZING THE FILE SYSTEM

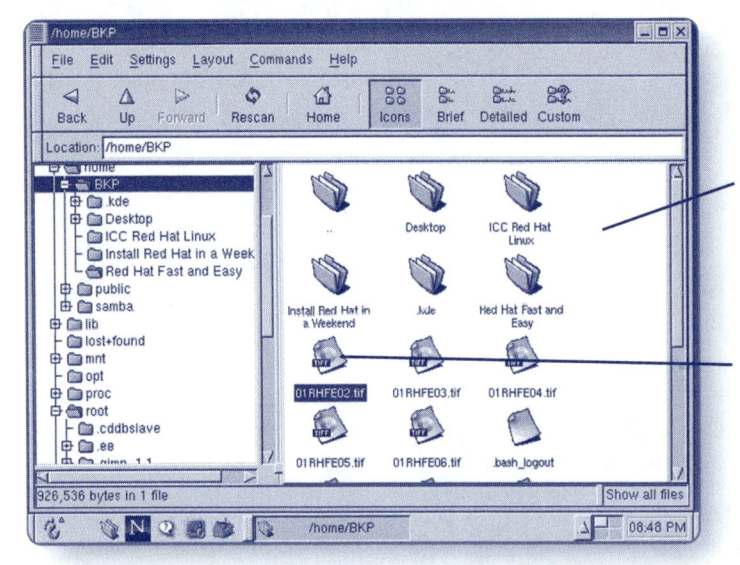

You can also use the drag-and-drop method to copy a file to another directory.

1. Click the **originating directory** in the tree view. The originating directory for the file will be displayed.

2. Press the **Ctrl** key and **click and hold** on a file. The file will be selected.

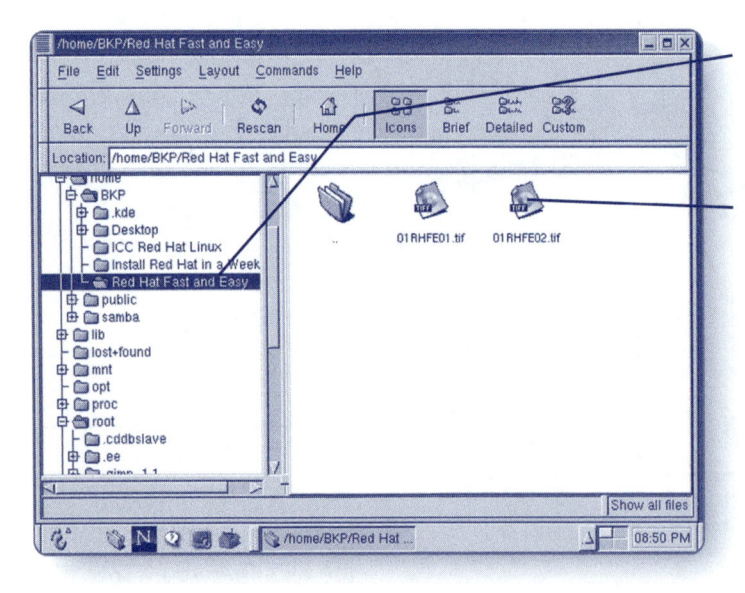

3. Move the **mouse pointer** to the destination directory. The directory will be selected.

4. Release the **mouse button**. The file will be moved.

Using a Control Menu

If you just can't get the hang of those drag-and-drop dance steps, you can also move and copy files using a menu.

COPYING AND MOVING FILES   119

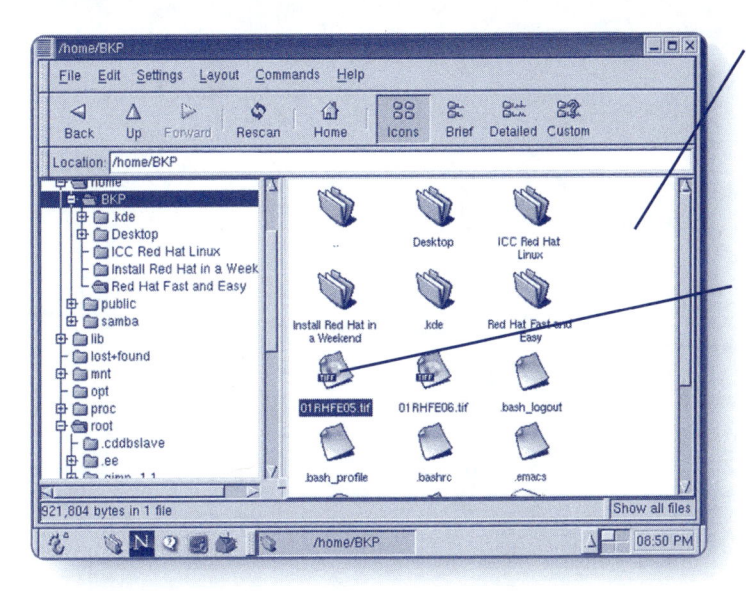

1. Open the **directory** that contains the file that you want to move or copy. The list of files contained in the directory will appear in the directory view.

2. Right-click on the **file** that you want to copy or move. A menu will appear.

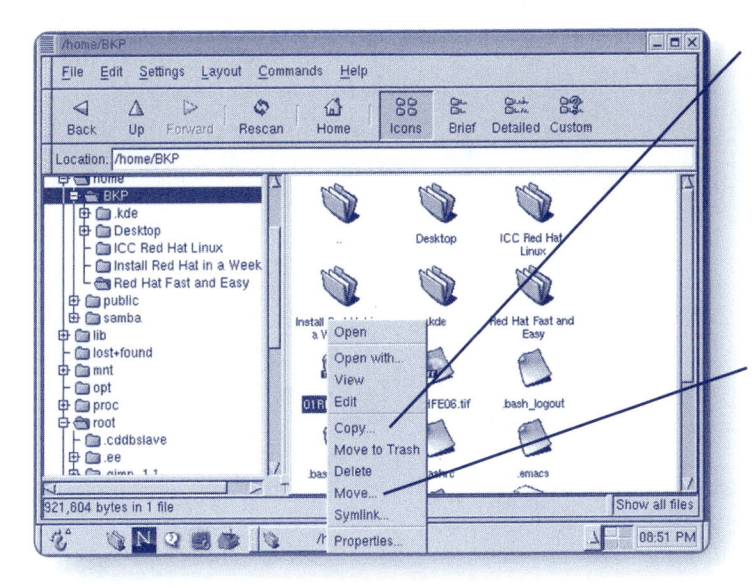

3a. Click on **Copy** if you want to make a copy of the file to place in another directory. The Copy dialog box will open and the Destination tab will be at the top of the stack.

or

3b. Click on **Move** if you want to move the file to a different directory. The Move dialog box will open and the Destination tab will be at the top of the stack.

NOTE

The Copy and Move dialog boxes work the same way.

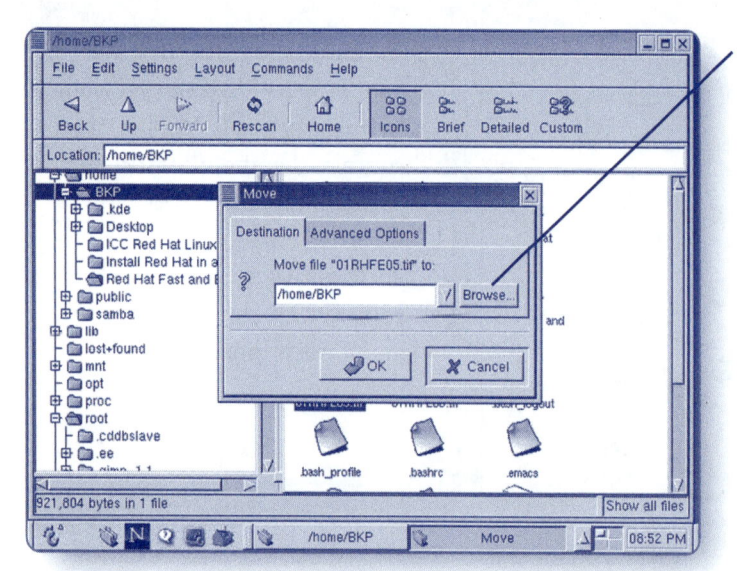

4. Click on the **Browse button**. The Find Destination Folder dialog box will open.

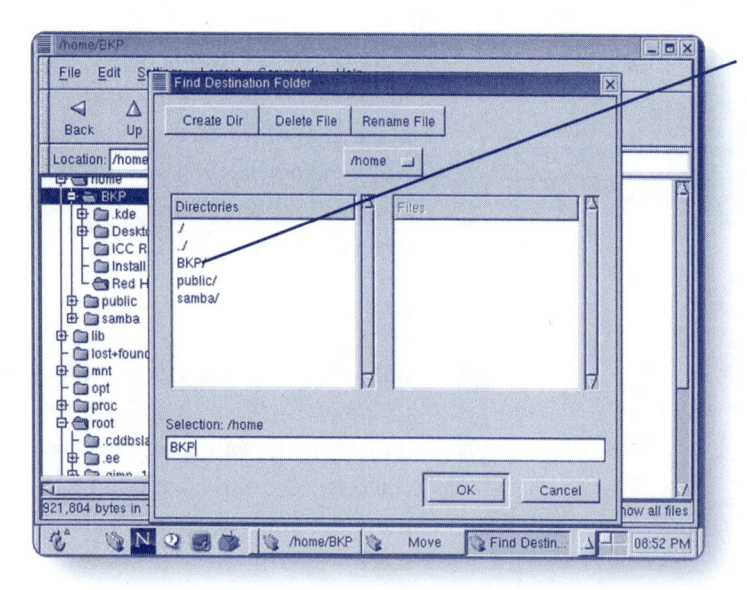

5. Double-click on your **home directory** in the Directories list. The list of directories in your user account will appear.

COPYING AND MOVING FILES   121

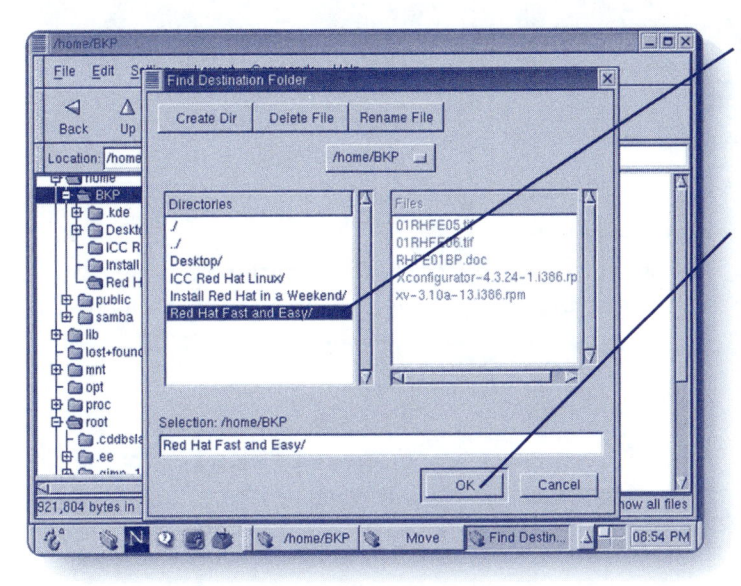

6. Click on the **directory** into which you want to move or copy the file. The directory will be selected.

7. Click on **OK**. The directory path will appear in the Copy file or Move file text boxes.

TIP

If you know the directory path, you can type it in the Copy file or Move file text box.

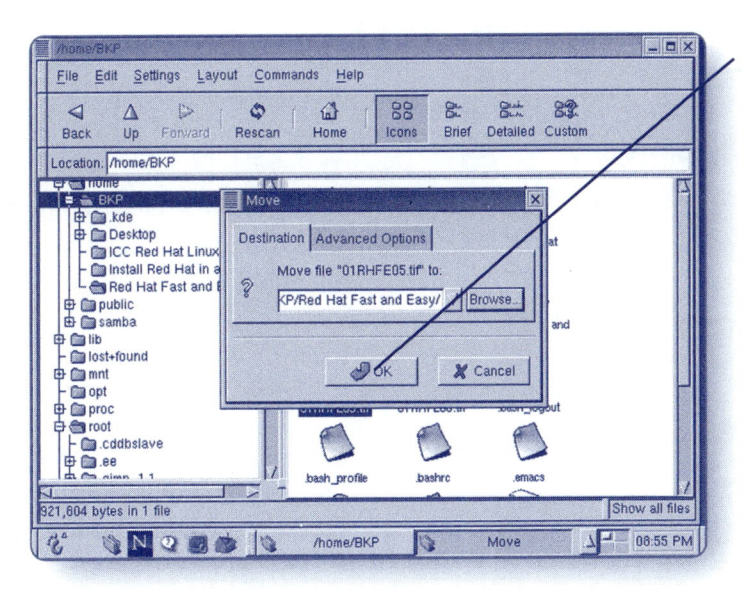

8. Click on **OK**. The file will be copied or moved to the selected directory.

CHAPTER 7: ORGANIZING THE FILE SYSTEM

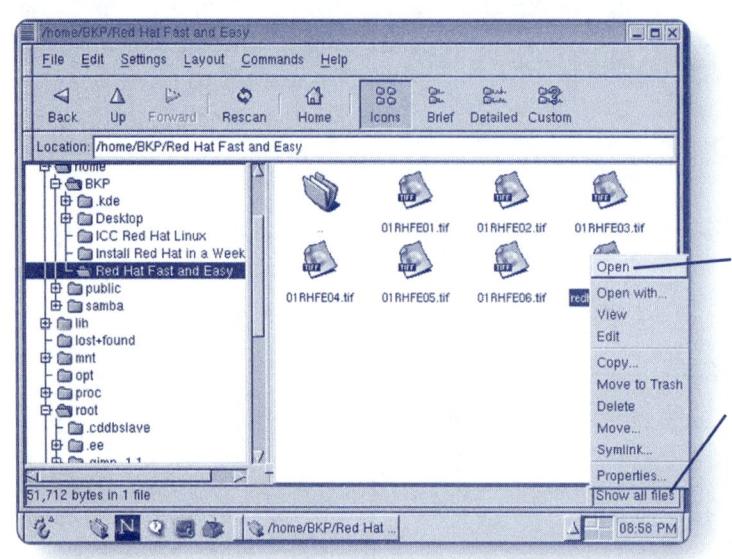

Renaming Files

You may decide to rename a file. You can easily change the file name.

1. Right-click on the **file** that you want to rename. A menu will appear.

2. Click on **Properties**. The Properties dialog box for the file will open.

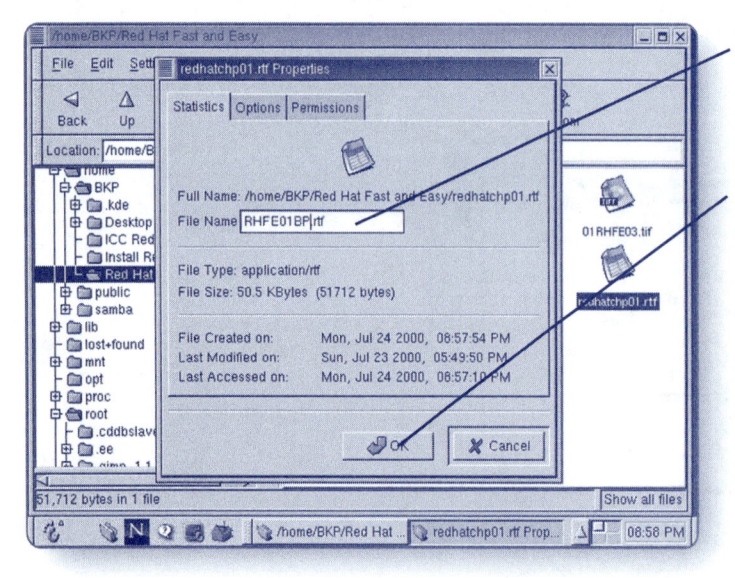

3. Click in the **File Name text box** and **type** a new name for the file.

4. Click on **OK**. The file will be renamed and the new file name will appear in the directory view.

TIP

You can change a directory name by displaying the directory in the directory view, right-clicking on the directory, and selecting Properties from the menu that appears.

Removing Files and Directories

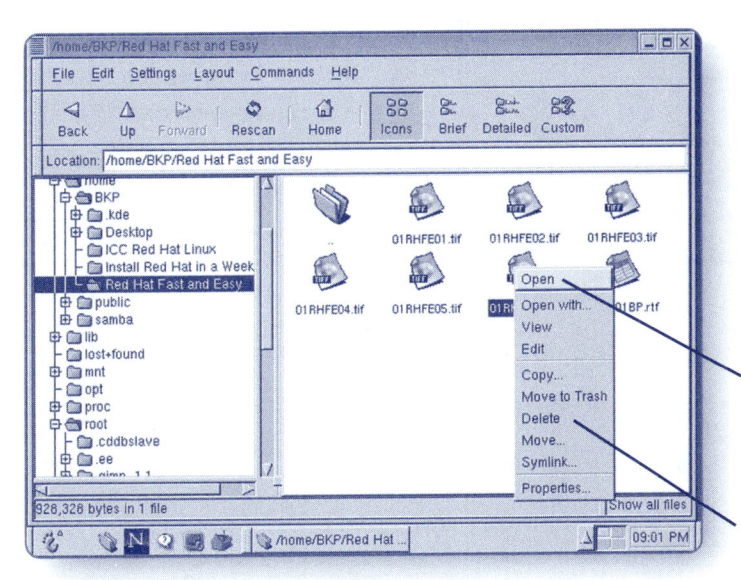

You may decide to delete some files and directories in your home directory. Before you can delete a directory, you'll first need to delete all the files from the directory.

Deleting Files

1. Right-click on the **file** that you want to delete. A menu will appear.

2. Click on **Delete**. A confirmation dialog box will open.

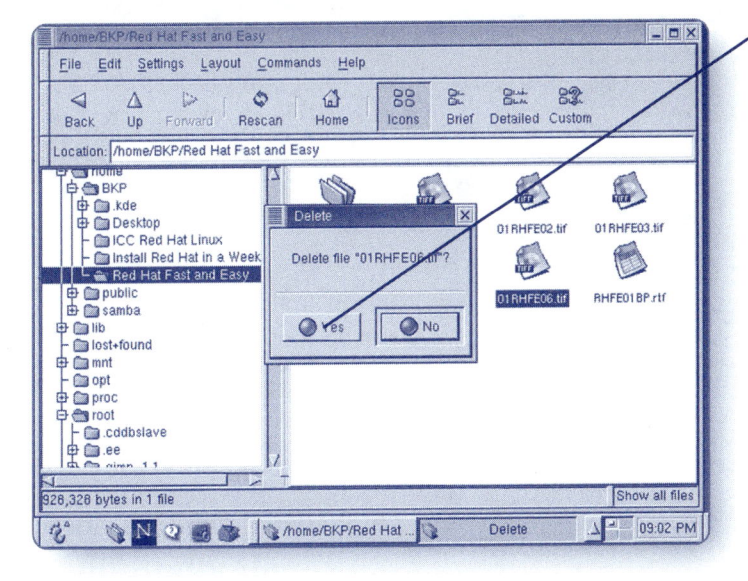

3. Click on **Yes**. The file will be deleted.

Working with Confirmation Dialog Boxes

To delete files, a confirmation box will ask if you want to perform the specified action. You can change the file manager so that confirmation boxes no longer open. You may want to wait until you are comfortable with Linux before you try this one.

124 CHAPTER 7: ORGANIZING THE FILE SYSTEM

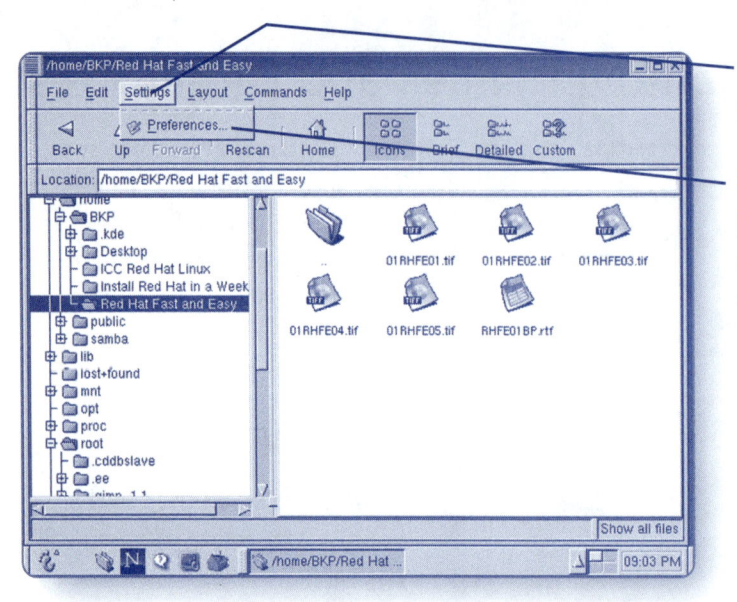

1. Click on **Settings**. The Settings menu will appear.

2. Click on **Preferences**. The Preferences dialog box will open and the File display tab will be at the top of the stack.

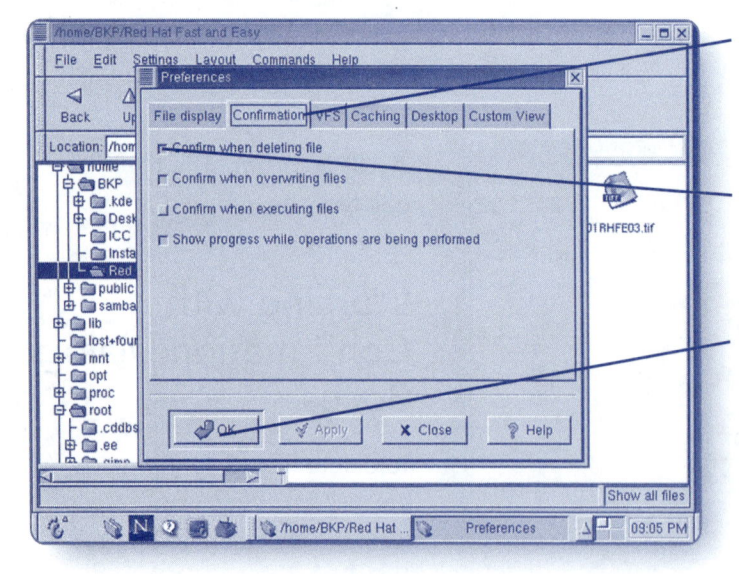

3. Click on the **Confirmation tab**. The Confirmation tab will come to the top of the stack.

4. Click on the **Confirm when deleting file check button**. The option will be cleared.

5. Click on **OK**. The Preferences dialog box will close and the confirmation box for deleting files will no longer display.

Finding Files in Your Home Directory

After moving and copying files all over your home directory, you may have some trouble trying to find a specific file.

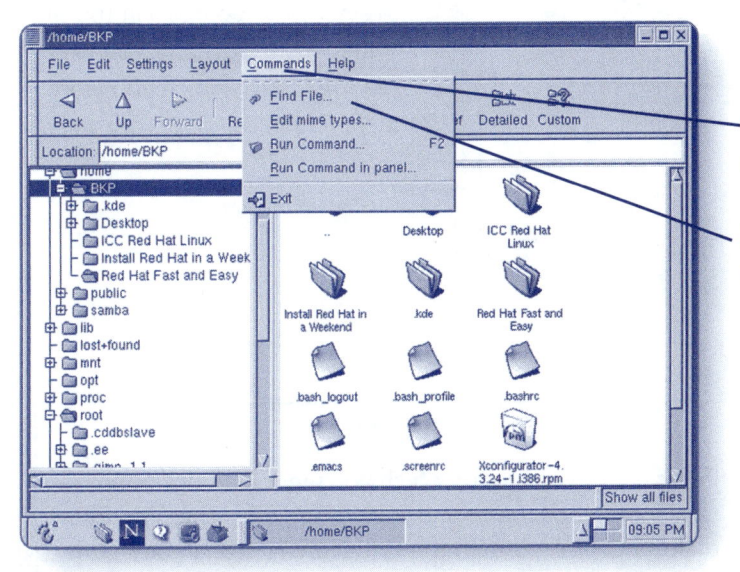

1. Click on **Commands**. The Commands menu will appear.

2. Click on **Find File**. The Find File dialog box will open.

NOTE

If you only know part of the file name, type that portion and include a wildcard character.

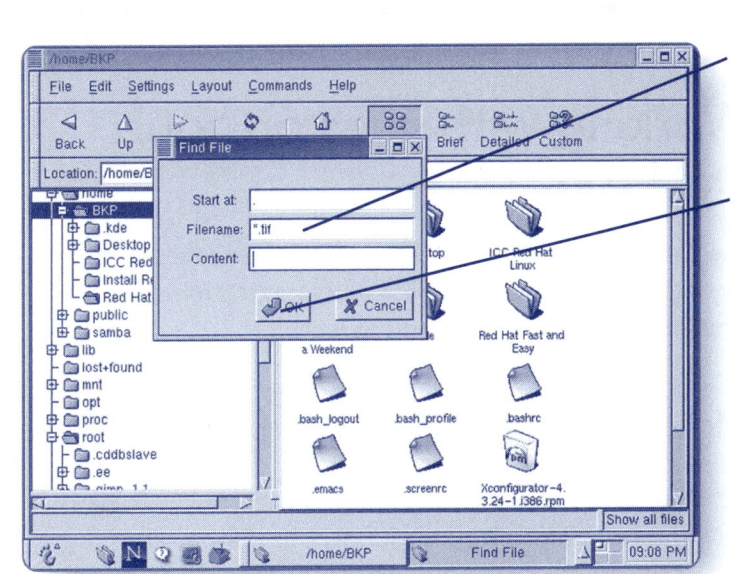

3. Click in the **Filename text box** and **type the name** of the file.

4. Click on **OK**. The Find file dialog box will open and show all directories in which the file can be found.

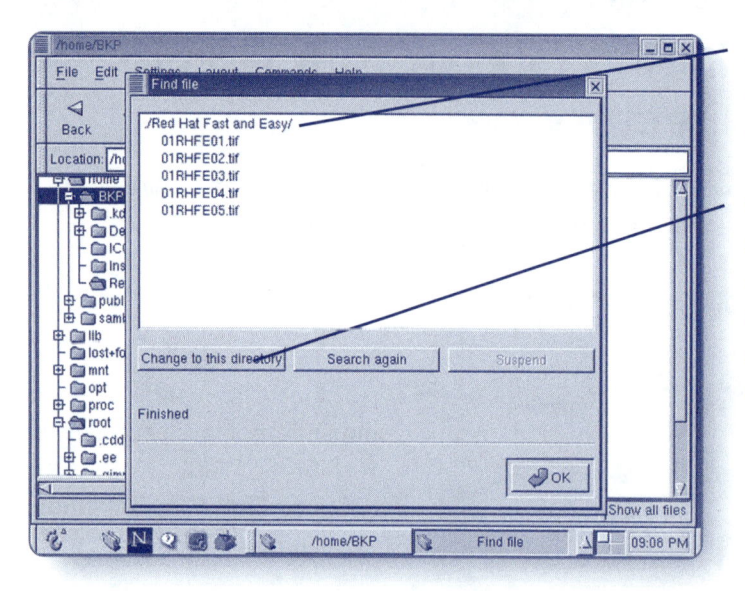

5. Click on the **directory** that contains the file you want. The directory will be selected.

6. Click on the **Change to this directory button**. The selected directory will be open in the file manager window and you will see the file for which you were searching in the directory view.

> **NOTE**
> If this is not the file for which you were looking, open the Commands menu and select Find File. The Find File dialog box will contain the last search criteria you entered.

> **NOTE**
> You can also move entire directories onto the desktop using this same drag and drop method.

Working with Files on Your Desktop

The file manager is not the only component of the graphical interface that can manage files. Your Desktop has some inherent file-management tools as well!

Moving a File to the Desktop

If you have a file that you use frequently and want to have it at your fingertips, move it onto your desktop.

WORKING WITH FILES ON YOUR DESKTOP 127

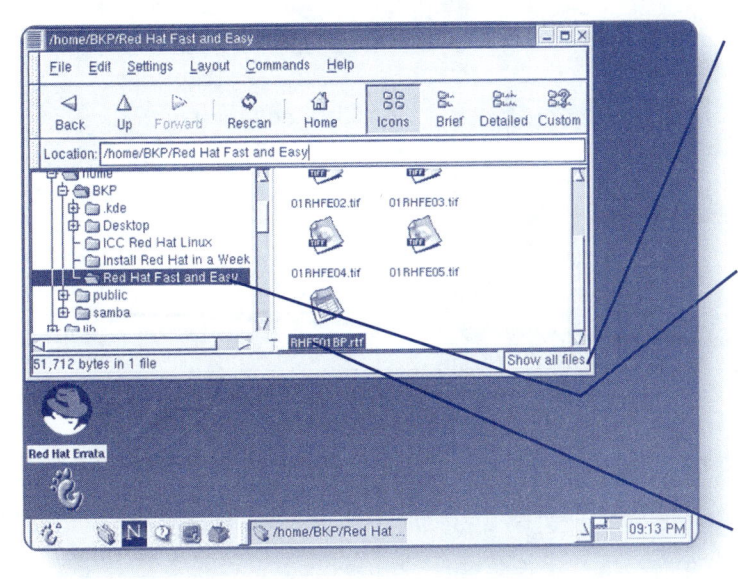

1. **Resize** the **file manager** so that the desktop area can be seen behind the window. The file manager window will be resized.

2. **Open** the **directory** that contains the file that you want to place on your desktop. The list of files contained in the directory will open in the directory view.

3. **Click** and **hold** the **mouse pointer** on the file. The file will be selected.

4. **Drag** the **file** to an empty area on the desktop.

5. **Release** the **mouse button**. An icon for the file will appear on your desktop.

Opening a File

It is not always necessary to open the Linux application before you can open a file. Open the file and select the application in which you want to work. For example, you may have a picture that you started in a simple computer drawing program (such as xpaint) and now you want to edit the picture in a more sophisticated image-editing program (like The Gimp).

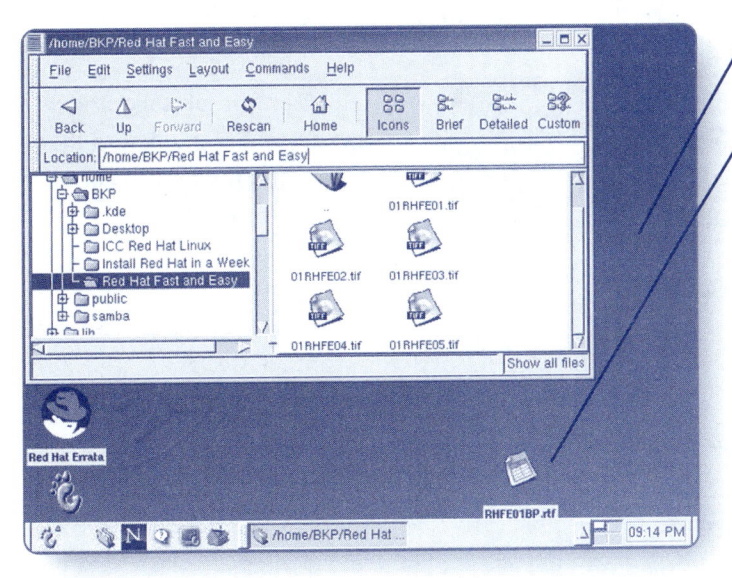

CHAPTER 7: ORGANIZING THE FILE SYSTEM

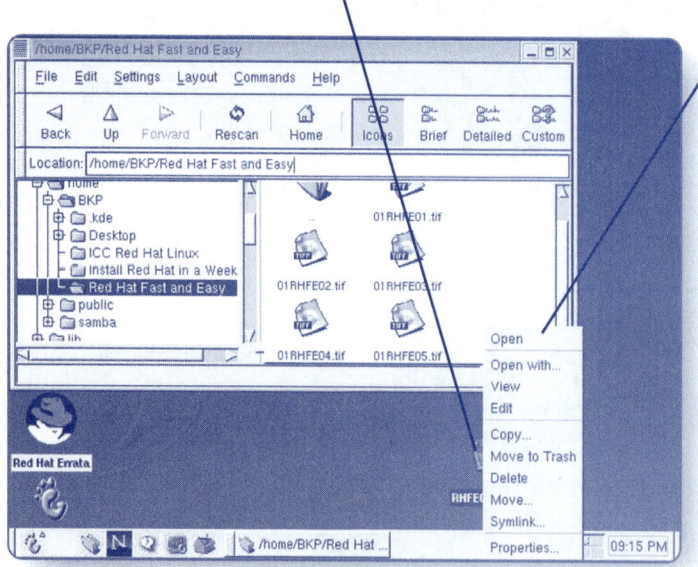

1. Right-click on a **file** to open. A menu will appear.

2. Click on **Open** with. The gmc dialog box will open.

TIP
To move the icon to a different place on your desktop, click and drag the icon to the new position.

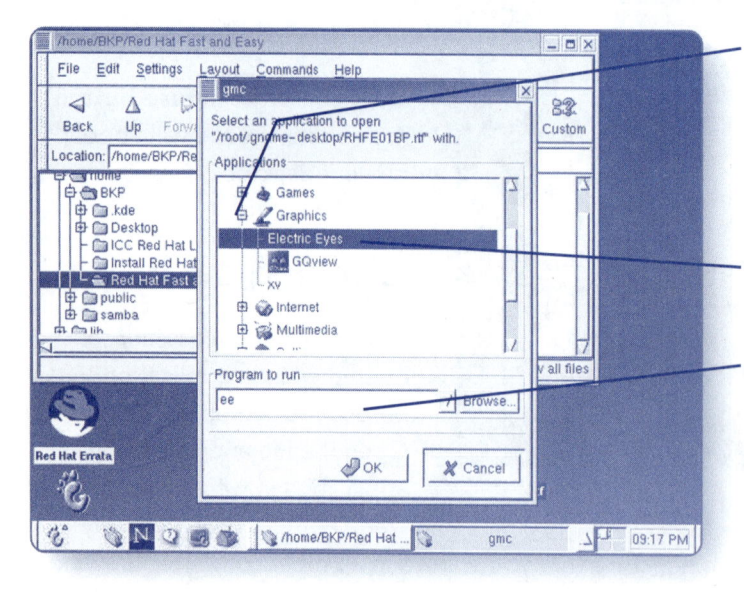

3. Click on the **plus sign** next to the system menu where the application is located. A list of the programs contained in that menu will appear.

4. Click on the **application** that you want to use. The application will be selected.

5. Click on **OK**. You'll see the file in the application window.

TIP
You can also open files from the file manager using this method.

8

Managing in a Multi-User Environment

Linux makes it easy for you to share one computer among several people. Each person is assigned an account and a password. Then, when each individual logs into Linux, the user will have a desktop and file system to customize. Each person's changes won't affect other users on the computer. Even though each user has a private area within Linux, all users can share files with each other. In this chapter, you'll learn how to:

- Create and edit user accounts
- Change your account password
- Form groups for file sharing
- Set file permissions for file sharing

Working with User Accounts

The first time you started Linux, you created a user account for yourself. You were shown a simple console command that would set up the account. There is more you can do, of course. You can also set up accounts so that each user on the system can share files and directories with other users. Before you begin working with user accounts, you must be logged in as the superuser or root.

Creating a New User Account

Each person using the Linux computer should have an account and password.

1. **Click** on the **Main Menu button**. The Main Menu will appear.

2. **Move** the **mouse pointer** to Programs. The Programs menu will appear.

3. **Move** the **mouse pointer** to System. The System menu will appear.

4. **Click** on **LinuxConf**. The Linuxconf window will open.

WORKING WITH USER ACCOUNTS 131

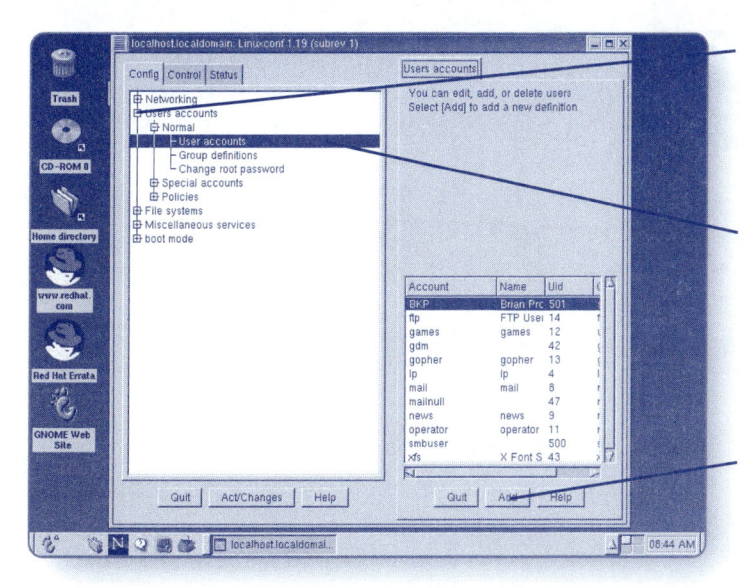

5. Click on the **plus sign** next to the User accounts category. A list of options for handling user accounts will appear.

6. Click on **User accounts** under the Normal option. The right pane will appear showing all of the user accounts that are currently set up on the system.

7. Click on the **Add button** in the User accounts pane. The User account creation pane will appear.

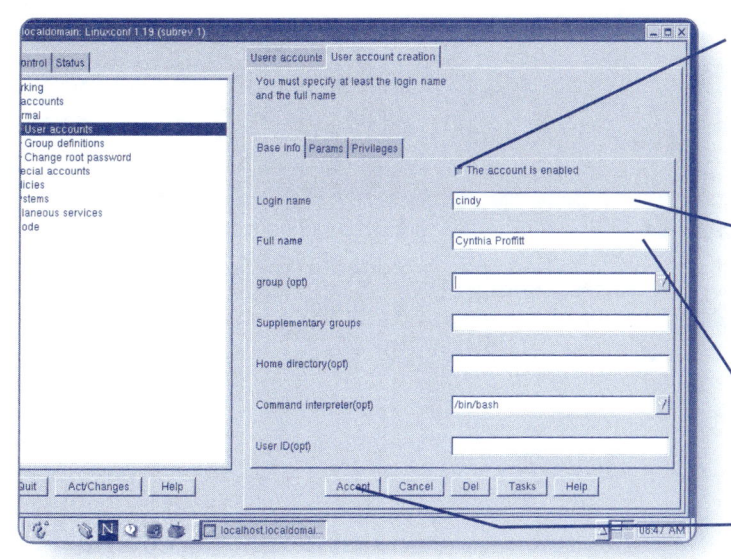

8. Click on the **check button** if The account is enabled is not selected (it should be). The check button will be selected.

9. Click in the **Login name text box** and **type** a **user name** for the person.

10. Click in the **Full name text box** and **type** the person's **first and last names**.

11. Click on the **Accept button**. The Changing password dialog box will open.

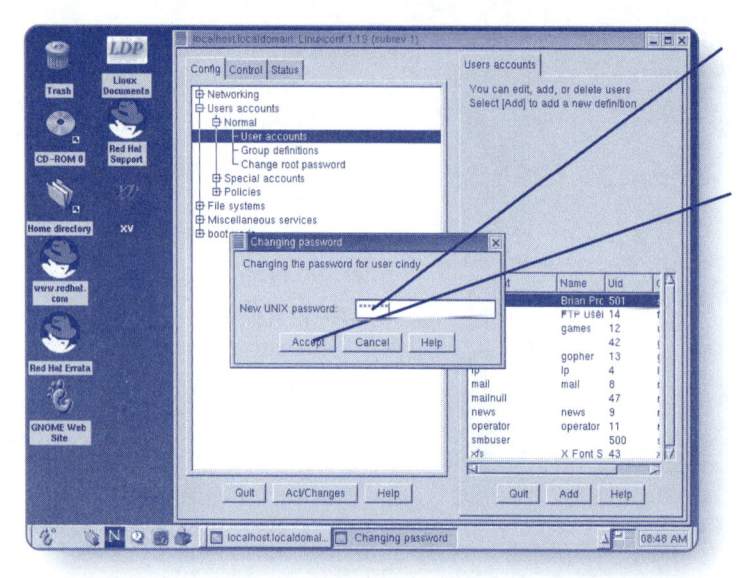

CHAPTER 8: MANAGING IN A MULTI-USER ENVIRONMENT

12. Type a **password** for the user account in the New Unix password text box.

13. Click on the **Accept button**. The Changing password pane will change.

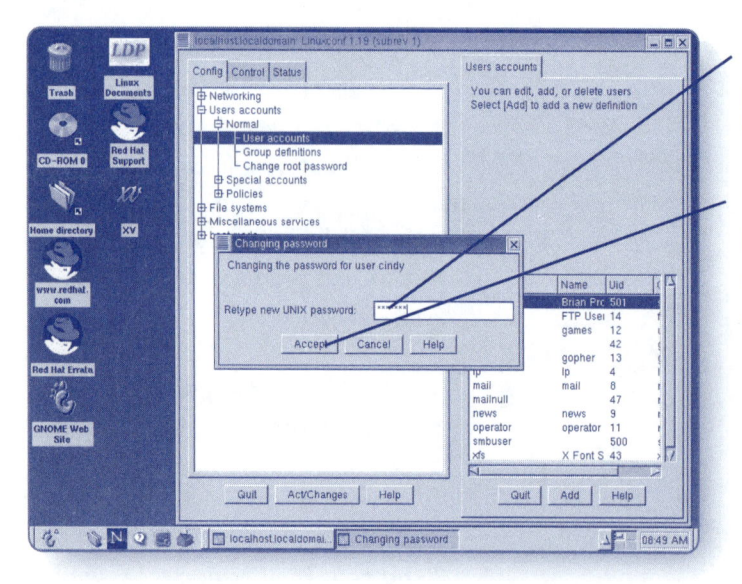

14. Retype the same **password** in the Retype new UNIX password: text box.

15. Click on the **Accept button**. The new user will be added to the list of user accounts.

WORKING WITH USER ACCOUNTS 133

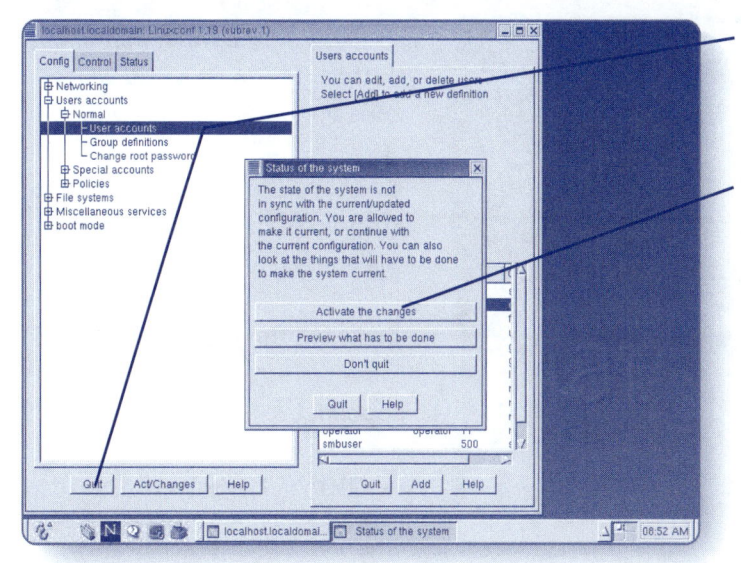

16. **Click** on the **Quit button**. The Status of the system dialog box will open.

17. **Click** the **Activate the changes button**. The user account will be added to your system, and the Linuxconf window will close.

Editing a User Account

Sometimes you'll need to change someone's name or password. Here's how you can change any needed details about the user.

134 CHAPTER 8: MANAGING IN A MULTI-USER ENVIRONMENT

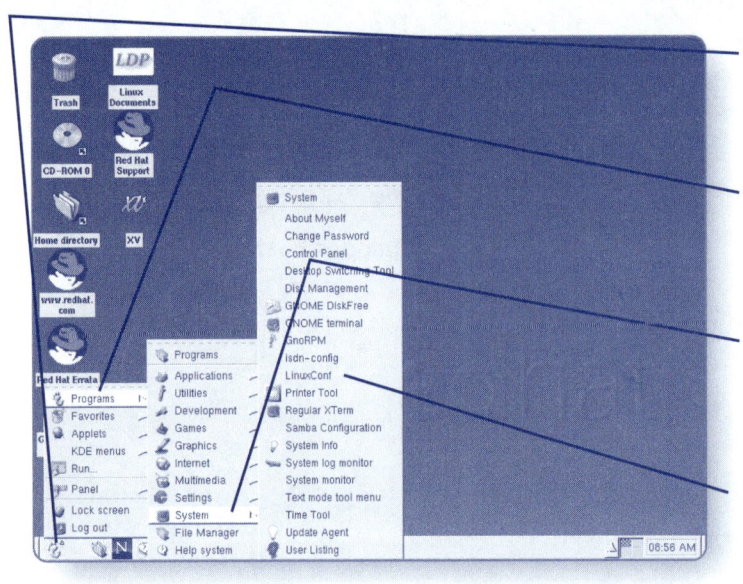

1. **Click** on the **Main Menu Button**. The Main Menu will appear.

2. **Move** the **mouse pointer** to Programs. The Programs menu will appear.

3. **Move** the **mouse pointer** to System. The System menu will appear.

4. **Click** on **LinuxConf**. The Linuxconf window will open.

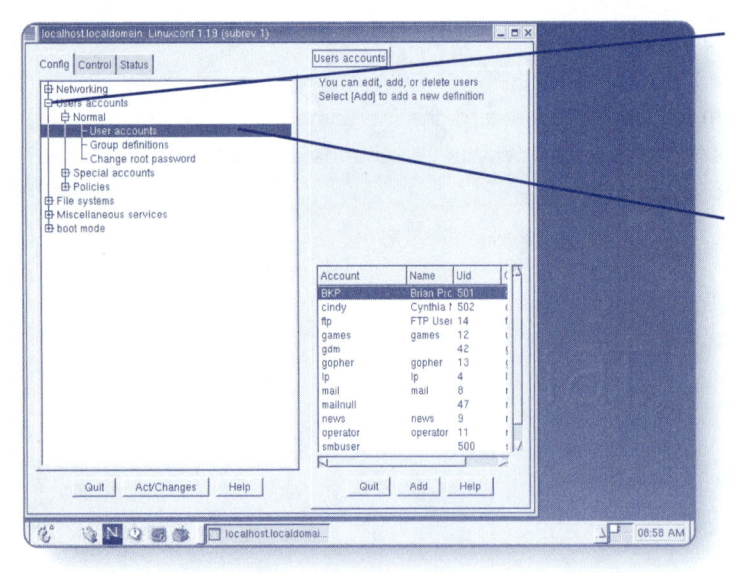

5. **Click** on the **plus sign** next to the User accounts category. A list of options for handling user accounts will appear.

6. **Click** on **User accounts** under the Normal option. The right pane will appear showing all of the user accounts that are currently set up on the system.

Changing User Information

Now that you have reached the user account pane, you can work from here to make your changes.

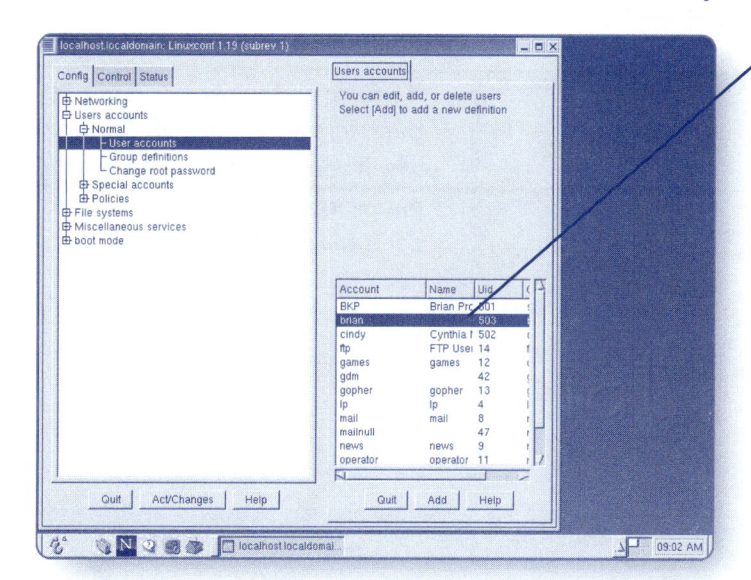

1. Click on the **user account** in the Users accounts pane to which you want to make changes. The User information pane will appear and you can make a variety of changes.

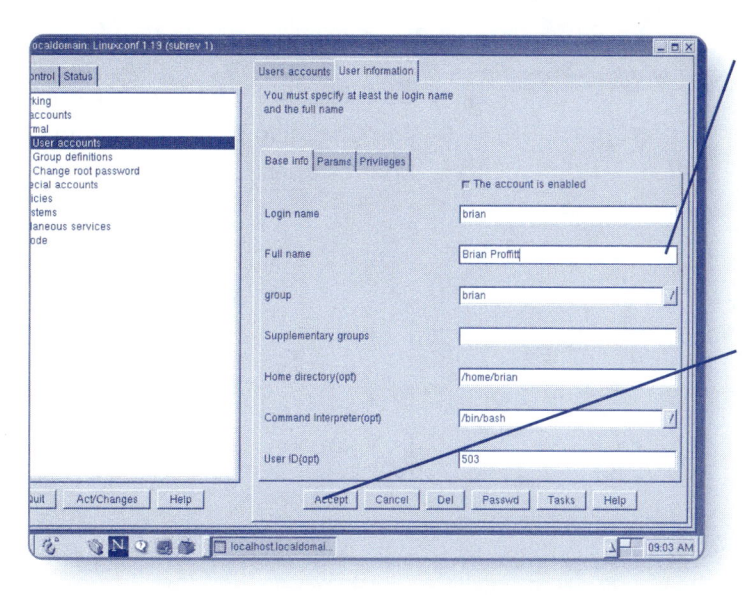

2. Click in the **Full name text box** and **type** the **first and last name** for the user. If you set up a user account using the method in Chapter 1, "Discovering Linux," this field will be blank.

3. Click on **Accept**. You'll be returned to the Users accounts pane.

Changing the Password

If a number of people are using the same computer, it's a good idea to have everyone change passwords on a regular basis.

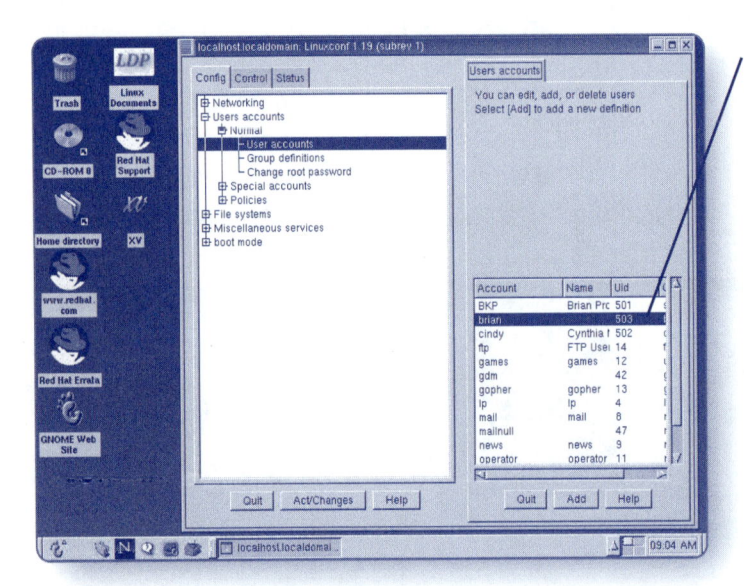

1. Click on the **user account** in the Users accounts pane for which you want to change the password. The User information pane will appear.

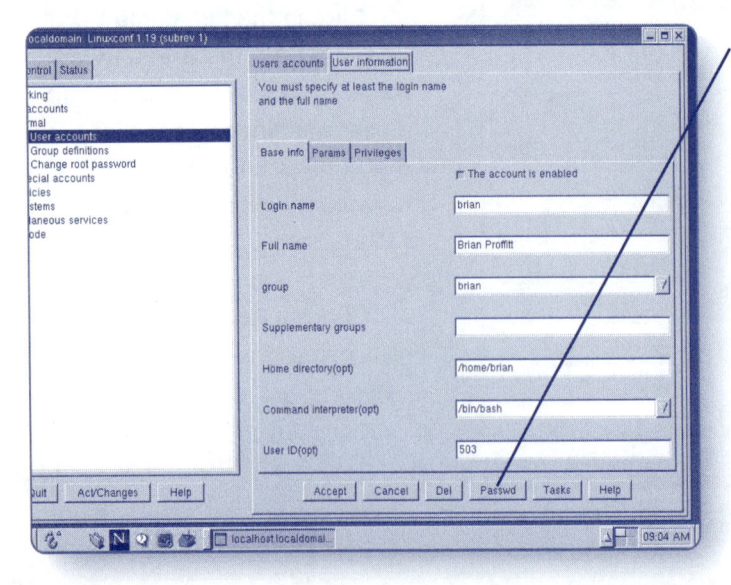

2. Click on the **Passwd button**. The Changing password dialog box will open.

WORKING WITH USER ACCOUNTS 137

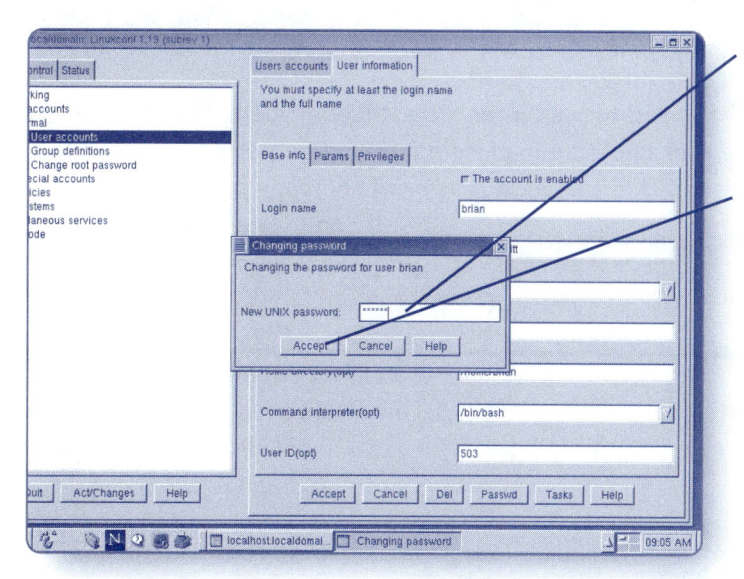

3. Type a different **password** in the New UNIX password text box.

4. Click on the **Accept button**. A confirmation pane will appear.

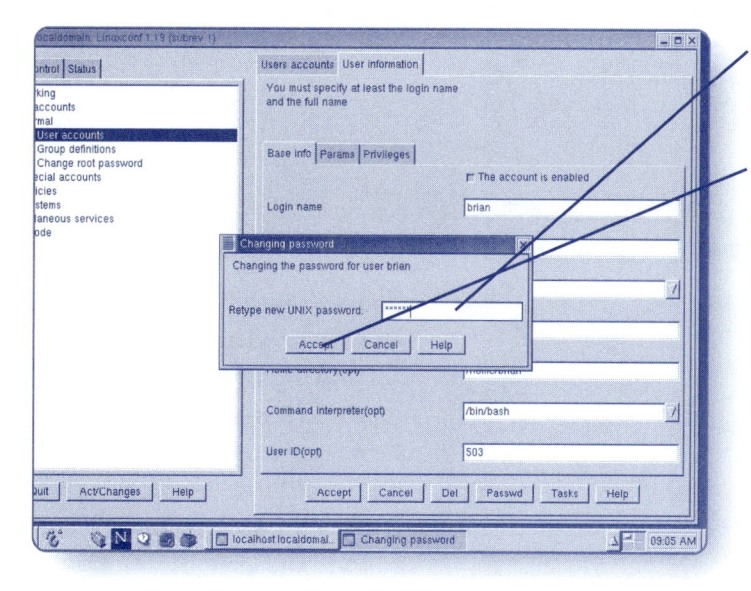

5. Type the same **password** that you typed in step 3.

6. Click on the **Accept button**. You will return to the list of user accounts.

Disabling a User's Account

If you need to put a user on restriction, you can easily keep the user's account in place but deny that person access to the system. This is especially useful if someone is on vacation and you don't want someone logging in with the vacationer's account.

1. Click on the **user account** in the Users accounts pane that you want to disable. The User information pane will appear.

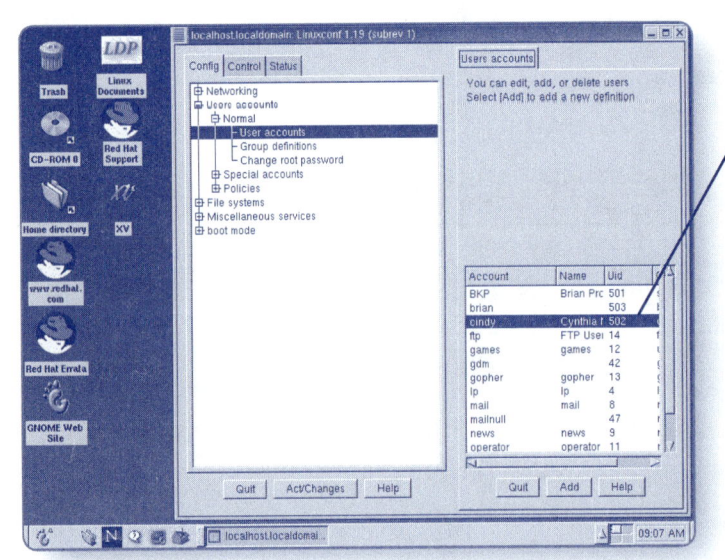

2. Click on the **The account is enabled check box**. The option will be cleared and any person trying to log in with this login name and password will not be given access to the system.

3. Click on **Accept**. You will return to the user list.

WORKING WITH USER ACCOUNTS 139

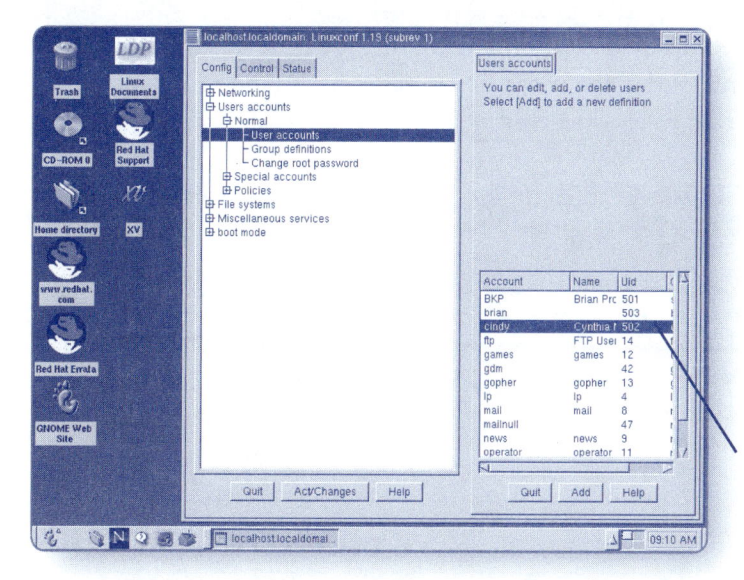

Deleting a User Account

When a person will no longer be using the Linux computer, you can delete the account. If other users will need the files created by the deleted user, these files can be saved and used by others.

1. In the Users accounts pane, **click** on the **user account** that you want to remove. The User information pane will appear.

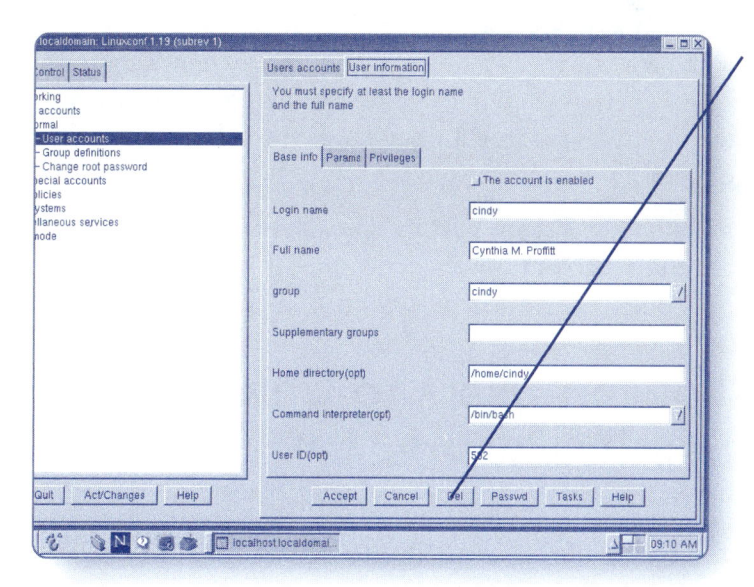

2. Click on the **Del button**. The Deleting account dialog box will open.

CHAPTER 8: MANAGING IN A MULTI-USER ENVIRONMENT

3. **Click** on an **option button** to specify how the files contained in the user's home directory will be handled. The option will be selected.

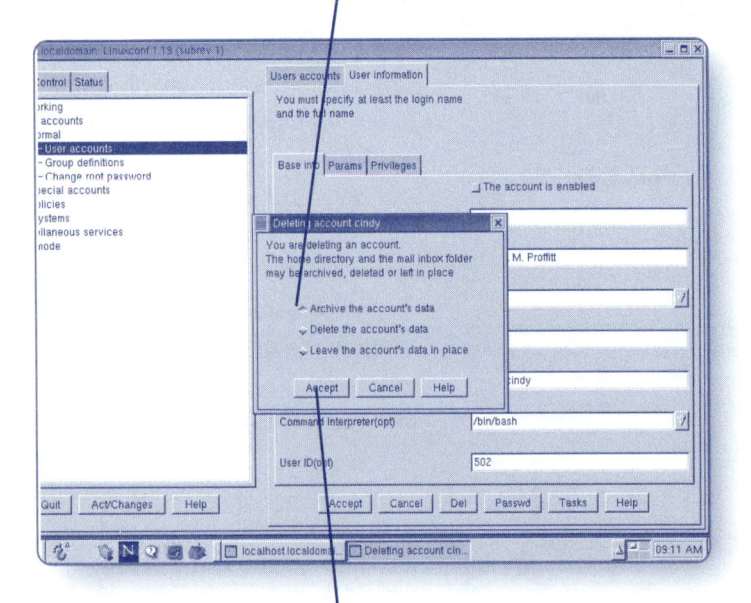

- **Archive the account's data.** This option compresses the files contained in the user's home directory into a single file. This file is placed in the /home directory, along with the directories for all of your user accounts, in a directory named /oldaccounts.

- **Delete the account's data.** This option removes the entire contents of the user's home directory.

- **Leave the account's data in place.** This option removes the user from the user list but leaves the user's home directory and contents in place.

4. **Click** on the **Accept button**. You will return to the user list and the user account will no longer appear in the list.

Allowing Users to Change Their Passwords

Individual users can change the password needed to access their user accounts from the Gnome interface. Before you do this for your own user account, log out of the root account, and log back in as a user.

ALLOWING USERS TO CHANGE THEIR PASSWORDS 141

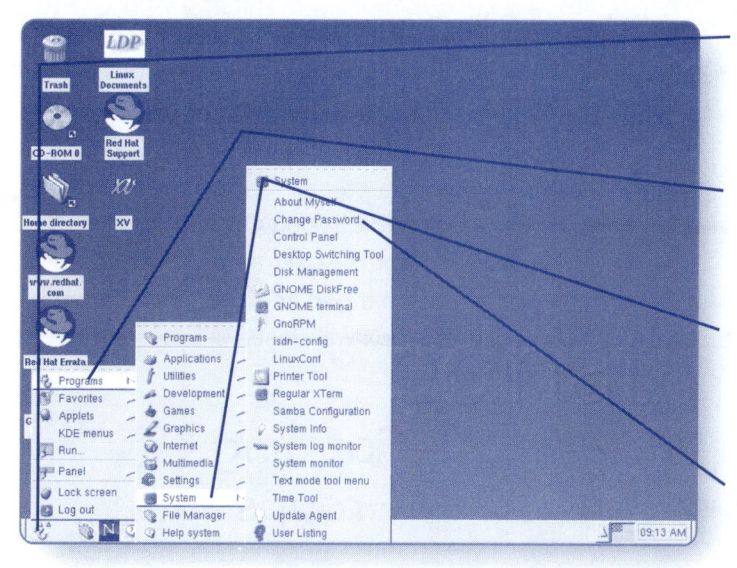

1. **Click** on the **Main Menu Button**. The Main Menu will appear.

2. Move the **mouse pointer** to Programs. The Programs menu will appear.

3. Move the **mouse pointer** to System. The System menu will appear.

4. Click on **Change Password**. The Input dialog box will open.

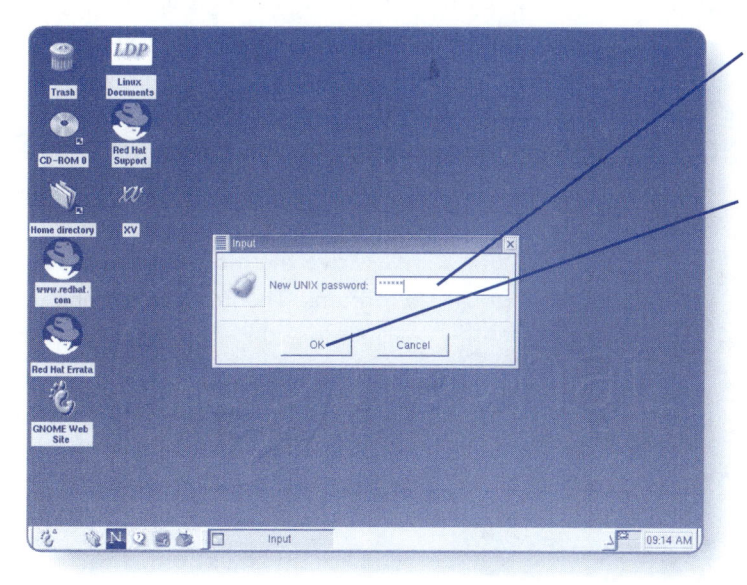

5. Type the **new password** used by the account in the New UNIX password text box.

6. Click on **OK**. Another Input dialog box will open.

CHAPTER 8: MANAGING IN A MULTI-USER ENVIRONMENT

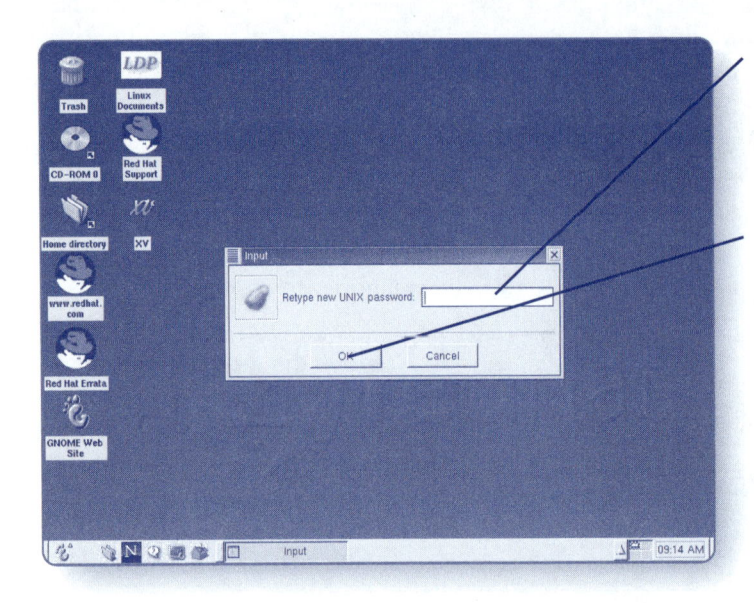

7. Retype the **new password** that the user wants to use in the Retype new UNIX password text box.

8. Click on **OK**. The password for the user account will be changed and the Input dialog box will close.

Forming Groups

Groups allow you to share files between users. When users belong to the same group, they can share files created by the members of the group. The person who created the file can specify the type of access available to other members of the group.

1. Click on the **Main Menu button**. The Main Menu will appear.

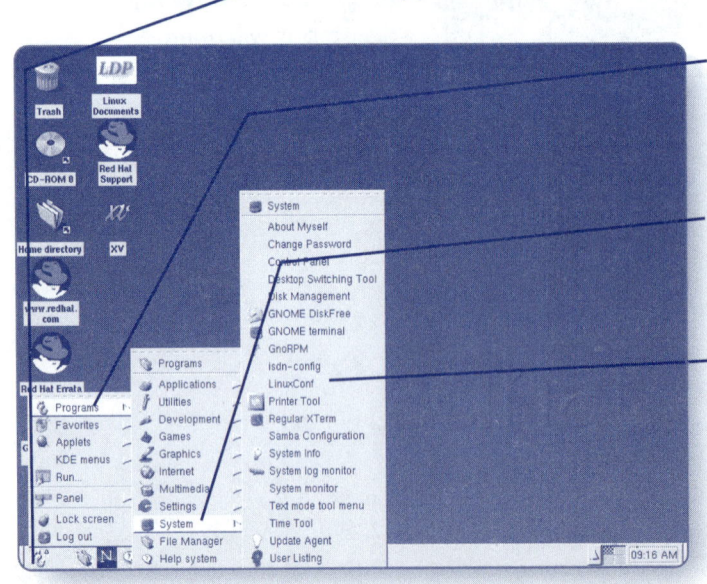

2. Move the **mouse pointer** to Programs. The Programs menu will appear.

3. Move the **mouse pointer** to System. The System menu will appear.

4. Click on **LinuxConf**. The Linuxconf window will open.

FORMING GROUPS 143

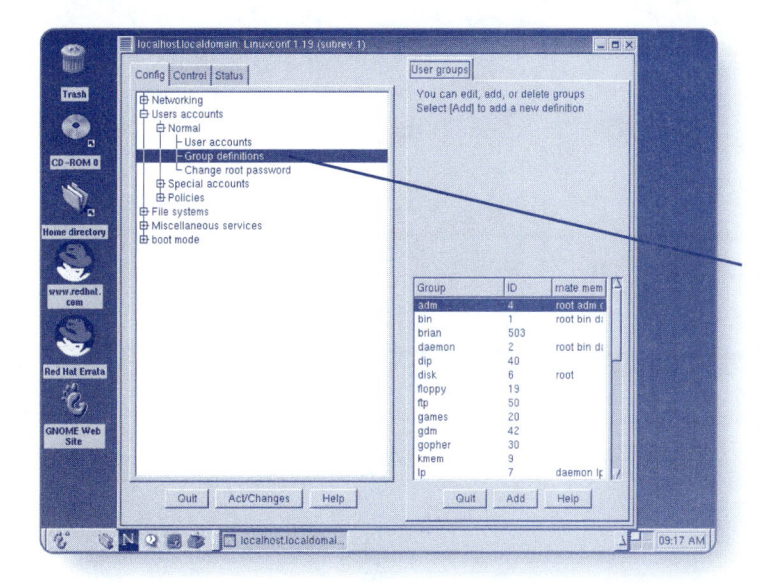

5. Scroll down the **Config list** in the left pane until you see the User accounts category. The list of configuration options for user accounts will be displayed.

6. Click on **Group definitions** under the Normal options. The right pane will appear showing all the user groups currently set up on the system.

Creating a Group

To create file access between users on the Linux system, the first step is to form a group. Not every user on the system needs to belong to a group—only those people who need to share files (such as a workgroup). Some users may belong to several groups.

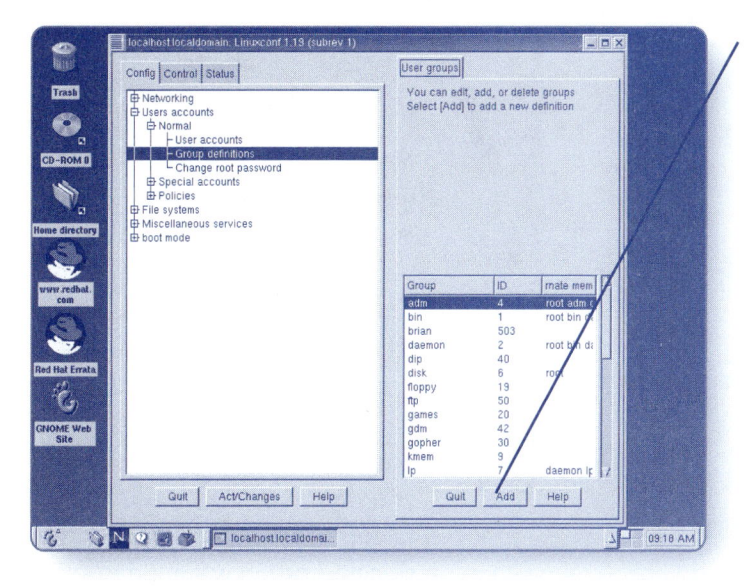

1. Click on the **Add button**. The Group specification pane will appear.

CHAPTER 8: MANAGING IN A MULTI-USER ENVIRONMENT

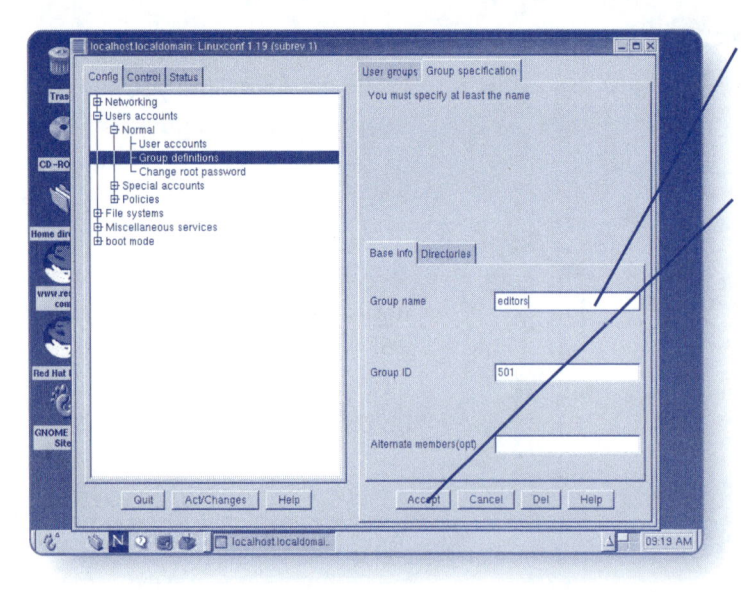

2. Click in the **Group name text box** and **type** a **name** for the group.

3. Click on the **Accept button**. You'll return to the list of user groups, where your new group will be displayed.

> **NOTE**
> To make changes to the group, click on the group in the User groups pane. From here you can delete a group or create a default directory for the group to use to store files.

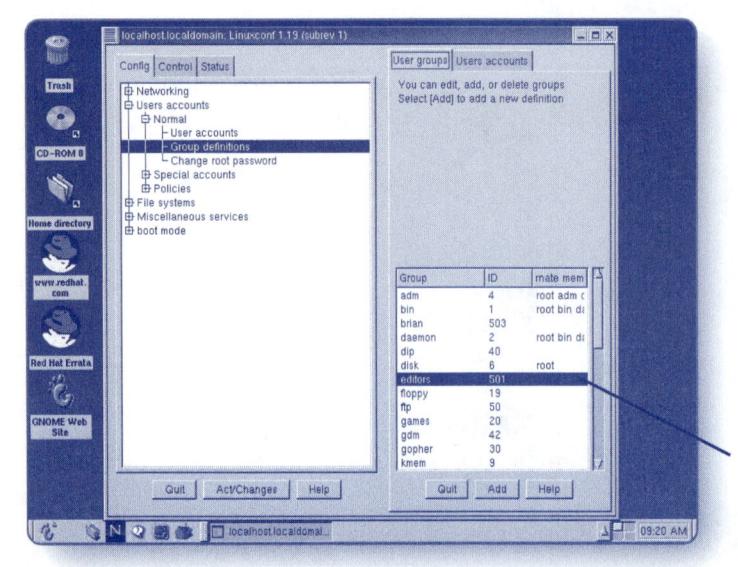

Assigning Users to a Group

Now that you've created a few groups, it's time to assign members to the group. Those people who have a reason to share files with each other should be placed in a separate group.

1. Click on the **group** to which you want to assign users. The Group specification pane for the selected group will appear.

FORMING GROUPS   145

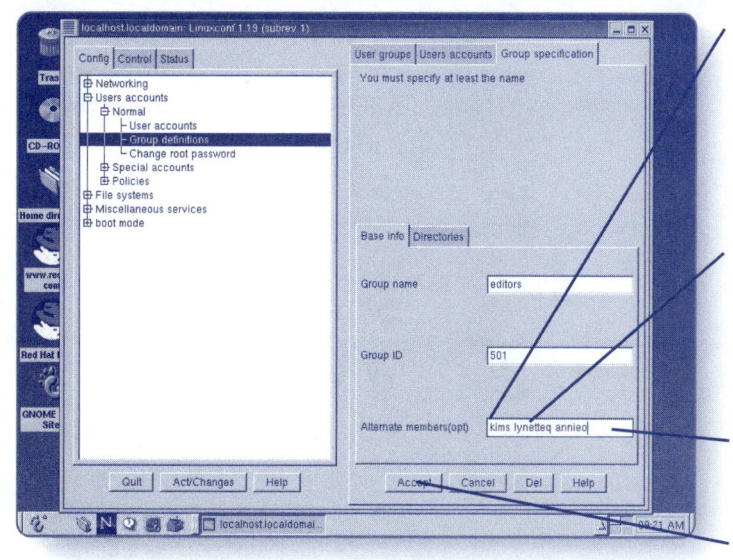

2. Click in the **Alternate members (opt) text box** and **type** the **user name** for the first person that you want to add to the group.

3. Press the **Spacebar** and **type** the **user name** for the second person that you want to add to the group.

4. Add more **user names** as needed.

5. Click on the **Accept button**. The User groups pane will appear.

> **TIP**
> You can assign a group to a user when you are editing the user's account.

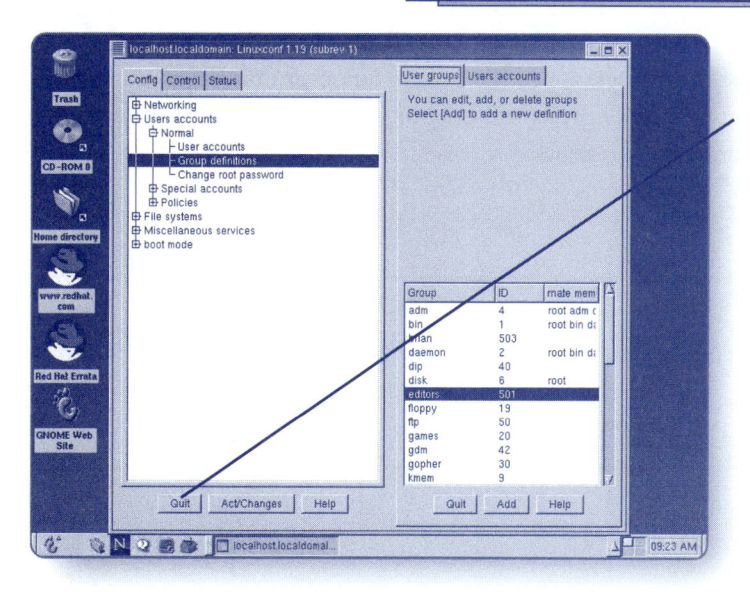

6. Click on the **Quit button**. The Status of the system dialog box will open.

CHAPTER 8: MANAGING IN A MULTI-USER ENVIRONMENT

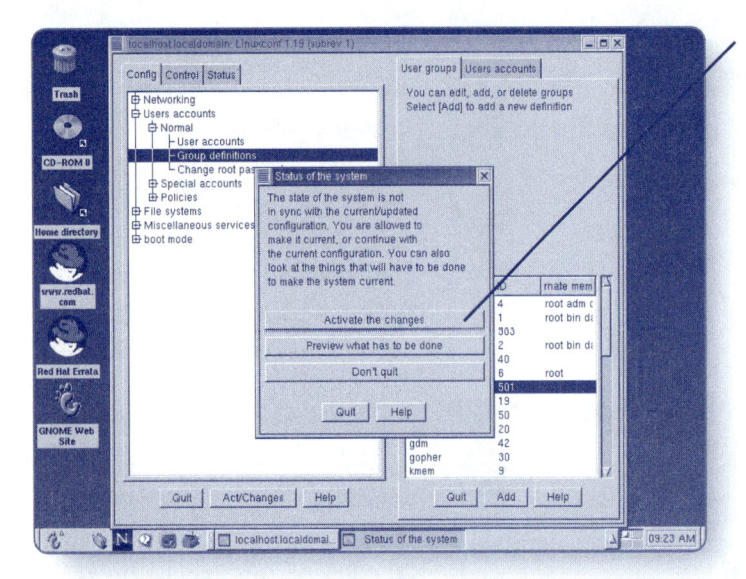

7. Click the **Activate the changes button**. The user group will be added to your system, and the Linuxconf window will close.

Sharing Files with a Group

Multi-user operating systems like Linux have different ways of handling file management than single-user systems like DOS. Sometimes you'll want to share things with other users. At the same time, you might not want to share everything with everyone, so you need to set up your files to discriminate about what you share and with whom. You'll want to be in your user account before you begin setting file permissions.

Setting File Permissions

The assignment of file permissions to control user access works on a system of file access being permitted or denied. You can easily give read-only or write-access to yourself or to members of a group.

> **TIP**
> You can set file permissions for several files at once. Select all the files that will need the same file permissions.

SHARING FILES WITH A GROUP 147

1. Double-click on the **Home directory icon** on the desktop. The File manager will open with your Home directory displayed.

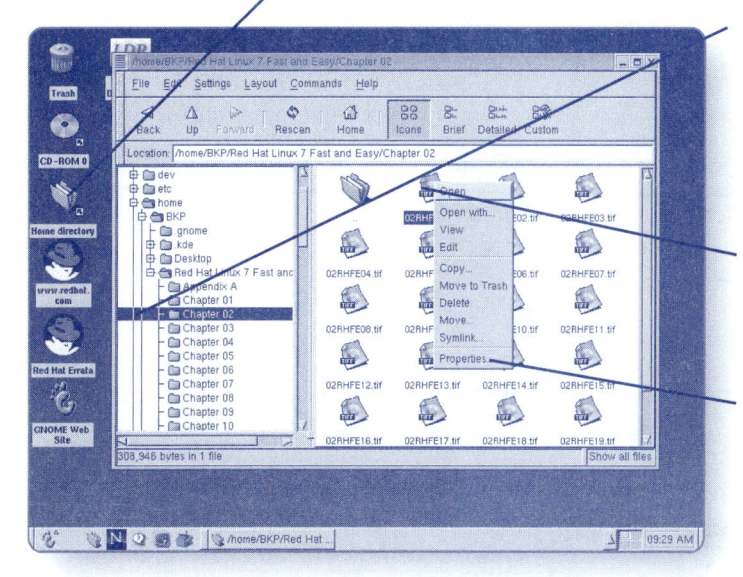

2. Click on the **directory** that contains the file you want to share with others in your group. The directory contents will open.

3. Right-click on the **file** that you want to share with others in a group. A menu will appear.

4. Click on **Properties**. The Properties dialog box for the selected file will open.

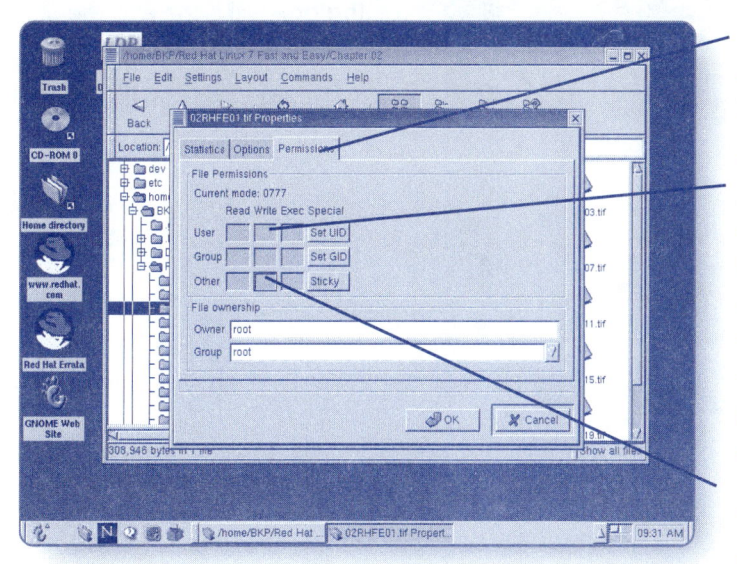

5. Click on the **Permissions tab**. The File Permissions tab will come to the top of the stack.

6. Click on the **Write check button** in the User area if the owner of the file does not want to be able to make any changes to the file. The check button will be cleared and the owner of the file will have read-only access.

7. Click on the **Write check button** in the Group area if the owner of the file wants other members of the group to be able to make changes to the file. The check button will be selected.

CHAPTER 8: MANAGING IN A MULTI-USER ENVIRONMENT

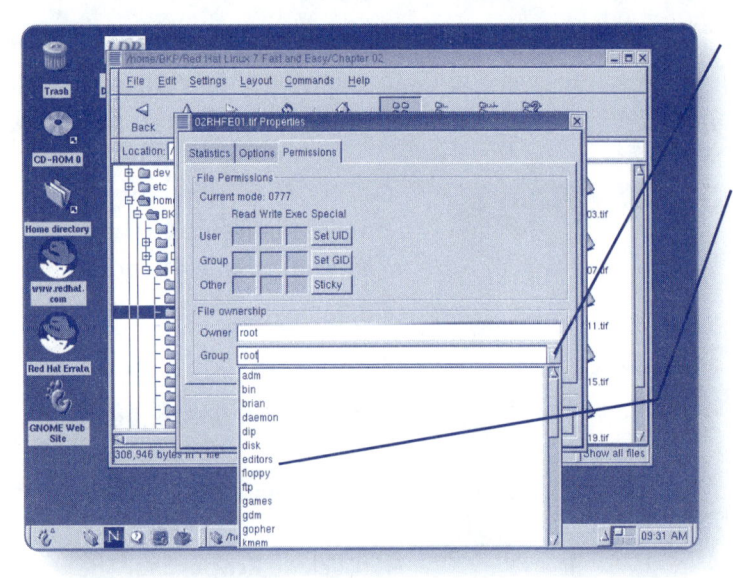

8. Click on the **down arrow** next to the Group list box. A drop-down list will appear.

9. Click on the **group** that needs to have access to the file. The selected group will appear in the list box.

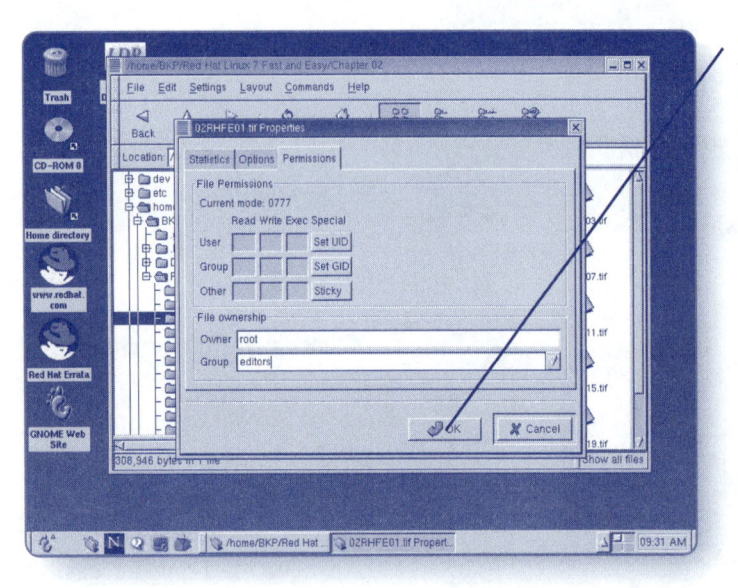

10. Click on **OK** if you are satisfied with your choices. The dialog box will close and the file permissions will be set

9

Maintaining Your Linux

The only time you'll want to log into Linux as the superuser is when you make changes to the entire Linux system, not just an individual user's account. There are a few things you can do to keep on top of your Linux system. One of the most important is having boot and recovery disks on hand. These two disks will help immensely when you run into a problem. In this chapter, you'll learn how to:

- Find information about your computer system
- Mount floppy drives to be used by Linux
- Create a recovery disk set
- Check for available disk space
- Change the time on your computer clock

Finding System Information

If you need to know some information about the system running your computer, there's an easy way to find it. You can find out which Linux distribution you're running along with the operating system version and kernel. You don't need to be in the superuser account to find this information—you can find it even if you are logged into a user account.

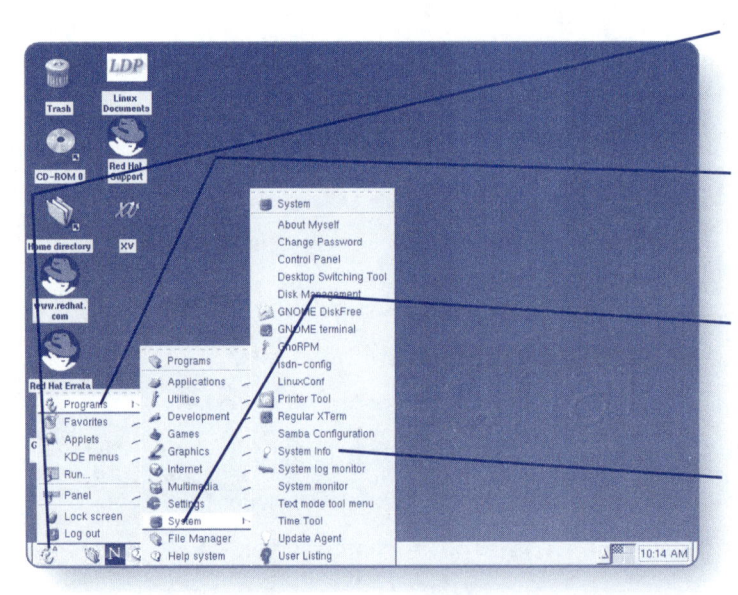

1. Click on the **Main Menu button**. The Main Menu will appear.

2. Move the **mouse pointer** to Programs. The Programs menu will appear.

3. Move the **mouse pointer** to System. The System menu will appear.

4. Click on **System Info**. The System Information window will open. At the bottom of the window, you'll see the Linux distribution name and version, the kernel number, and some information about your computer and its current usage.

FINDING SYSTEM INFORMATION 151

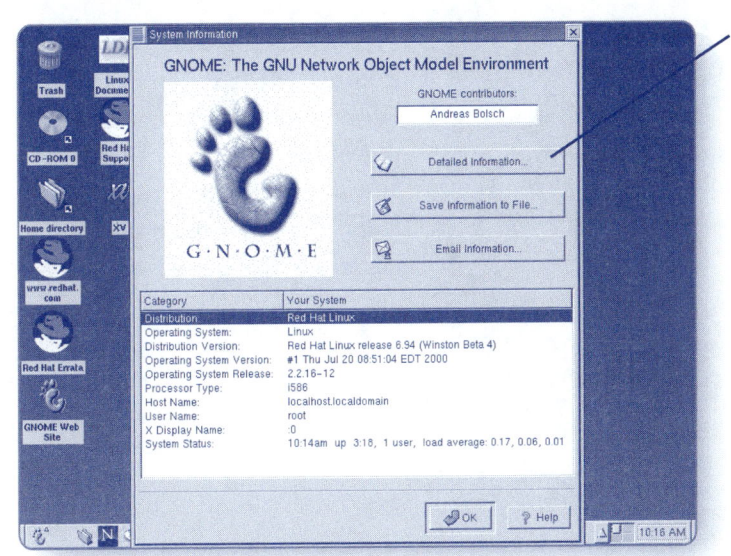

5. Click on the **Detailed Information button**. The Detail System Information dialog box will open and the Disk Information tab will be at the top of the stack. Note the total hard drive space and the amount of free space.

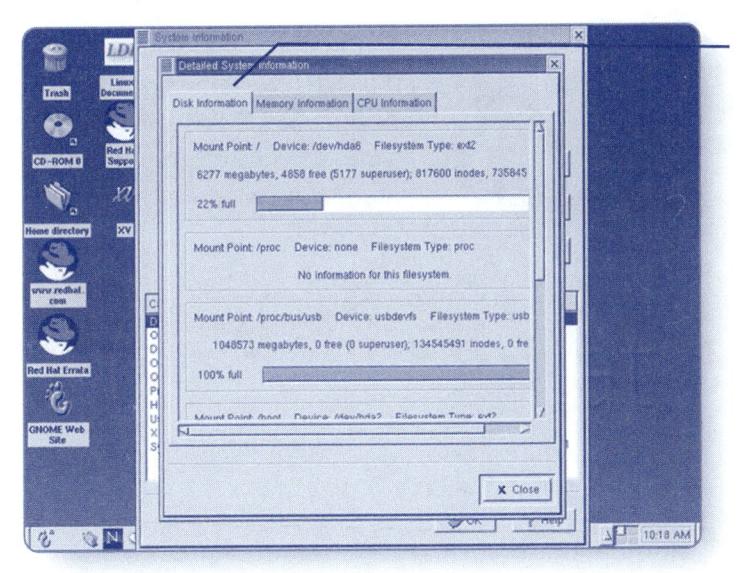

6. Click on the **Memory Information tab**. The memory Information tab will come to the top of the stack. The Total Memory is the amount of RAM installed on your system. You'll also notice how much memory is currently being used.

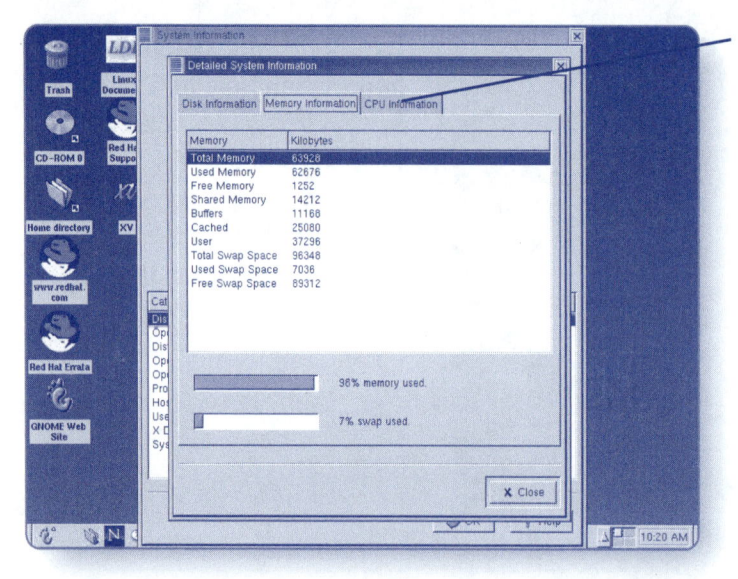

7. Click on the **CPU Information tab**. The CPU Information tab will come to the top of the stack. All of the information relating to your computer's processor chip is located in this pane.

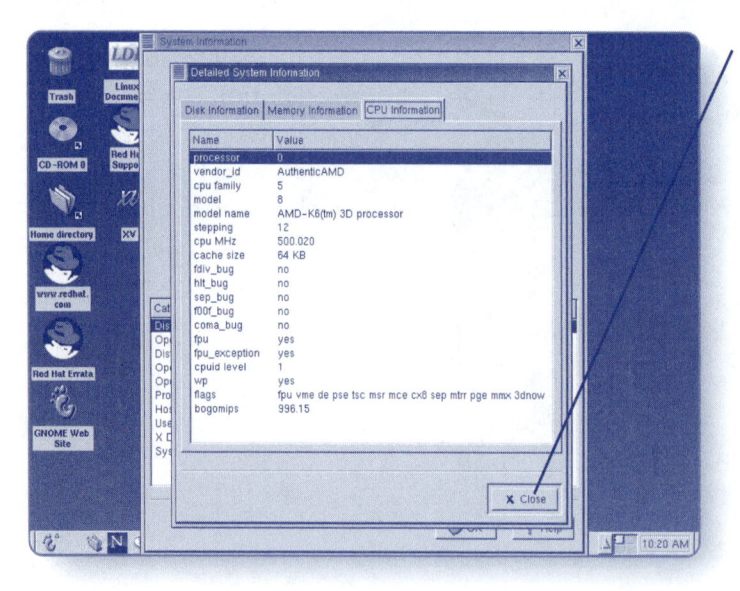

8. Click on the **Close button**. The Detail System Information dialog box will close and you'll return to the System Information window.

MOUNTING A FLOPPY DISK DRIVE

> **TIP**
>
> If you want to print the information, click on the Save Information to File button. You can save the information as a text file and print it later.

9. Click on **OK**. The System Information window will close.

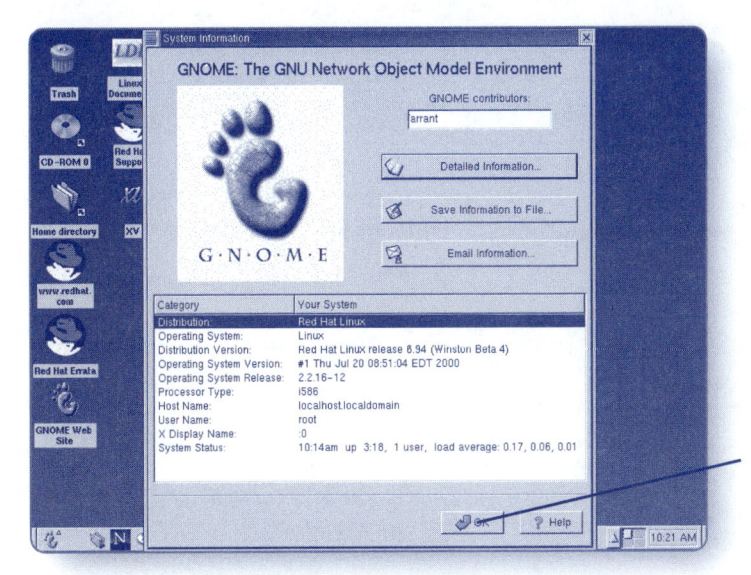

Mounting a Floppy Disk Drive

Before you can copy files from the Linux file system to a floppy disk, you'll need to mount your computer's floppy disk drive. By mounting the drive, you are telling Linux where the drive resides and what type of file system it uses. You have a choice of two types of file systems. You can either use Linux-formatted disks to use on other Linux machines, or you can create a DOS file system so that you can transfer files between a Linux computer and a DOS or Windows computer.

Creating a Linux Floppy Drive

You must be logged in as superuser or root to mount a drive.

CHAPTER 9: MAINTAINING YOUR LINUX

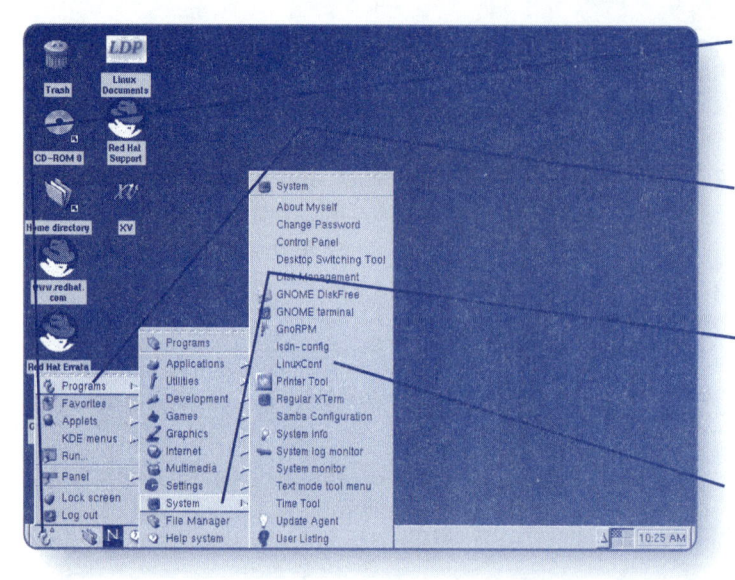

1. Click on the **Main Menu button**. The Main Menu will appear.

2. Move the **mouse pointer** to Programs. The Programs menu will appear.

3. Move the **mouse pointer** to System. The System menu will appear.

4. Click on **LinuxConf**. The Linuxconf window will open.

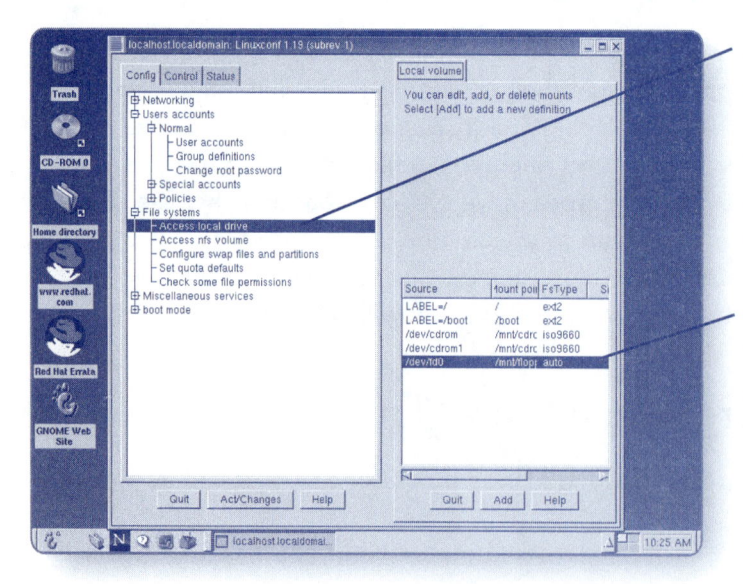

5. Scroll down to the **File systems category** and **click** on the **Access local drive option**. The Local volume pane will appear to the right of the window.

6. Click on **/dev/fd0**. The Volume specification pane will appear.

MOUNTING A FLOPPY DISK DRIVE

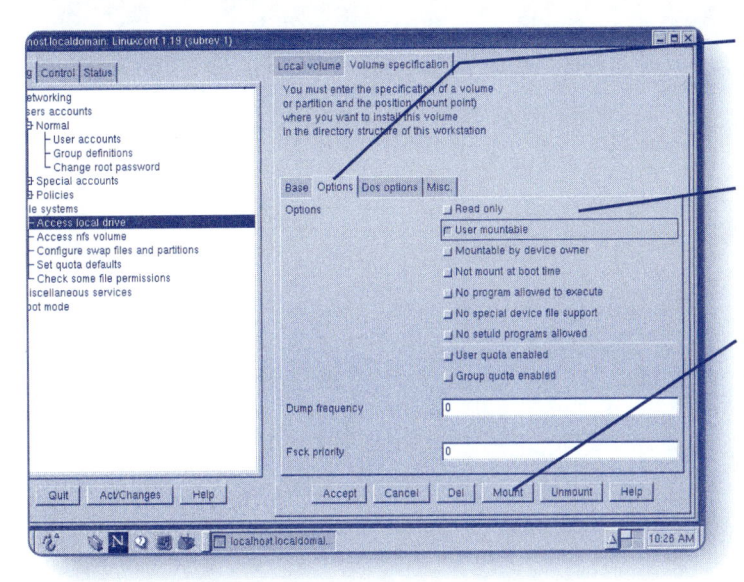

7. **Click** on the **Options tab**. The Options tab will come to the top of the stack.

8. **Click** on the **User mountable option button**. The option will be selected.

9. **Click** on the **Mount button**. The Mount file system dialog box will open.

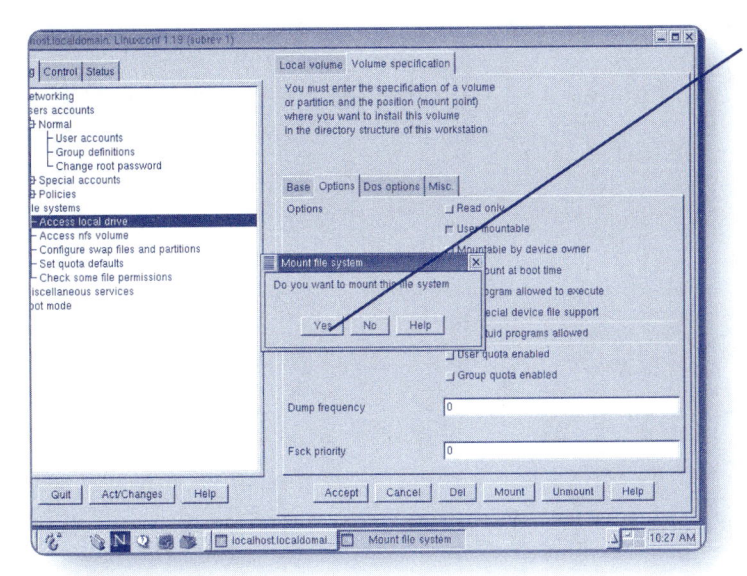

10. **Click** on the **Yes button**. The Please note pane will appear.

CHAPTER 9: MAINTAINING YOUR LINUX

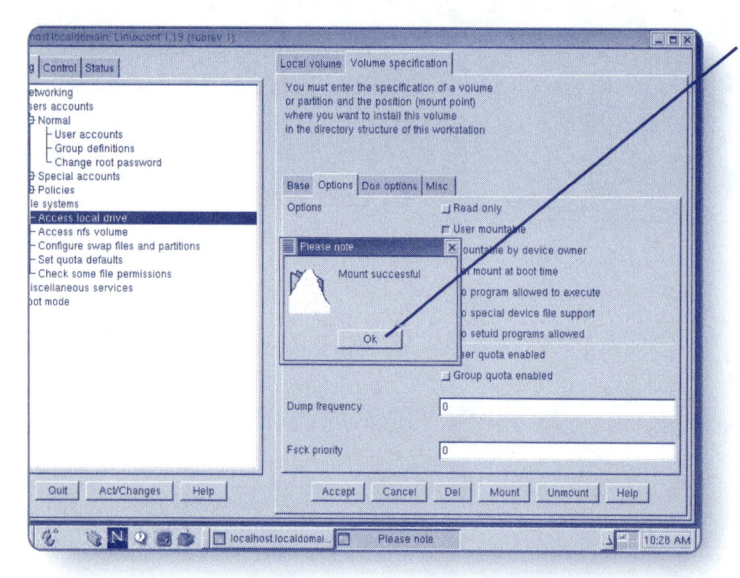

11. Click on the **OK button**. You will return to the Volume specification pane.

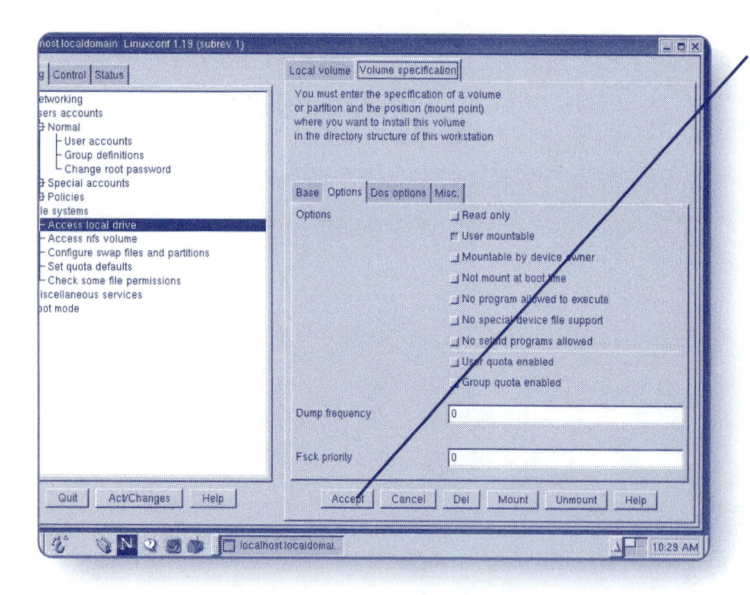

12. Click on the **Accept button**. You will return to the Local volume.

MOUNTING A FLOPPY DISK DRIVE

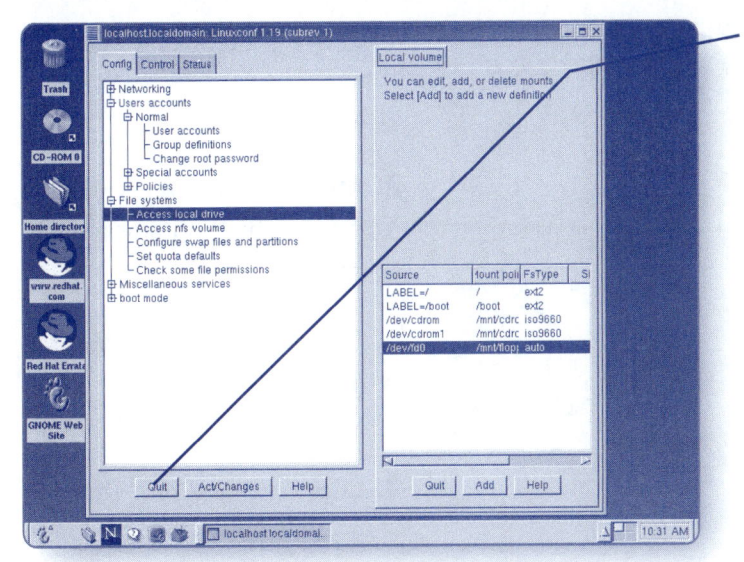

13. Click on the **Quit button**. The Status of the system dialog box will open.

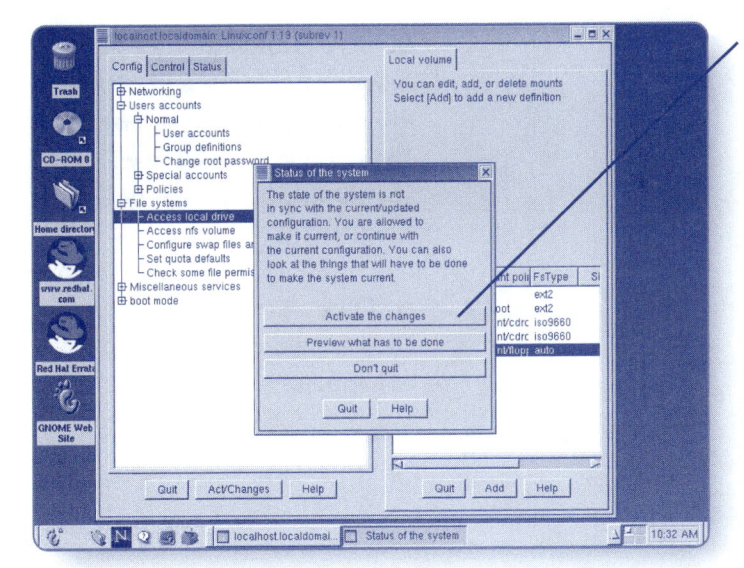

14. Click on the **Activate the changes button**. The user account will be added to your system, and the Linuxconf window will close.

Creating a DOS Floppy Drive

If you want to copy files onto a floppy disk and use that disk on a computer that uses DOS or Windows, you'll want to set the file system for the floppy drive to operate in MS-DOS Format.

CHAPTER 9: MAINTAINING YOUR LINUX

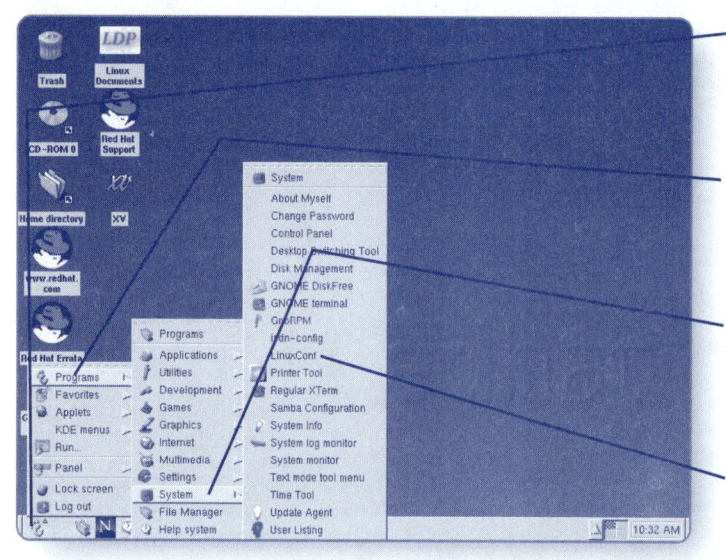

1. **Click** on the **Main Menu button**. The Main Menu will appear.

2. **Move** the **mouse pointer** to Programs. The Programs menu will appear.

3. **Move** the **mouse pointer** to System. The System menu will appear.

4. **Click** on **LinuxConf**. The Linuxconf window will open.

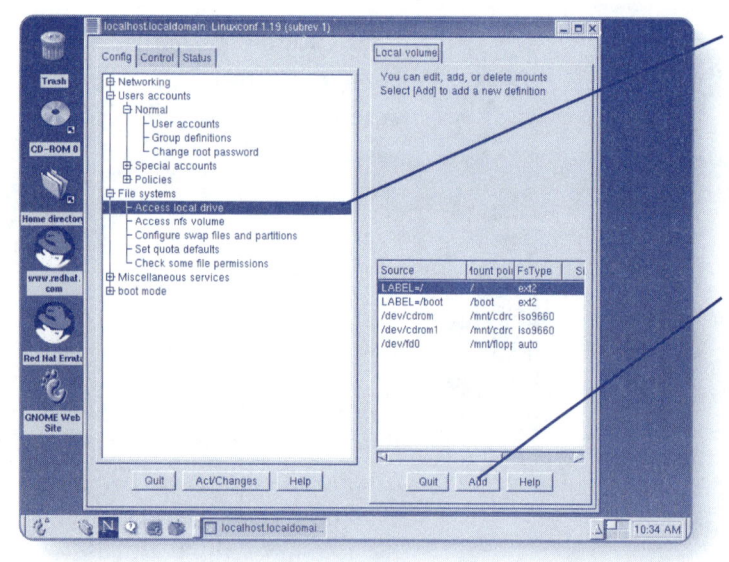

5. **Scroll down** to the **File systems category** and **click** on the **Access local drive option**. The Local volume pane will appear to the right of the window.

6. **Click** on the **Add button**. The Volume specification pane will appear.

MOUNTING A FLOPPY DISK DRIVE

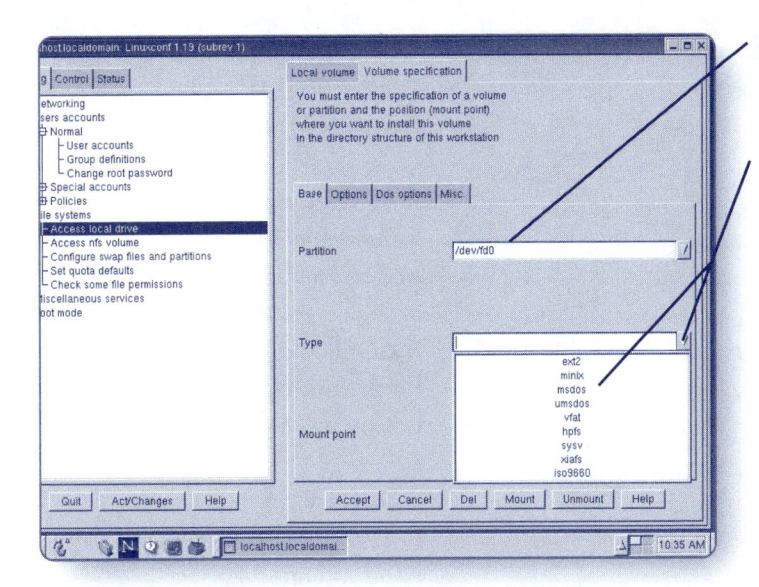

7. Click in the **Partition text box** and **type /dev/fd0**.

8. Click on the **down arrow** next to the Type list box and **click** on **msdos**. The selected type will appear in the list box.

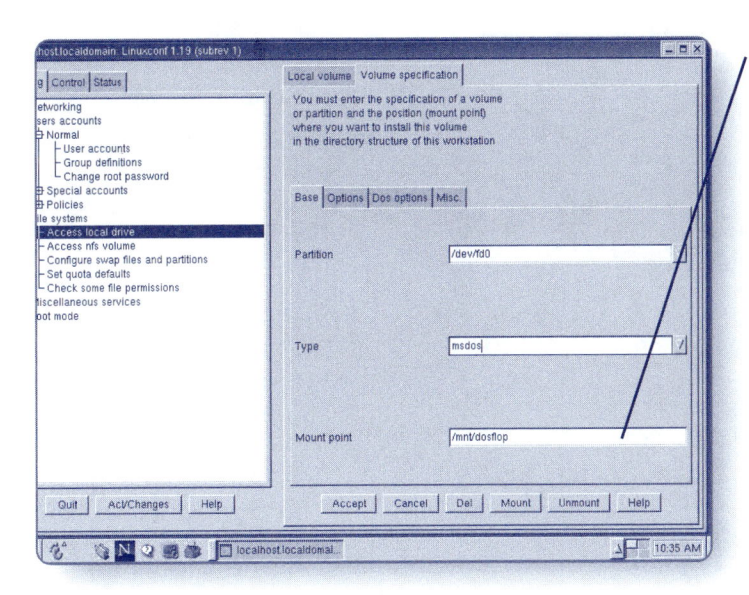

9. Click in the **Mount point text box** and **type /mnt/dosflop**.

CHAPTER 9: MAINTAINING YOUR LINUX

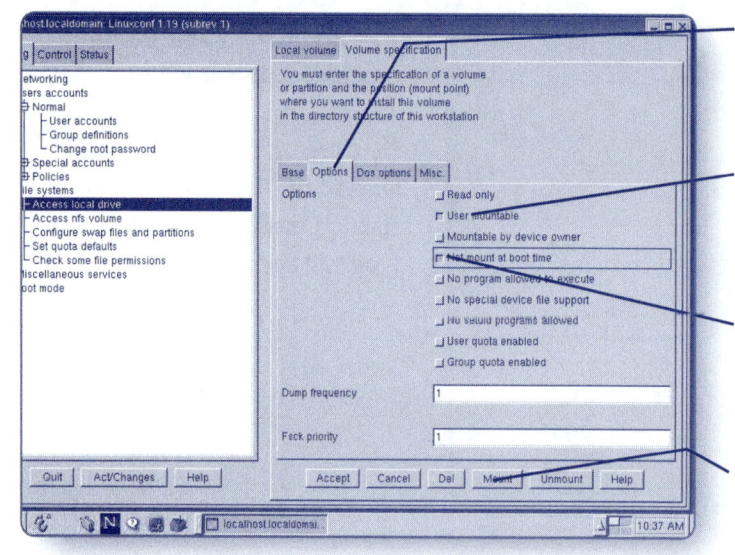

10. Click on the **Options tab**. The Options tab will come to the top of the stack.

11. Click on the **User mountable option button**. The option will be selected.

12. Click on the **Not mount at boot time option button**. The option will be selected.

13. Click on the **Mount button**. The Mount file system pane will appear.

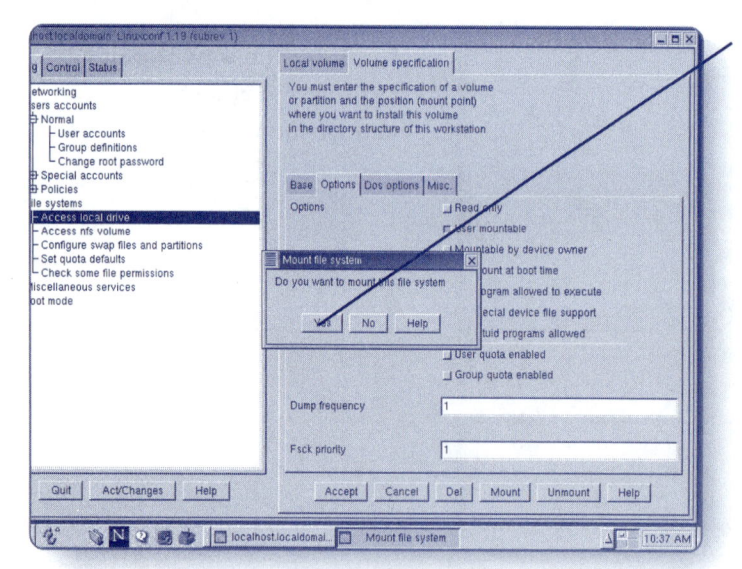

14. Click on the **Yes button**. The Please note pane will appear.

MOUNTING A FLOPPY DISK DRIVE   161

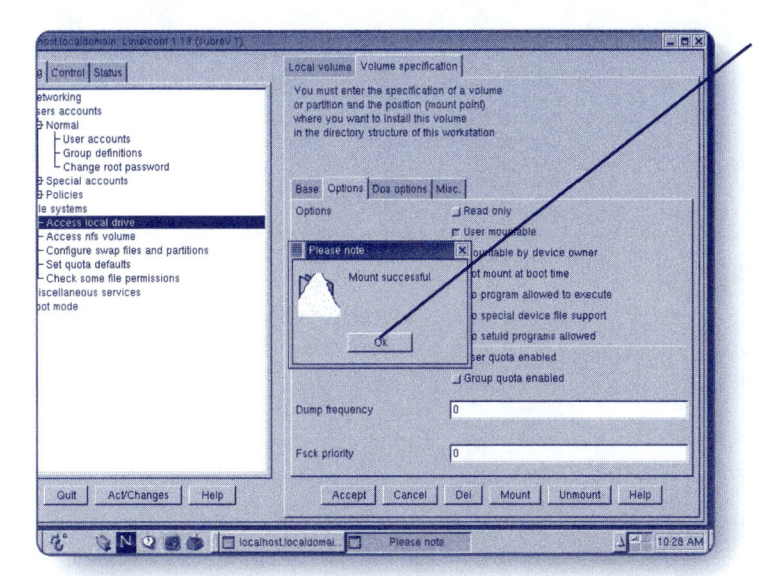

15. **Click** on the **OK button**. You will return to the Volume specification pane.

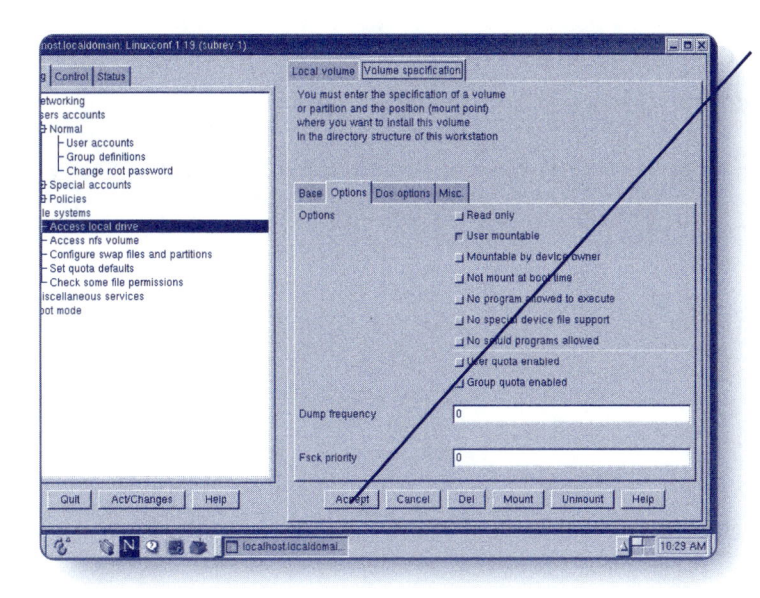

16. **Click** on the **Accept button**. You will return to the Local volume.

CHAPTER 9: MAINTAINING YOUR LINUX

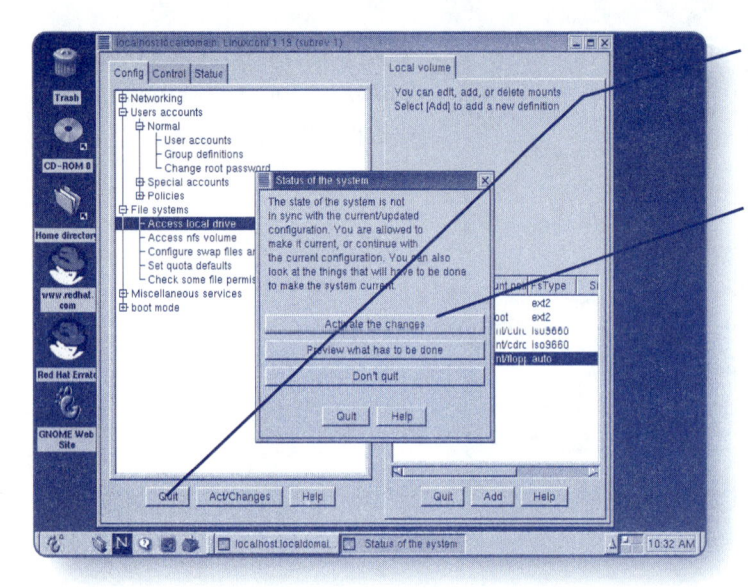

17. **Click** on the **Quit button**. The Status of the system dialog box will open.

18. **Click** the **Activate the changes button**. The user account will be added to your system, and the Linuxconf window will close.

Mounting the Floppy Drive in the User Account

The floppy drive needs to be mounted before a user can have access to the floppy drive from their account.

MOUNTING A FLOPPY DISK DRIVE

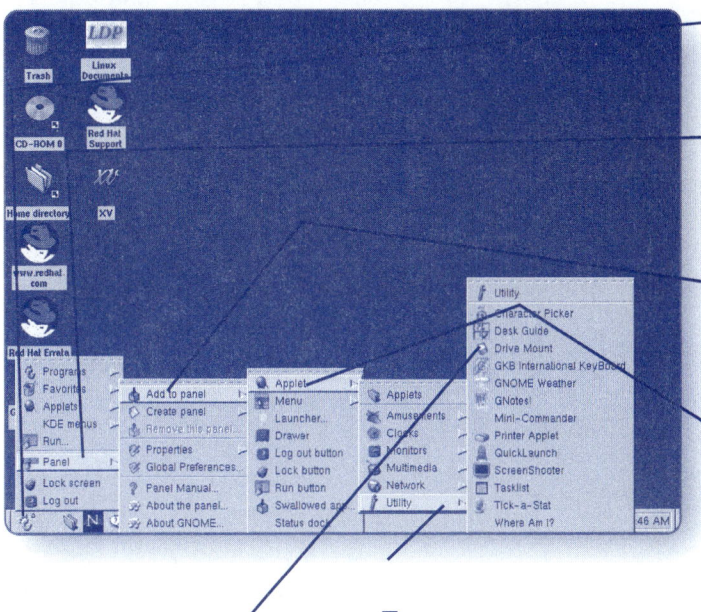

1. Click on the **Main Menu button**. The Main Menu will appear.

2. Move the **mouse pointer** to Panel. The Panel menu will appear.

3. Move the **mouse pointer** to Add to panel. The Add to panel menu will appear.

4. Move the **mouse pointer** to Applet. The Applet menu will appear.

5. Move the **mouse pointer** to Utility. The Utility menu will appear.

6. Click on **Drive Mount**. A floppy drive icon will be added to the Gnome Panel.

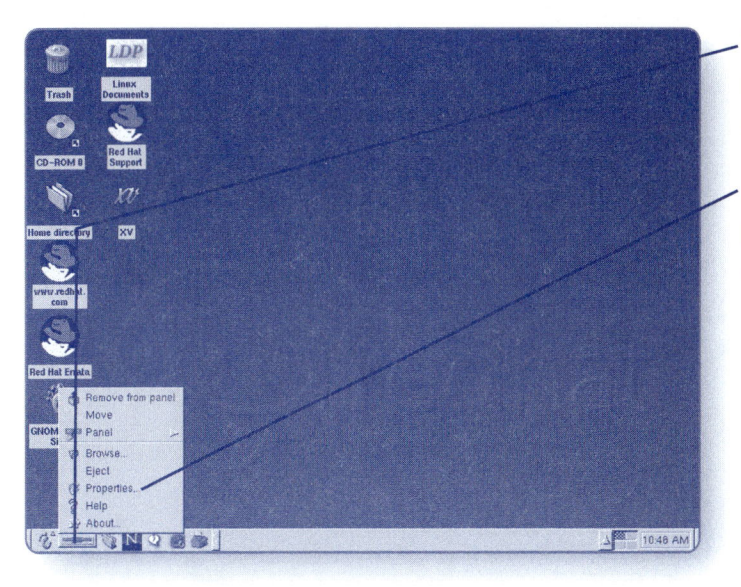

7. Right-click on the **Drive Mount applet icon**. A menu will appear.

8. Click on **Properties**. The Drive Mount Applet Properties dialog box will open.

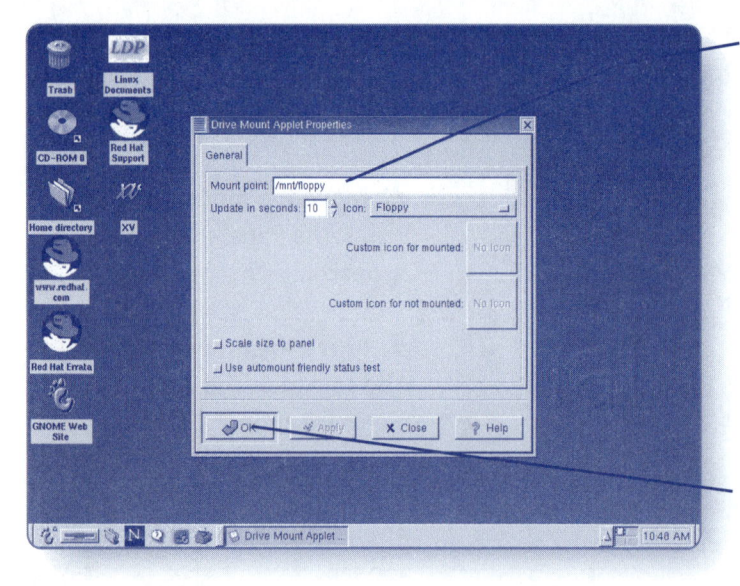

9a. If you want to mount the Linux floppy drive, **click** in the **Mount point text box** and **type /mnt/floppy**.

or

9b. If you want to mount the MS-DOS floppy drive, **click** in the **Mount point text box** and **type /mnt/dosflop**.

10. Click on **OK**. The Drive Mount Settings dialog box will close. If you hold the mouse pointer over the floppy icon on the Gnome panel, you'll see a tool tip that says the floppy drive is mounted.

Browsing the Floppy Drive

Now that you can quickly mount the floppy drive, you can browse a floppy's contents in a flash.

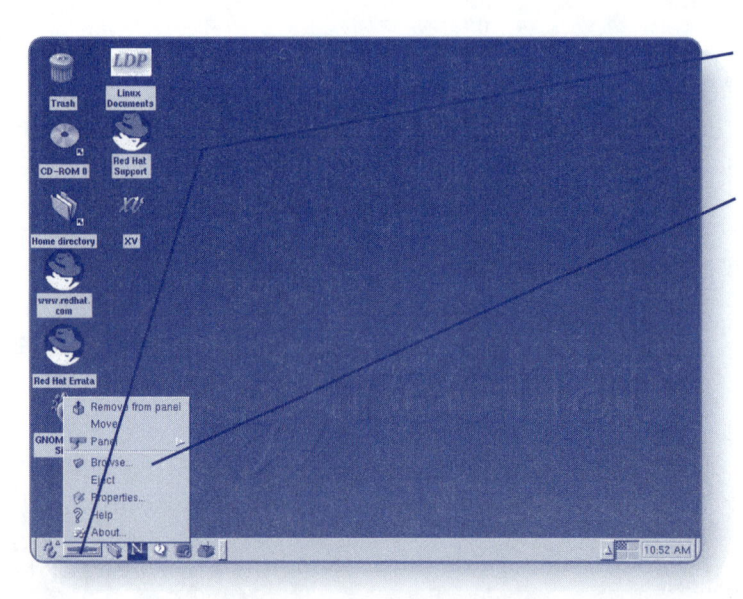

1. Right-click on the **Drive Mount applet icon**. A menu will appear.

2. Click on **Browse**. The Gnome file manager window will open to look at the floppy's contents.

Preparing a Boot Disk

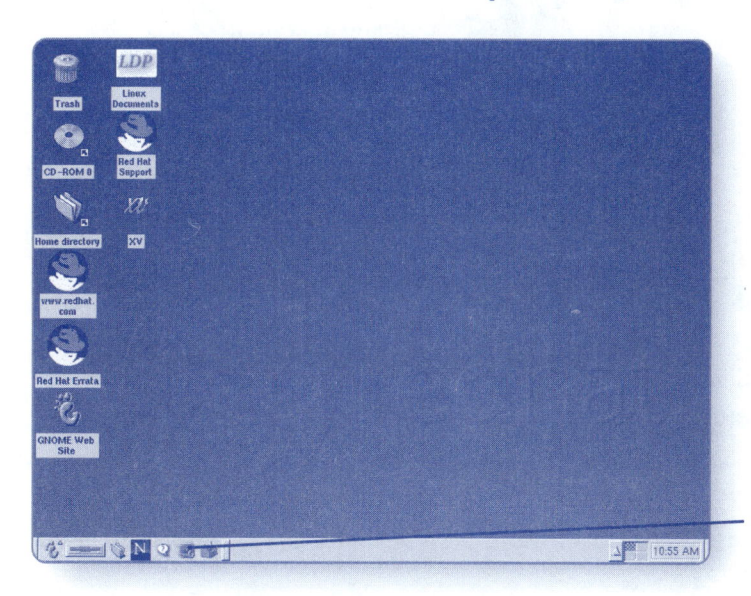

When you installed Linux, you were given the opportunity to create a boot disk. If you didn't create one at that time, you can still give yourself some peace of mind by creating a boot disk now.

1. Insert a **floppy disk** into your computer's floppy disk drive. You'll want to label this disk "Boot Image Disk".

2. Click on the **Gnome Terminal icon** on the Gnome Panel. The Terminal window will open on your screen.

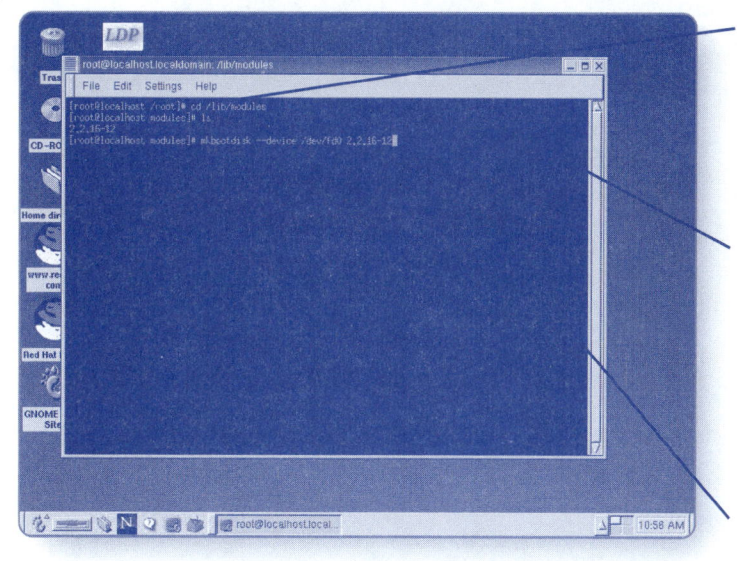

3. Type cd /lib/modules and **press Enter**. The directory will be changed to the modules directory where the files needed for the boot disk are located.

4. Type ls and **press Enter**. The kernel version number for your Linux operating system will be displayed and you will know which kernel to copy to the boot disk.

5. Type mkbootdisk —device /dev/fd0 2.2.16-12 and **press Enter**. A confirmation prompt will appear.

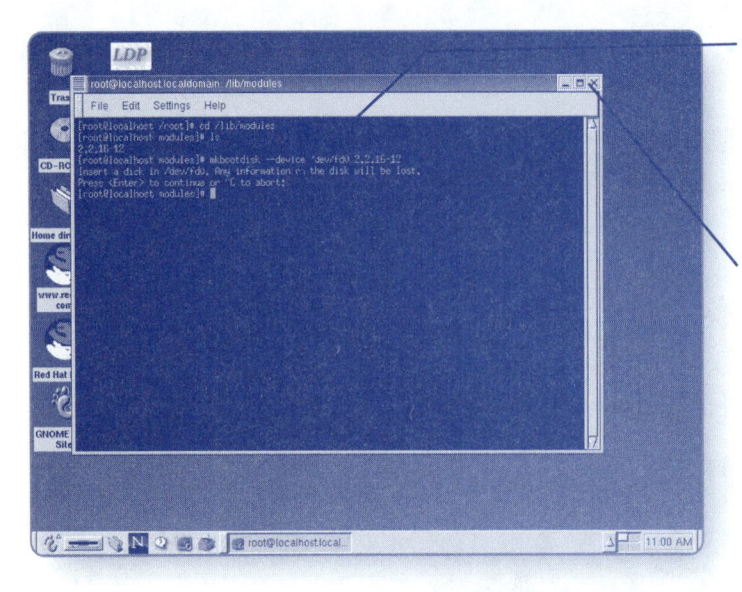

6. Press Enter. The boot information will be copied to the disk. When the process is complete, you'll return to the command prompt.

7. Click on the **Kill button**. The Terminal window will close.

Checking for Available Disk Space

The Gnome DiskFree is a small utility that shows you how much free space is available on the different partitions and hard drives on your computer system.

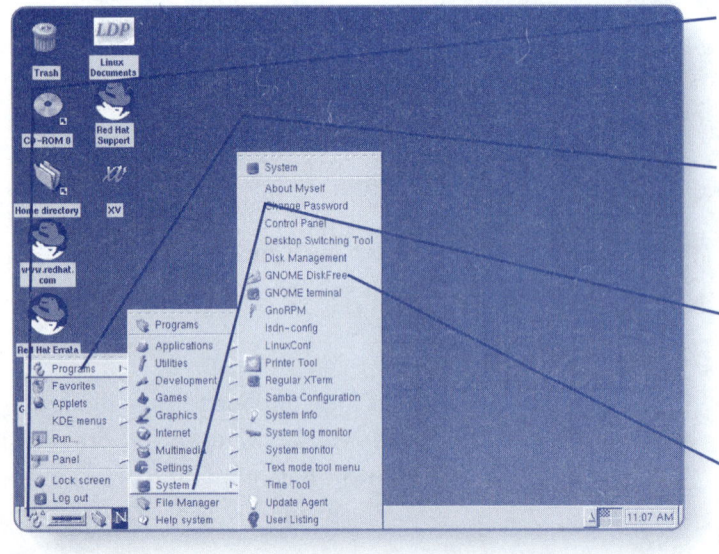

1. Click on the **Main Menu button**. The Main Menu will appear.

2. Move the **mouse pointer** to Programs. The Programs menu will appear.

3. Move the **mouse pointer** to System. The Systems menu will appear.

4. Click on **GNOME DiskFree**. The GDiskFree application will open.

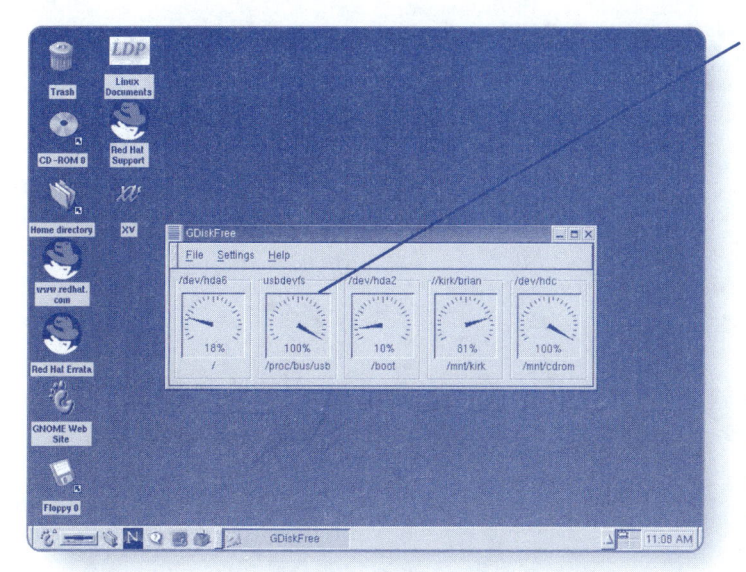

RESETTING THE CLOCK

Notice the different dials for each partition and hard drive. The dials show you the amount of free space available.

Resetting the Clock

You may find that the clock on the Gnome Panel is off by a few minutes. Here's what you can do to keep the exact time.

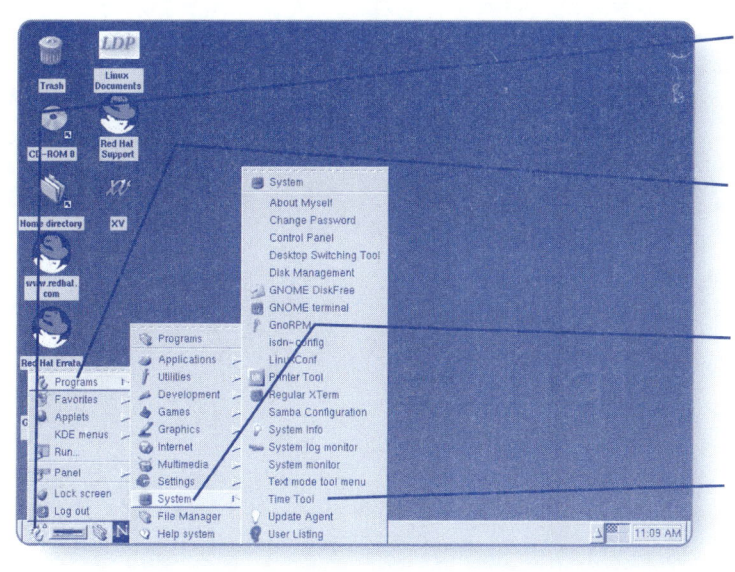

1. Click on the **Main Menu button**. The Main Menu will appear.

2. Move the **mouse pointer** to Programs. The Programs menu will appear.

3. Move the **mouse pointer** to System. The Systems menu will appear.

4. Click on **Time Tool**. The Time Machine will open.

CHAPTER 9: MAINTAINING YOUR LINUX

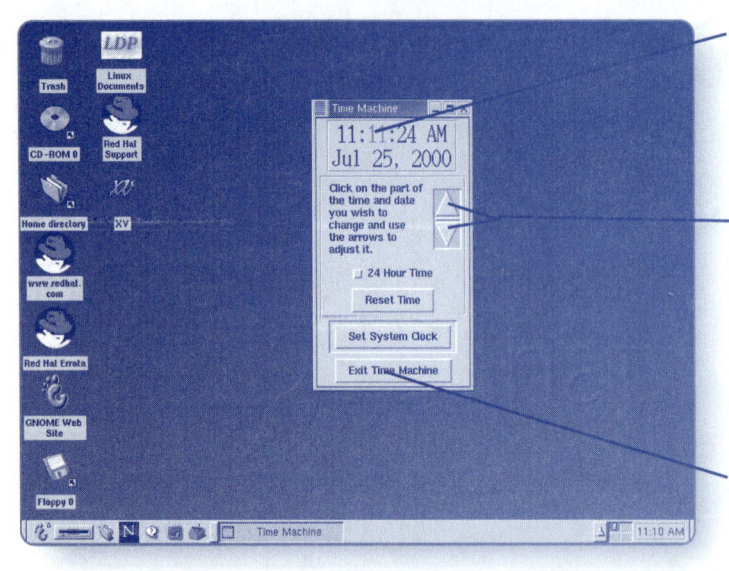

5. **Click** on the **hour, minute,** or **date** that you want to change. The hour or date will be selected.

6. **Click** the **up** and **down arrows** until the time you want is displayed.

7. Change any other time or date **elements**.

8. Click on the **Exit Time Machine button**. The Time Machine will close and your system clock will be updated to show the change.

Part II Review Questions

1. Where are your user files located in the Linux file system? *See "Opening the File System" in Chapter 6*

2. What are the three different ways in which you can view the contents of a directory? *See "Browsing the File System" in Chapter 6*

3. In which directory on the Linux file system will you be storing most of the files you created? *See "Creating Directories" in Chapter 7*

4. How do you make a copy of a file and move it to another directory? *See "Copying and Moving Files" in Chapter 7*

5. Which Linux utility allows you to create and edit user accounts? *See "Working with User Accounts" in Chapter 8*

6. Can users on the Linux system change their own passwords? *See "Allowing Users to Change Their Password" in Chapter 8*

7. How do you add users to a group so that they can share files? *See "Forming Groups" in Chapter 8*

8. What kinds of information can you find out about your computer and Linux system? *See "Finding System Information" in Chapter 9*

9. Name the two types of file systems that can be used to mount floppy disks. *See "Mounting a Floppy Disk Drive" in Chapter 9*

10. Why is it important to create a boot disk? *See "Preparing a Boot Disk" in Chapter 9*

PART III

Making Linux Work for You

Chapter 10
 Working with Files **173**

Chapter 11
 Working in the Console **183**

Chapter 12
 Getting Organized Using Linux **195**

Chapter 13
 Printing Files **217**

Chapter 14
 Sounding Off with Your Computer **225**

10

Working with Files

Now that you've had some fun playing with the Linux operating system and the Gnome user interface, it's time to try your hand at some of the applications that were installed with your Linux. All software applications allow you to create a new file and to save that file on your computer's hard drive. In previous chapters, you learned about the Linux file system and how to move around within the file system. Now it's time to use an application to see how the Linux applications interact with the file system. In this chapter, you'll learn how to:

- Open gnotepad+ and create a new file
- Perform basic text selection and editing commands
- Save a file
- Close and reopen a file

Creating a New File

You first need to open a Linux application and create a new file. Some applications will open with a blank page, whereas other applications make you create your own blank page. You'll learn how to use gnotepad+ to perform basic file tasks in Linux.

1. Click on the **Main Menu button**. The main menu will appear.

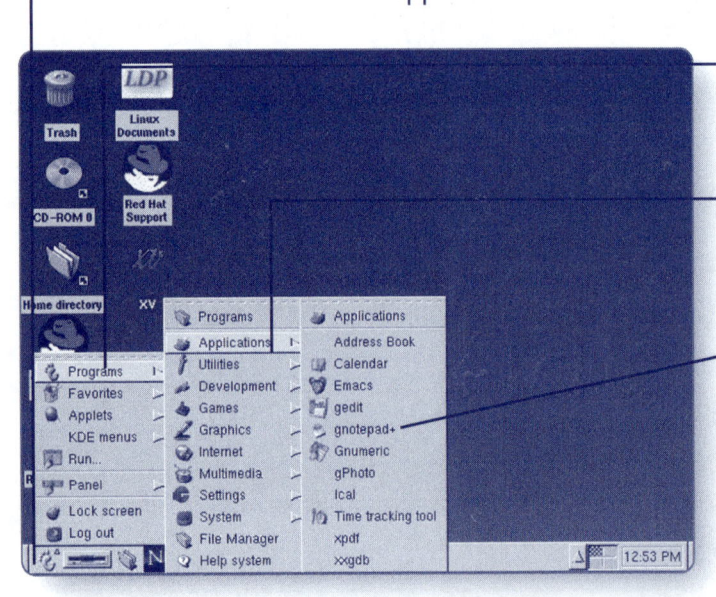

2. Move the **mouse pointer** to Programs. The Programs menu will appear.

3. Move the **mouse pointer** to Applications. The Applications menu will appear.

4. Click on **gnotepad+**. The gnotepad application will open and a blank page will appear ready for you to start typing.

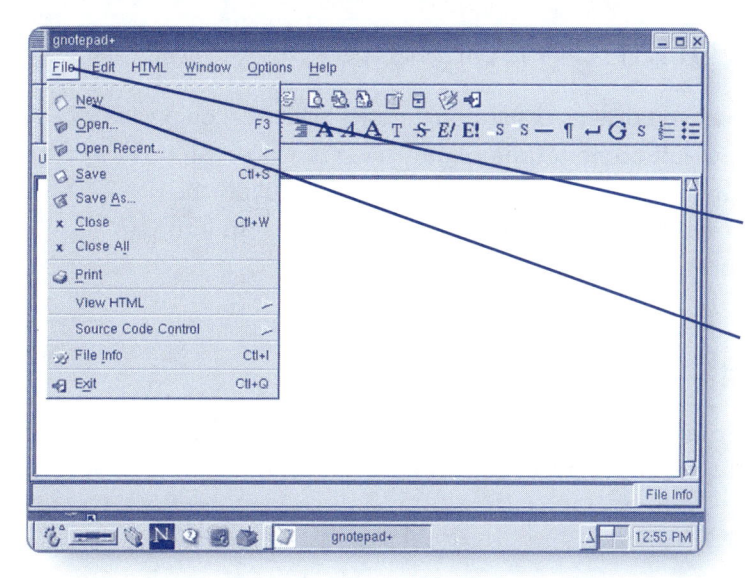

CREATING A NEW FILE 175

Some Linux applications do not display a blank page. If this is the case, you'll need to open a new document.

5. Click on **File**. The File menu will appear.

6. Click on **New**. A blank page will open in the application window.

NOTE

Some applications display a toolbar that contains buttons for a number of frequently used commands. Hold the mouse pointer over a toolbar button to display a tool tip that explains the command a button executes.

7. Click on the **New File button**. Another blank page will open in the application window.

Working with Text

When you open a blank page, notice a vertical bar in the upper-left corner of the page. This is the insertion point and it is where text will appear as you type. To follow the instructions that follow, type a few paragraphs into the gnotepad+ window.

Selecting Text

Before you can begin editing text in most applications, you need to know how to select text.

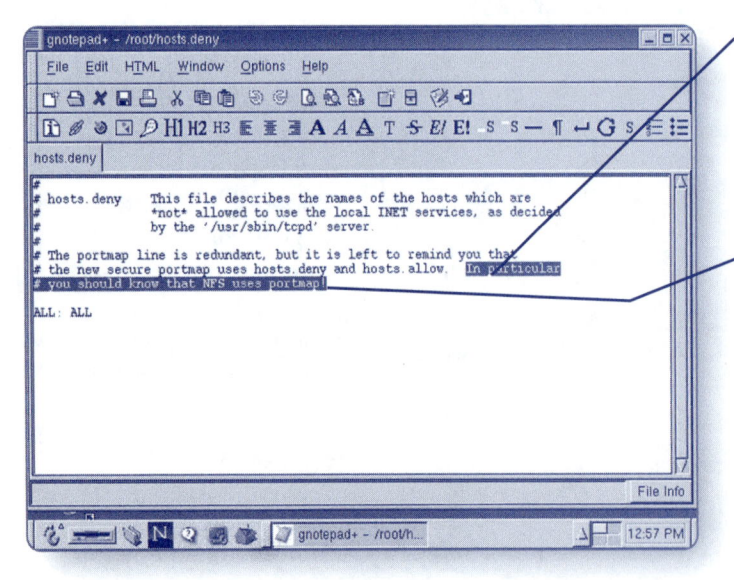

1. **Click** and **hold** the **mouse pointer** at the place where you want to begin the selection. The insertion bar will appear in the selected position.

2. **Drag** the **mouse** to the **end** of the selection. The selected text will be highlighted.

WORKING WITH TEXT   177

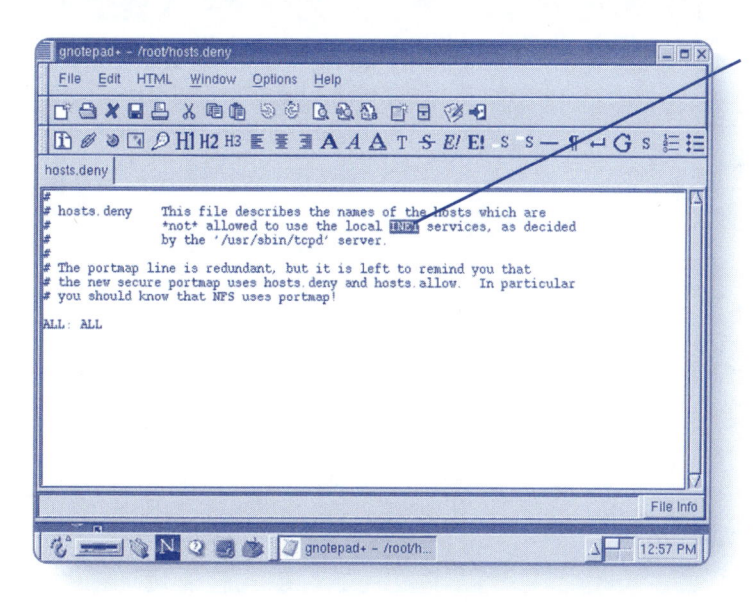

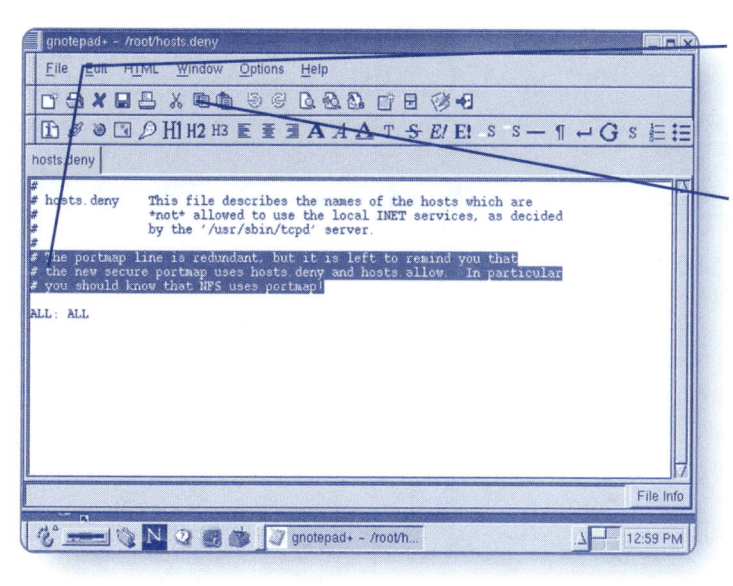

3. Try out **these shortcut** methods for selecting text.

- To select one word, click twice on the word.
- To select a paragraph, click three times on the paragraph.

Copying and Deleting Text

You'll use the copy and delete functions when you are rearranging text. You'll also get some practice using toolbar buttons.

1. Highlight the **text** that you want to copy. The text will be selected.

2. Click on the **Copy Text button**. The text will be copied to the Clipboard.

CHAPTER 10: WORKING WITH FILES

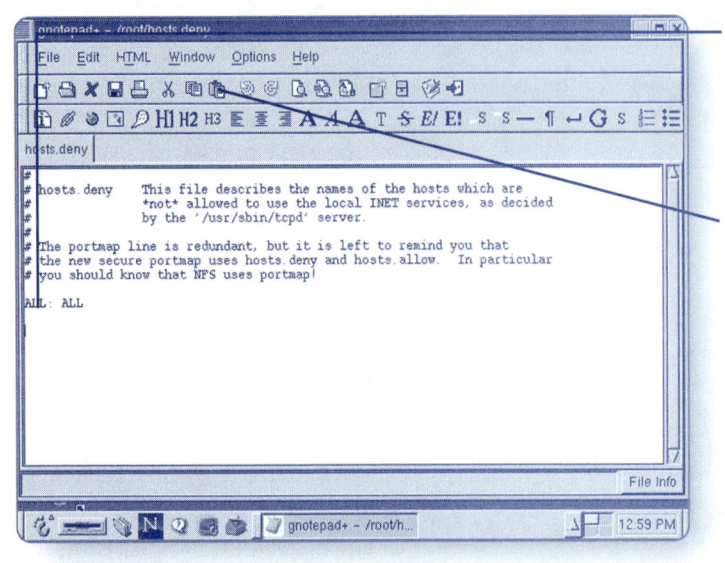

3. Click on the **place** where you want to place a copy of the text. The insertion bar will appear in the selected position.

4. Click on the **Paste Text button**. The text will be copied to the new position.

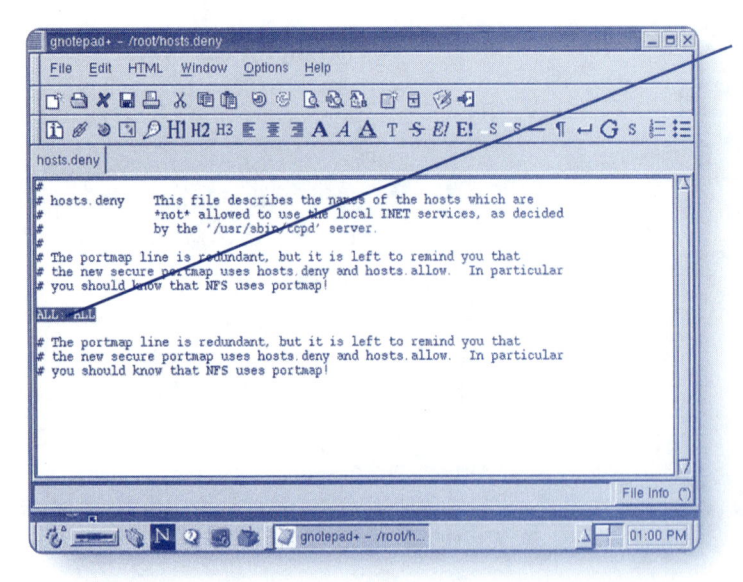

5. Highlight the **text** that you want to delete. The text will be selected.

6. Press the **Delete key**. The text will be deleted.

> ### TIP
> If you made a mistake and want to reverse the last action you performed, click on the Undo button. You can undo more than one action.

Saving a File

The importance of saving your work cannot be emphasized enough. Anyone who uses a computer has lost valuable work at one time or another. Save your work regularly; it only takes a few mouse clicks to save hours of lost work.

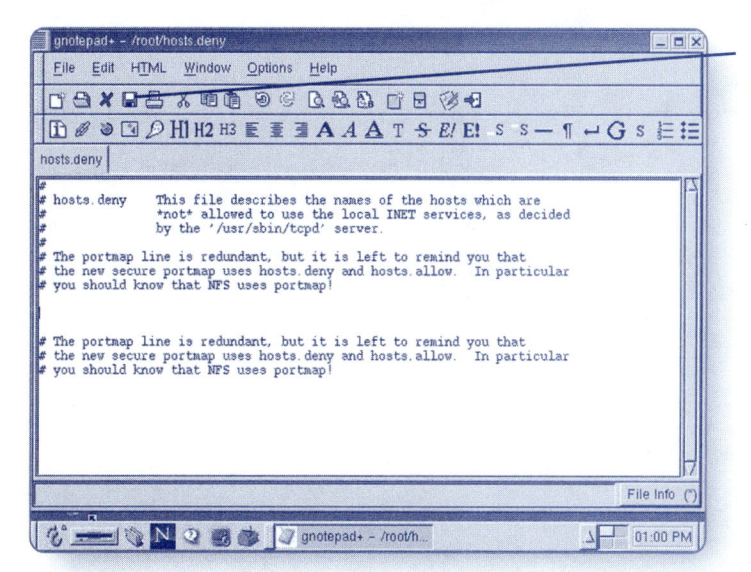

1. Click on the **Save File button**. The Save As dialog box will open.

TIP

If you want to have another copy of a document, open the File menu and select Save As. You can then save the document using a different file name.

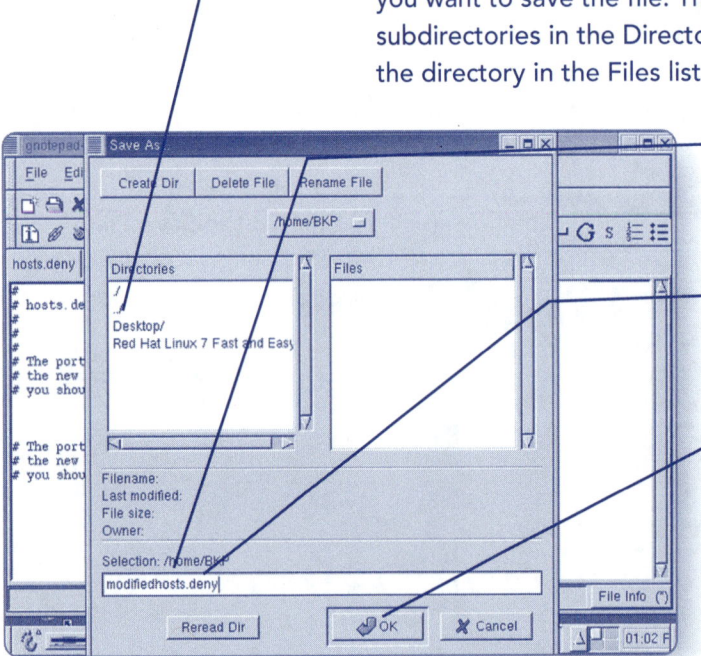

2. Double-click on the **directory** in the Directories list where you want to save the file. The directory will open to show the subdirectories in the Directories list and the files contained in the directory in the Files list.

3. Click in the **Selection text box**. The insertion point will be in the text box.

4. Type a **name** for the **file**. The name will appear in the text box.

5. Click on **OK**. The file will be saved in the directory you specified.

TIP

If you want to go back to a previous directory that you had open, click on the list box and select a directory from the list.

Closing a File

When you are finished working with a document, you can close the file. It's easy to close the file but still leave your application open.

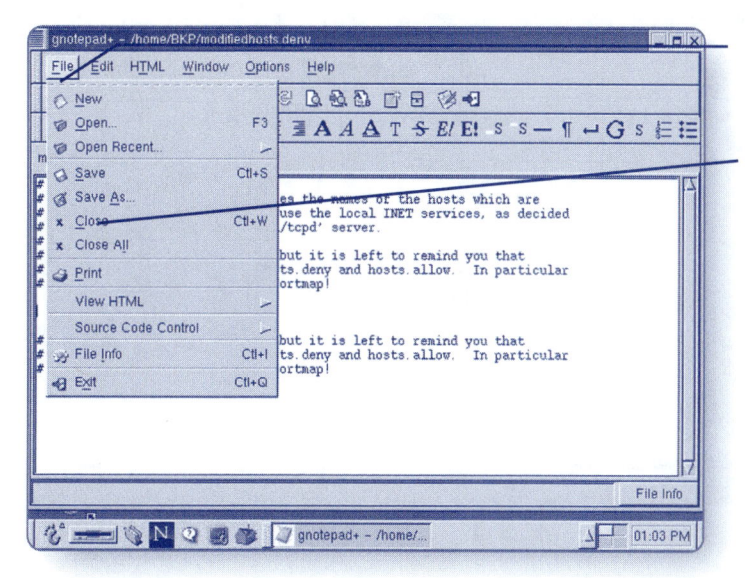

1. Click on **File**. The File menu will appear.

2. Click on **Close**. The file will close and the gnotepad+ window will stay open.

Opening an Existing File

You can open any document that you've saved. You'll need to go back to the file system and remember where you put the file.

1. Click on the **Open File button**. The Open File dialog box will open.

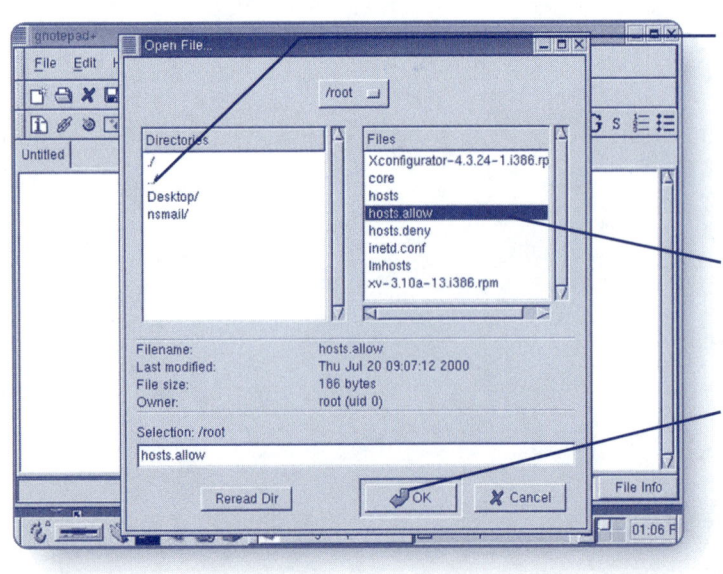

2. Double-click on the **directory** where the file is located. The list of files contained in that directory will appear.

3. Click on the **file** that you want to open. The file will be selected.

4. Click on **OK**. The file will open in the application window and you can resume working on the file.

11

Working in the Console

As Linux continues to grow in the marketplace, less and less emphasis is being placed on what makes Linux a great and stable operating system. Linux, after all, is a command-line operating system. X Window, window managers like Sawmill, and desktop environments like Gnome just run on top of Linux. The real power of Linux lies in the console. And, as you'll soon learn, you don't have to be a geek to use it. In this chapter, you'll learn how to:

- Switch between the console and X Window
- Organize directories from the console
- Manage files from the console

Entering Console Mode

The console mode of Linux is a bit different from the terminal emulation application. For one thing, the console runs completely without the benefit of X Window, so operations in the console are much faster. You can also start up several consoles at a time, to get true-multitasking performance from your computer.

1. Press the **Ctrl+Alt+F1 keys** simultaneously. The console will appear.

2. Type your **username** at the localhost login prompt and **press** the **Enter key**. The Password prompt will appear.

3. Type the **password** for the user and **press** the **Enter key**. A message will appear showing when you last logged into your Linux system and the [user@localhost user]$ prompt will display.

4. Press the **Alt+F7** keys simultaneously. X Window will be displayed as you last left it.

> **TIP**
>
> If you press Ctrl+Alt and any function key from F1 to F6 simultaneously, you will get an independent console each time. This will allow you to run separate operations from up to six different command lines.

Managing Directories

When the console is first opened, the prompt is set to the home directory of the user who logged in. The files you need, however, may not be in that directory. Here's how to get to them and make new directories to hold your files.

Changing Directories

Changing directories in the console is simplicity itself. All you need is a two-letter command: cd.

1. Type ls and **press Enter**. This command will list all of the files and directories in the current directory.

> **NOTE**
>
> Files in a listing are shown in light green. Directories are displayed in dark blue. Everything typed in the console is case-sensitive!

CHAPTER 11: WORKING IN THE CONSOLE

2. Type cd and the **directory name** and **press Enter**. The prompt will change to reflect the shift.

> **TIP**
>
> If you have a really long directory name, such as the one in this example, you can use wildcards to make your typing faster. Instead of cd Red Hat Linux Fast and Easy, you can type cd Red*, which is a lot easier.

3. Type ls and **press Enter**. This command will list all of the files and directories in the current directory.

4. Type cd and the **directory name** (with wildcards if need be) and **press Enter**. The prompt will change to reflect the shift.

MANAGING DIRECTORIES

5. Type cd and **press Enter**. The prompt will take you immediately to your home directory.

6. Type cd - and **press Enter**. The prompt will take you immediately to the last directory you were in.

CHAPTER 11: WORKING IN THE CONSOLE

7. Type cd .. and **press Enter**. The prompt will take you up to the next-highest level directory.

8. Type cd ../../ and **press Enter**. The prompt will take you two directory levels up in the filesystem.

9. Type cd / and **press Enter**. The prompt will take you up to the highest level directory in the filesystem: root (/).

> **TIP**
>
> Moving around the directories may get confusing. If you ever get "lost", just type pwd to see where in the filesystem your prompt is.

Making Directories

As if you don't have enough directories to move about in, here's how to make more! Navigate to the directory in which you want to make a new directory before starting this procedure.

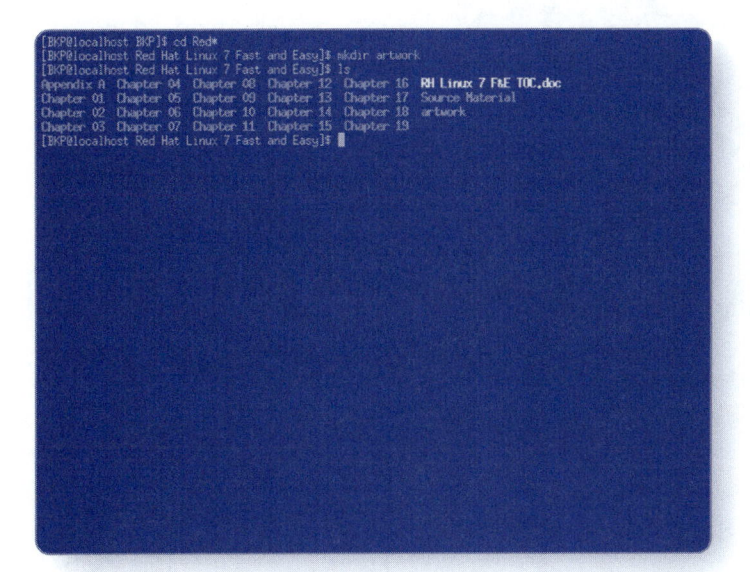

1. **Type mkdir** and a **directory name** and **press Enter**. This command will create a new directory.

2. **Type ls** and **press Enter**. This command will list all of the files and directories in the current directory, including the new subdirectory.

> ### NOTE
> Be sure your account has the ownership and permissions to create new directories within the directory you are working.

Removing Directories

After a directory is emptied, you should delete it from your system.

1. Type **rmdir** and a **directory name** and **press Enter**. This command will create a new directory.

2. Type **ls** and **press Enter**. This command will list all of the files and directories in the current directory, including the absence of the deleted directory.

NOTE
All files in a directory must be deleted before the directory can be removed.

Managing Files

Working with files in the console is not too hard, as long as you remember that everything in the console is case-sensitive. Using wildcards is a huge help as well.

Copying Files

Copying files from place to place is a common practice. Use the cp command to get your files where they need to be.

MANAGING FILES 191

1. Type cp and the **filename** of the file you want to copy. The command will appear at the prompt.

2. Type a **destination directory name** and **press Enter**. This command will copy the file to the destination directory.

3. Type cp, the **filenames** (using wildcards) of the files you want to copy, and the **destination directory**. The command will appear at the prompt.

4. Press Enter. This command will copy the files to the destination directory.

TIP
To avoid a lot of retyping, use the up and down arrow keys to cycle through all of the commands entered in the current session. Then, simply edit the command to something new if need be and press Enter.

Moving Files

Like copying, moving files is pretty easy. The only difference is that one single copy of your file(s) will exist on your PC when all is said and done.

1. Type mv and the **filename** of the file you want to move. The command will appear at the prompt.

2. Type a **destination directory name** and **press Enter**. This command will move the file to the destination directory.

3. Type mv, the **filenames** (using wildcards) of the files you want to move, and the **destination directory**. The command will appear at the prompt.

4. Press Enter. This command will move the files to the destination directory.

Renaming Files

Renaming files does not have to be a tedious proposition, as you will see in this section.

1. Type mv and the **filename** of the file you want to rename. The command will appear at the prompt.

2. Type a **new name** and **press Enter**. This command will rename the file within the same directory.

Deleting Files

Sometimes you just have to throw out all of the old stuff that accumulates on your PC. If you hate housekeeping, has Linux got a command for you!

1. Type rm and the **filename** of the file you want to delete. The command will appear at the prompt.

2. Press Enter. This command will delete the files from your system permanently.

CHAPTER 11: WORKING IN THE CONSOLE

```
[BKP@localhost BKP]$ cd Red*/Chap*12
[BKP@localhost Chapter 12]$ ls
11RHFE03.tif  11RHFE05.tif  11RHFE07.tif  11RHFE09.tif  11RHFE11.tif
11RHFE04.tif  11RHFE06.tif  11RHFE08.tif  11RHFE10.tif  12RHFE02.tif
[BKP@localhost Chapter 12]$ rm 12RHFE02.tif
[BKP@localhost Chapter 12]$ rm 11*
[BKP@localhost Chapter 12]$
```

3. Type rm and the **filenames** (using wildcards) of the files you want to delete. The command will appear at the prompt.

4. Press Enter. This command will delete the file from your system permanently.

12

Getting Organized Using Linux

Red Hat Linux comes installed with several applications that can help you keep your personal and business life organized. Seems like there's always a checkbook to balance, invoices to tally, important dates to remember, or appointments to keep. A calculator and a calendar can come in handy. To keep track of friends, family, and business acquaintances, you'll want to keep an address book, which keeps valuable personal and business information in one place. In this chapter, you'll learn how to:

- Use the calculator
- Keep a calendar of important events
- Maintain names and addresses in the address book

Adding It up with the Calculator

Calculators are a part of everyday life. You'll need them when it's time to balance the checkbooks, work out a monthly spending budget, figure expense reports, and more.

Turning on the Calculator

The calculator is not directly accessible from the Gnome interface[em] you have to start it from the Terminal. If you'll be using the calculator often, you may want to add a launcher to the Gnome panel to find the calculator fast and easy. If you need help adding a launcher, refer to Chapter 5, "Managing Your Desktop".

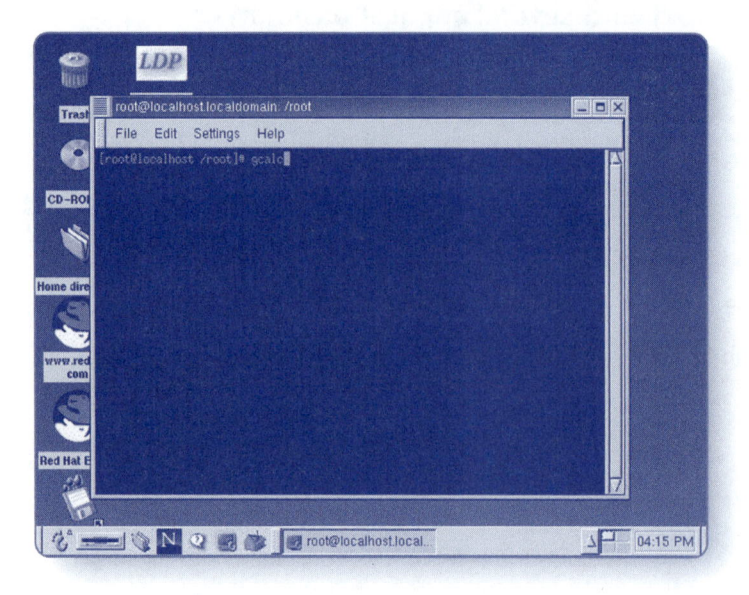

1. Click on the **Gnome terminal emulator button**. The Terminal window will open.

2. Type gcalc and press Enter. The Gnome Calculator will appear on your desktop.

ADDING IT UP WITH THE CALCULATOR

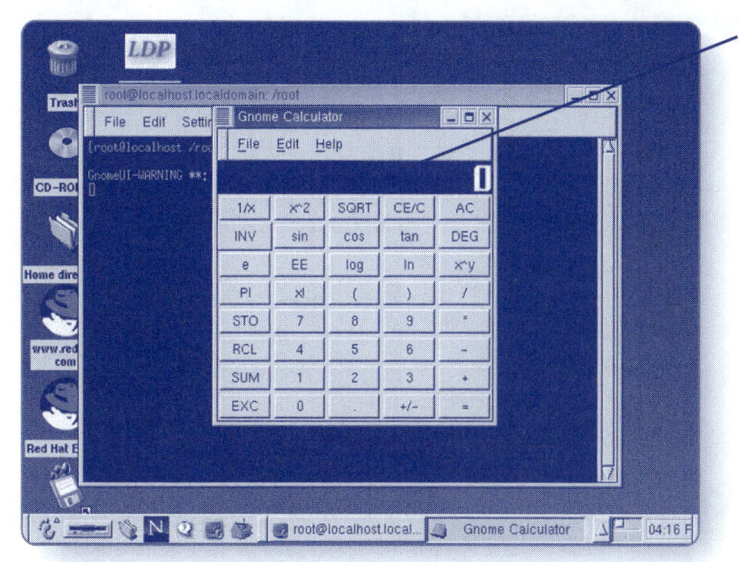

This calculator can do more than your ordinary desktop calculator. It can perform high level mathematical calculations (such as algebraic notation, logarithmic functions, financial functions, and other complex numbers). You can even use the manual that came with your handheld calculator and apply many of those instructions to this handy Linux calculator. Or, you might check out the library or used bookstore for a calculator manual.

Performing Simple Math Calculations

You might need a calculator for tasks such as adding up household budget items or balancing a checkbook. This calculator is easy to find and can help you get the job done. If you're a traveling engineer and don't want to clutter your laptop carrying case with a lot of "stuff," this calculator can perform all the calculations you'll need. Or, if you're a student on an allowance, use this calculator instead of doling out the spare cash.

CHAPTER 12: GETTING ORGANIZED USING LINUX

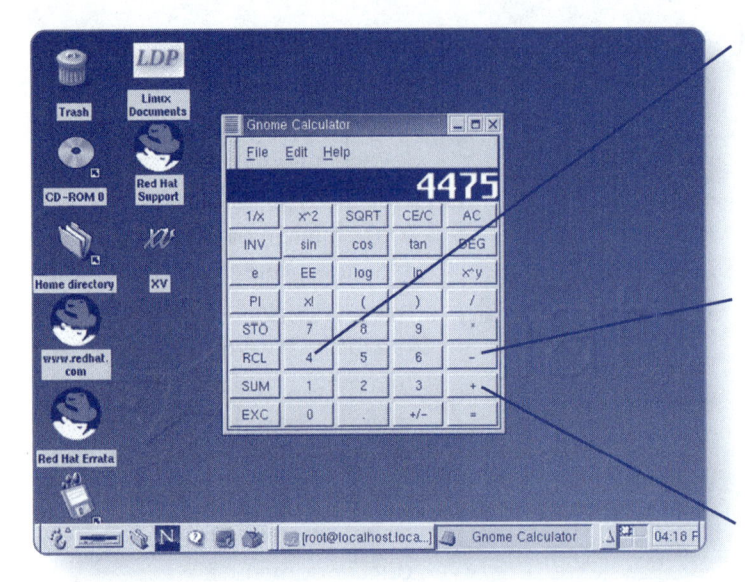

1. Click on the **number keys** that correspond with the first number in the calculation. The number will appear in the display area at the top of the calculator.

2a. Click on the **– key** if you want to subtract the next number from the first.

or

2b. Click on the **+ key** if you want to add the next number to the first.

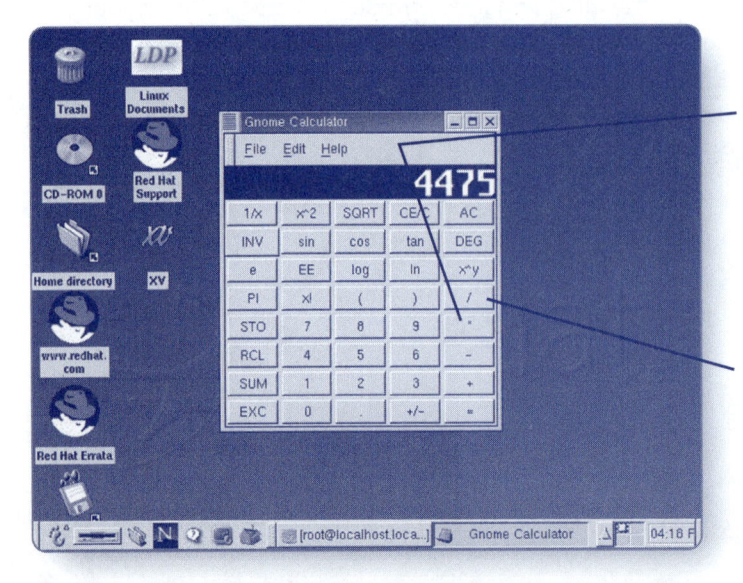

or

2c. Click on the *** key** if you want to multiply the first number by the next number you'll be entering.

or

2d. Click on the **/ key** if you want to divide the first number by the next number you'll be entering.

ADDING IT UP WITH THE CALCULATOR 199

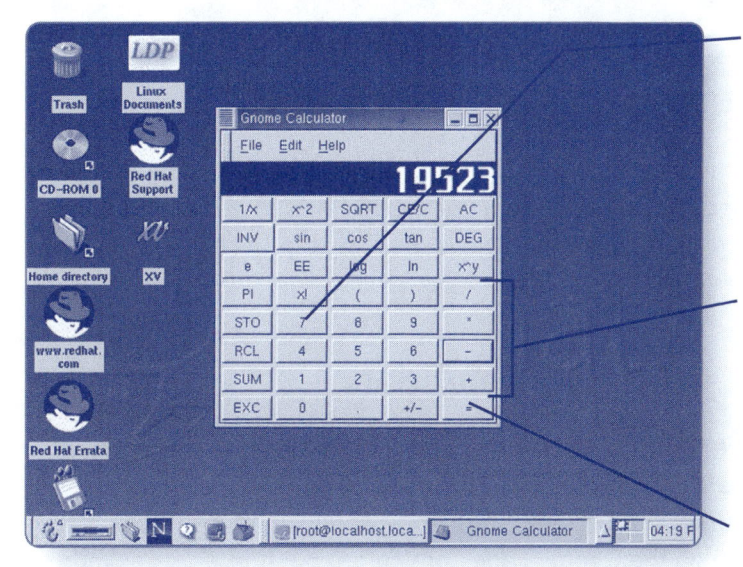

3. Click on the **number keys** that correspond with the next number in the calculation. The number will appear in the display area at the top of the calculator.

4. Add, subtract, multiply, or divide any **remaining numbers** in your calculation. The numbers will be computed in the calculation.

5. Click on the **= key**. The total for your calculation will appear in the calculator display.

> **NOTE**
> You can also use the numeric keypad on your keyboard.

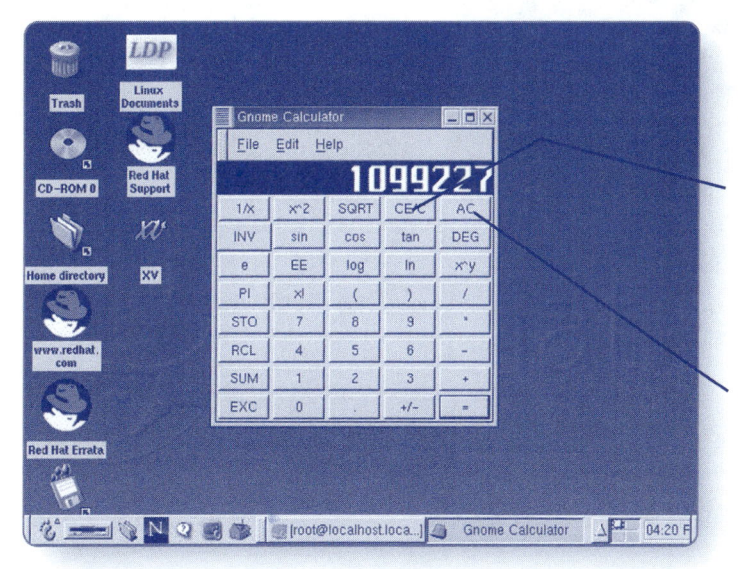

Here are a couple of tips to help you work with the Gnome Calculator:

- If you've entered the wrong number and want to clear the number (or the entry) without clearing the computation, press the CE/C key.

- If you want to clear the display so that you can start a new calculation, press the AC key.

Keeping Track of Important Dates

Some days it's just too hard to remember everything that needs to be done, all the places to be seen, and the people to meet. Keeping a calendar is the first step to organizing all these important events.

Starting the Calendar

Like the other Linux programs that you've seen throughout this book, the Calendar can be found on the Main menu. If you use the Calendar frequently, you may want to make it an icon on the Gnome Panel, or you can put it in a drawer with other important applications and files.

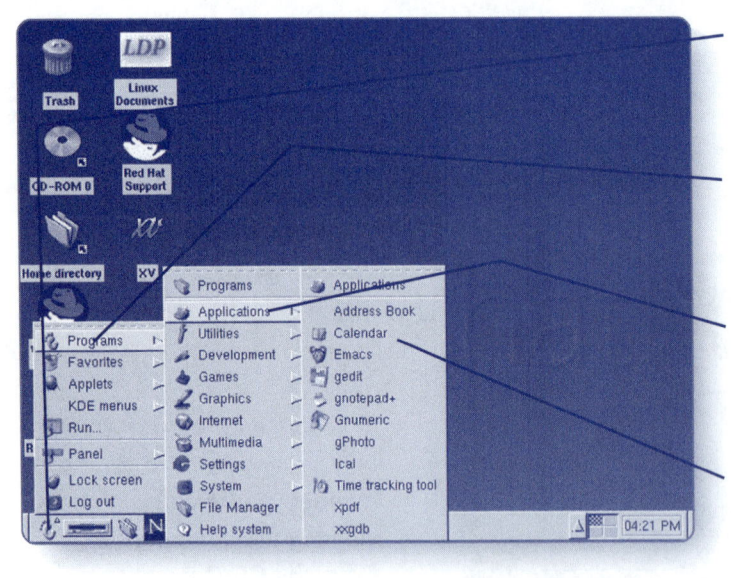

1. Click on the **Main Menu Button**. The Main Menu will appear.

2. Move the **mouse pointer** to Programs. The Programs menu will appear.

3. Move the **mouse pointer** to Applications. The Applications menu will appear.

4. Click on **Calendar**. The Calendar application will open.

Changing the Time View

When you open the calendar, you'll notice that it uses a 24-hour clock. This is great if you're in the military, or in Europe, where the 24-hour clock is more commonly used. Here's how to change it to a 12-hour clock. You can also change the hours that display on the calendar.

1. Click on **Settings**. The Settings menu will appear.

2. Click on **Preferences**. The Preferences dialog box will open.

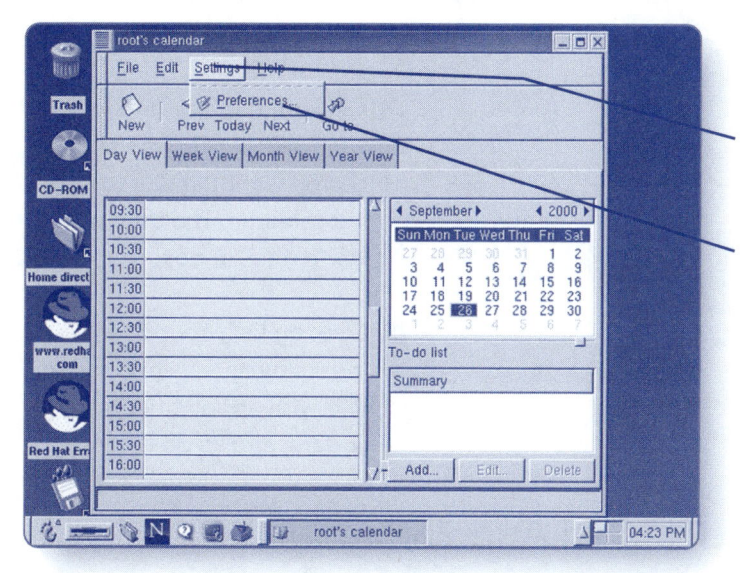

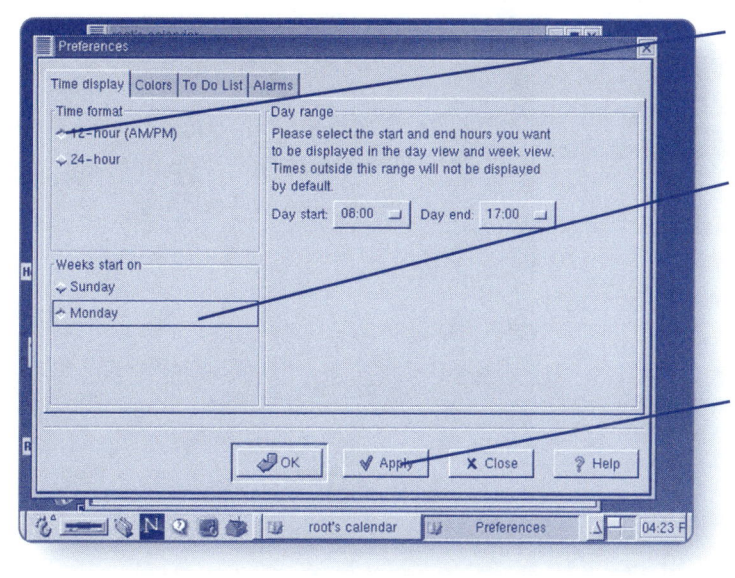

3. Click on the **12-hour (AM/PM) option button**. The option will be selected.

4. Click on the **Monday option button** if you want to change the day on which the week starts. The option will be selected.

5. Click on **Apply**. You'll see the calendar change to a 12-hour format on the calendar.

CHAPTER 12: GETTING ORGANIZED USING LINUX

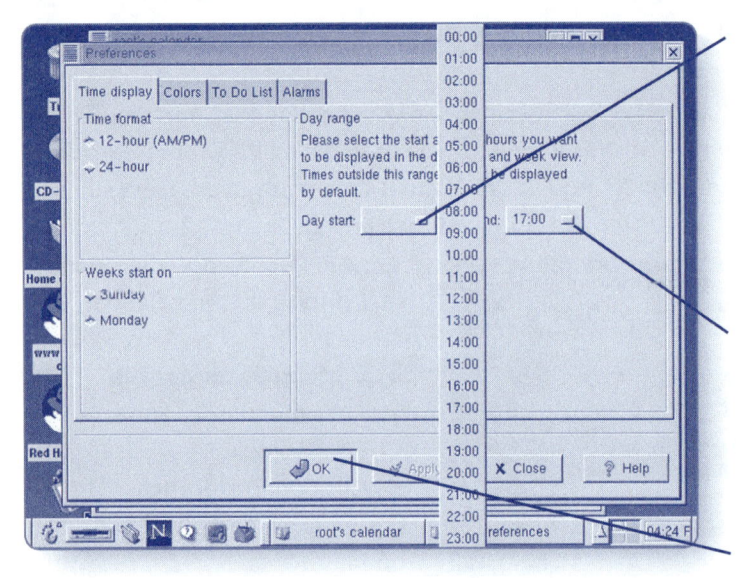

6. Click on the **Day start list box** and **select** the **time** (the calendar is still using a 24-hour time format to select the time) at which you want the day to start on the calendar. The time will appear in the list box.

7. Click on the **Day end list box** and **select** the **time** at which you want the day to end on the calendar. The time will appear in the list box.

8. Click on **OK**. Your calendar will be ready and waiting for you to fill it with appointments, reminders, and to-do lists.

Adding an Appointment

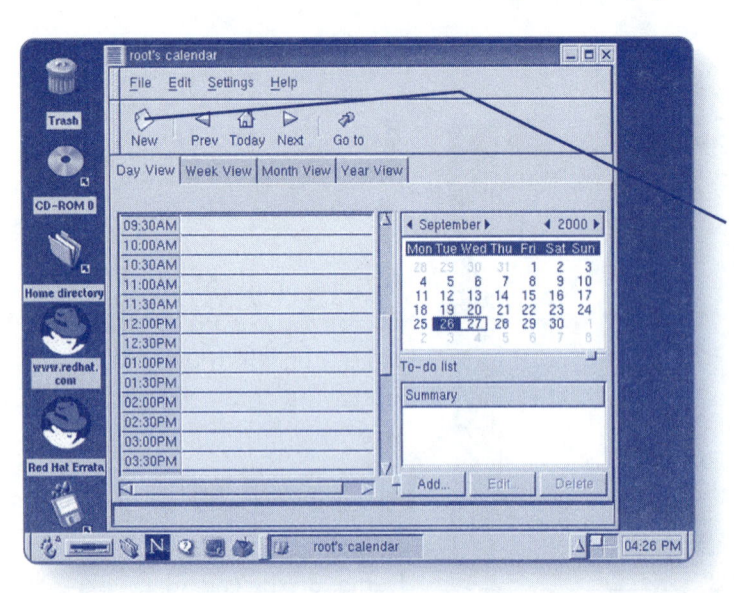

If you have a reason for being at a designated place at a certain time on a specific date, keep track of it in the calendar.

1. Click on the **New button**. The Create new appointment dialog box will open.

KEEPING TRACK OF IMPORTANT DATES **203**

2. Click in the **Summary text box** and **type** a **description** of the appointment, persons attending the appointment, or notes needed for the appointment.

3. Click in the **Start time text box** and **type** the **date** on which the appointment is scheduled to begin. Use slashes (for example, mm/dd/yy).

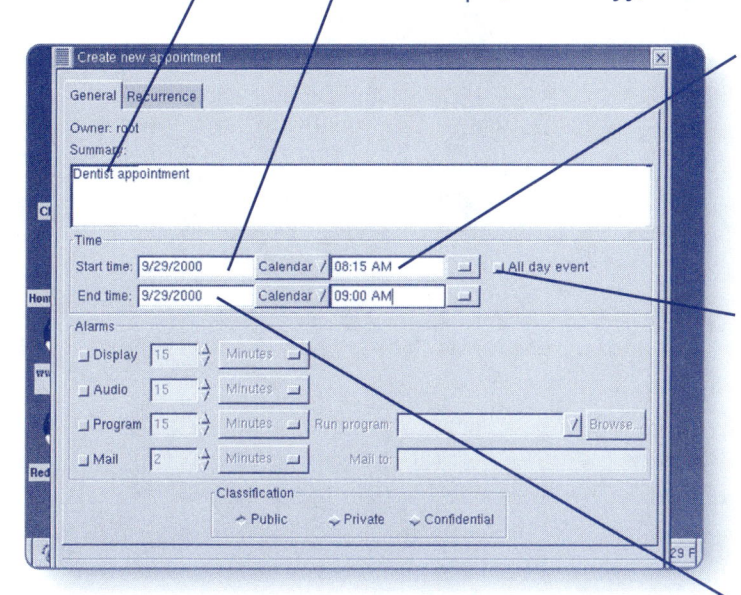

4a. Click in the second **Start time text box** and **type** the **time** at which the appointment is scheduled.

or

4b. Click on the **All day event check button** if you need to block out the entire day for the appointment. The option will be selected.

5. Click in the **End time text boxes** and **type** the **date** and **time** at which the appointment is scheduled to end.

> **NOTE**
> You can use the drop-down lists to select the date and time for the appointment.

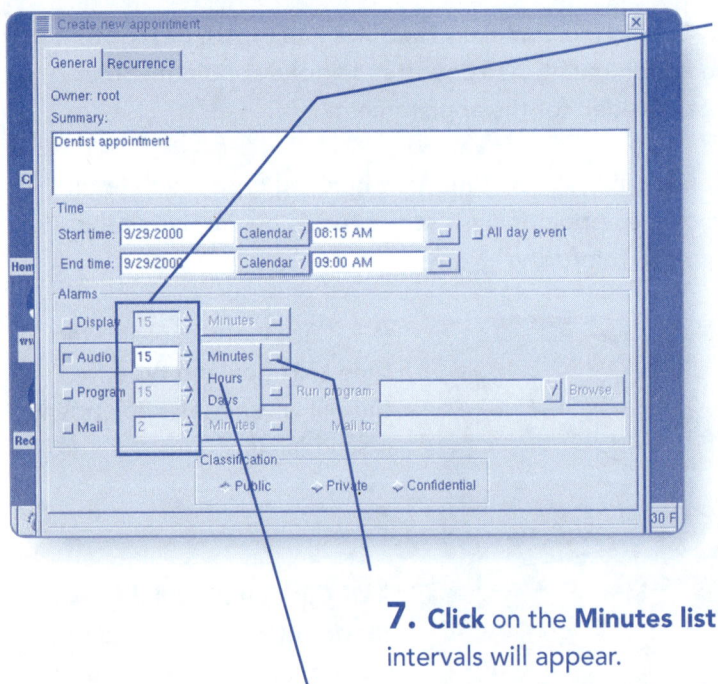

6. Choose from a **notification option** if you want to be automatically notified in advance of an upcoming appointment.

- If you would like a pop-up menu to let you know an appointment is near, click on the Display check button.

- To have a sound played to remind you of an appointment, click on the Audio check button.

7. Click on the **Minutes list box button**. A list of time intervals will appear.

8. Click on the **time interval** you want to use for the notification. The interval will appear in the list box.

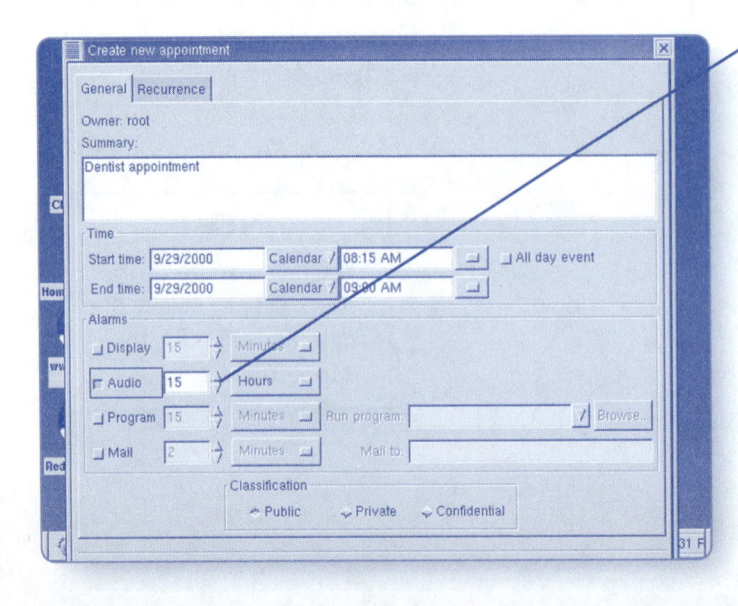

9. Click on the **up** and **down arrows** to **select** the **number** of intervals (selected in step 8) in advance that you'd like to be reminded of the appointment.

10. Click on **OK**. The appointment will be added to your calendar.

KEEPING TRACK OF IMPORTANT DATES 205

> **NOTE**
> If this appointment will be a regular occurrence, click on the Recurrence tab and set up the appointment so that it is repeated in the calendar.

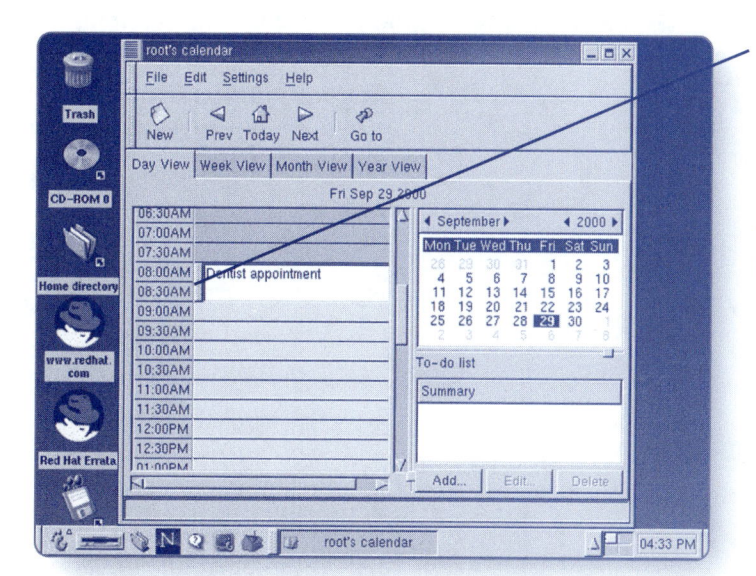

Your appointment will appear in a box on the Day View of the calendar. If you added a notification alarm to the appointment, a bell icon will be to the right of the appointment box.

> **NOTE**
> You can edit or delete the appointment. Right-click on the appointment box and select the appropriate command from the menu that appears.

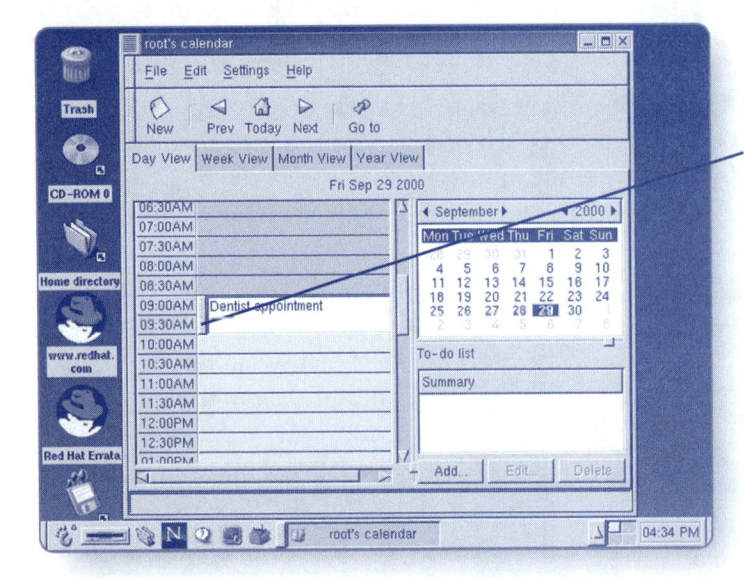

Here's a few tips for editing appointments:

- To move an appointment to a different time during the same day, click inside the appointment box to display the box outline. Click and drag the left side outline until the appointment box is moved to the desired location.

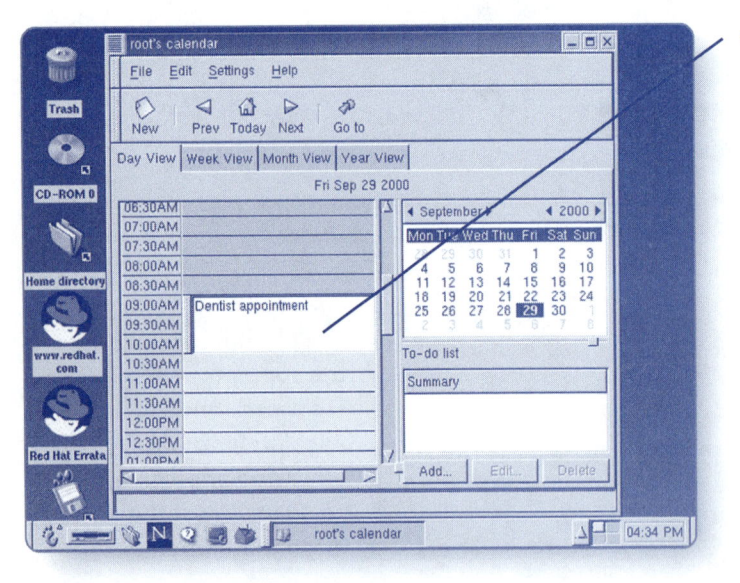

- To change the time span for an appointment, click inside the appointment box to display the box outline. Click and drag the top outline to move the start time or click and drag the bottom outline to move the end time.

Maintaining an Address Book

The Gnome address book is the electronic equivalent of a card file or the little black book you keep in your wallet. But, it is much more sophisticated. Along with being able to store information about friends, family, and business associates, you can sort and view addresses in a variety of ways.

Opening the Address Book

Use the Gnome address book to keep track of your contacts. Taking the time now to learn about the address book features will make the job of maintaining it a snap.

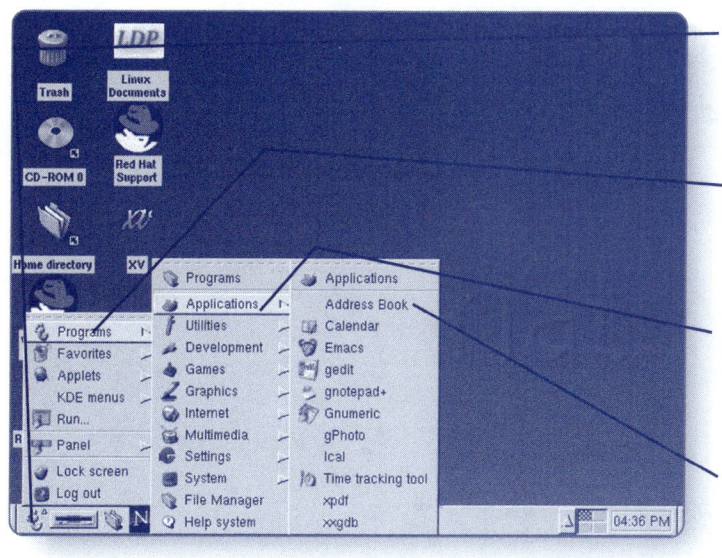

1. Click on the **Main Menu Button**. The Main Menu will appear.

2. Move the **mouse pointer** to Programs. The Programs menu will appear.

3. Move the **mouse pointer** to Applications. The Applications menu will appear.

4. Click on **Address Book**. The GnomeCard application will open.

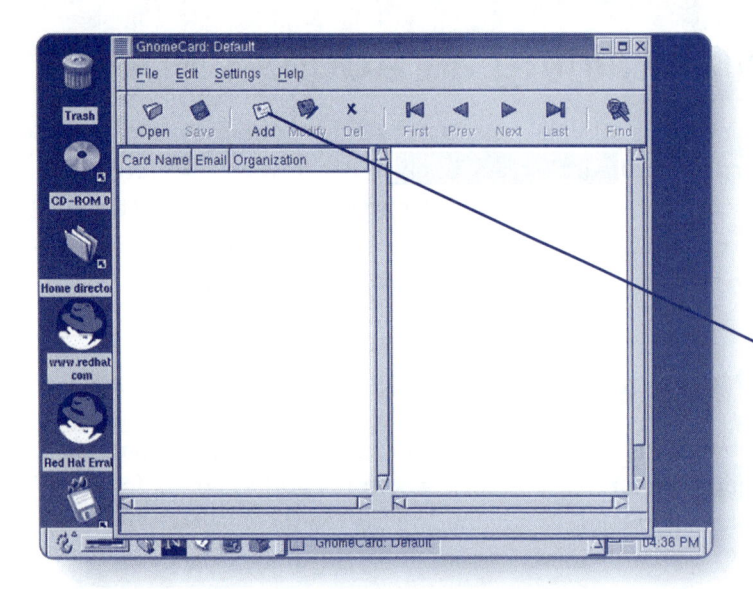

Adding an Address

Adding new names and addresses to the address book is as simple as clicking on a button and typing information into a dialog box.

1. Click on the **Add button**. The gnomecard dialog box will open.

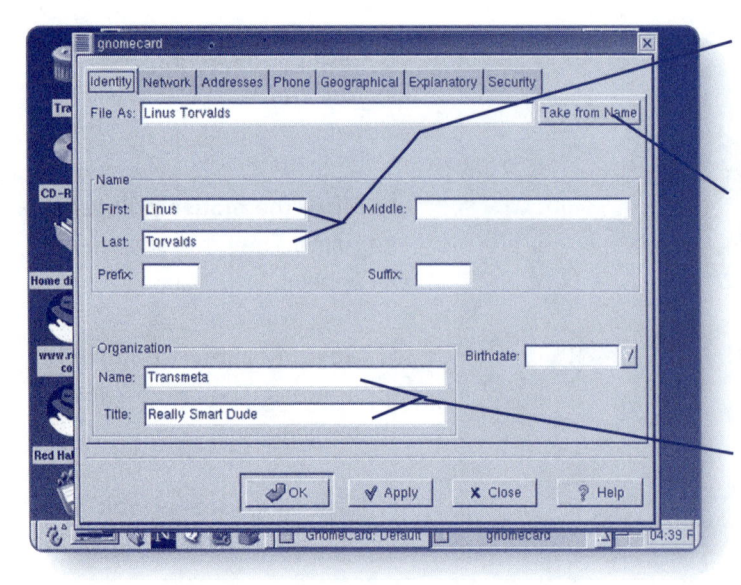

2. Type the **full name** of your contact in the First, Middle, and Last text boxes.

3. Click on the **Take from Name button**. The contact's name will appear in the File As text box. This is how you will see the contact's name listed in the list of addresses.

4. Fill in other **fields** as needed.

MAINTAINING AN ADDRESS BOOK

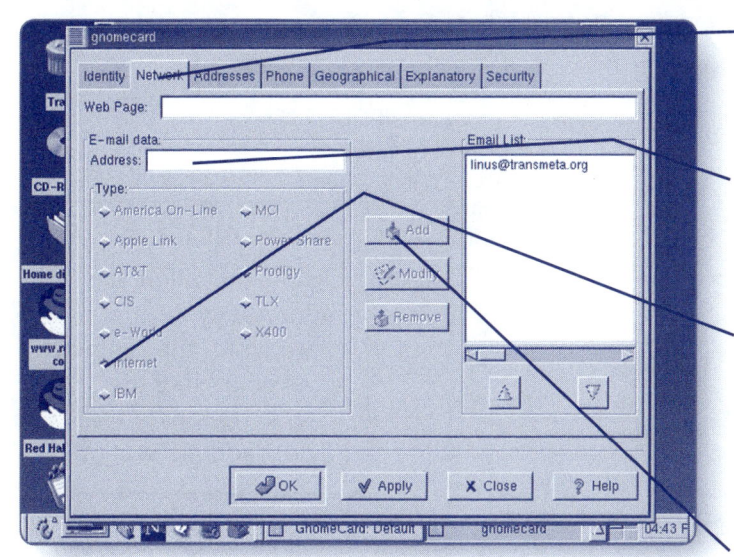

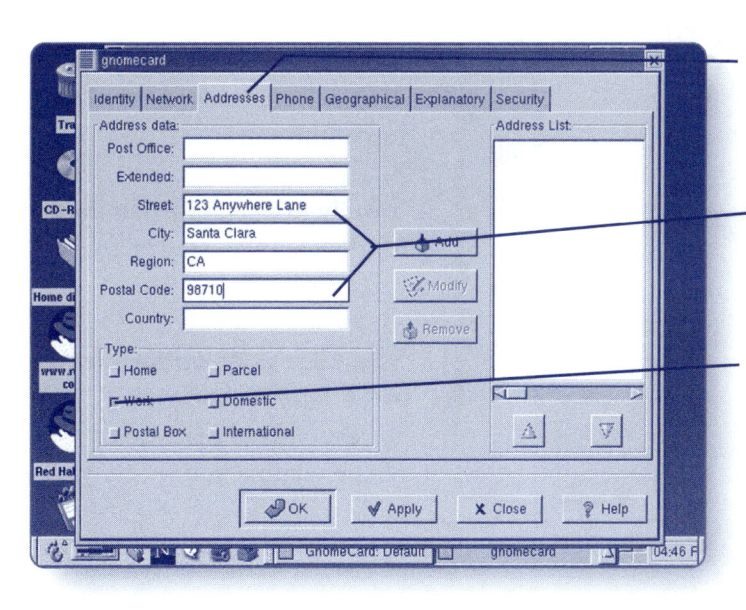

5. Click on the **Network tab**. The Network tab will come to the top of the stack.

6. Type the **e-mail address** for the contact in the Address text box.

7. Click on an **option button** in the Type section that corresponds to the type of e-mail you are entering for the contact.

8. Click the **Add button**. The e-mail address will be applied to the e-mail list.

9. Click on the **Addresses tab**. The Addresses tab will come to the top of the stack.

10. Type the **street** and **city information** for the contact in the corresponding text boxes.

11. Click on an **option button** in the Type section that corresponds to the type of address you want to enter for the contact.

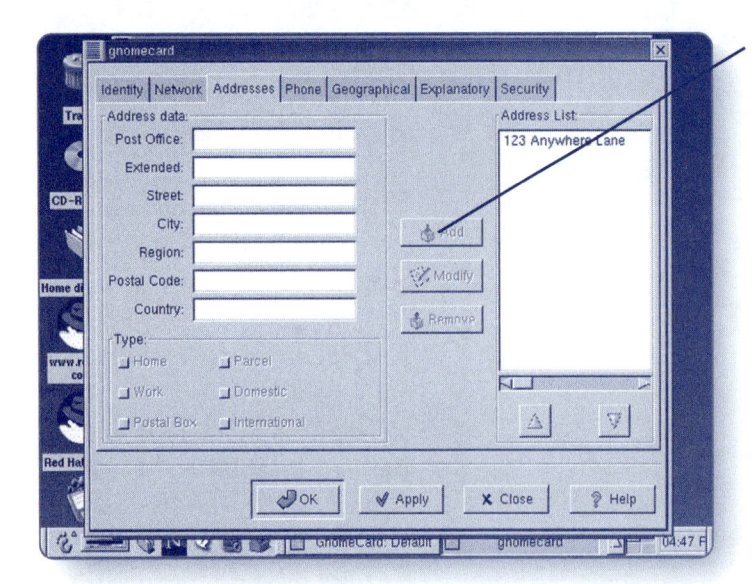

12. **Click** the **Add button**. The address will be applied to the address list.

> **NOTE**
>
> To see the different addresses you've entered for the contact, click on each of the option buttons in the Select address section.

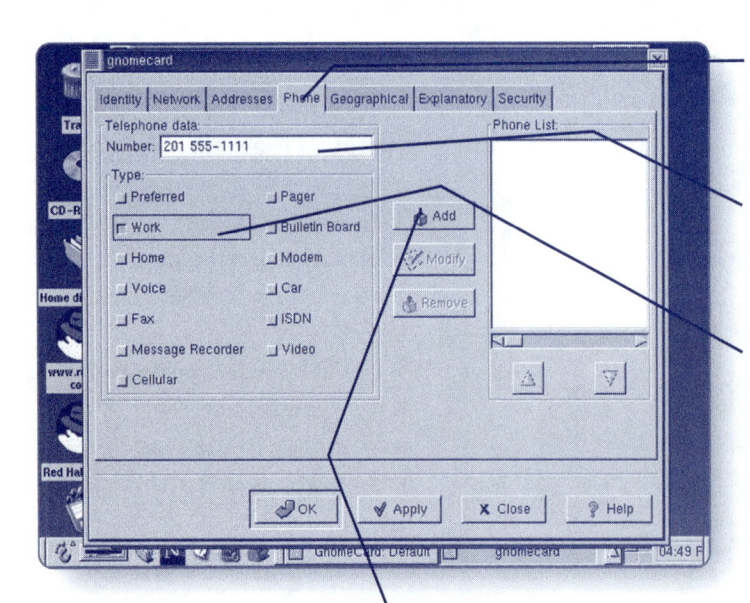

13. **Click** on the **Phone tab**. The Phone tab will come to the top of the stack.

14. **Type** the **phone number** for the contact in the Number text box.

15. **Click** on an **option button** in the Type section that corresponds to the type of phone number you will be adding for the contact. The option will be selected.

16. **Click** the **Add button**. The address will be applied to the phone list.

MAINTAINING AN ADDRESS BOOK

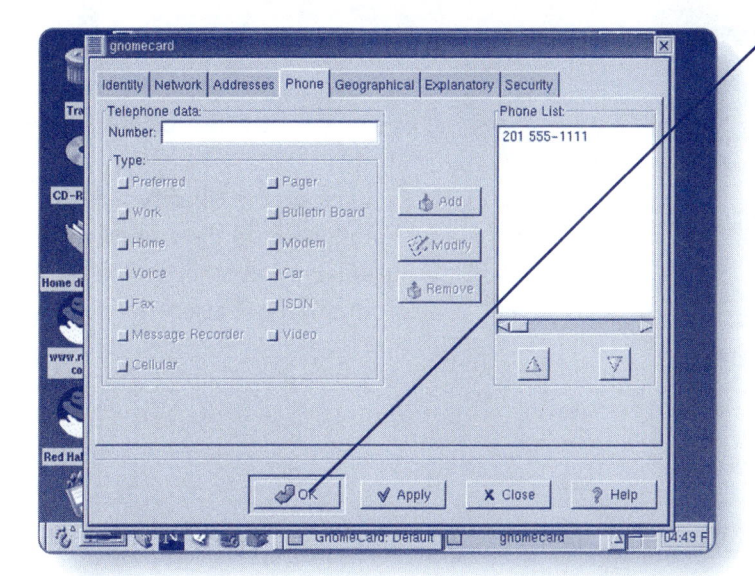

17. **Click** on **OK**. The contact will appear in the address book.

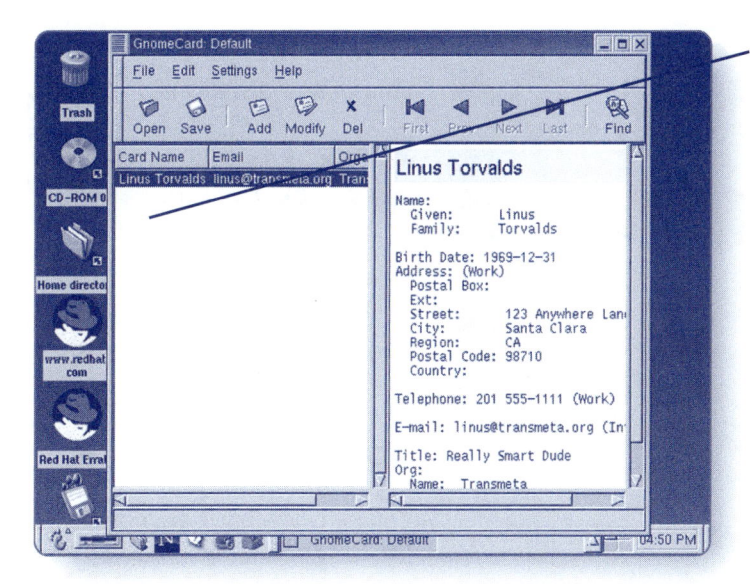

18. **Add** other **contacts** as needed. The contact will appear in the address list.

Updating Address Information

If you need to make changes to a person's address listing, just follow these easy steps.

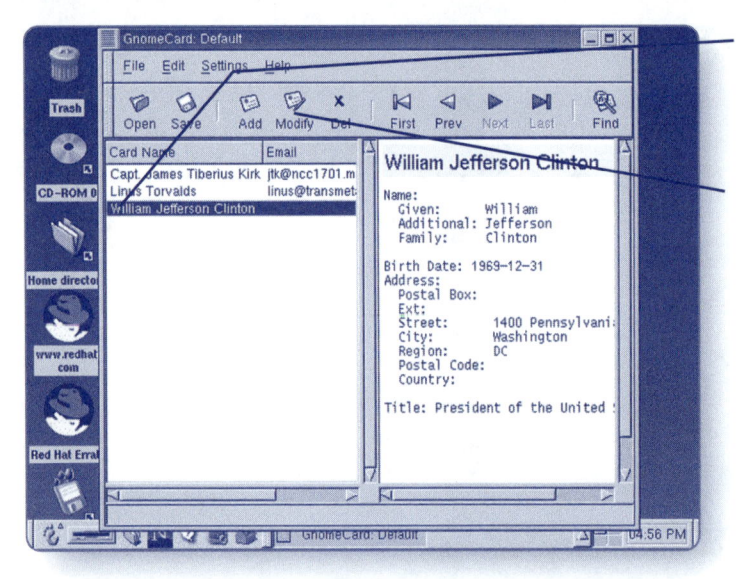

1. **Click** on the **contact** whose information you want to change. The contact will be selected.

2. **Click** on the **Modify button**. The gnomecard dialog box with the selected contact's address information will open.

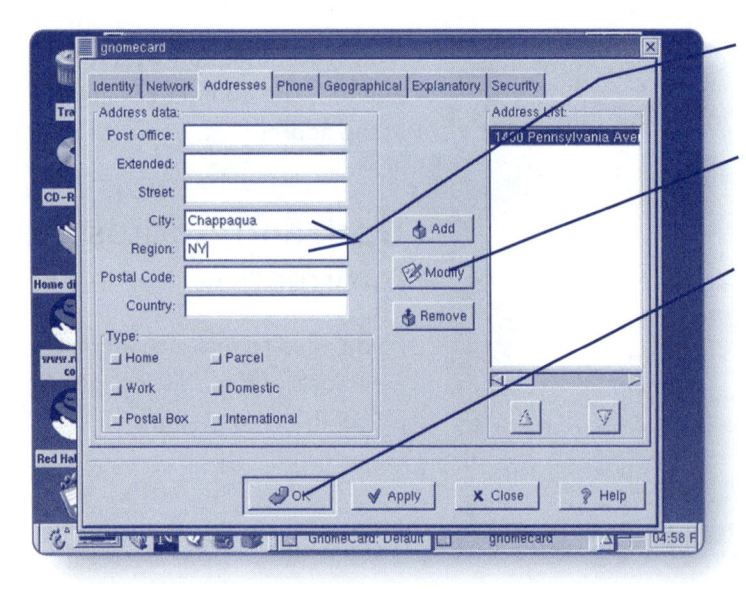

3. **Make** the necessary **changes** or **additions**.

4. **Click** the **Modify button**. The altered data will be recorded.

5. **Click** on **OK**. The contact's information will be updated.

Sorting Addresses

You can view a list of contacts by name, e-mail address, or company name.

MAINTAINING AN ADDRESS BOOK   213

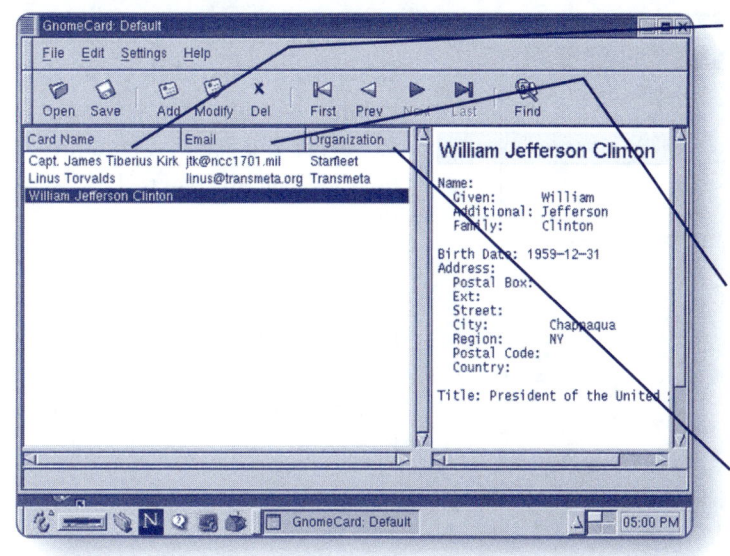

1. Click on the **Card Name column heading**. The list of contacts will be sorted by the name you used as the card name and will display in alphabetical order.

2. Click on the **Email column heading**. The list of contacts will be sorted by e-mail address in alphabetical order.

3. Click on the **Organization column heading**. The list of contacts will be sorted by the contacts' company names in alphabetical order.

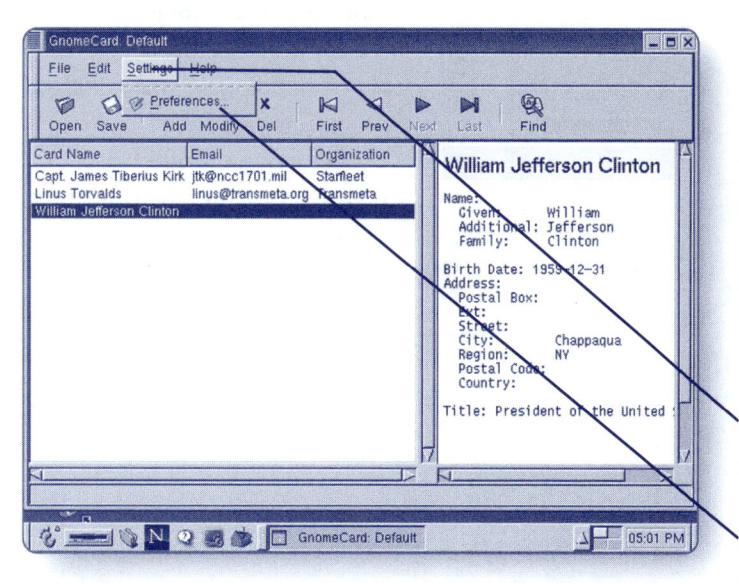

Adding Column Headings

You can add additional column headings to the contacts' list. Look through the list of column headings to see which ones will help you work with your address list easier.

1. Click on **Settings**. The Settings menu will appear.

2. Click on **Preferences**. The gnomecard dialog box will open.

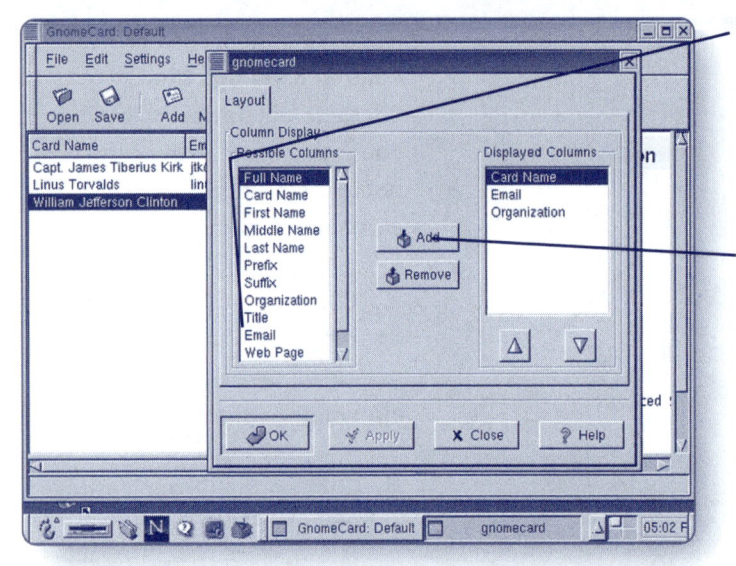

3. Scroll through the **Possible Columns list** and **click** on a **column heading** that you want to add to the list. The column heading will be selected.

4. Click on **Add**. The column heading will be added to the bottom of the Displayed Columns list. You can also change the order of the column headings.

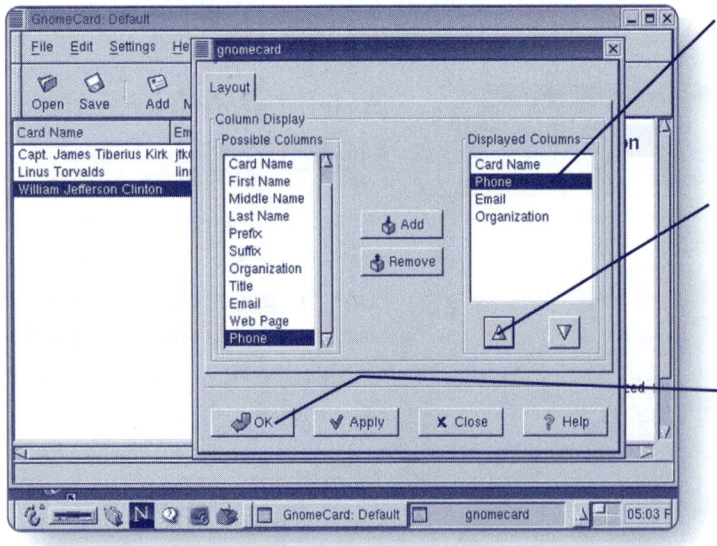

5. Click on the **column heading** in the Displayed Columns list that you want to move. The column heading will be selected.

6. Click on the **Move Up** or **Move Dn button**. The position of the column will be moved in the list.

7. Click on **OK**. The dialog box will close and your changes will be made.

MAINTAINING AN ADDRESS BOOK 215

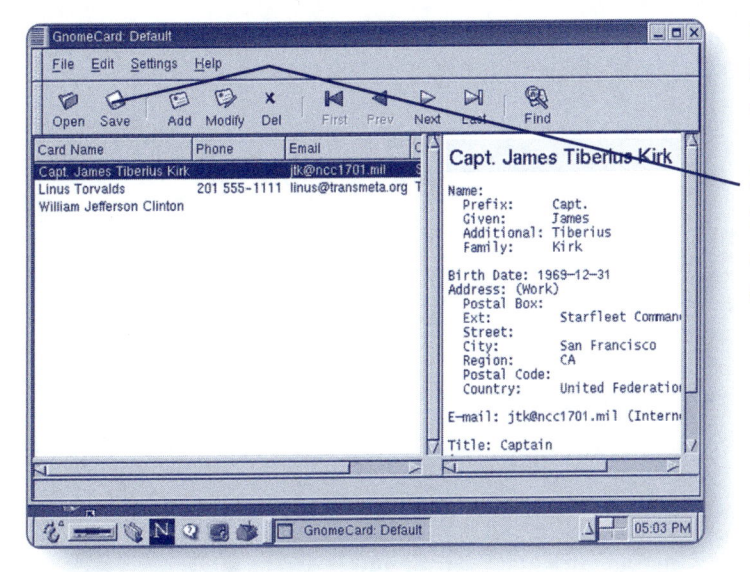

You'll see the new column headings and the reordered columns.

8. Click on the **Save button**. Your address book will be saved and you can safely close the Gnome address book.

> **NOTE**
>
> You can use the navigation toolbar buttons to move through the list of contacts.

13

Printing Files

Because Red Hat Linux is a multi-user/multi-tasking operating system, it offers many benefits to the user not found in single-user operating systems. One of the biggest benefits is the printing system. Printing in Linux is more feature-rich, flexible, and powerful than printing in a DOS or Windows environment. Linux uses an easily configurable spooling subsystem to control printing. The system enables printing to any printer available. It can be a local (attached) printer, a printer attached to another Linux machine, a network printer, or even a Windows 95/98/NT network printer. In this chapter, you'll learn how to:

- Set up a printer that is attached to your computer
- Print files using drag and drop

Configuring a Local Printer

The Red Hat Printer Tool provides a graphical front-end for the Linux PrintTool applet and will help you to set up a printer. It provides some of the information automatically, and lets you select the rest from easy graphical menus. To access the Red Hat Linux Print System Manager, you must first log in as a superuser or root.

> **TIP**
> Remember to be careful while you're in root.

Setting Up the Printer

Setting up a printer in Linux may seem a little cryptic, but it's not too bad!

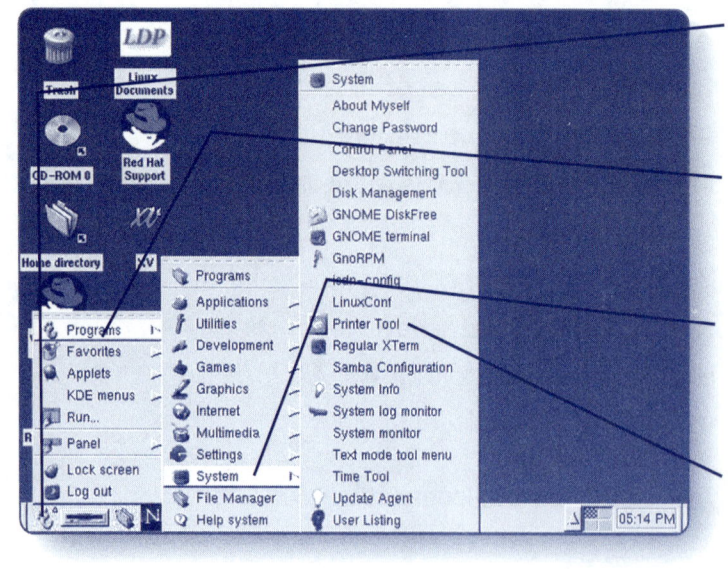

1. Click on the **Main Menu** button. The Main Menu will appear.

2. Move the **mouse pointer** to **Programs**. The Programs menu will appear.

3. Move the **mouse pointer** to **System**. The System menu will appear.

4. Click on **Printer Tool**. The Red Hat Linux Print System Manager will appear.

CONFIGURING A LOCAL PRINTER 219

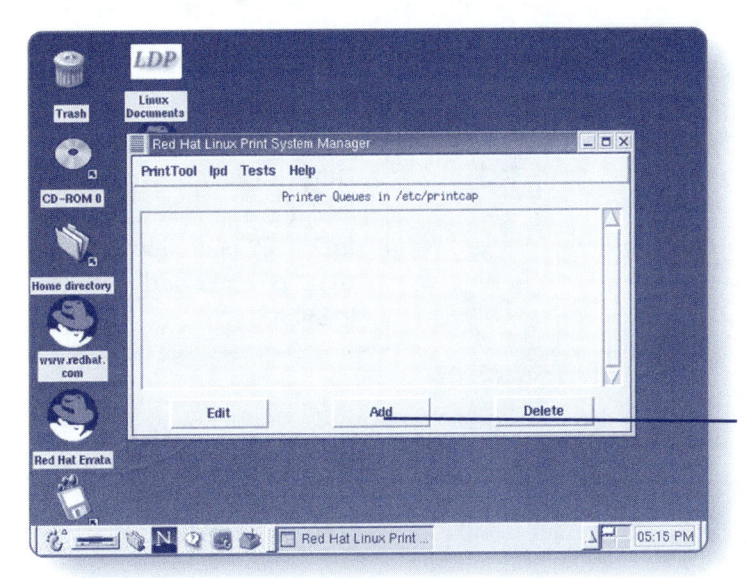

NOTE

You may see a series of Error dialog boxes. Press Ignore to skip these messages and continue to the printer tool.

5. **Click** on **Add**. The Add a Printer Entry dialog box will open.

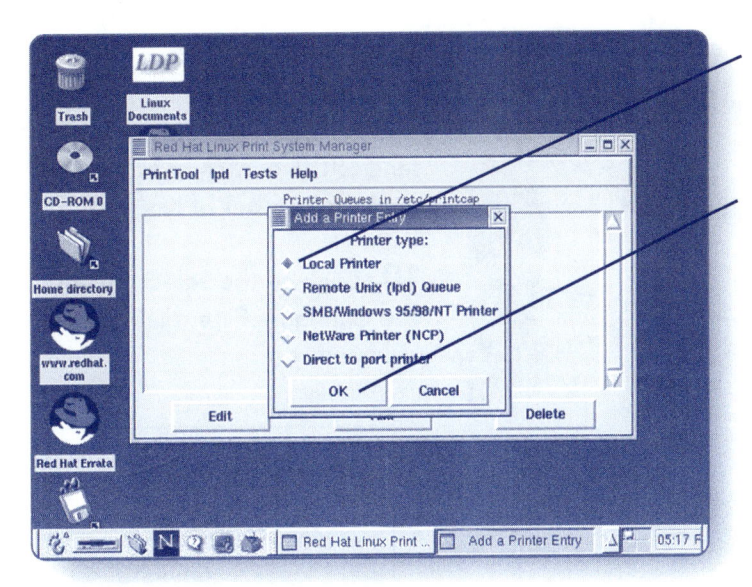

6. **Click** on the **Local Printer option button**. The option will be selected.

7. **Click** on **OK**. An Info dialog box will open showing the list of auto-detected printer ports.

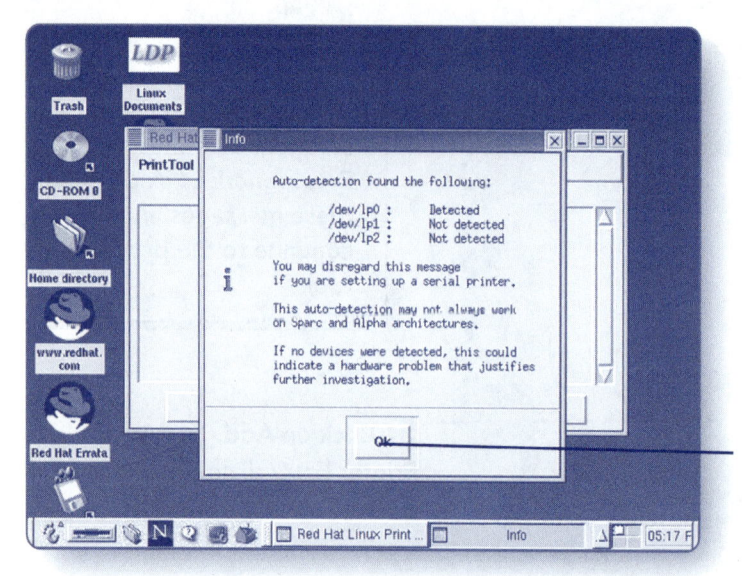

CHAPTER 13 PRINTING FILES

NOTE

Linux numbers parallel ports differently than DOS. If Linux detected lp0, it is equivalent to lpt1 in DOS. Following that, lp1=lpt2 and lp2=lpt3.

8. Click on **OK**. The Edit Local Printer Entry dialog box will open.

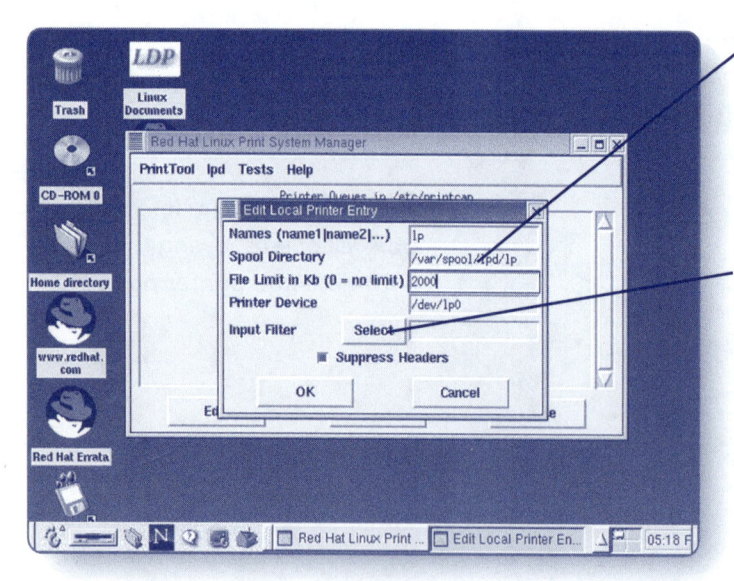

9. Click in the **text box** next to File Limit in Kb to limit the size files that your user accounts can send to the printer and then **type** the **number** of Kb.

10. Click on the **Select button**. The Configure Filter dialog box will open.

NOTE

Many printers emulate other printers and most of those can emulate the HP printers. If your printer is on the list, select it, if not, try and find one that closely matches it.

CONFIGURING A LOCAL PRINTER 221

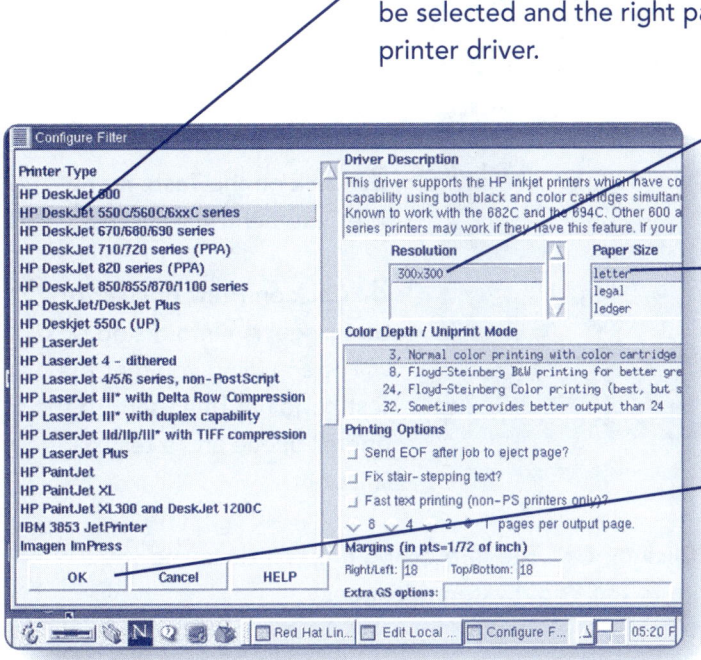

11. Click on a **printer** in the Printer Type list. The printer will be selected and the right panel will display details for the printer driver.

12. Click on a **resolution** for the default print resolution. The resolution will be selected.

13. Click on the **paper size** you will be using most of the time. The paper size will be selected.

14. Click on **OK**. You will be taken back to the Edit Local Printer Entry dialog box.

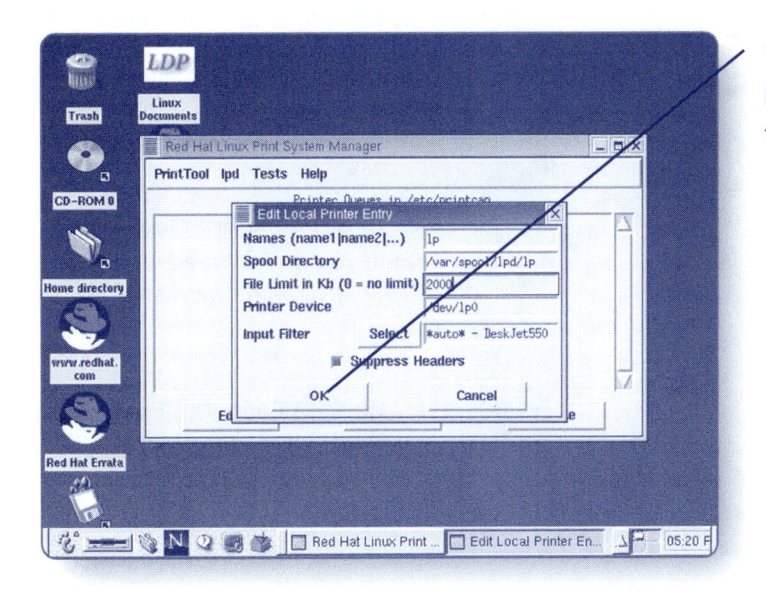

15. Click on **OK**. The dialog box will close and you'll return to the Print System Manager.

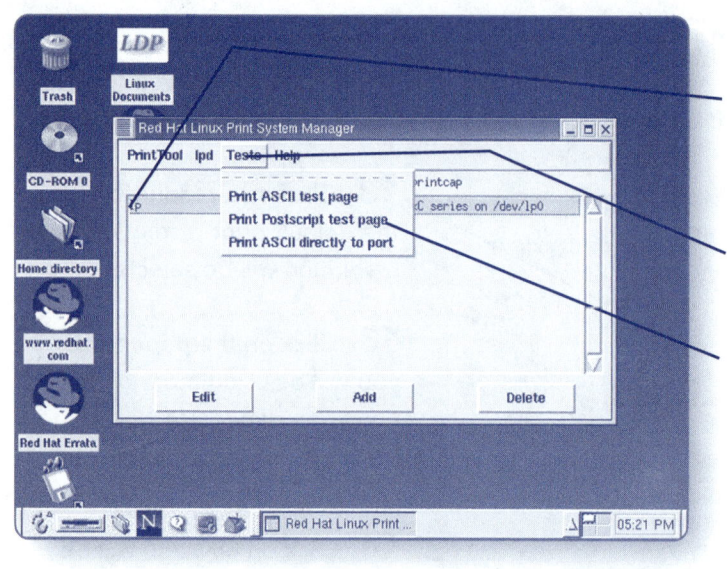

CHAPTER 13 PRINTING FILES

Testing the Printer

1. Click on the **printer** you just added. The printer will be selected.

2. Click on the **Tests menu**. The Test menu will appear.

3. Click on **Print Postscript test page**. An Info dialog box will open telling you that the test page has been sent to the printer queue and a test page will print.

4. Click on **OK**. The Info dialog box will close and you'll return to the Print System Manager.

> **TIP**
> Look over the test page and see if it looks right. If not, click on the Edit button and try a different printer.

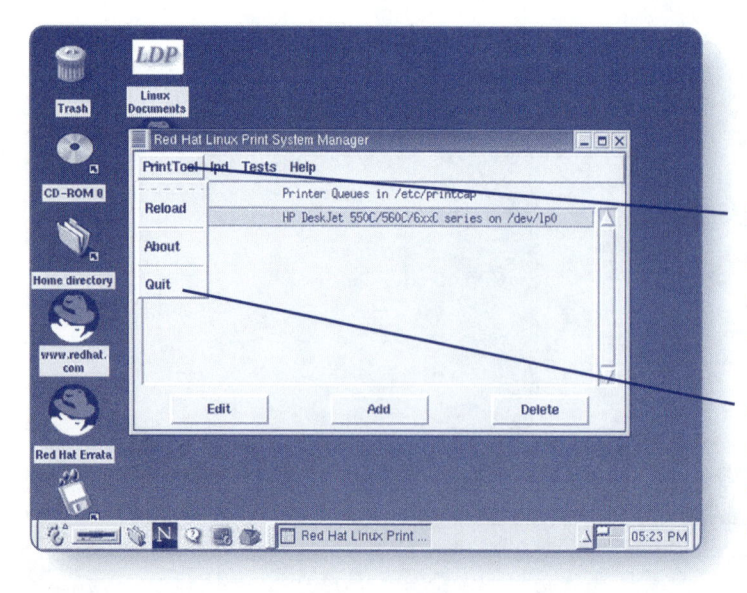

5. Click on the **PrintTool menu** when you are satisfied with the result. The PrintTool menu will appear.

6. Click on **Quit**. The PrintTool utility will close. Now, your user accounts are ready to use the printer.

Printing Files

Now that the system knows that you have a printer, all users will have access to it. Before they can have access to the printer, they'll need to add a printer applet to their Gnome Panel. Once they have the applet, it's a matter of drag and drop to print a file.

1. Click on the **Main Menu button**. The Main Menu will appear.

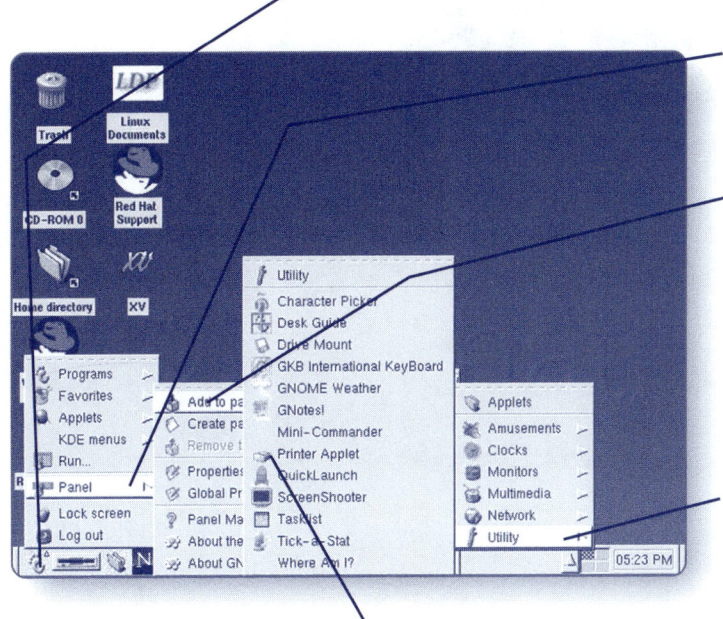

2. Move the **mouse pointer** to Panel. The Panel menu will appear.

3. Move the **mouse pointer** to Add to panel. The Add to panel menu will appear.

4. Move the **mouse pointer** to Applet. The Applet menu will appear.

5. Move the **mouse pointer** to Utility. The Utility menu will appear.

6. Click on **Printer Applet**. A printer icon will appear on the Gnome Panel.

CHAPTER 13 PRINTING FILES

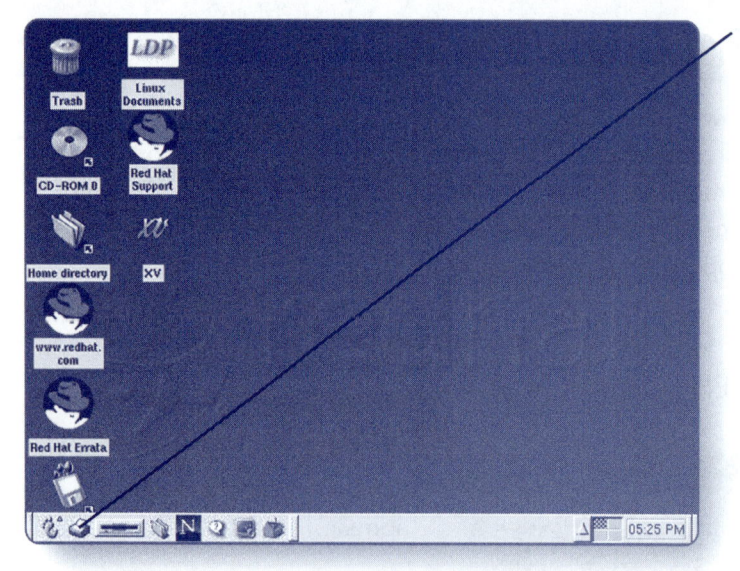

Your printer is now ready. To print, open the file manager, drag the file that you want to print over the top of the icon and drop the file. After a few moments, it will print.

14

Sounding Off with Your Computer

If you have a multimedia computer (that is, a computer with speakers, a CD-ROM drive, and a sound card), you can make your computer play a variety of sounds. You can set alarms and warning bells to let you know you performed a certain event or made a mistake. If you have a music CD collection, you can enjoy listening to music while you work at your computer. In this chapter, you'll learn how to:

- Configure your sound card if Red Hat has not done it already
- Set a different sound for the keyboard bell
- Change the system event sounds
- Play your music collection on the CD player:

Configuring Your Sound Card

One of the more persistent configuration problems Red Hat Linux used to have was getting the sound cards to work. Many a new user would bang their heads in frustration trying to get a peep out of their speakers. Today, this is not a major concern. Red Hat 7 automatically configures the sound card upon installation.

However, Murphy's Law and just plain chaos sometimes conspire against us and require us to manually configure a sound card. The good news is, Linux comes with a great application to make this task a breeze.

> **NOTE**
> sndconfig *must* be run in console mode. It is being run in the Terminal window for illustration purposes only!

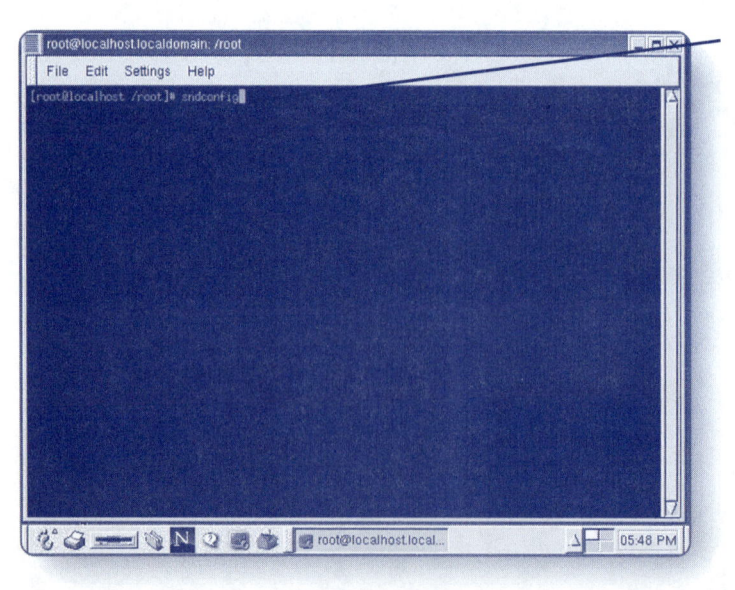

1. In the console, **type sndconfig**. The sndconfig application will start at the Introduction screen.

CONFIGURING YOUR SOUND CARD

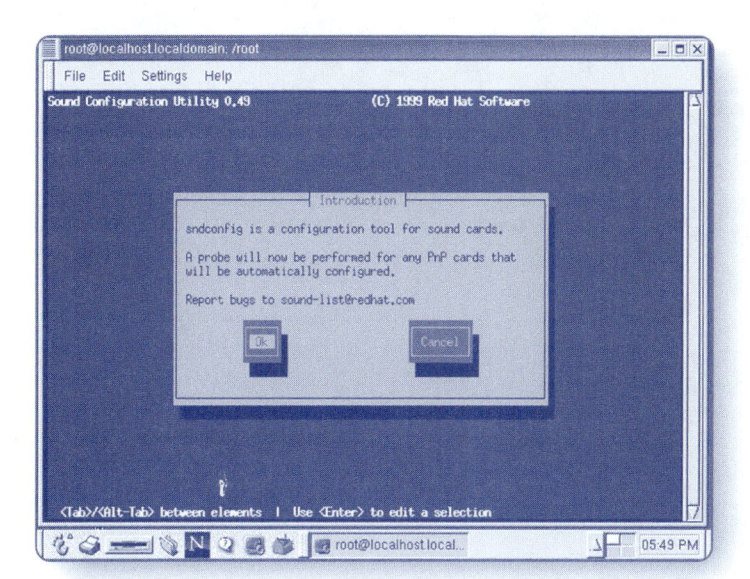

2. Press the **Enter** key. The PCI Probe Results screen will appear.

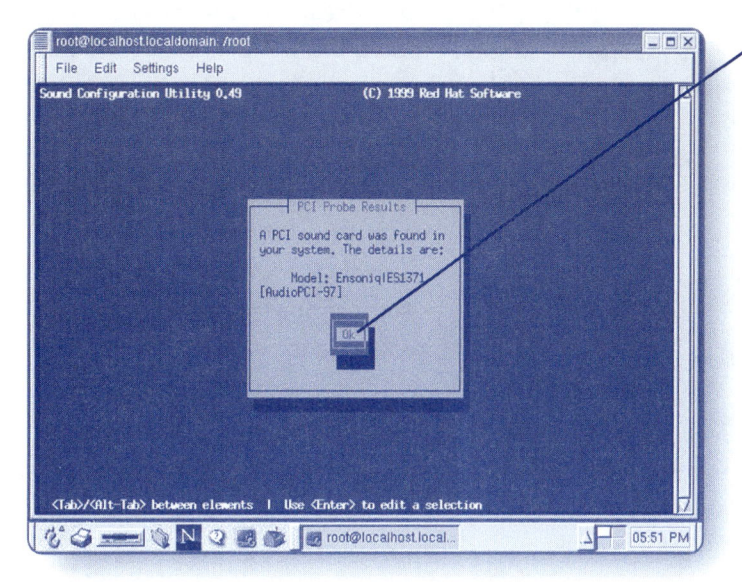

3. Confirm the **results** of the probe.

4. Press the **Enter** key. The Sound Card Test screen will appear.

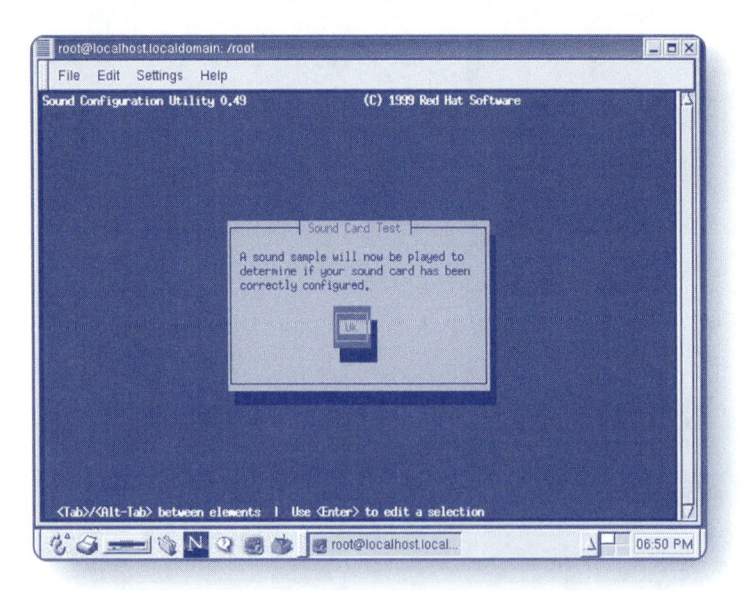

5. Press the **Enter** key. A short sound sample should be heard through your speakers, followed by the display of the Test Result screen.

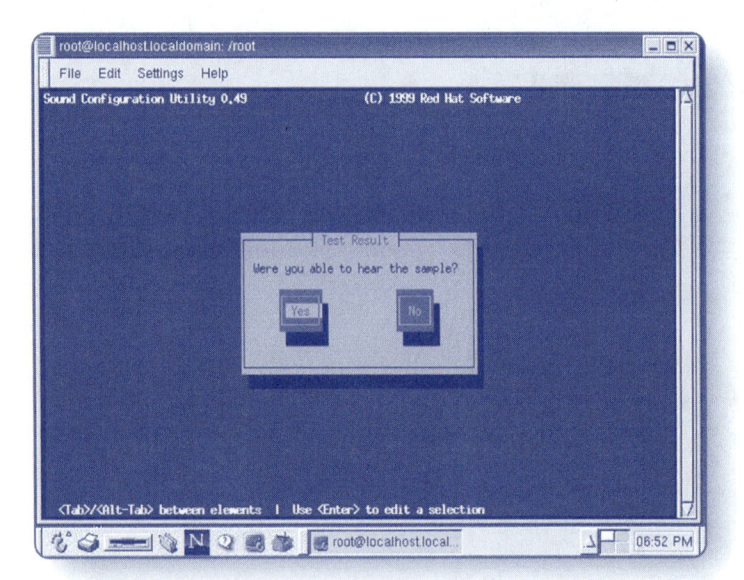

6a. Press the **Enter key** if you heard the sample. Sndconfig will end here.

or

6b. Press the **Tab key** and then the **Enter key**. The Autoconfiguration failed screen will appear.

> **NOTE**
> With some sound cards, you may be prompted to complete a MIDI sound test as well. Follow the prompts of the sndconfig application to execute this test.

CONFIGURING YOUR SOUND CARD

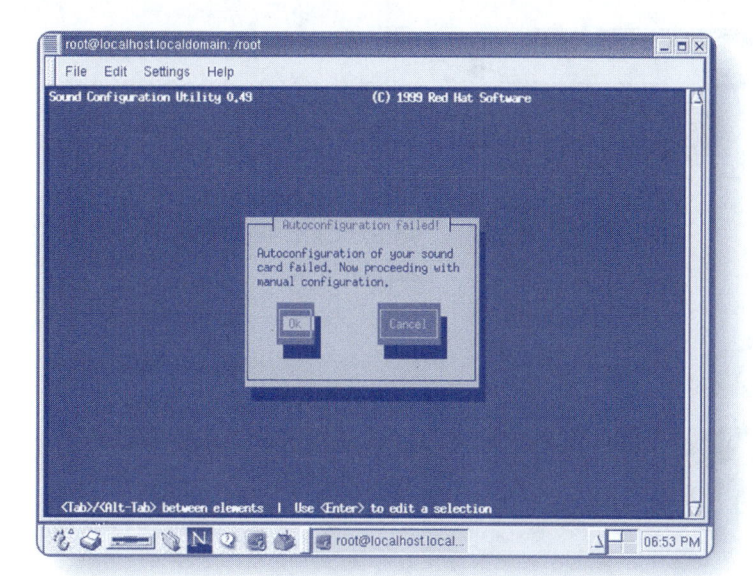

7. Press the **Enter** key. The Card Type screen will appear.

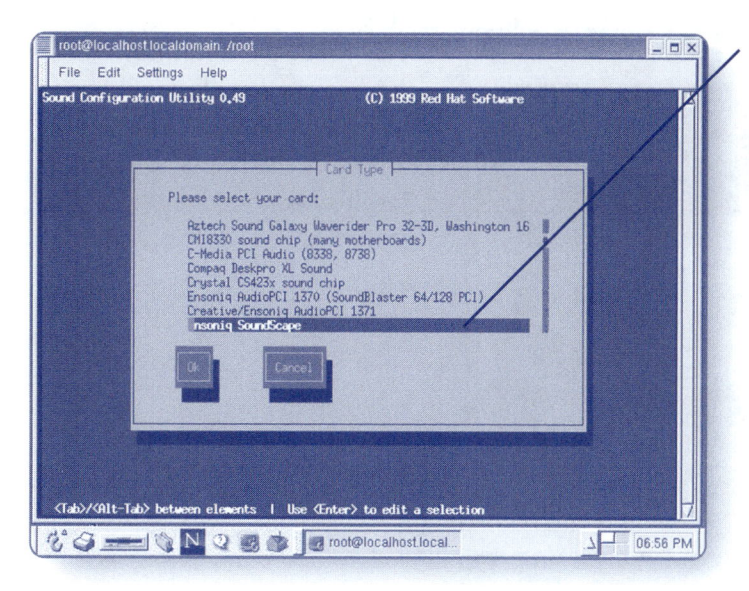

8. Press the **arrow keys** to select the listing that matches your card. The listing will be highlighted.

9. Press the **Enter** key. The Card Settings screen will appear.

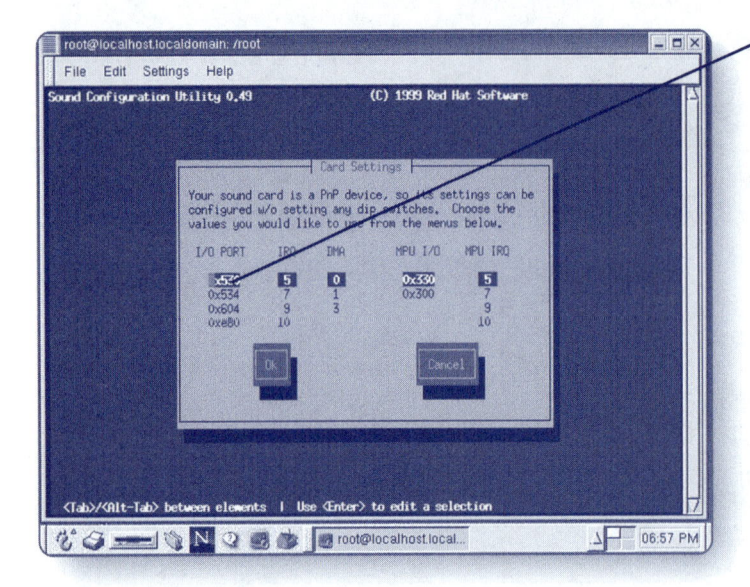

10. Press the **arrow keys** to select the correct port settings. The settings will be highlighted.

11. Press the **Enter** key. The Sound Card Test screen will appear again.

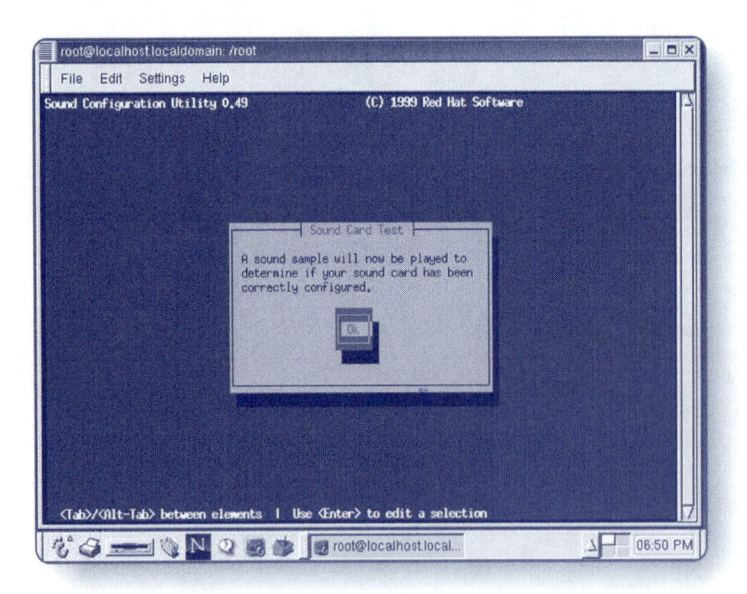

12. Press the **Enter** key. A short sound sample should be heard through your speakers, flowed by the display of the Test Result screen.

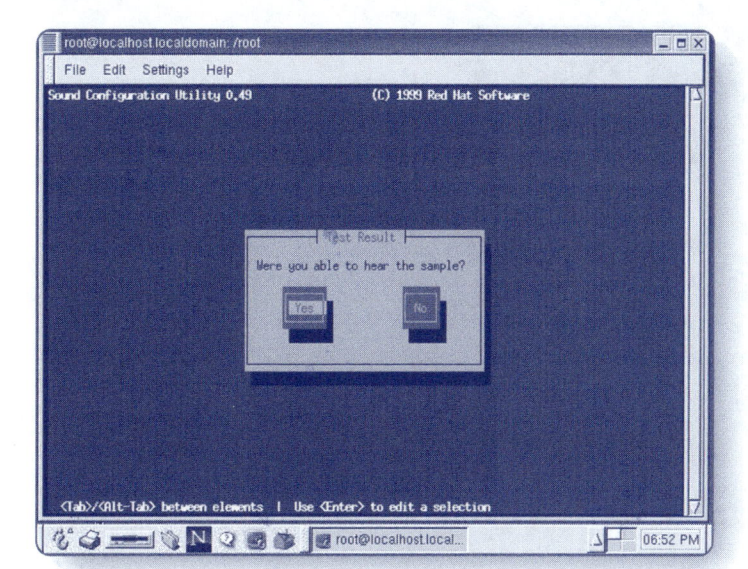

13. Press the **Enter key** if you heard the sample. Sndconfig will close.

Setting System Sounds

Once your sound card is configured, you may start hearing your computer make a number of beeping, clanging, buzzing, and popping sounds. No, your computer isn't falling apart. These sounds are telling you that you performed a certain event, or that you made an error. Depending on where your computer is located and your personal preferences, you may want to change the sounds your computer makes.

Changing the Keyboard Bell

The keyboard bell is actually a warning that a keyboard input was made in error. Experiment with the tone of the bell until you find a sound you like. You can make your keyboard bell a tenor or a baritone.

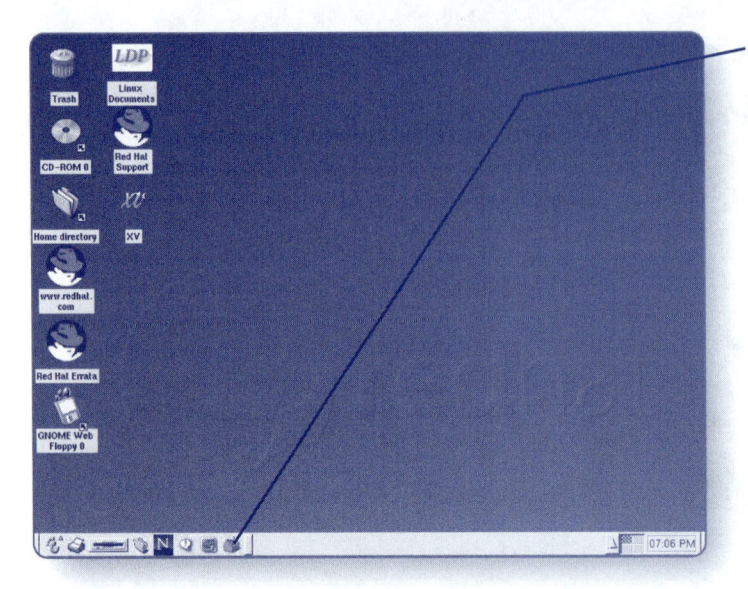

1. **Click** on the **Gnome Control Center icon** on the Gnome Panel. The Control Center window will open.

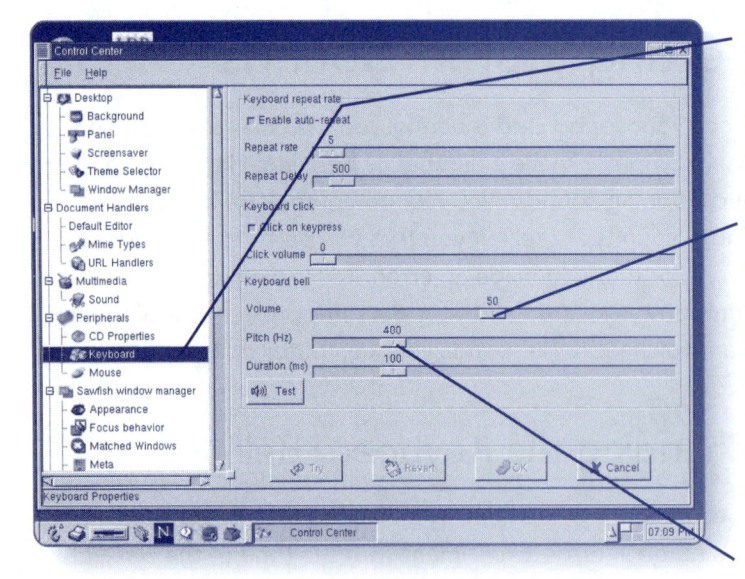

2. **Click** on **Keyboard**. The Keyboard pane will appear in the right pane of the Control Center window.

3. **Click** and **drag** the **Volume slider** to change the volume of the bell that sounds when a keyboard error is made. Dragging the slider to the left will turn the volume down. Dragging the slider to the right will turn the volume up.

4. **Click** and **drag** the **Pitch slider** to change the musical note that plays. Dragging the slider to the left will play a lower key. Dragging the slider to the right will play a higher key.

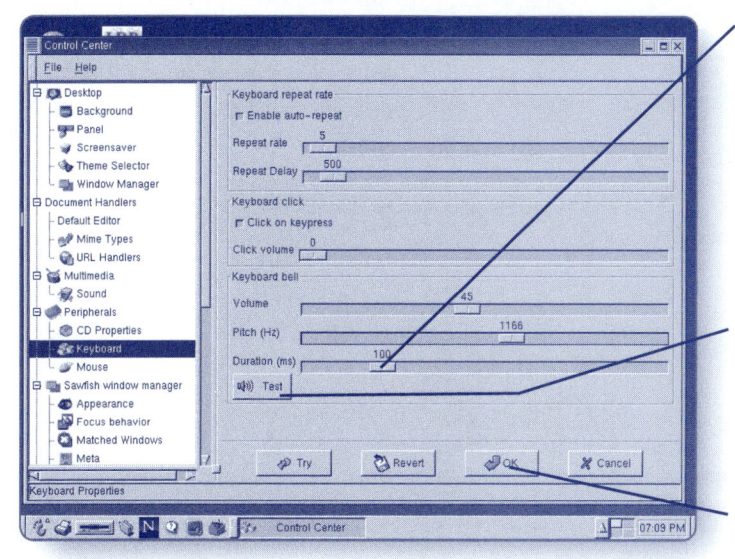

SETTING SYSTEM SOUNDS 233

5. Click and **drag** the **Duration slider** to change the amount of time you hear the keyboard sound. Dragging the slider to the left plays a shorter sound. Dragging the slider to the right plays a longer sound.

6. Click on the **Test button**. You'll hear how your changes affect the sound of the keyboard bell.

7. Click on **OK**. Your changes will be applied.

Changing Sound Events

You can change the sounds your computer makes when you perform such tasks such as executing menu commands or logging out of Gnome. There are also sound events associated with the various Linux games. If all the noise is getting to you, you can turn off the sounds completely. If you don't hear any sounds, it may be because your sound card is not configured for Red Hat Linux. Try using the sndconfig application as detailed earlier in this chapter.

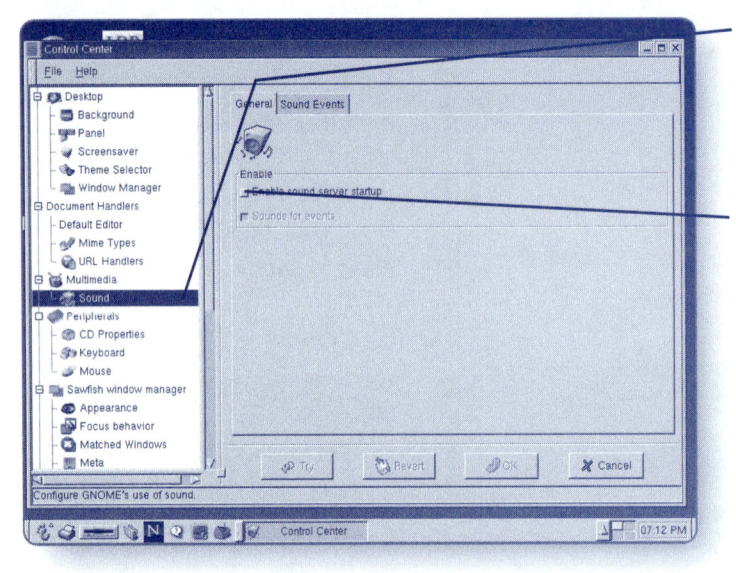

1. Click on **Sound**. The Sound pane will appear on the right side of the Control Center window.

2. Click on the **Enable sound server startup button**. The option will be selected.

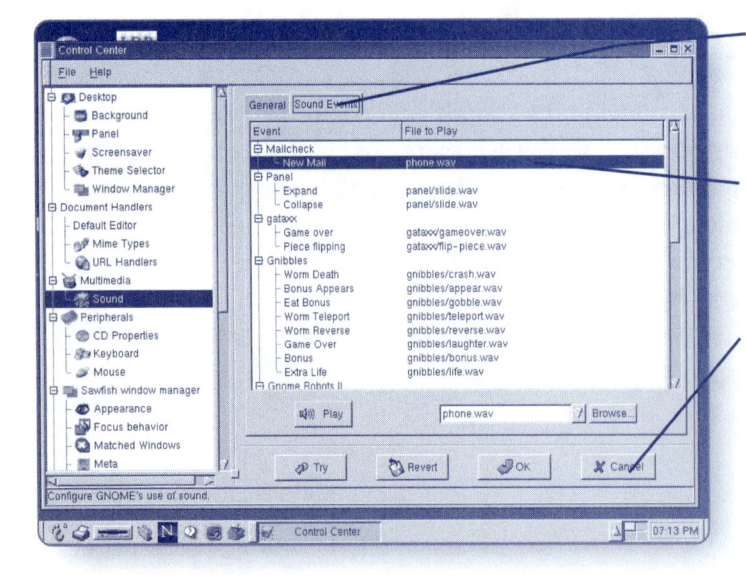

3. Click on the **Sound Events tab**. The Sound Events tab will come to the top of the stack.

4. Click on the **sound event** that you want to change. The sound event will be highlighted.

5. Click on the **Browse button**. The Select sound file dialog box will open.

NOTE

If you don't want a sound associated with an event, delete the directory path and file name in the text box.

SETTING SYSTEM SOUNDS   235

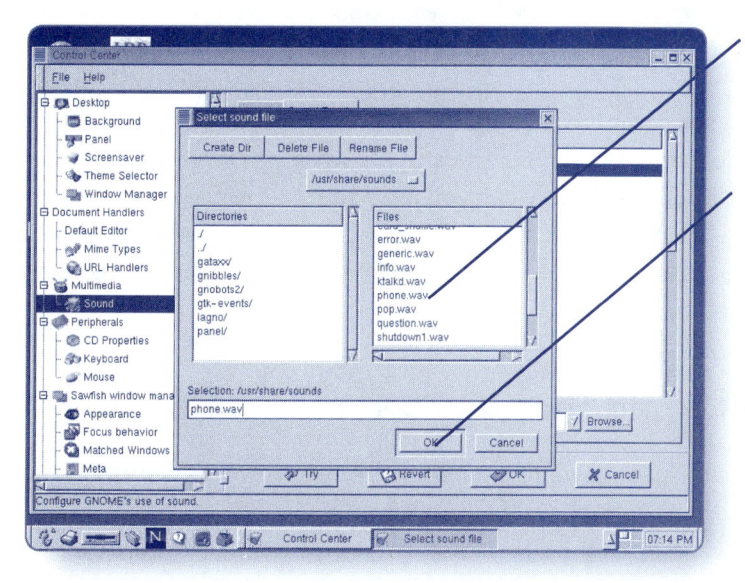

6. Click on the **sound file** that you want to use for the sound event. The file will be selected.

7. Click on **OK**. The new sound will appear next to the event you selected.

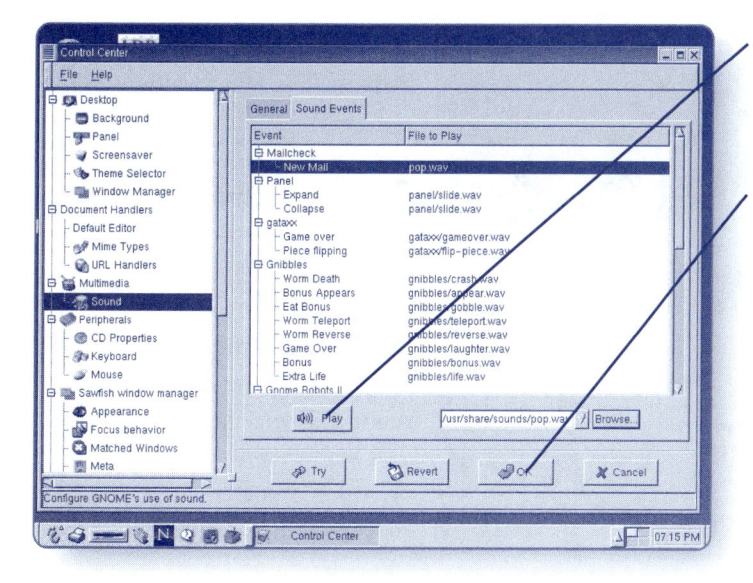

8. Click on the **Play button**. You'll hear the sound you selected.

9. Click on **OK**. Your changes will be made.

Tuning Up with the CD Player

If your computer has a CD-ROM drive, a sound card, and speakers, you can play music CDs while you work at your computer. Not only can you just listen to the CD in the order the tracks appear on the CD, but you can also switch between tracks and have all of the titles from the CD uploaded to your screen.

Starting the CD Player

It's time to play a few tunes, so get your favorite music CD ready and crank up the jukebox.

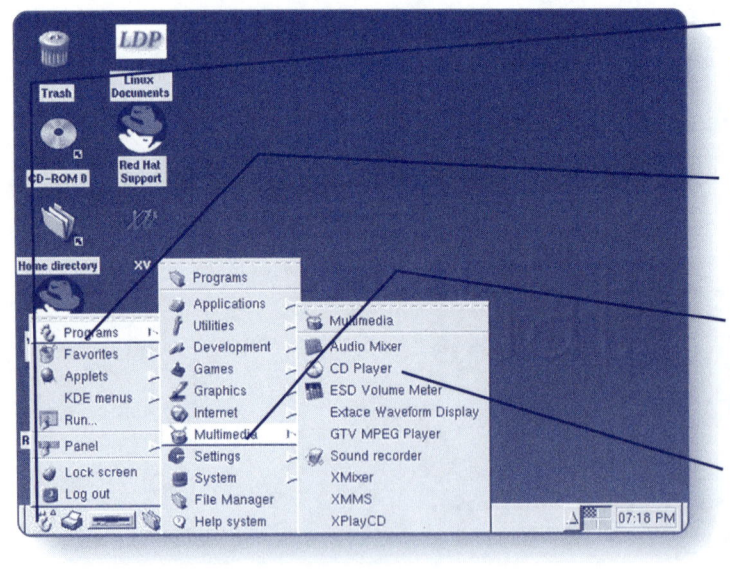

1. Click on the **Main Menu button**. The Main Menu will appear.

2. Move the **mouse pointer** to Programs. The Programs menu will appear.

3. Move the **mouse pointer** to Multimedia. The Multimedia menu will appear.

4. Click on **CD Player**. The CD player will appear on your desktop.

TUNING UP WITH THE CD PLAYER 237

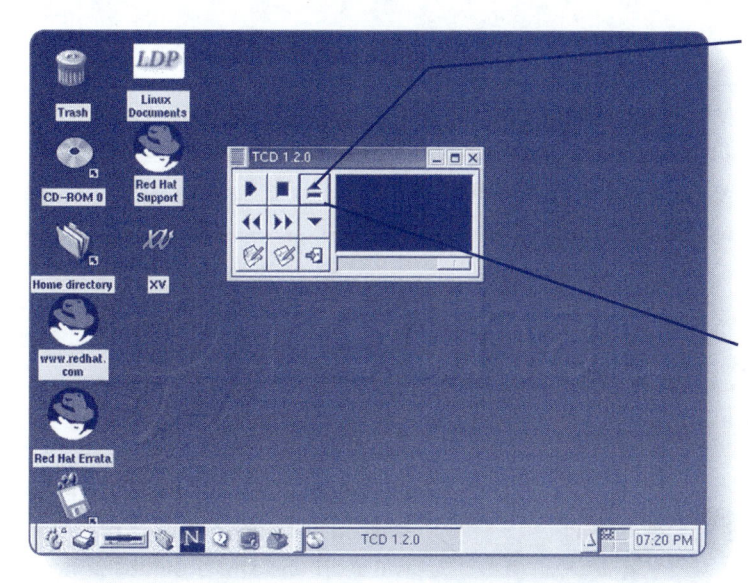

5. Click on the **Eject button**. The CD carriage for your CD-ROM drive will slide out of the computer.

6. Place the **music CD** in the CD carriage.

7. Click on the **Eject button** on your computer's CD-ROM drive. The carriage will close.

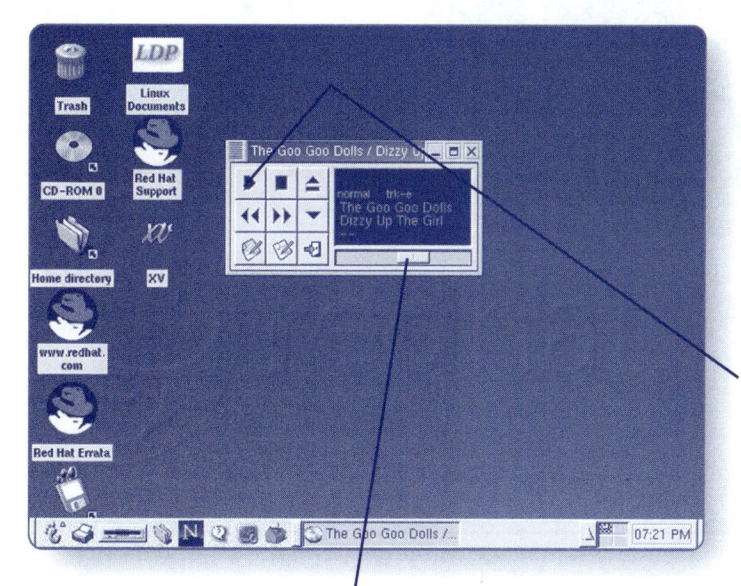

Playing Music CDs

Now that you have a CD in the CD-ROM drive and the CD player turned on, it's time to learn how to use the CD player to start playing the CD and switch between songs.

1. Click on the **Play button**. You'll begin to hear music come from your computer speakers. Notice that the button changes. Click on this button a second time to pause the song.

2. Click and **drag** on the **Volume slider**. Dragging the slider to the right will make the music louder. Dragging the slider to the left will turn the volume down.

> **NOTE**
> You can also use the volume control on your speakers (it may also be located on the monitor) to set the volume for the CD player.

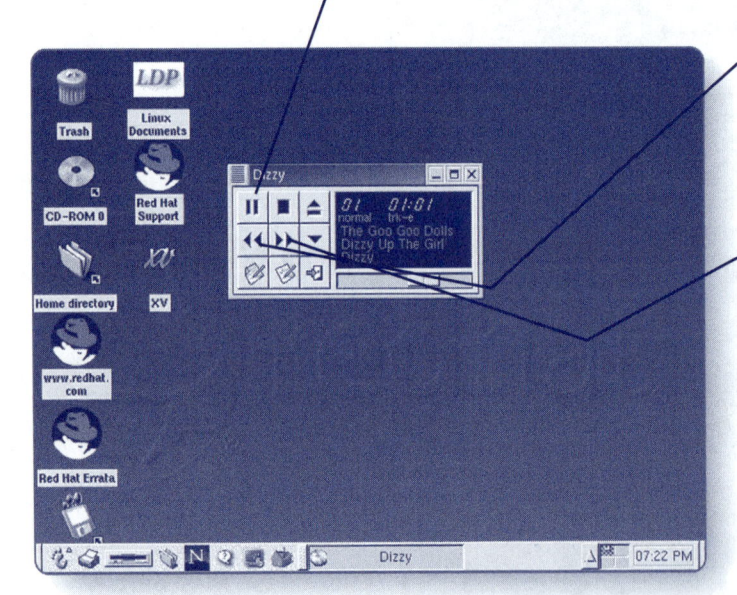

3. Click on the **Pause button**. The music will stop playing but the CD player will remember where it left off.

4. Click on the **Skip backwards button**. The song that is playing will stop and the previous song on the CD play list will begin playing.

5. Click on the **Skip forwards button**. The song that is playing will stop and the next song on the CD play list will begin playing.

> **TIP**
> If you have Internet access, you may not need to type in all this information. Connect to your Internet service provider and click on the CDDB Status button. If the album is in the database, all the information will be filled in for you.

TUNING UP WITH THE CD PLAYER 239

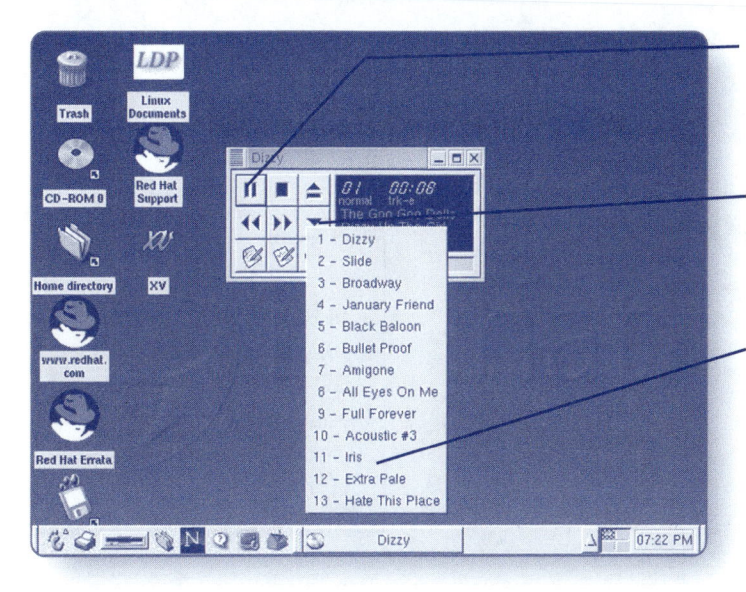

6. Click on the **Play button**. The CD will begin playing at the place where it was paused.

7. Click on the **Track Selection button**. A list of the track numbers on the CD will appear.

8. Click on the **track** that you want to listen to. The selected track will begin playing.

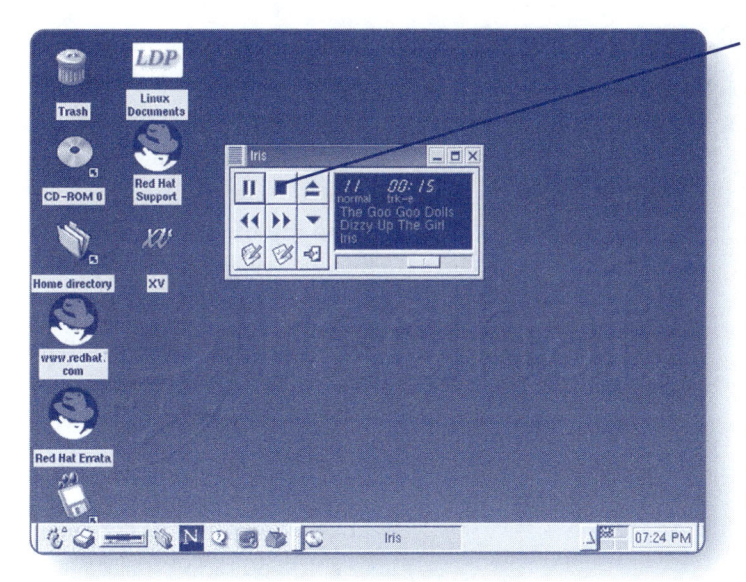

9. Click on the **Stop button** when you're finished listening to the CD. The music will stop.

Keeping a Play List for Your Favorite CDs

The CD player will keep a list of songs that appear on a CD. A universal database on the Internet called CDDB will likely have the song information on your CD, but you may need to type it in yourself. You'll be able to see this information each time you put that CD in the CD player. You won't need to keep going back to the album cover to find the song list.

CHAPTER 14: SOUNDING OFF WITH YOUR COMPUTER

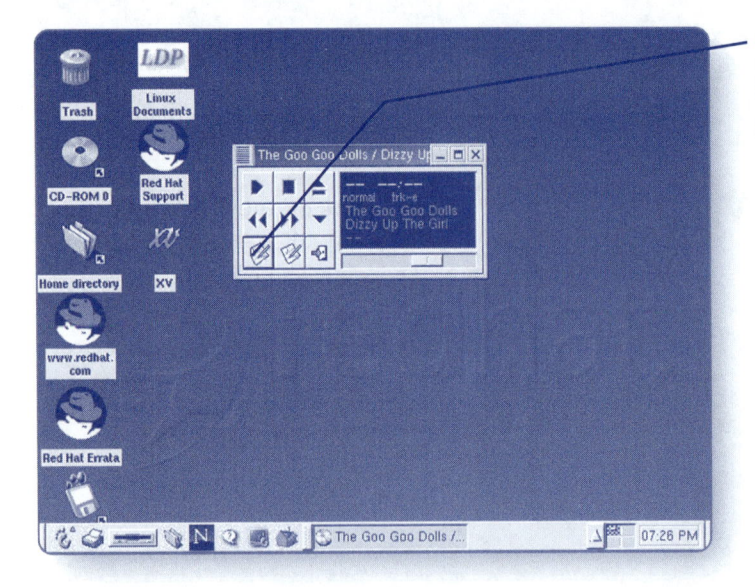

1. Click on the **Open Track Editor button**. The Track Editor dialog box will open.

NOTE

Before you begin, make sure the CD is in the CD-ROM drive and that you have the album jacket with the song list in front of you.

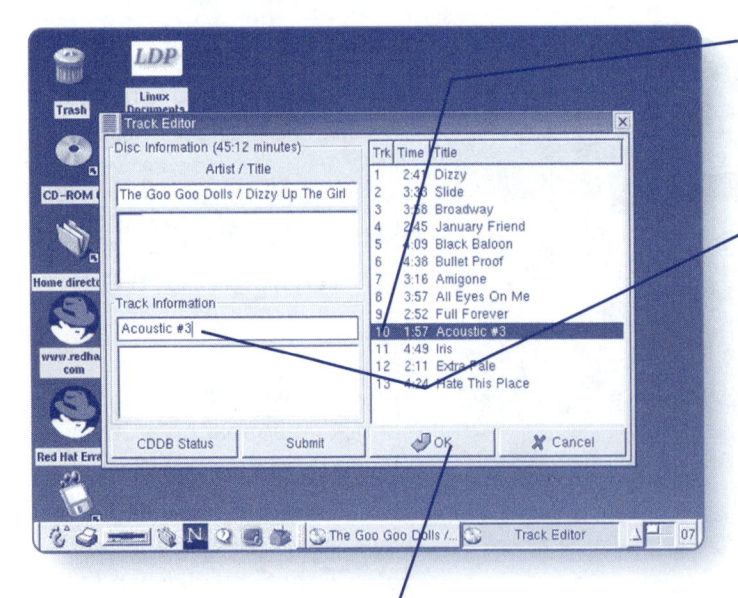

2. Click on the **track number** in the Track List to which you want to add a song title. The track number will be selected.

3. Type the **title** of the song that corresponds to that track.

4. Add song titles to the other tracks on the CD. The entire play list will be added to the Track Editor.

5. Look over the **play list** and make sure you didn't make any typing mistakes. If you did, click on the track that contains the error and fix it in the Track Information text box.

6. Click on **OK** when you are finished. The Track Editor will close.

Part III Review Questions

1. What menu in an application normally contains the command that saves files? *See "Creating a New File" in Chapter 10*

2. What are three different methods of selecting text? *See "Working with Text" in Chapter 10*

3. How do you create a new directory in the console mode? *See "Managing Directories" in Chapter 11*

4. How can you move multiple files in the console mode? *See "Managing Files" in Chapter 11*

5. Where can you find a Linux program that will help you keep your appointments organized? *See "Keeping Track of Important Dates" in Chapter 12*

6. How do you add a new address listing to the Gnome address book? *See "Maintaining an Address Book" in Chapter 12*

7. Where do you find the print tool that configures a printer for you? *See "Configuring a Local Printer" in Chapter 13*

8. How do you place an icon on the Gnome Panel so that you can easily print files? *See "Printing Files" in Chapter 13*

9. What are the two types of system sounds that you can change for your computer? *See "Setting System Sounds" in Chapter 14*

10. How can you get sound on your PC? *See "Configuring Your Sound Card" in Chapter 14*

PART IV

Tuning Up Your Linux

Chapter 15
 Adding Applications to Linux 245

Chapter 16
 Getting On the Internet 255

Chapter 17
 Surfing the Web 263

15

Adding Applications to Your Linux

Now that Linux is installed and configured on your computer, you can begin to enjoy some of the benefits. Linux is a wonderful playground with a wealth of things to do. Linux can help you with many of your tasks—you can use it both to install new applications and to upgrade old applications. You can also replace, update, or repair files in the installed programs. In this chapter, you'll learn how to:

- Verify that your applications are correctly installed
- Install an application with Gnome RPM

Starting the Gnome RPM

The Gnome RPM, or GnoRPM, is a graphical front-end to the Red Hat Package Management System. Most Linux users will already be familiar with the Red Hat Package management system; but for those who aren't, the GnoRPM tool is the answer. You must be logged in as the superuser or root to install, upgrade, or uninstall applications. Users may verify and query packages to determine their status.

In this chapter, you will use the PowerTools CD, which came with your boxed Red Hat 7 application. This CD is chock-full of useful applications for the Red hat platform.

1. Place the **Red Hat Linux Powertool CD** in your computer's CD-ROM drive. The drive will automatically mount.

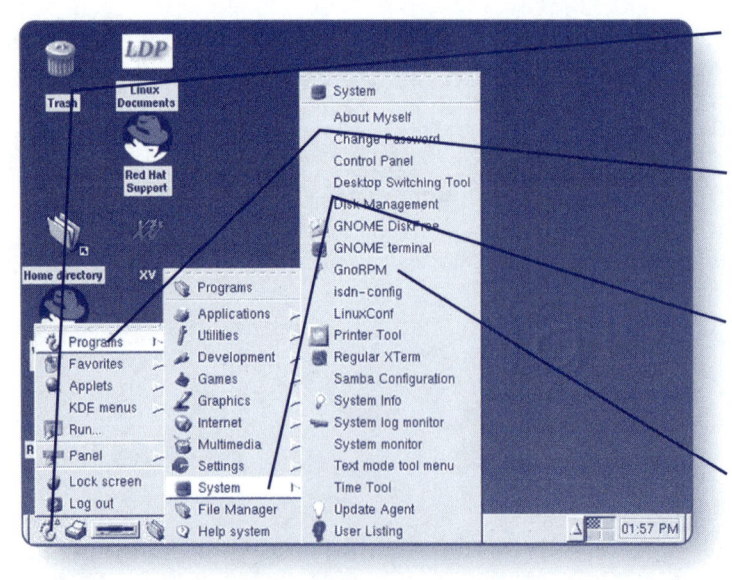

2. Click on the **Main Menu button**. The Main Menu will appear.

3. Move the **mouse pointer** to Programs. The Programs menu will appear.

4. Move the **mouse pointer** to System. The System menu will appear.

5. Click on **GnoRPM**. The Gnome RPM window will open.

Take a minute to get familiar with the Gnome RPM window. The first packages that show up in the package panel are the packages that you already have installed on your system from the original installation.

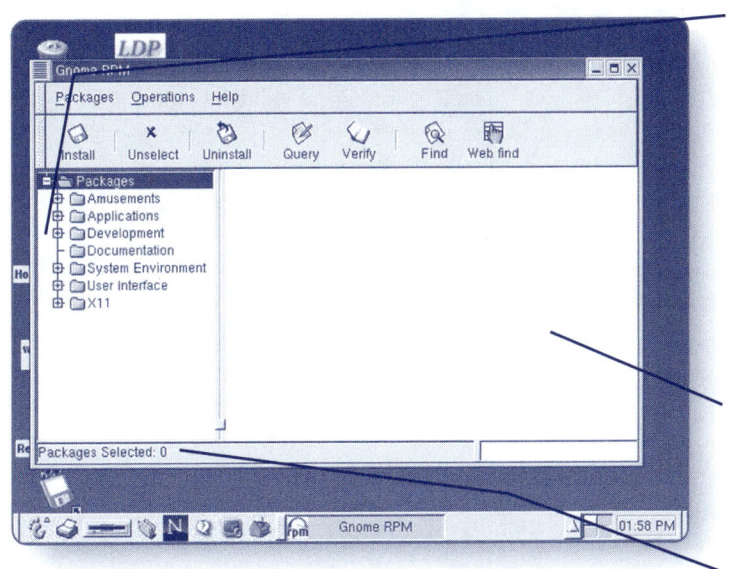

- **Package panel.** This panel groups packages that perform similar functions into categories. These packages are applications that are available for you to install and use. Click on the plus sign next to a category to expand the list to show the subcategories.

- **Display window.** This window shows the different applications that are available in a selected category.

- **Status bar.** This bar shows how many packages are selected.

Verifying Installed Packages

If you suspect that one of your applications isn't working correctly, Gnome RPM is just the tool to verify it. GnoRPM is a graphical tool that verifies that an application is complete and working correctly. If needed, you can replace files and whole packages, as well as determine if all the packages available from the installation were installed.

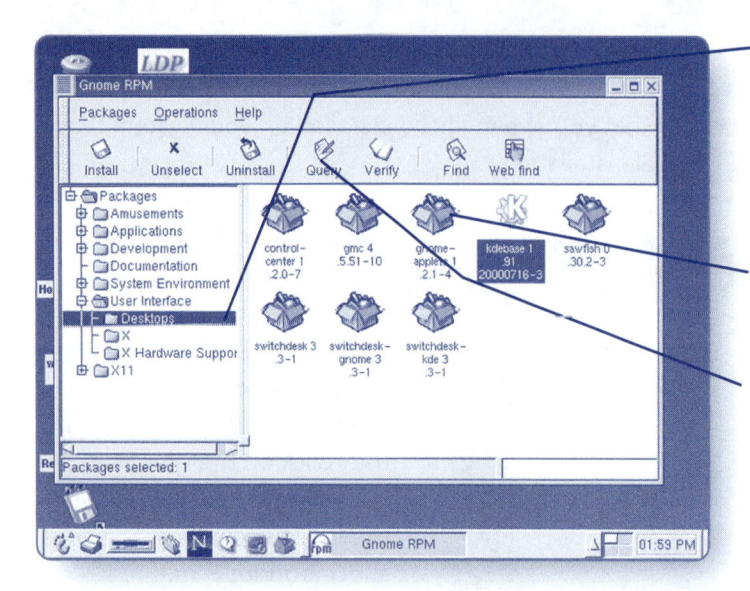

1. Click on the **category** in the Package Panel that contains the one that you want to verify. A list of the packages contained in that category will appear.

2. Click on a **package**. The package will be selected.

3. Click on the **Query button**. The Package Info dialog box will open.

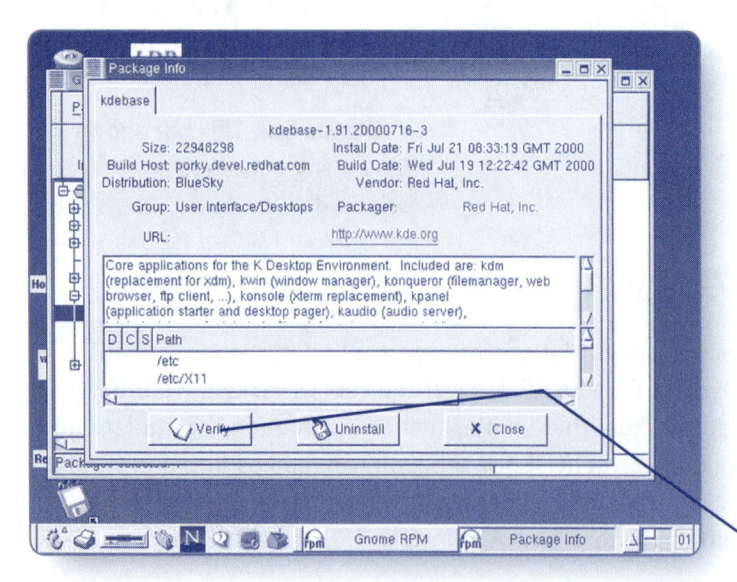

In the Package Info dialog box, you can find out the build date of the package, its size, the files contained within it, and where they are installed in the Linux file system. At the bottom of the dialog box are buttons to verify the condition of the installed application package and to automatically install or uninstall packages after you have verified them.

4. Click on the **Verify button**. The Verifying Packages dialog box will open.

INSTALLING A PACKAGE 249

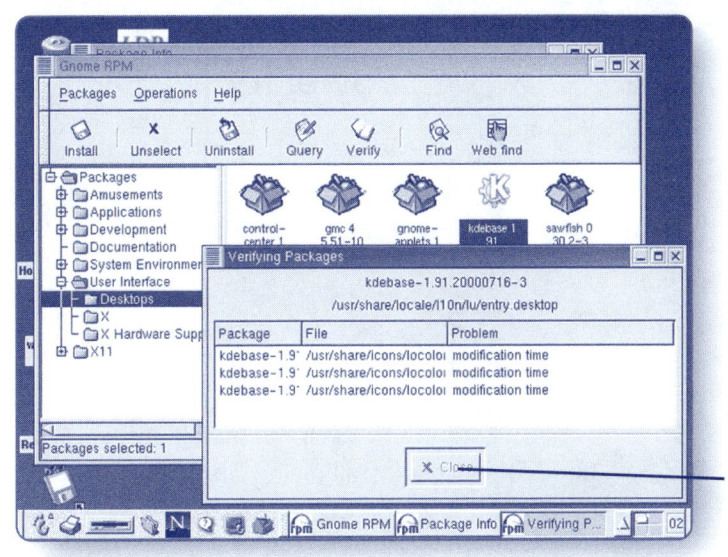

The Verifying Packages dialog box will indicate the progress of the verification as the package is checked. If all the files in the package are intact, the dialog will return nothing. If one or more has become corrupted, it will be reported along with a description of the problem. You can then re-install the package and correct the problem.

5. Click on the **Close button**. You'll return to the Package Info dialog box.

6. Click on the **Close button**. The Package Info dialog box will close and you'll return to the Gnome RPM.

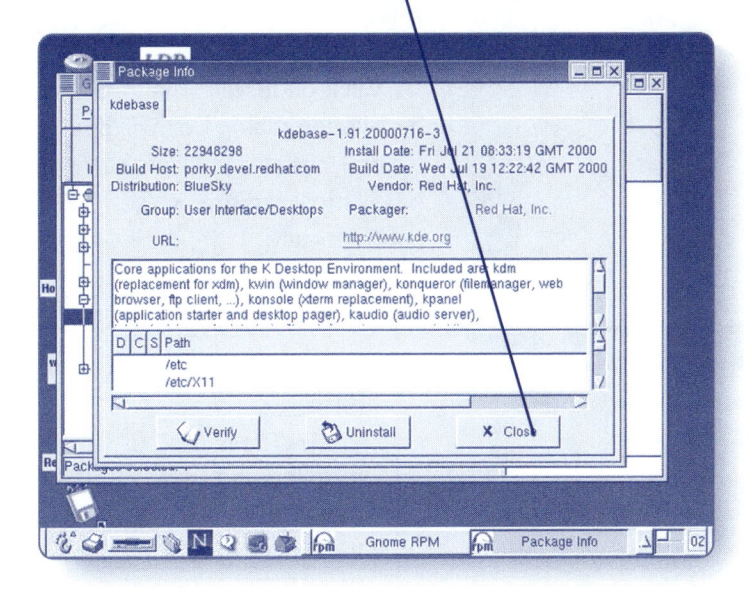

Installing a Package

The Package Management System provides the path and means for obtaining new applications and upgrades, as well as fixes for old applications and adding and removing modules to the Linux kernel.

CHAPTER 15: ADDING APPLICATIONS TO YOUR LINUX

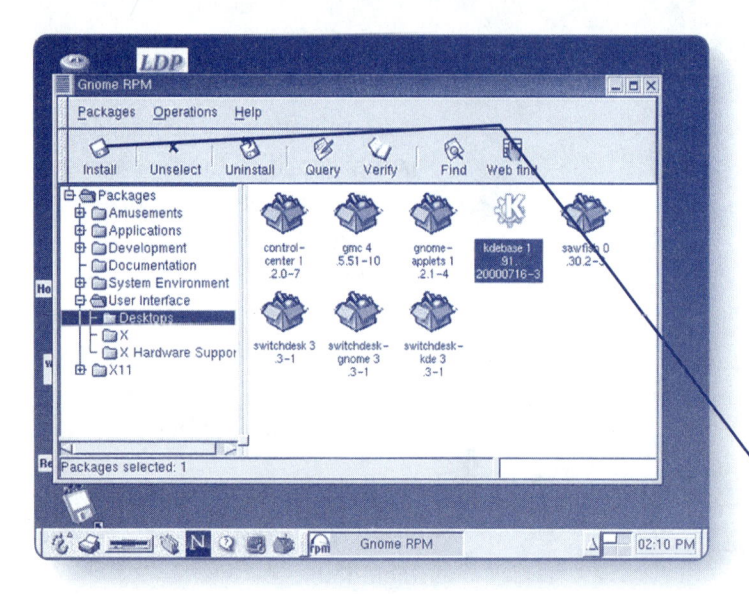

Installing from the PowerTools CD

To get started with Gnome RPM, you're going to load an application from the Red Hat 7.0 PowerTools CD and install it on your system.

1. Click the **Install button**. The Install dialog box will open and the CD will be read.

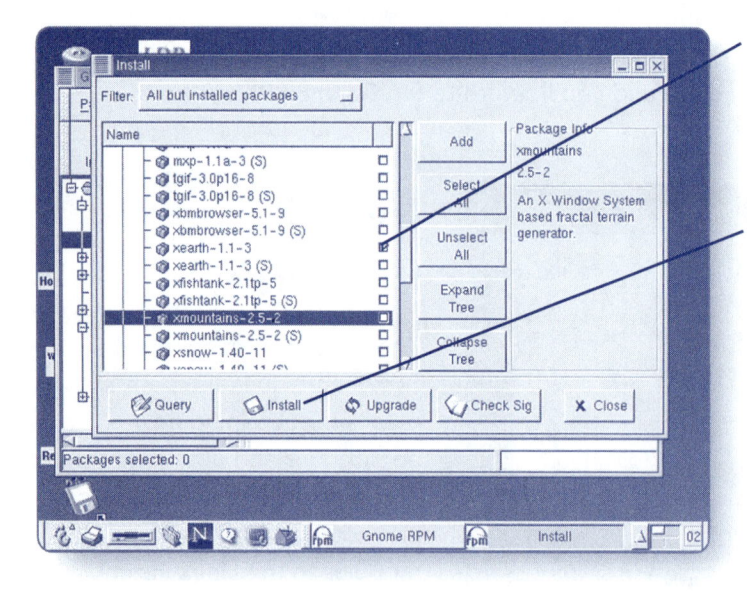

2. Click on the **check box** next to the package you would like to install. The package will be selected for installation.

3. Click on **Install**. The Package Installation dialog box will open to mark the progress of the installation and then close automatically.

> **NOTE**
>
> Packages noted with an (S) are source code RPMs. These can be installed and then modified by advanced users. Unless you are a programmer, ignore them.

INSTALLING A PACKAGE   251

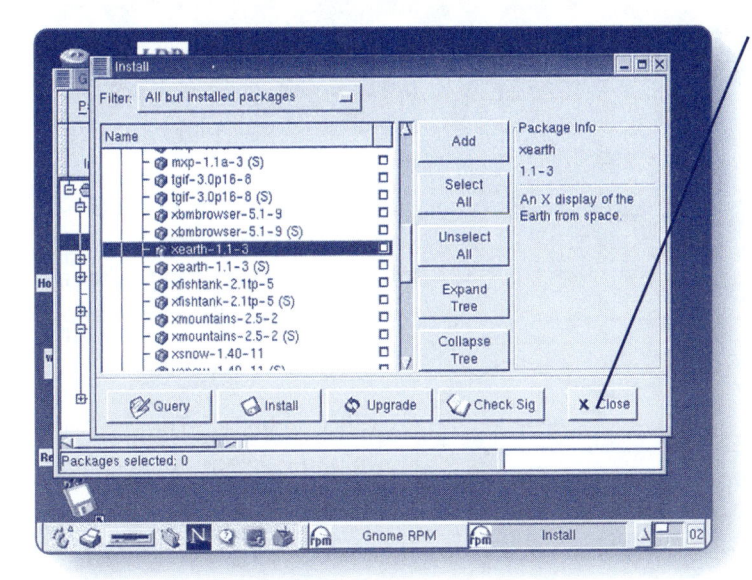

4. Click on **Close**. The Install dialog box will close and the application is ready to be run.

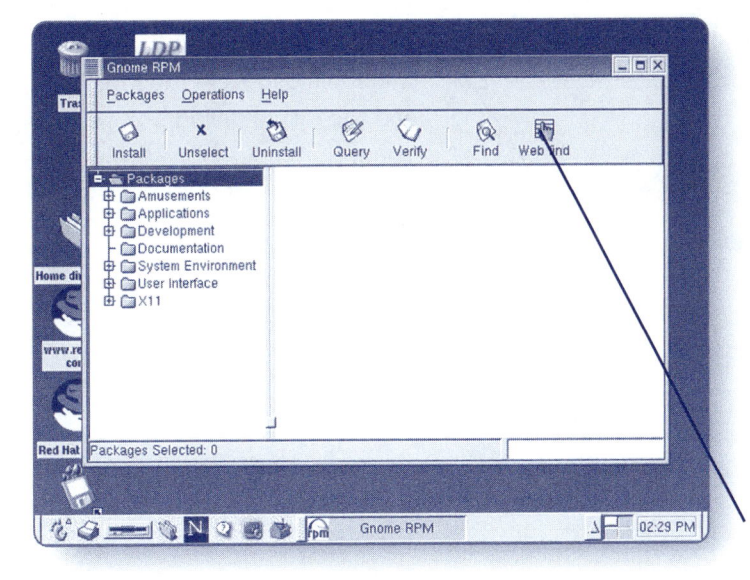

Installing from Third-Party RPMs

You are not just limited to installing RPMs that are provided by Red Hat. If you find an RPM out on the Internet, you can download it and install with Gnome RPM in just a few minutes. Gnome RPM will even help you find the latest releases of RPMs on the Internet.

1. Click the **Web find button**. The RPM Find dialog box will open.

CHAPTER 15: ADDING APPLICATIONS TO YOUR LINUX

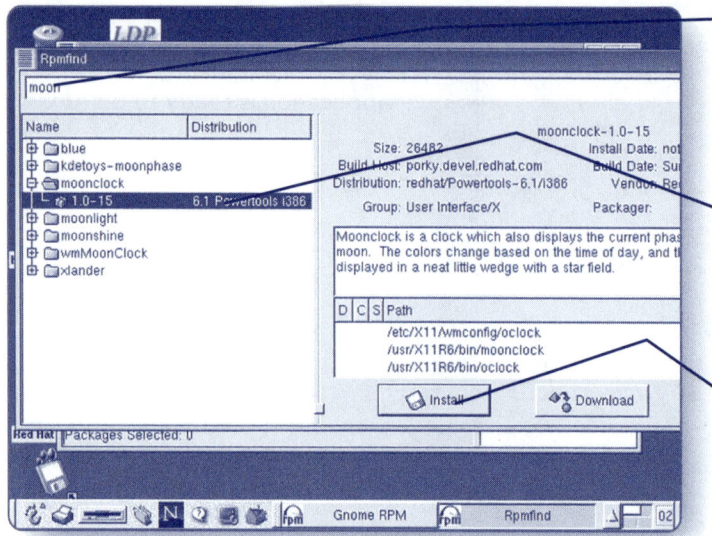

2. Type a **search term** and press **Enter**. The results of the search will be displayed in the file tree.

3. Click on a **package**. Information about the package will be shown in the information fields.

4. Click on **Install**. The Download Packages dialog box will open.

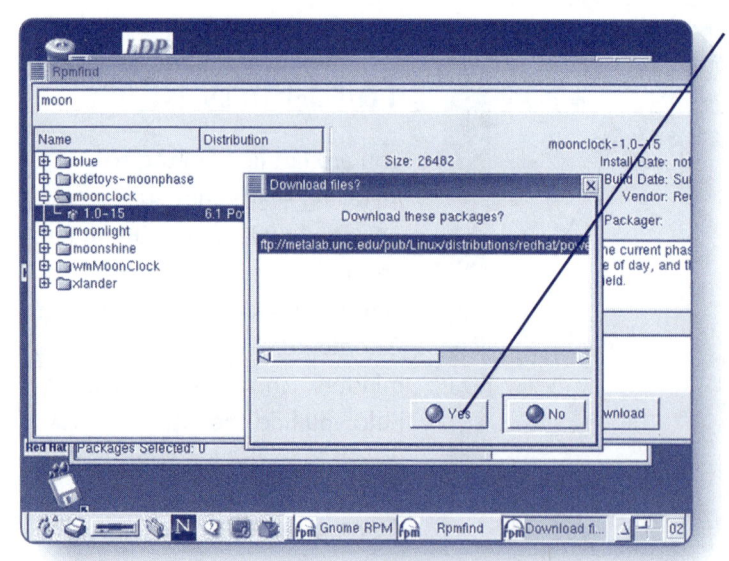

5. Click on **Yes**. The package will download from the Internet and the Install dialog box will open.

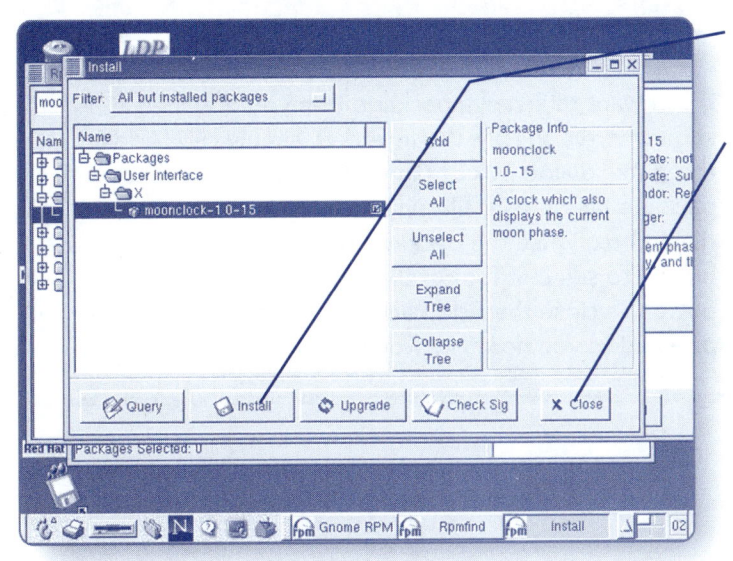

INSTALLING A PACKAGE 253

6. Click on **Install**. The package will be installed.

7. Click on **Close**. The Install dialog box will close.

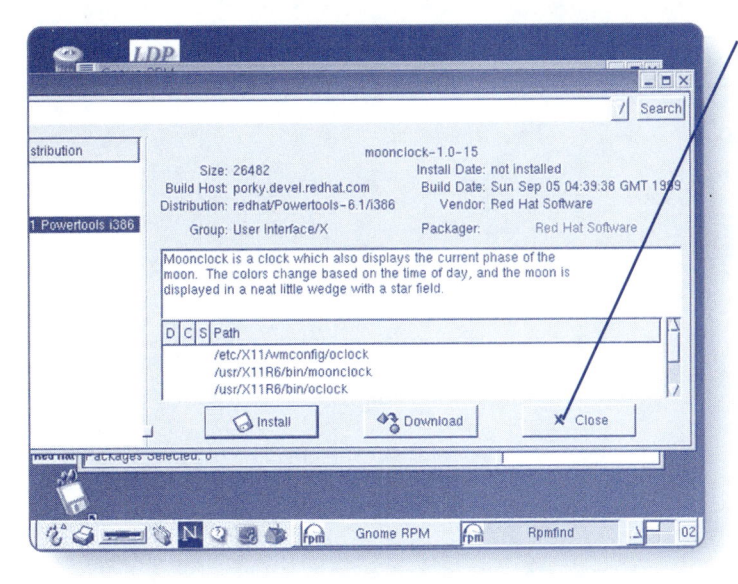

8. Click on **Close**. The RPM Find dialog box will close.

> **NOTE**
>
> If you want to install a package that you obtained somewhere else (say, the Internet), simply click Add in the Install dialog box of GnoRPM. Then locate your package file on your file system in the Add Packages dialog box. Once the package is selected, click the Add button to select it for installation, click the Close button to close the Add Packages dialog box, and then proceed as you normally would in GnoRPM.

16

Getting On the Internet

Before you begin to enter the Web, you'll need to set up an account with an ISP (Internet Service Provider). The ISP will then provide important information that is needed to set up the dial-up connection on your computer. You'll need a username or ID, password, access phone number, IP (Internet Protocol) addresses, and mail and news server names. After you configure the connection, you can use the UserNet dialer utility to get connected. In this chapter, you'll learn how to:

- Set up your dial-up connection
- Connect to the Internet

Creating the Connection

Once an account is set up with an ISP and you have all the required information to create the dial-up connection, it is time to log into Linux as a superuser or root and build a dial-up connection. This section will show how to configure the most popular connection, a PPP (*Point-to-Point Protocol*).

Setting Up a PPP Connection

You first must log in as root, and if you're using an external modem, make sure that the modem is turned on. Linux will automatically detect the location of your modem.

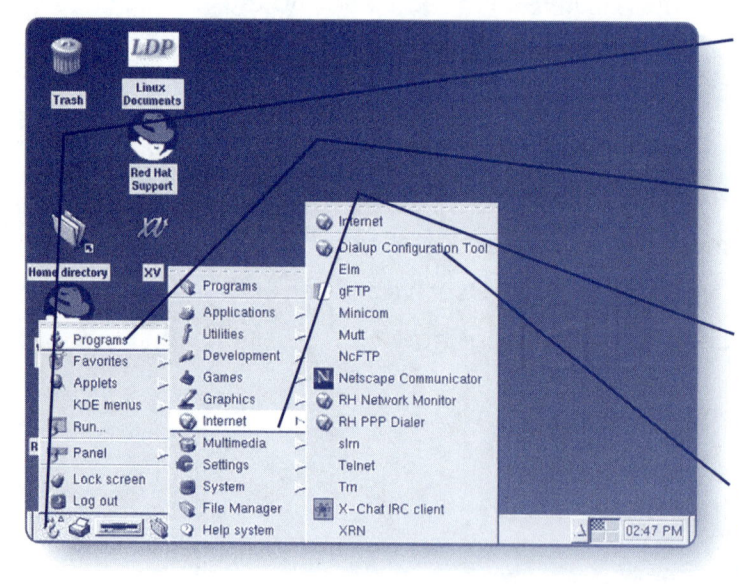

1. Click on the **Main Menu Button**. The Main Menu will appear.

2. Move the **mouse pointer** to the Programs menu. The Programs menu will appear.

3. Move the **mouse pointer** to the Internet menu. The Internet menu will appear.

4. Click on **Dialup Configuration Tool**. The Add New Internet Connection dialog box will open.

CREATING THE CONNECTION

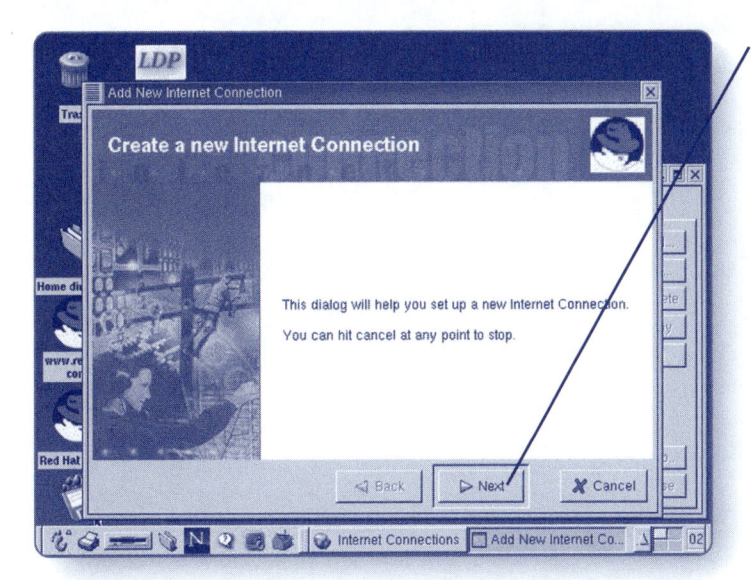

5. Click on **Next.** The Phone Number and Name dialog box will open.

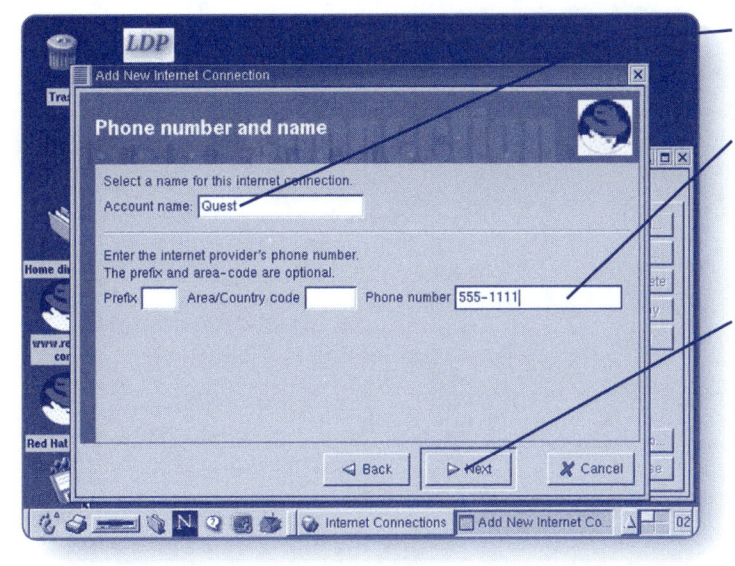

6. Type a **name** for the account in the Account Name field.

7. Type a **phone number** in the Phone Number field. Use the Prefix and Area Code fields if necessary.

8. Click on **Next.** The User Name and Password dialog box will open.

CHAPTER 16: GETTING STARTED WITH LINUX

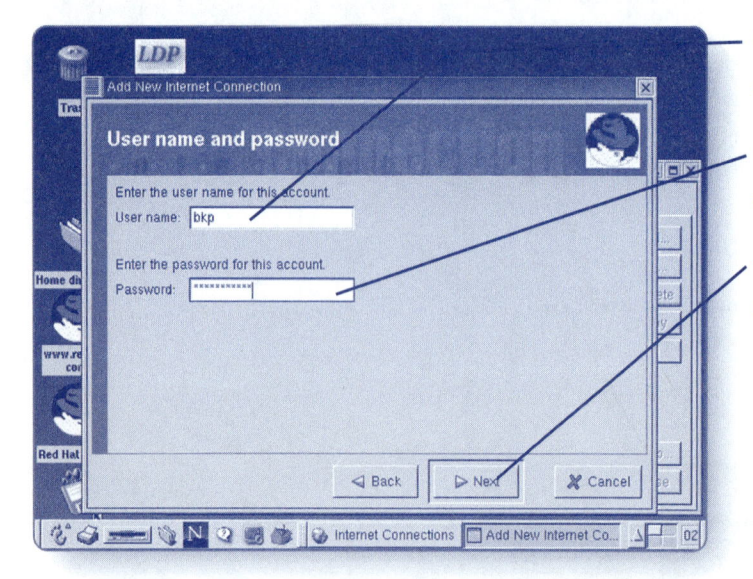

9. Type a **username** for the account in the User Name field.

10. Type the **password** for the account in the Password field.

11. Click on **Next.** The Other Options dialog box will open.

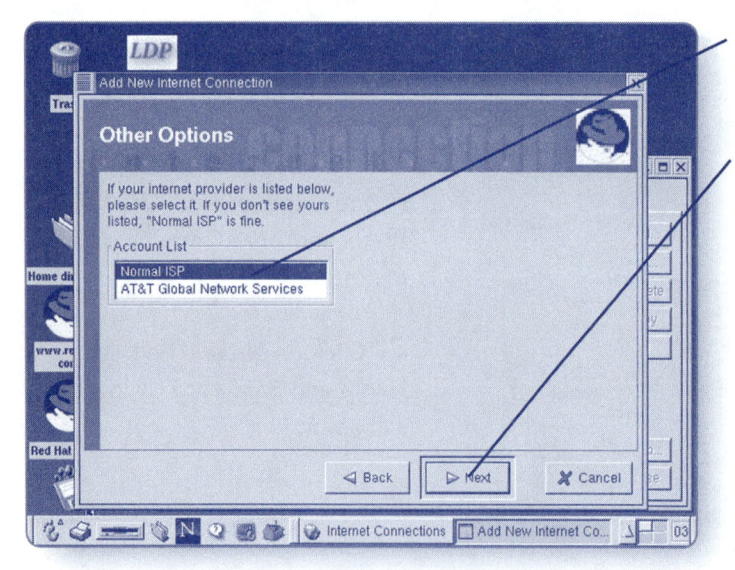

12. Click on your ISP type. The option will be highlighted.

13. Click on **Next.** The Create the Account dialog box will open.

CREATING THE CONNECTION 259

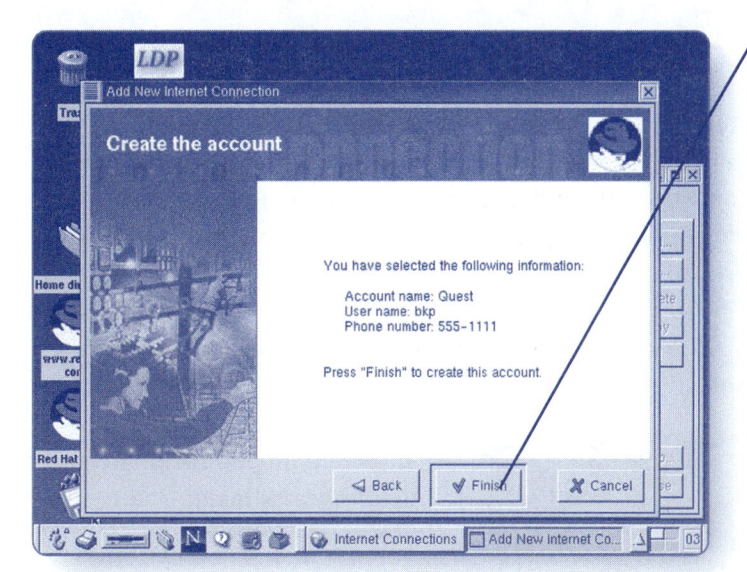

14. Click on **Finish**. The account will be created and the Add New Internet Connection dialog box will close to reveal the Internet Connections window.

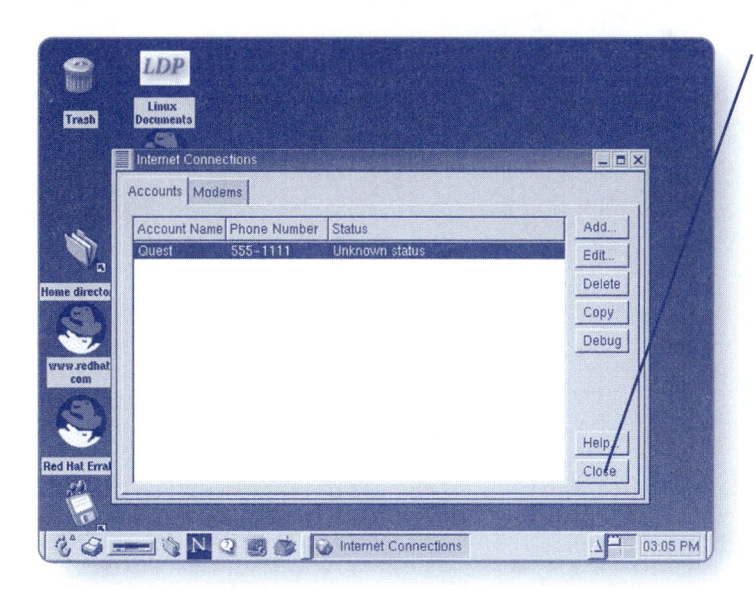

15. Click on **Close**. The Internet Connections window will close.

Connecting to Your ISP

After the dial-up connection has been configured, you can use the PPP Dialer utility to dial up your ISP and make the Internet connection. The PPP Dialer utility is a simple dialer that connects you in just a few short clicks. Remember, if you're using an external modem, make sure the modem is turned on.

1. Click on the **Main Menu button**. The Main Menu will appear.

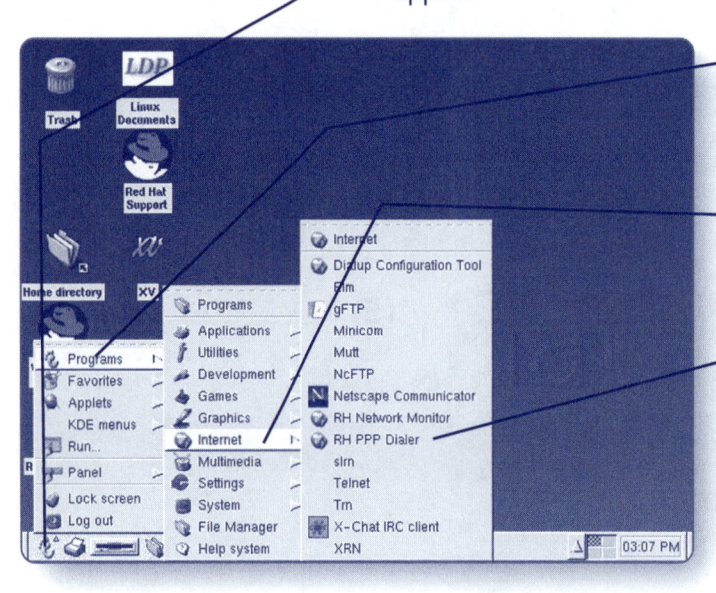

2. Move the **mouse pointer** to the Programs menu. The Programs menu will appear.

3. Move the **mouse pointer** to the Internet menu. The Internet menu will appear.

4. Click on **RH PPP Dialer**. The Choose dialog box will open.

CONNECTING TO YOUR ISP

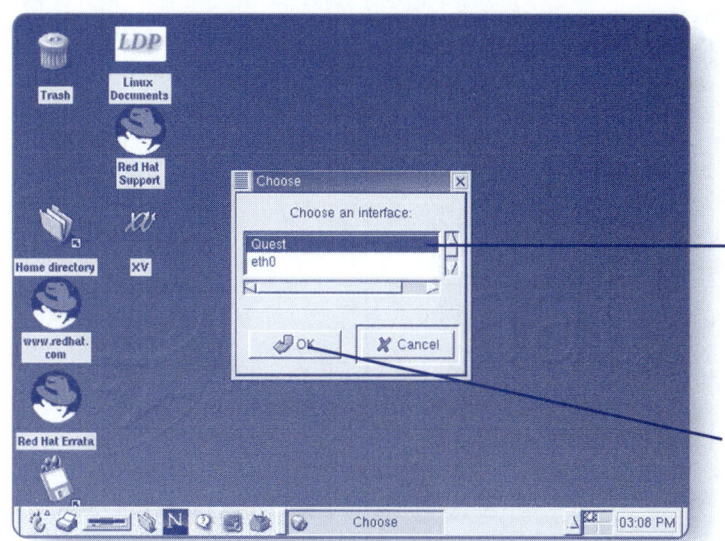

This dialog box shows one dial-up connection, the one we created in the last section. Additional dial-up connections can be added easily.

5. Click on the **dial-up connection** that you want to access. The option will be highlighted.

6. Click on **OK**. The Change Connection Status dialog box will open.

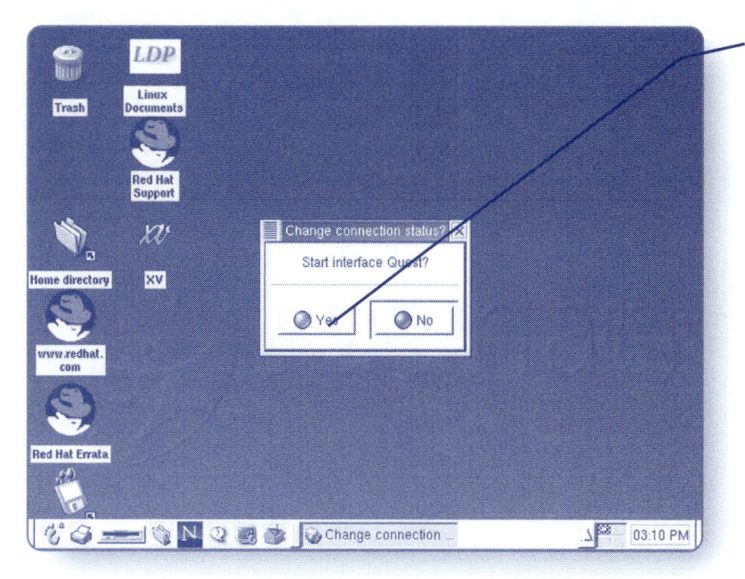

7. Click on **Yes.** The Internet Connection monitor will open.

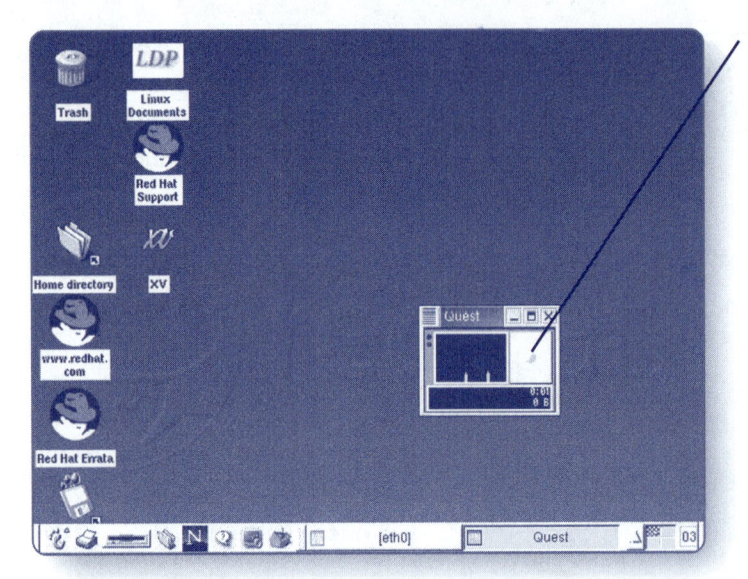

8. Click on the **Disconnect button**. The connection to the Internet will be shut down.

> **TIP**
> If you surf the Net often, you may want to place the RH PPP Dialer utility on the Gnome Panel as a launcher. See Chapter 5, "Managing Your Desktop," for a refresher.

17

Surfing the Web

Now that you've made the connection to your Internet Service Provider (ISP), you'll need a Web browser, e-mail program, and newsgroup reader so you can travel on the Web and stay in contact with other people. You'll find all these capabilities, and more, in Netscape Communicator. If you've used the Windows or Macintosh version of Communicator, you'll feel right at home. For those who have worked with Microsoft Internet Explorer, this chapter can help you make the switch to Navigator. In this chapter, you'll learn how to:

- Use Netscape Navigator to visit Web sites
- Set up Communicator to access e-mail and newsgroups
- Send and receive e-mail
- Browse the newsgroups

Using the Netscape Navigator Web Browser

Netscape Navigator is one of several Linux Web browsers that you can use to surf the Web. If you come from a Windows or Macintosh background, you'll find Navigator to be a familiar face and a quick way to get up and running on the Web. Also, it's easy to find a launcher for Navigator.

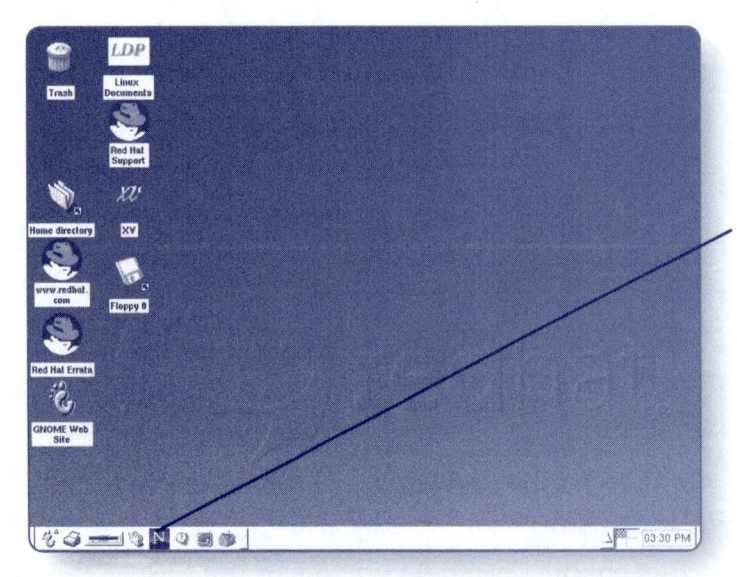

1. Connect to your **ISP**. You can use the RH PPP utility from Chapter 16, "Getting on the Internet".

2. Click on the **Netscape Communicator icon** on the Gnome Panel. The Netscape Navigator Web browser will open.

Accessing Web Pages

Begin by typing a Web address, or URL (Uniform Resourse Locator), into the Location text box. You may know of different addresses that you'd like to try, but if not, try the Prima Tech home page at www.prima-tech.com.

USING THE NETSCAPE NAVIGATOR WEB BROWSER   265

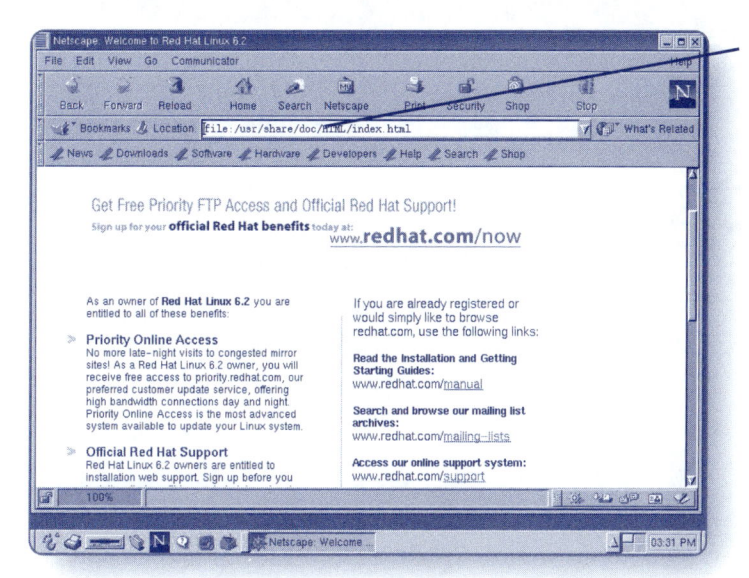

1. Double-click in the **Location box**. The URL that is currently in the Location box will be selected.

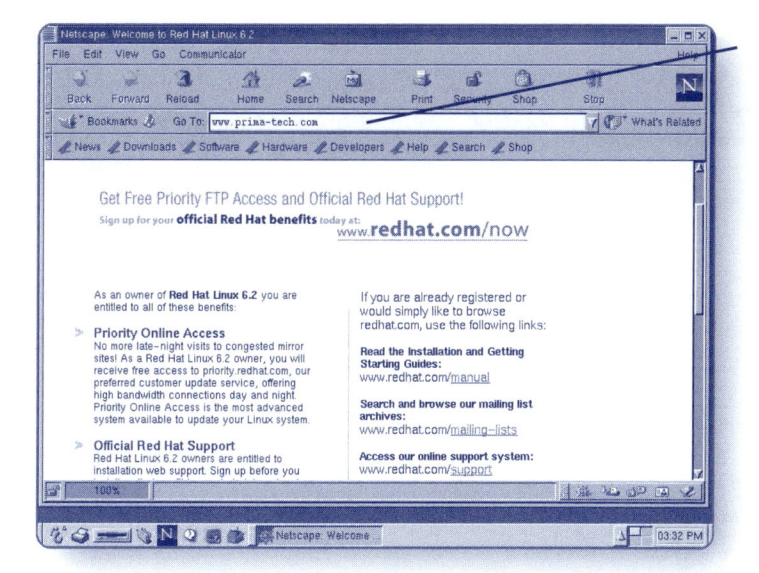

2. Type the **URL** of the Web page you want to visit. The first URL will disappear and the URL you type will display.

3. Press the **Enter key** when you are finished typing the URL. The Web page will open in the browser window.

> **NOTE**
>
> It is not necessary to type the "http://" or "www" part of the address because Navigator will take care of that part for you.

CHAPTER 17: SURFING THE WEB

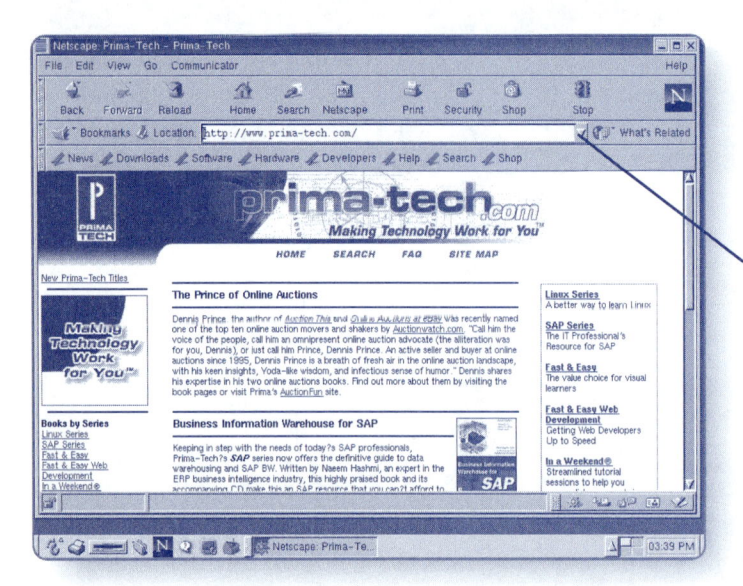

If you've typed Web addresses previously in the Location box, Navigator keeps track of these Web addresses in the Location box drop-down menu.

4. Click on the **down arrow** to the right of the Location box. A list of URLs that you previously typed in the location box will appear.

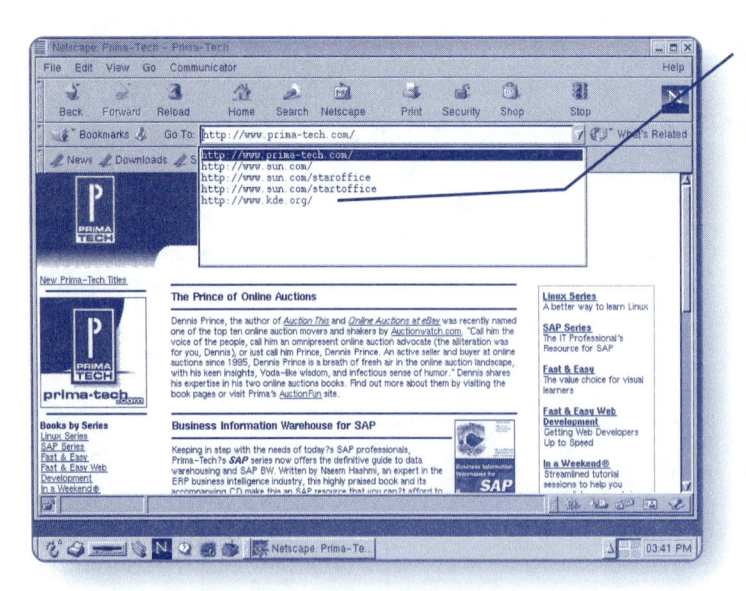

5. Click on a **URL**. The associated Web page will open in the browser window.

TIP

If you're searching for information and a page that you are visiting is close, but not quite what you were looking for, click on the What's Related button. A list of Web sites that are similar to the one currently displayed in the browser window will appear.

Changing Your Home Page

The home page is the first Web page you see when you open the Navigator browser. The first time you use Navigator, Red Hat creates a home page for you. You can change it to something that is more useful or interesting to you.

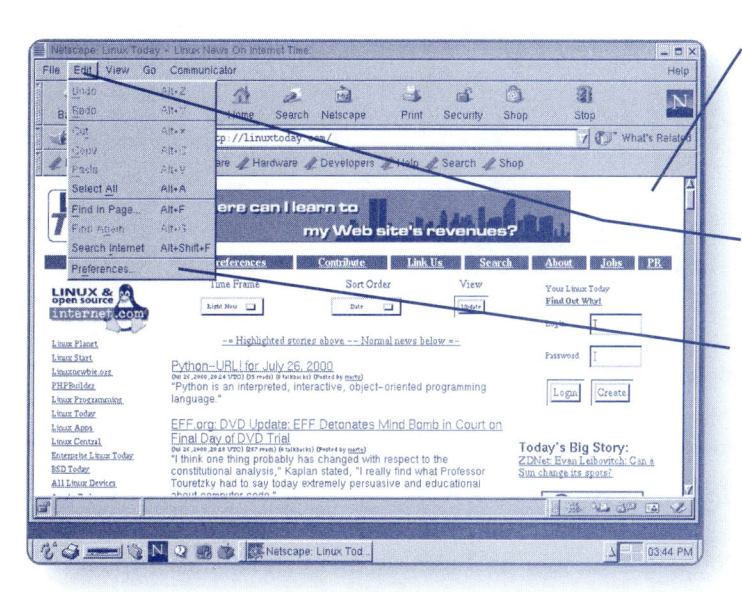

1. Open the **Web page** that you want to use as a home page. The Web page will appear in the browser window.

2. Click on **Edit**. The Edit menu will appear.

3. Click on **Preferences**. The Preferences dialog box will open.

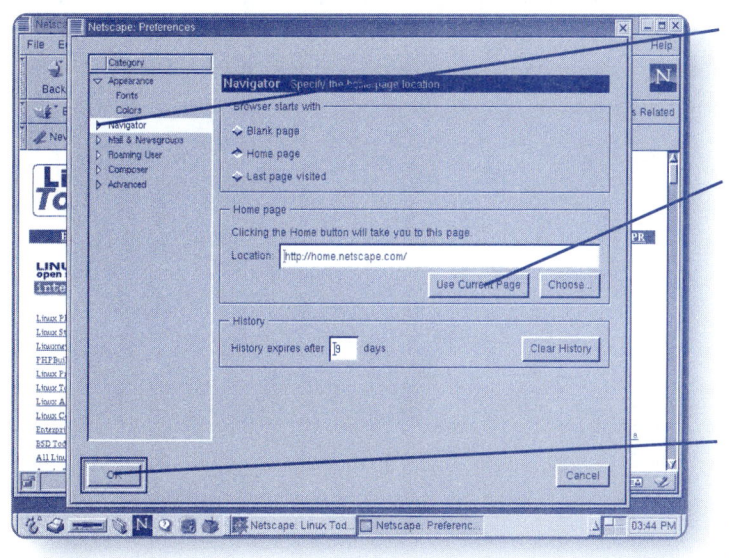

4. Click on the **Navigator category**. The Specify the home page location pane will open.

5. Click on the **Use Current Page button**. The URL in the Location text box will change to match the URL of the page displayed in the browser window.

6. Click on **OK**. The Preferences dialog box will close and you'll return to the browser window.

> **NOTE**
>
> When you're cruising around the Web, you can return to your home page easily with just a click of the Home button. Your default home page will open in the browser window.

Keeping a List of Frequently Visited Web Sites

If you visit a number of Web sites on a regular basis, you'll want to keep a list of those sites for future references. A tool called Bookmarks will keep all the Web pages organized in one convenient place. If you don't want one big list of bookmarks, you can create folders in which to file the bookmarks.

USING THE NETSCAPE NAVIGATOR WEB BROWSER   269

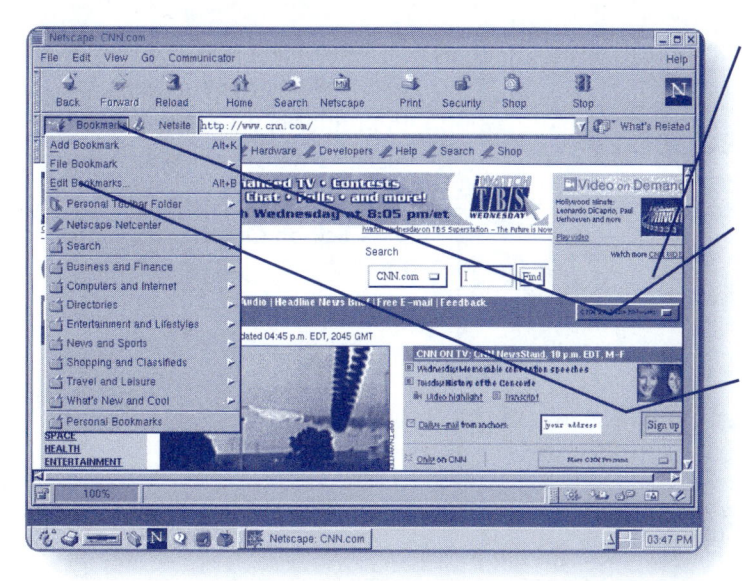

1. Open the **Web page** that you want to add to the Bookmarks list. The Web page will open in the browser window.

2. Click on the **Bookmarks button**. The Bookmarks menu will appear.

3. Click on **Edit Bookmarks**. The Communicator Bookmarks for [username] account dialog box will open.

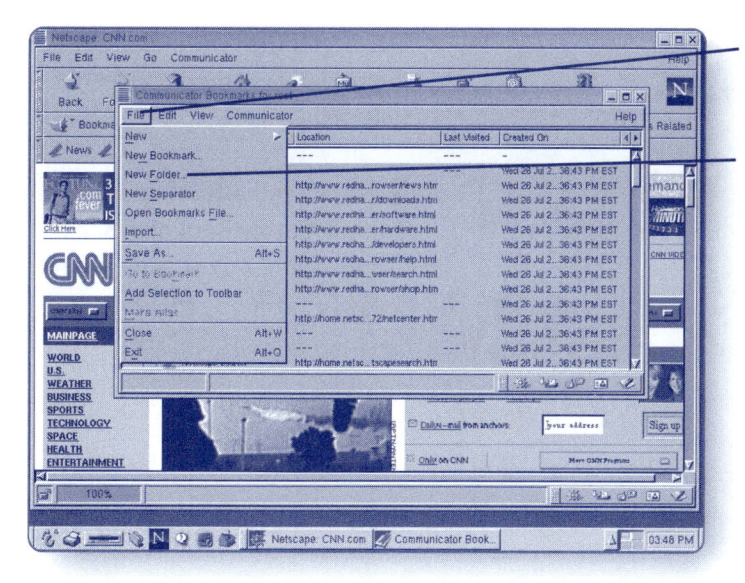

4. Click on **File**. The File menu will appear.

5. Click on **New Folder**. The Bookmark Properties dialog box will open.

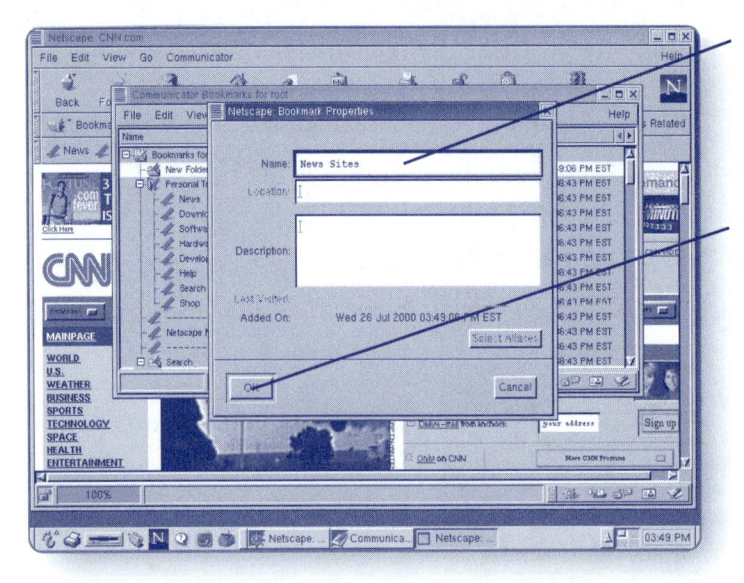

6. Select the **text** in the Name text box and **type** a **name** for the folder in which you want to place some of your bookmarks.

7. Click on **OK**. The folder will be created.

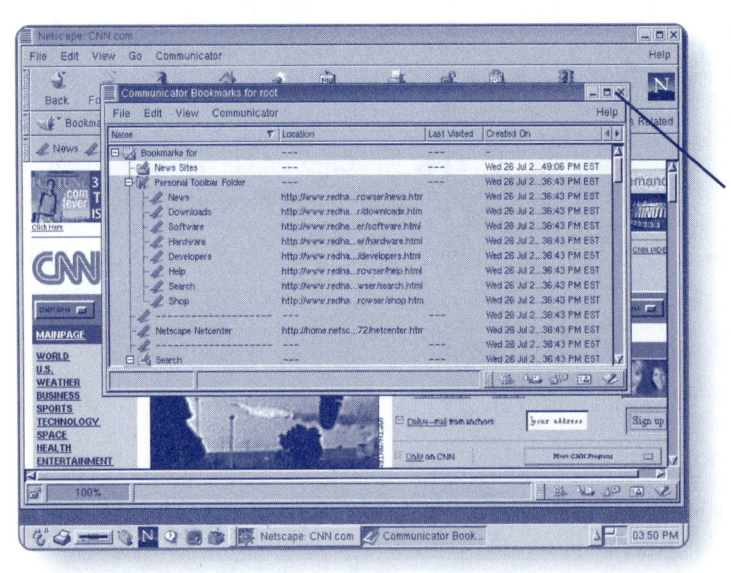

The new folder will appear in the bookmarks menu and will be selected.

8. Click on the **Kill button**. The Communicator Bookmarks dialog box will close and you're ready to file a bookmark into the folder.

USING THE NETSCAPE NAVIGATOR WEB BROWSER 271

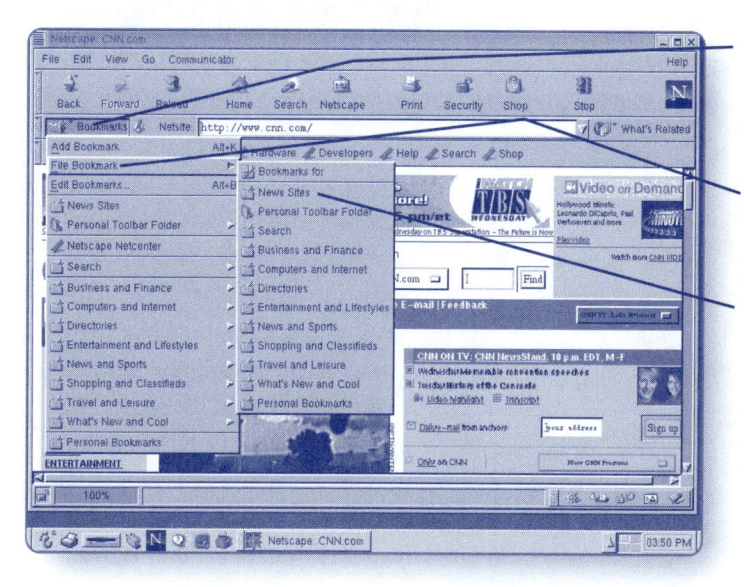

9. Click on the **Bookmarks button**. The Bookmarks menu will appear.

10. Click on **File Bookmark**. A second menu will appear.

11. Click on the **folder** into which you want to place the bookmark. The bookmark will be stored in the selected folder.

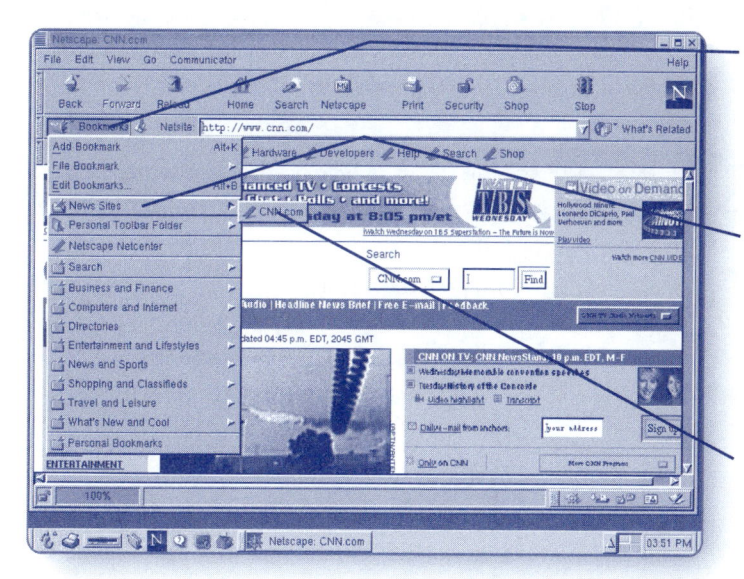

12. Click on the **Bookmarks button** to access a bookmark. The Bookmarks menu will appear.

13. Click on the **folder** that contains the bookmark that you want to view. A list of the Web sites contained in the folder will appear.

14. Click on the **Web site**. The Web site will open in the browser window.

Setting Up E-mail and News Accounts

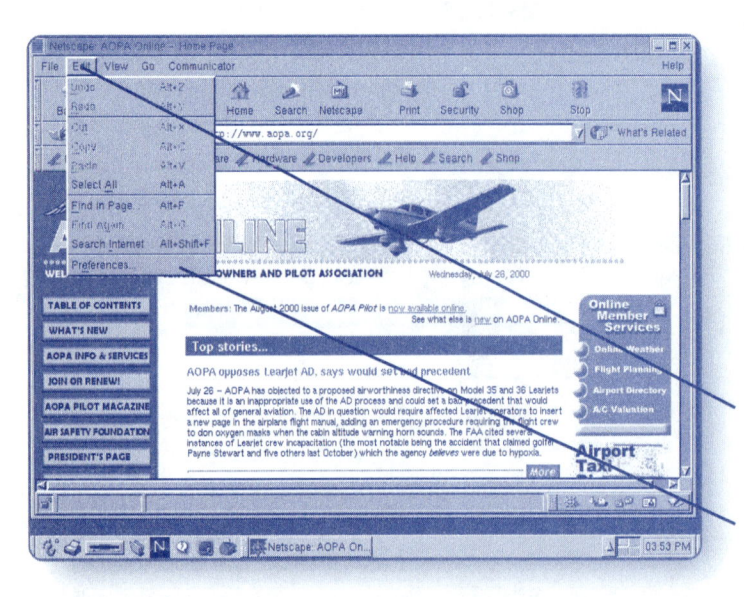

When you set up your Internet account, the ISP assigned you a username and password to access their service. They should have also given you a mail server and news server address. You'll need these when you set up Communicator to work with e-mail and newsgroups.

1. Click on **Edit**. The Edit menu will appear.

2. Click on **Preferences**. The Preferences dialog box will open.

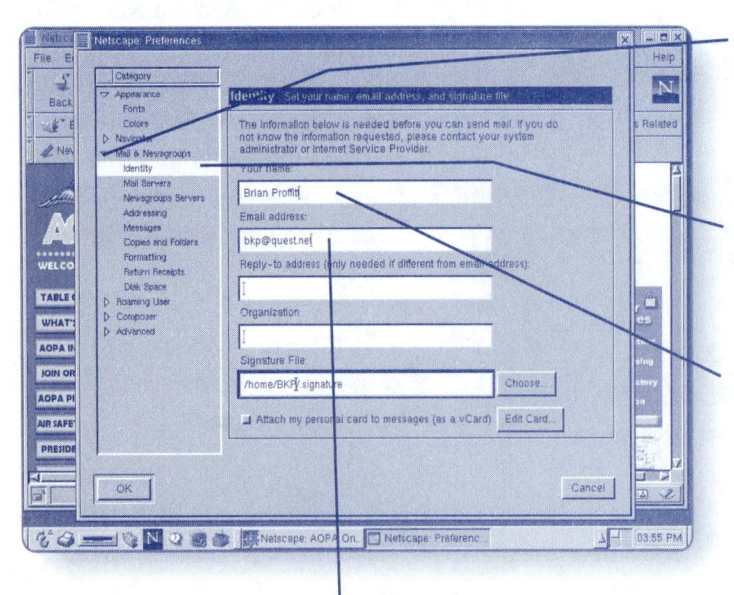

3. Click on the **arrow** next to the Mail & Newsgroups category. The category list will expand.

4. Click on the **Identity subcategory**. The Identity pane will open.

5. Select the **text** in the Your name text box and **type** your **name**. What you type in this box is what will appear in the header information for all your outgoing messages.

6. Select the **text** in the Email address text box and **type** your **e-mail address**.

SETTING UP E-MAIL AND NEWS ACCOUNTS

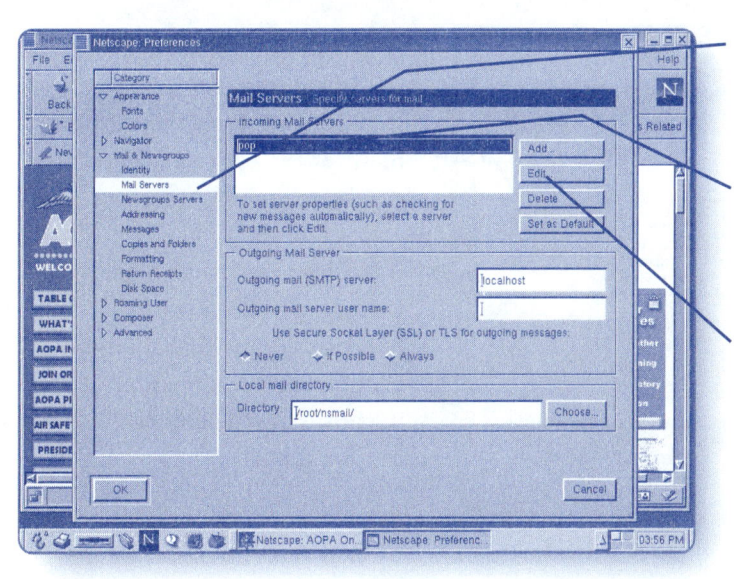

7. Click on the **Mail Servers subcategory**. The Mail Servers pane will appear.

8. Click on the **server** listed in the Incoming Mail Servers list box. The server will be selected.

9. Click on the **Edit button**. The Netscape dialog box will open.

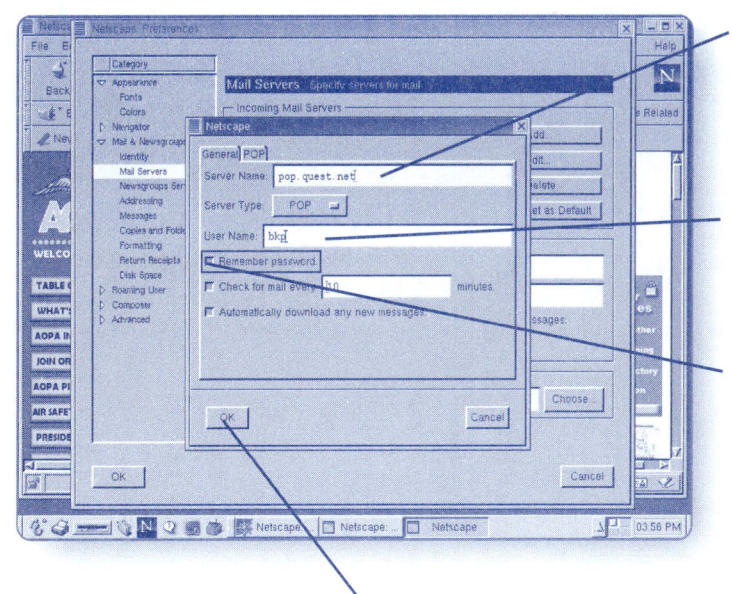

10. Select the **text** in the Server Name text box and **type** the **mail server address** given to you by your ISP.

11. Click in the **User Name text box** and **type** the **user ID** assigned to you by your ISP.

12. Click on the **check button** next to Remember password if you want Communicator to remember your password. The option will be selected.

13. Click on **OK**. You will return to the Preferences dialog box.

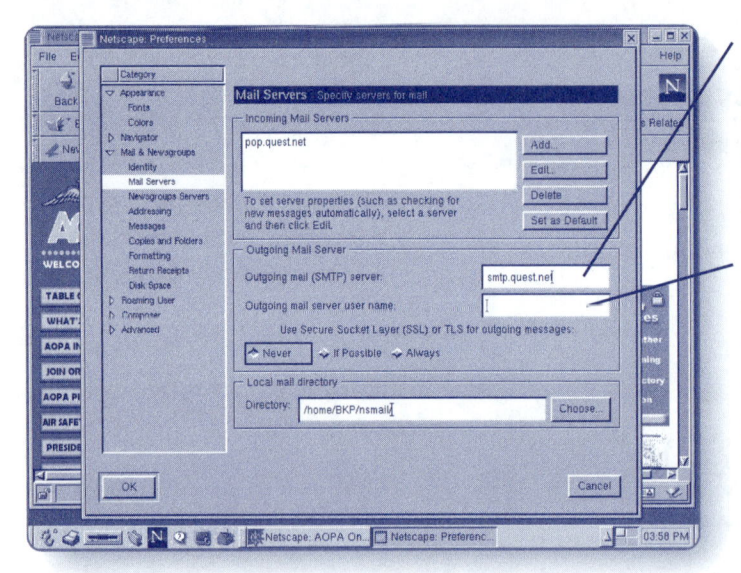

14. Select the **text** in the Outgoing mail (SMTP) server text box and **type** the **outgoing mail server address** given to you by your ISP.

15. Type the **user name** in the Outgoing mail server user name text box if your ISP requires a username for verification purposes when sending outgoing mail.

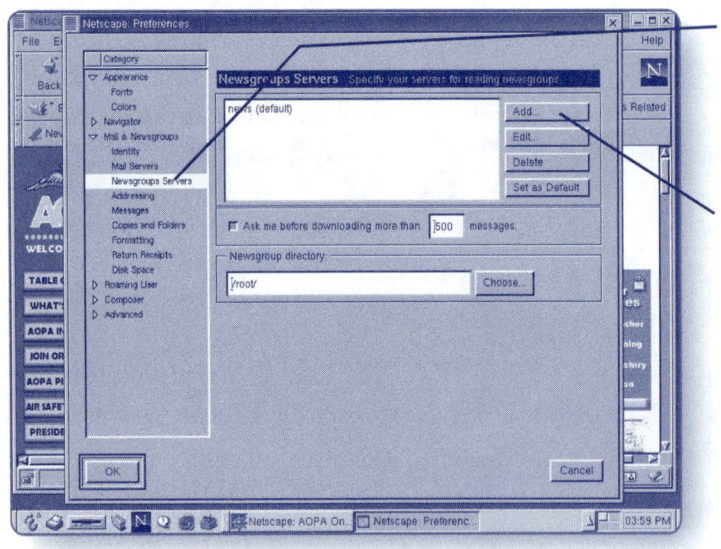

16. Click on the **Newsgroups Servers subcategory**. The Newsgroups Servers pane will open.

17. Click on the **Add button**. The Netscape dialog box will open.

SETTING UP E-MAIL AND NEWS ACCOUNTS

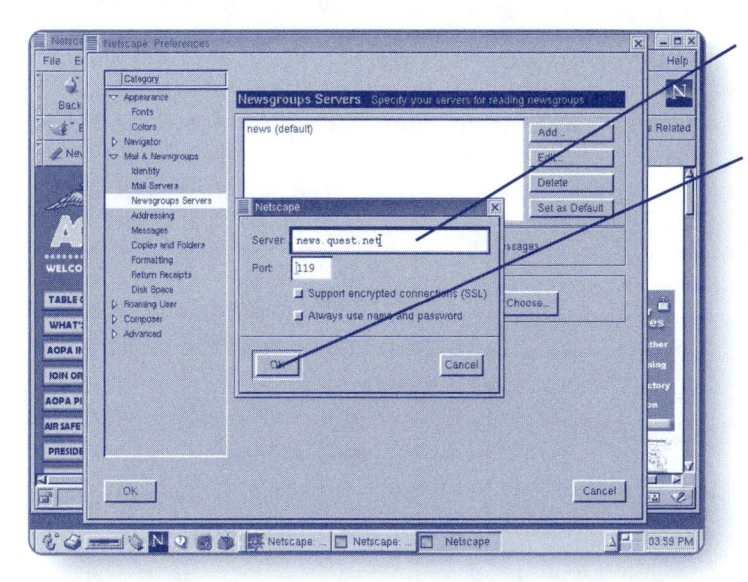

18. Type the **news server name** in the Server text box.

19. Click on **OK**. The news server will be added to the list of servers.

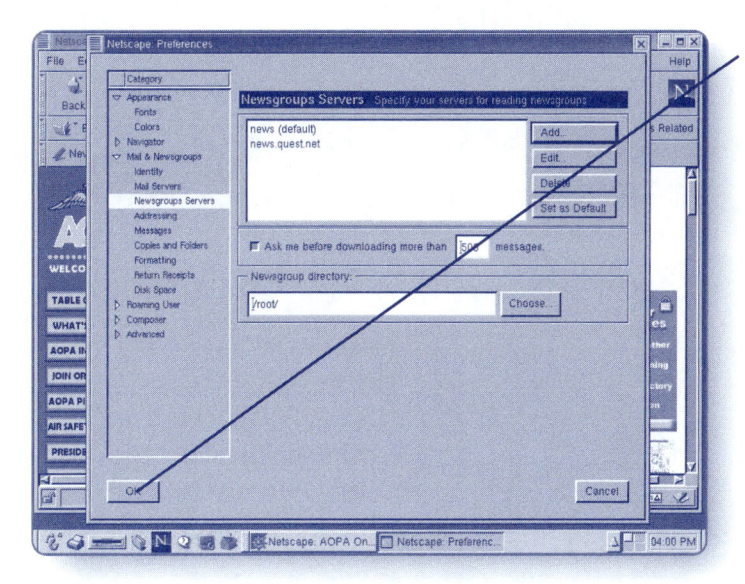

20. Click on **OK**. You're now ready to send and receive e-mail and browse through the newsgroups.

Managing E-mail

Now that you have Communicator set up for e-mail and news, it's time to go online and check to see if you have any messages waiting for you. Before you begin, you'll need to open Netscape Messenger.

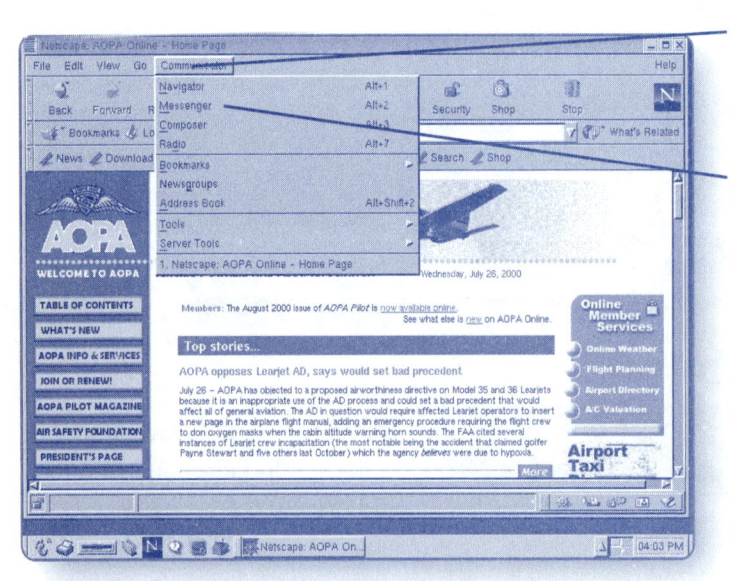

1. Click on **Communicator**. The Communicator menu will appear.

2. Click on **Messenger**. The Netscape Mail & Newsgroups window will open.

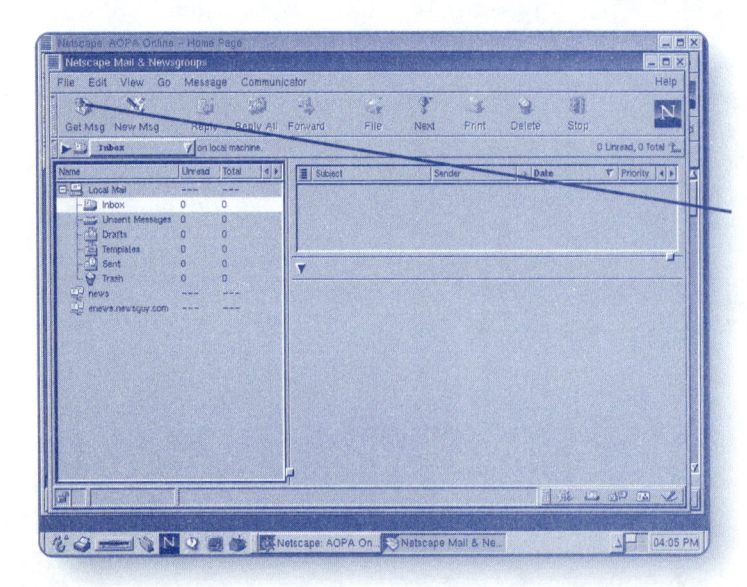

Receiving Messages

In just one click, all your e-mail will be delivered to you.

1. Click on the **Get Msg button**. A Password dialog box will open.

MANAGING E-MAIL

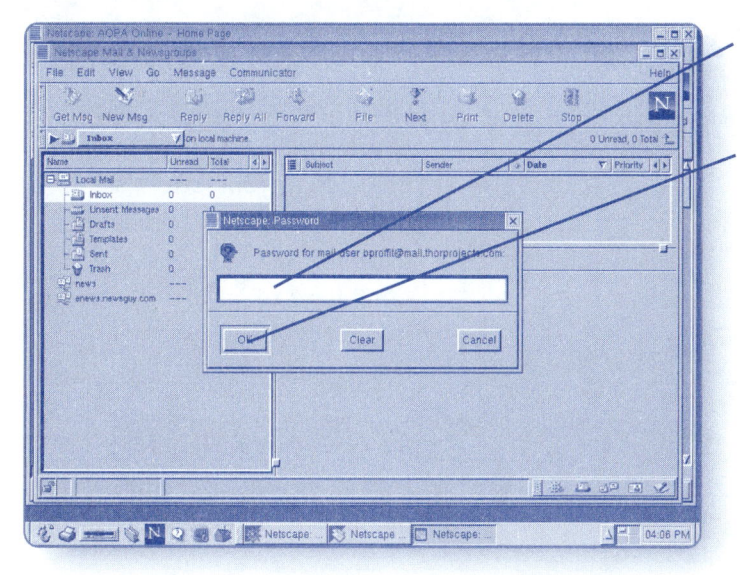

2. Type the **password** assigned to you by your ISP.

3. Click on **OK**. A download dialog box will open and any new messages will be downloaded.

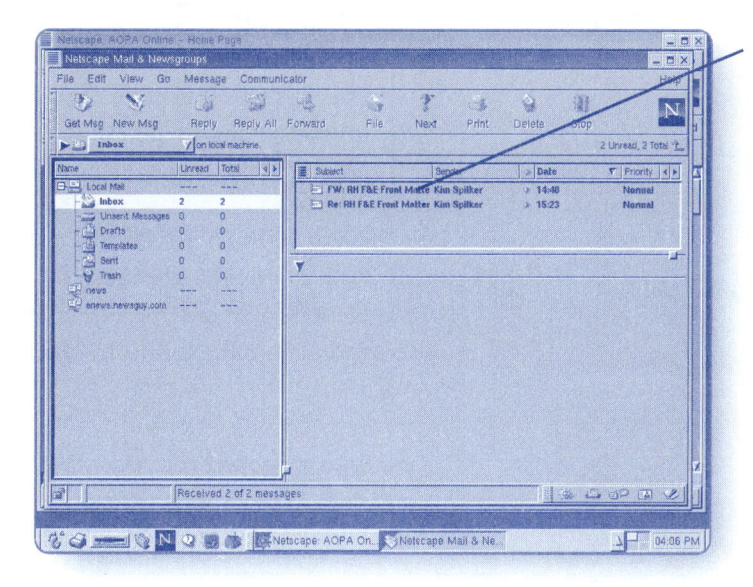

4. Click on the **message** that you want to read. The body of the message will appear.

5. Read through the **message** and decide what action to take.

> **NOTE**
> If it's junk mail, click on the Delete button.

Sending Messages

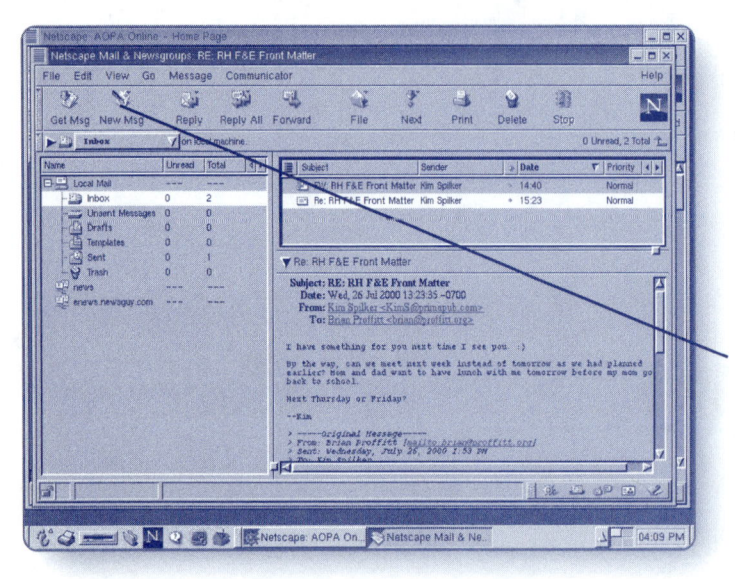

Gone are the days of stamps, envelopes, and trips to the post office. Now your letters are delivered to their recipient in a matter of seconds, and you don't have to make a special trip into town to replenish your stamp supply.

1. Click on the **New Msg button**. A Compose window will appear.

> **NOTE**
> If you want to reply to a message, select the message and then click on the Reply button.

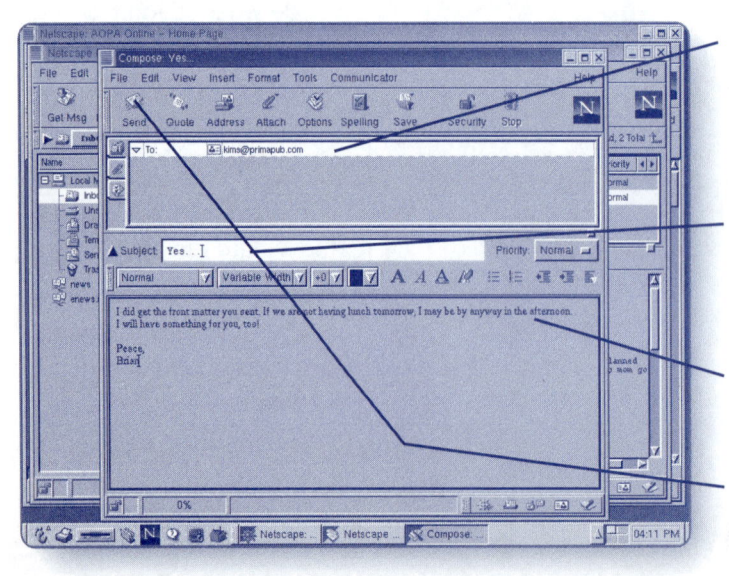

2. Type the **e-mail address** of the person to whom you want to send a message in the To text box.

3. Type a **subject** for your message in the Subject text area.

4. Type your **message** in the message pane.

5. Click on the **Send button**. Your message will be off to its intended recipient.

Lurking through the Newsgroups

Finding and joining one of the news bulletin board discussion groups on your favorite subject is easier than you think. With thousands of groups from which to choose, there's something in the newsgroups for everyone. If you want to learn more about computers, check out the myriad of computer-related newsgroups. You can usually find someone willing to help you solve a problem, answer a question about how to use a software program, or discuss the future of computers.

Subscribing to Newsgroups

Before you can participate in newsgroup discussions, you'll need to make the newsgroup messages easy to view and readily available. You can do this by subscribing to the various newsgroups that interest you.

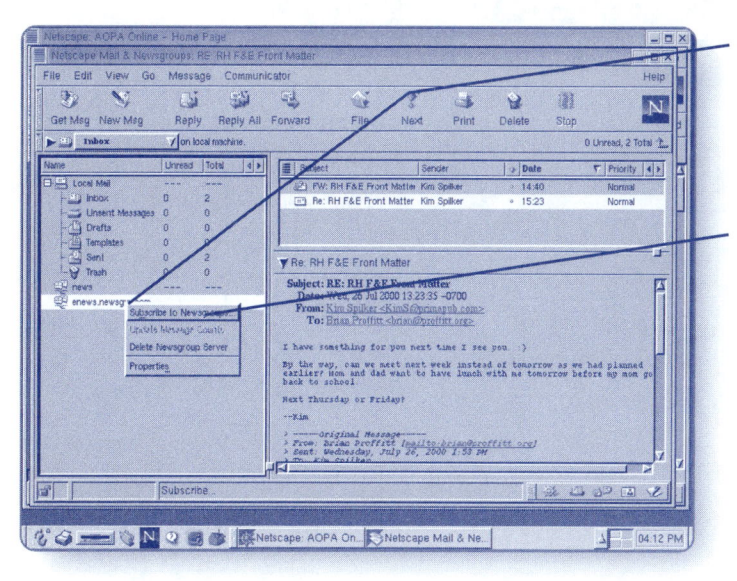

1. Right-click on the **news server** from which you want to download a list of newsgroups. A menu will appear.

2. Click on **Subscribe to Newsgroups**. The Netscape dialog box will open and the list of newsgroups will begin downloading from the server. This may take a while, depending on how many newsgroups are supplied by the news server. When the download has finished, the list of newsgroups will appear.

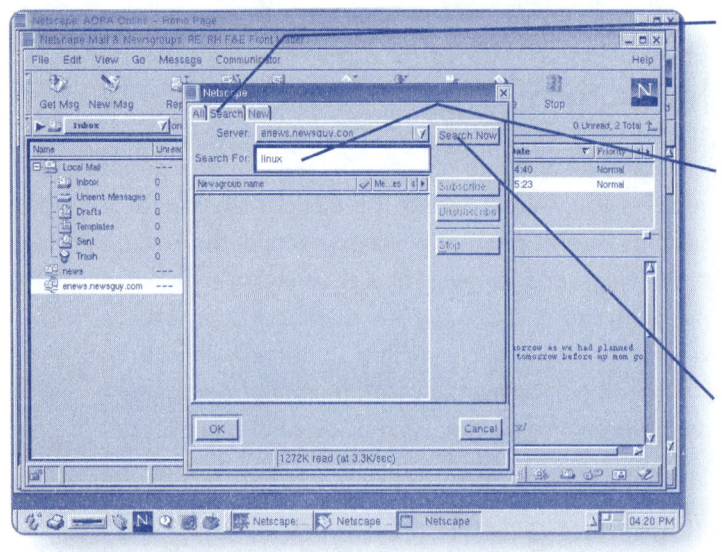

3. Click on the **Search tab**. The Search tab will come to the top of the stack.

4. Type a **keyword** that describes the type of newsgroups in which you're interested into the Search For text box.

5. Click on the **Search Now button**. Newsgroups that contain matching words will appear in the Newsgroup name list.

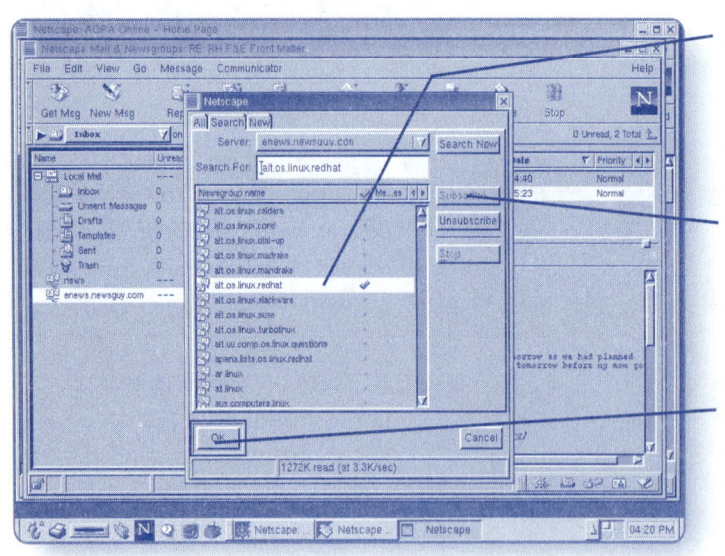

6. Click on the **newsgroup** to which you want to subscribe. The newsgroup will be highlighted.

7. Click on the **Subscribe button**. A check mark will appear to the right of the newsgroup name.

8. Click on **OK**. The newsgroup will appear under the news server in the Netscape Mail & Newsgroups window.

Reading Newsgroup Messages

To read the messages in the group(s) to which you have subscribed, follow these steps.

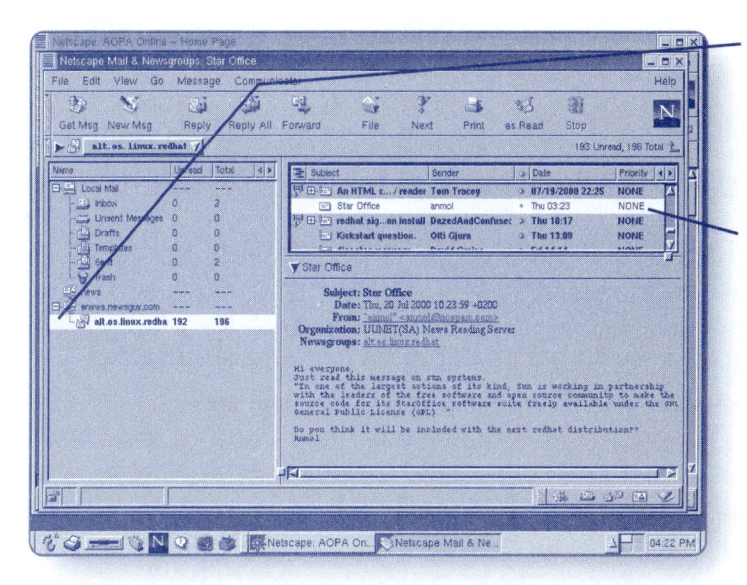

1. Click on the **name** of a subscribed newsgroup. The newsgroup headers will start downloading to your computer.

2. Click on the **newsgroup message** that you want to read. The message will open in the preview pane.

Part IV Review Questions

1. How do you check to see if an application is installed correctly? *See "Verifying Installed Packages" in Chapter 15*

2. Where is one place that you can find applications to install on your Linux? *See "Installing a Package" in Chapter 15*

3. How do you install applications found on the Internet? *See "Installing a Package" in Chapter 15*

4. Which user on the Linux system has the ability to create an Internet connection? *See "Creating the Connection" in Chapter 16*

5. What tool makes Internet configuration easy? *See "Creating the Connection" in Chapter 16*

6. What is the easiest dialer you can use to connect to your ISP? *See "Connecting to Your ISP" in Chapter 16*

7. How can you keep a list of Web sites that you visit frequently? *See "Using the Netscape Navigator Web Browser" in Chapter 17*

8. What information do you need from your ISP in order to set up your mail and news accounts? *See "Setting Up E-mail and News Accounts" in Chapter 17*

9. How do you send an e-mail message? *See "Managing E-mail" in Chapter 17*

10. How do you read newsgroup messages? *See "Lurking Through the Newsgroups" in Chapter 17*

PART V

Appendix

Appendix A
 Installing Linux 285

A
Installing Linux

Over the many Linux distributions since its beginning, much effort has been made to simplify the installation process. In the past, the long and involved installation process was a barrier that kept many people from installing and experimenting with Linux. Things are much better now and even somewhat automated, which takes a lot of the difficulty out of the task. However, even with an improved installation, you should still take the time to understand your computer's configuration and gain a little knowledge of what will happen during a Linux installation. Please read all the documentation before you begin. This appendix will show you how to perform the easiest Linux installation—running Linux as the sole operating system on your computer. In this appendix, you'll learn how to:

- Determine which installation method you want
- Prepare for the installation process
- Install the Red Hat Linux operating system

Understanding Your Installation Options

Linux is a very flexible operating system that can be easily modeled to meet your specific needs. Choices made during the installation process guide the setup program in selecting which software to load and configure. The installation process is enhanced by Linux's ability to probe your computer and provide answers to some of its own questions. Many of the choices you need to make are highlighted for you as you progress through the installation.

Another way in which the installation process has been simplified is the introduction of installation classes. You have three choices for the type of installation you can perform.

- The Workstation option is for those who are new to Linux and want an easy and automated installation. You'll also want to use this option if you are planning to use your Linux computer as a stand-alone workspace or as a workstation connected to a network.
- If you'll be using your Linux computer to run your network, you'll want to choose the Server option.
- If your requirements for the operation of your Linux computer do not really fit either of these two options, you may elect to install Linux by using the Custom option. You should be knowledgeable about your needs and have some experience configuring operating systems to use this option.

It should be noted that this appendix shows you a simple, stand-alone, Workstation installation with Red Hat Linux 7 as the *only operating system*. If you have an old computer that doesn't seem to be performing well, this is a great opportunity to try out Linux and add some useful life to an older computer.

> **TIP**
>
> If you want to run multiple operating systems on one computer, you will need to prepare a new partition for Linux on your current hard drive. A partition is a section of hard drive reserved for one particular file system. Since Windows and Linux use different file systems, they each need their own partition. You can switch between Linux and another operating system by using the Linux loader utility called LILO, which is a graphic screen that pops up when your PC first boots.
>
> Because of the complexity of a dual-boot installation, I recommend you pick up *Install, Configure, and Customize Red Hat Linux 7* (Prima, 2000).

Getting Ready

Before you begin, take time to plan and organize your Linux installation. If you come from a Windows or Mac background, you'll find a significant, but not insurmountable, learning curve ahead of you. But you'll also find that Linux has enormous potential. Please make sure that you understand the installation process and your computer's configuration before you begin. Read the Installation and Getting Ready manuals provided by Red Hat. Hit the Web and read through the Linux newsgroups, go to Red Hat's Web site and look at all of the resources available there. (www.redhat.com)

You may want to think about keeping a Linux journal. Find a notebook or ring binder in which you can keep notes. Record everything you can about your computer's configuration. Write down the steps you followed during the Linux installation. Keep up with your Linux journal even after the installation. Keep notes about changes you made to the system, peripherals attached to the system, user accounts, problems you encounter, and any solutions.

Determining Your System Devices

To help Linux configure itself properly, and to help you avoid surprises, you need to collect some basic information about the hardware installed on your computer.

The main reason for this is that unlike Microsoft Windows, Linux is not widely supported by the manufacturers of hardware. Support for hardware comes instead from dedicated Linux users and programmers who are churning out hardware drivers for Linux every day.

The information you require may be found in the manuals that came with the computer or with the particular peripheral. It can also be obtained from the manufacturer or vendor. Or, if you have Microsoft Windows 95 or later on your computer, you can look in the System Properties. And, remember, this is good stuff to keep in your Linux journal.

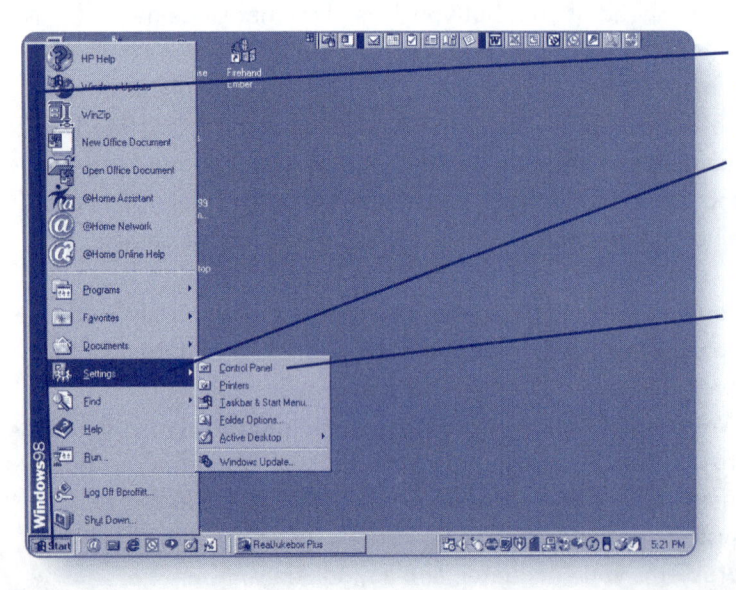

1. In Windows 95/98, **Click** on **Start**. The Start menu will appear.

2. Move the **mouse pointer** to Settings. The Settings menu will appear.

3. Click on **Control Panel**. The Control Panel will appear.

DETERMINING YOUR SYSTEM DEVICES 289

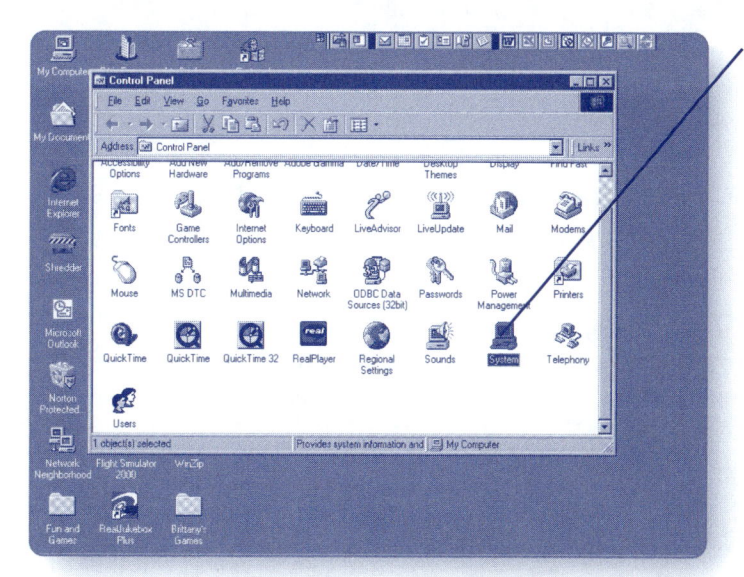

4. Double-click on the **System icon**. The System Properties dialog box will open.

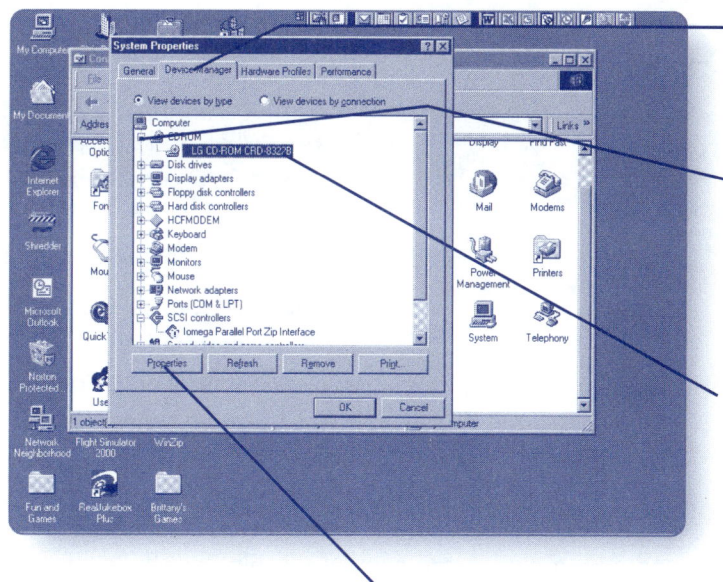

5. Click on the **Device Manager tab**. The Device Manager tab will come to the top of the stack.

6. Click the **Plus sign** next to a device. The device type will expand to show the devices of that type that are installed on your computer.

7. Click on the **device** about which you need hardware information. The device will be selected.

8. Click on the **Properties button**. The Properties dialog box for the selected device will open.

APPENDIX A: INSTALLING LINUX

You'll need to know certain information about a number of devices. Write down the following information for each device:

- **CD-ROM drives**. Write down the interface type (IDE, SCSI, or other) and be sure and write down the manufacturer and model number of any in the 'other' category.

- **Display adapter**. You'll need the make and model and how much memory it has (most display adapters are auto-detected).

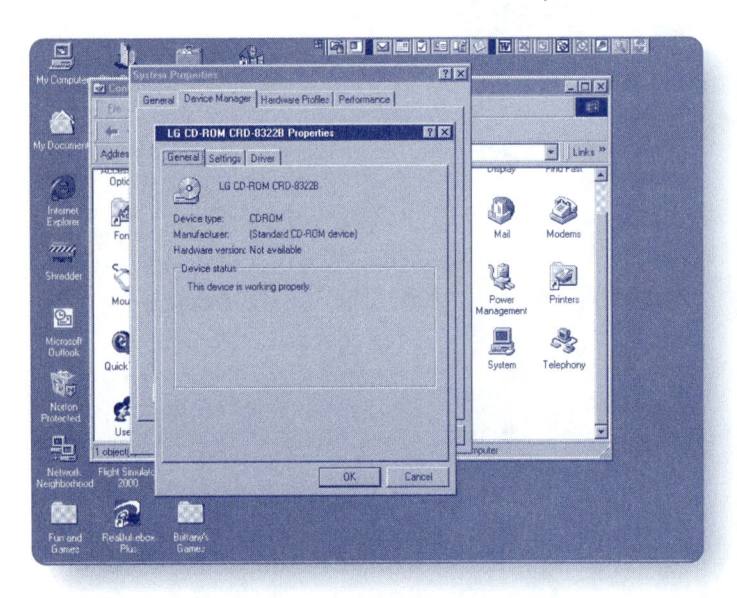

- **Hard drives**. Write down the number of hard disk drives, how they are numbered, what size they are, and whether the drives are IDE or SCSI.

- **Modem**. Take down the make and model number, speed, and communications port (COM port).

- **Mouse**. What kind of mouse is yours: A PS-2 compatible one or a serial mouse, with one, two, or three buttons?

- **Network adapters**. You will need the information about your card's make and model if you are to be connected to a network.

- **SCSI controllers**. Jot down the make and model numbers.

- **Sound, video, and game controllers**. Find out the names of the manufacturers and the model numbers.

- **Monitor**. You should know your monitor's make and model number and the vertical and horizontal refresh rate parameters.

Now that you have all this information, you need to check your computer hardware with the Red Hat Linux Hardware Compatibility List. You can find it on the Web at www.redhat.com/corp/support/hardware/index.html. If you have incompatible hardware, try to determine how this will affect the installation before you begin. You'll find very few internal modems that are compatible, because of their proprietary Windows drivers.

Loading the Linux Operating System

Now's the moment you've been waiting for. You've read all the documentation, learned everything you can about your computer and peripherals, and prepared a hard drive just for the Linux installation. It's time to grab that CD and get the show on the road.

> **NOTE**
> The installation shown in this appendix is the text installation of Red Hat 7. It is similar to the Anaconda graphical installation, only not as pretty. Use this installation if your video card or monitor initially has trouble displaying the graphical installation.

APPENDIX A: INSTALLING LINUX

1. Insert the **Red Hat Linux 7 CD-ROM number 1** into your computer's CD-ROM drive.

2. Turn off the **power** to your computer, wait a few seconds, and then **turn on** the **power**. Your computer will restart and the Welcome screen will appear.

> **CAUTION**
> If your computer is already running Windows or another operating system, be sure to follow proper shutdown procedures.

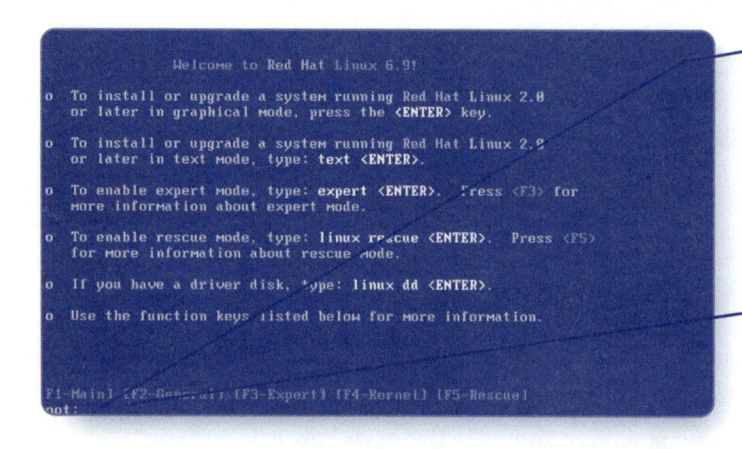

3a. Press the **Enter key**. The Language Selection screen will appear in the graphical installation.

or

3b. Type text and **press** the **Enter key**. The Language Selection screen will appear in the text installation.

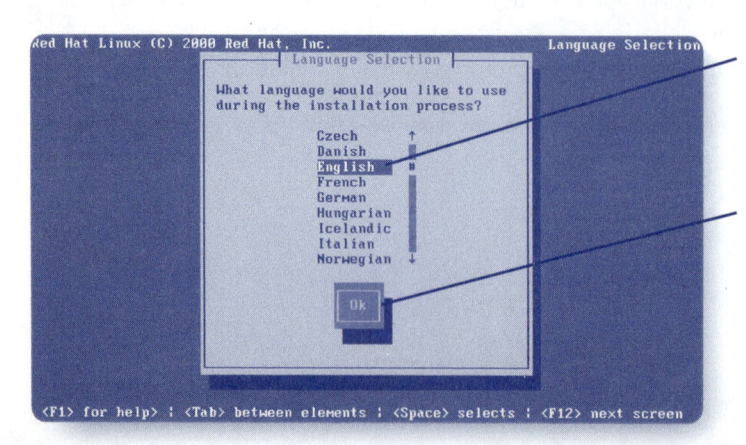

4. Press the **arrow keys** to select a preferred language. The default is English.

5. Press the **Enter key**. The Keyboard Selection screen will appear.

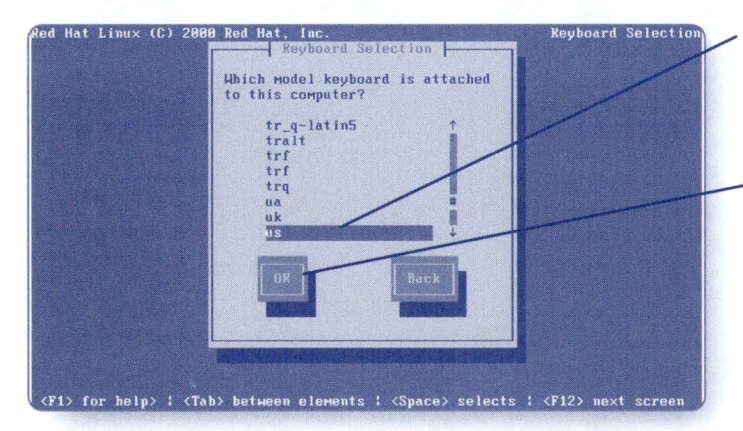

LOADING THE LINUX OPERATING SYSTEM 293

6. Press the **arrow keys** to select the keyboard model. The default is us.

7. Press the **Enter key**. The Red Hat Welcome screen will appear.

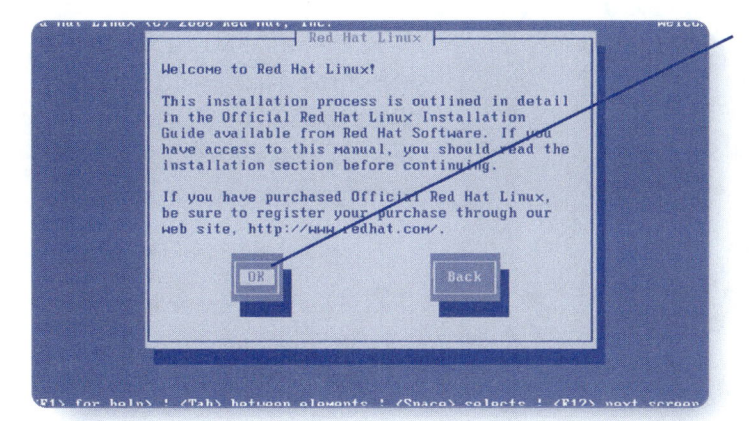

8. Press the **Enter key**. The Installation Type screen will appear.

APPENDIX A: INSTALLING LINUX

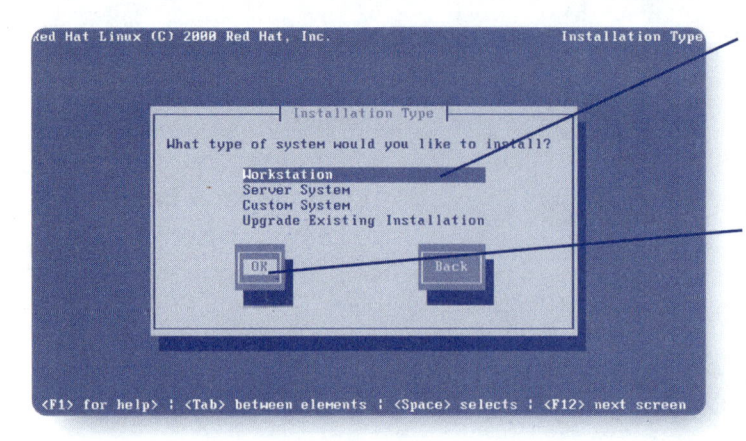

9. Press the **arrow keys** to select the installation type. The recommended option is Workstation.

10. Press the **Enter key**. The Automatic Partitioning screen will appear.

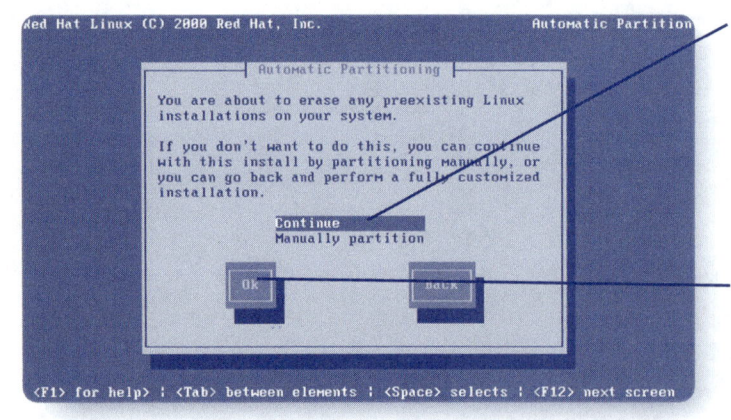

11. Press the **arrow keys** to select the partitioning option. Since this will be a single-operating system PC, the recommended option is Continue.

12. Press the **Enter key**. The Mouse Selection screen will appear.

> **NOTE**
> If you do want to share Windows and Linux on the same PC, then you should choose the manual install option.

LOADING THE LINUX OPERATING SYSTEM   295

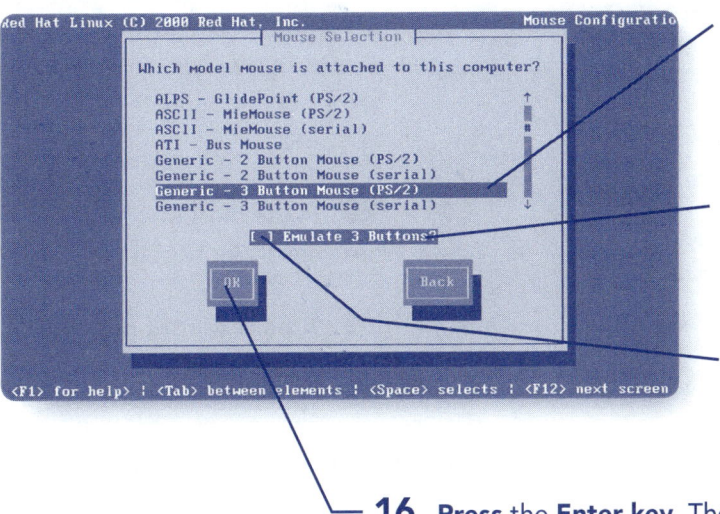

13. Press the **arrow keys** to select the mouse type. The recommended option is one of the Generic options.

14. Press the **Tab key**. The Emulate 3 buttons option will be highlighted.

15. Press the **Spacebar**. The Emulate 3 buttons option will be selected.

16. Press the **Enter key**. The Time Zone Selection screen will appear.

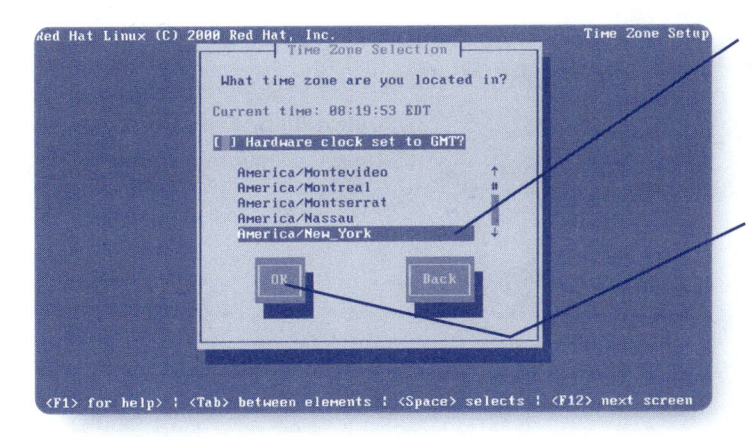

17. Press the **arrow keys** to select the time zone. The zones are oriented to major world cities.

18. Press the **Enter key**. The Root Password screen will appear.

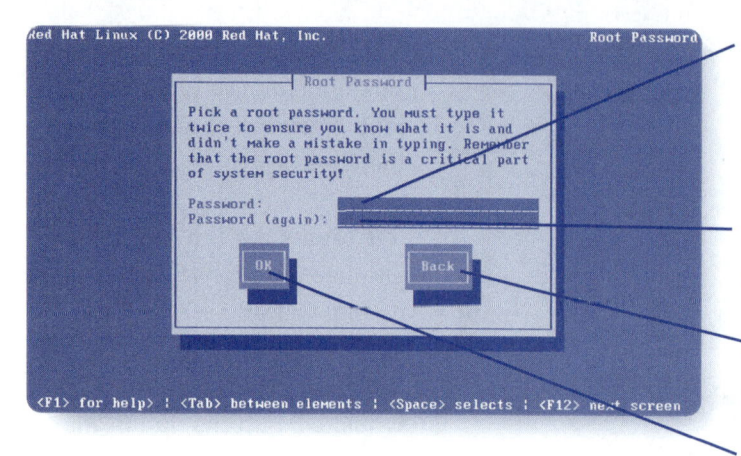

19. **Type** your **root password**. Be sure it is something easily remembered, but not easily deduced.

20. **Press** the **Tab key**. The next field is highlighted.

21. **Type** your **root password** again.

22. **Press** the **Enter key**. The Add User screen will appear.

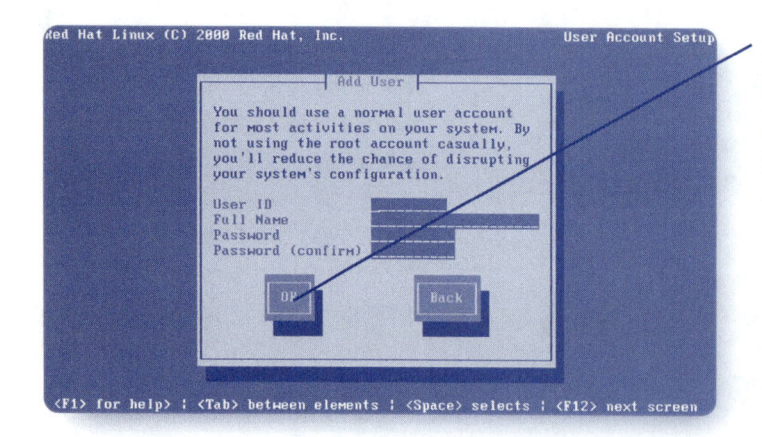

23. **Press** the **Enter key**. The Package Group Selection screen will appear, after the installation program reads packages.

NOTE

Adding new users to your PC is discussed in Chapter 1, "Discovering Linux", so this can be skipped for now.

LOADING THE LINUX OPERATING SYSTEM

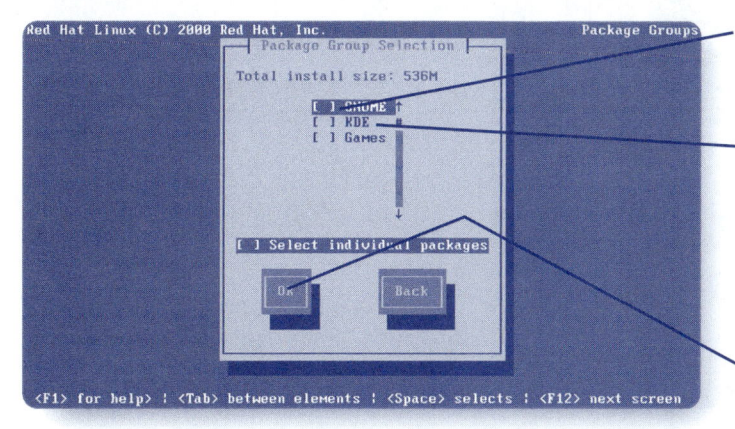

24. Press the **Spacebar**. The Gnome option will be selected.

25. Press the **arrow keys** and the **spacebar** to select other package groups. If you have the room, I recommend all three groups.

26. Press the **Enter key**. The Video Card Selection screen will appear, after the installation program runs a dependency check.

> **NOTE**
> A dependency check makes sure that all of the packages will have every file they need to successfully install their applications.

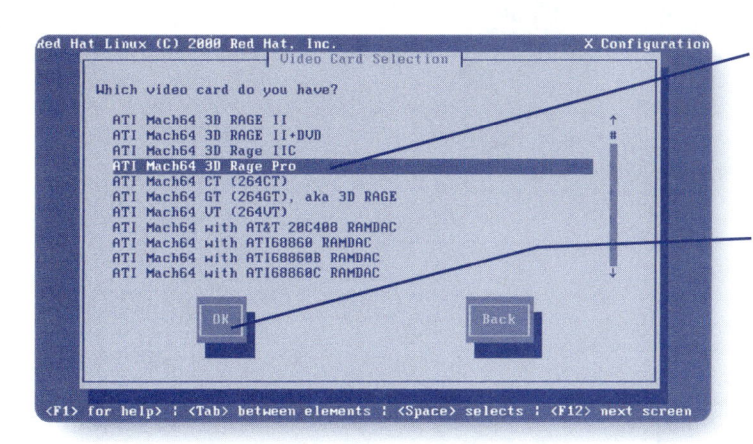

27. Press the **arrow keys** to select the correct video card. Be sure you select one that closely matches your installed card.

28. Press the **Enter key**. The Installation screen will appear.

APPENDIX A: INSTALLING LINUX

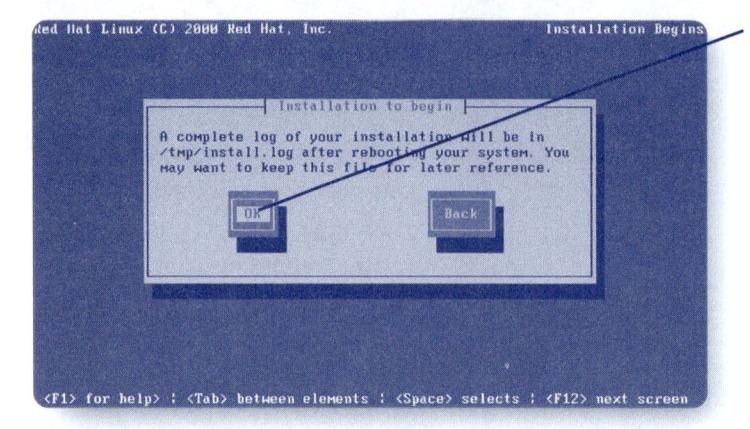

29. Press the **Enter key**. After several minutes of file copying, the Bootdisk screen will appear.

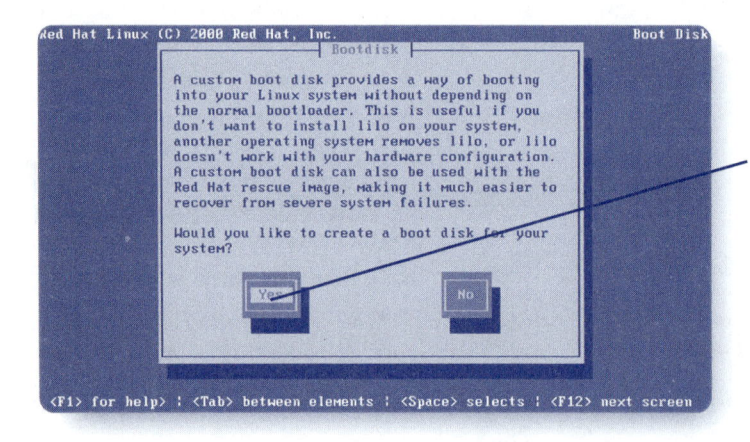

30. Insert a **blank floppy disk** into the floppy drive.

31. Press the **Enter key**. After a few minutes of file copying, the Complete screen will appear.

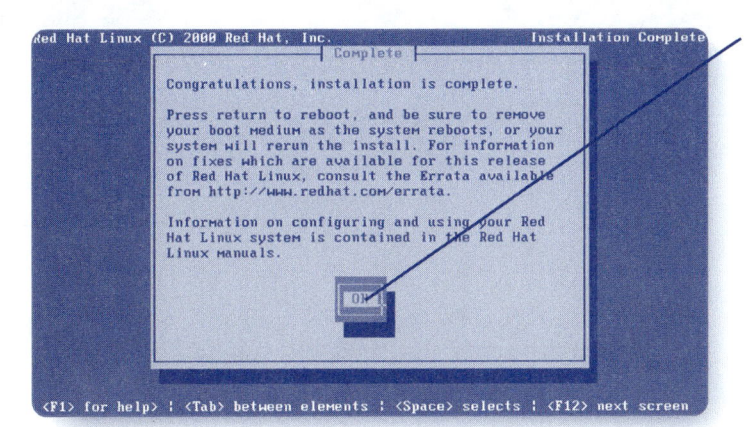

32. Press the **Enter key**. Congratulations, you've installed Red Hat Linux!

33. Remove any **CDs** and **floppy disks** from their drives as the system reboots. This will prevent the installation program from running again.

Glossary

A

absolute path. Specifies the exact directory in the directory tree where a file or subdirectory is stored. The absolute path includes the entire path that is required to access the file. The absolute path begins with the root directory.

access rights. These are also known as file permissions. These define which users have access to which files, directories, and peripherals in the system, and the type of access each user is allowed.

active window. The window in which an application will run or in which a task will be performed.

anonymous FTP. A way in which any person can access the public areas of an FTP site to transfer data files. To access these public areas, use "anonymous" as the user name and your e-mail address as the password.

application. A software program that performs a specific task or function, such as word processing, bookkeeping, or graphics.

Application Starter button. The button located on the Kpanel that looks like a gear. This button displays a menu containing applications, utilities, the File Manager, help, and log out options.

archive. To put data files in a place where they are protected from loss. Use a backup program to copy the files onto a removable media that can be kept in a safe deposit box or fireproof safe.

B

background process. A function (such as a print job or automatic save) that does not require interaction from the user. When a function is running in the background, the user can work with another application without any noticeable effect on performance.

backup. To make a copy of files that are stored on the computer's hard drive onto another medium, such as a floppy disk, magnetic tape, or CD-ROM. If the files on the hard disk become damaged or lost, it is possible to restore the files from the backup.

boot. The process your computer goes through when it is turned on so that the operating system loads.

boot disk. A floppy disk that is created during the installation process so that the Linux operating system can start in the event that the Linux Loader (LILO) does not work on the system.

boot image floppy. A floppy disk that will boot the computer and load a small Linux operating system. This floppy disk may be needed before installation of the entire Linux distribution.

C

cache memory. A storage area for data as it moves between the computer's RAM memory and the processor chip. Cache memory is needed to keep the processor working at full potential. Most computers have either 128K or 256K of cache memory. This speed indicates how fast the processor moves data in and out of cache memory.

command line. This is a text mode display where Linux commands are typed and then executed by pressing the Enter key. Command line operations can be performed from a terminal window, a terminal emulator, a console, or an x-term window. The easiest to work with is the x-term window because it can be opened inside the Gnome interface and it is not necessary to log out of the interface to perform functions that cannot be executed with the interface.

current directory. The directory or folder in which all file and directory commands operate. The current directory will usually be the Home directory.

D

daemon. A process that sits in the background and waits until something activates it. For example, the update daemon starts on a regular cycle to flush the buffer cache; the Sendmail daemon starts when mail is sent over the network.

desktop. The background that displays behind all the different screen elements (such as windows, dialog boxes, and applications) used in the Linux operating system.

desktop environment. The software that supplies visual tools and utilities to use "on top" of a window manager in Linux. Red Hat Linux 7 uses the Gnome and KDE desktop environments.

device drivers. Small software programs that provide access to system devices and resources such as disk drives, modems, graphics cards, and printers.

dial-up networking. A method of connecting to the Internet or to some other computer or network through a dial-up modem.

directory. A unique address in the computer's file system where files are stored. Linux uses several conventions for indicating the location of the directory in relation to other directories. Directories and subdirectories are separated by a forward slash (/), which is different from DOS and Windows systems. A single forward slash indicates that the user is at the root directory. The current directory in which the user is working is indicated by a single period (.). The directory that is above the current directory is indicated by two periods (..).

distribution. A set of prepackaged Linux software made available by a vendor. The package contains the Linux operating system, the set of GNU software applications and utilities, and other software programs developed by the vendor.

dynamic IP address. An Internet Protocol address assigned when the dial-up connection is made. This means that each time the user connects to the Internet, the user will get a different IP address.

E

encryption. A procedure used in cryptography to convert text into cipher to keep anyone but the intended recipient from reading the message. There are many types of data encryption that are the basis of network security. Data Encryption Standard and public key encryption are common.

executable file. A single file used to open a program.

F

FDISK (DOS). A DOS utility that allows the creation and management of partitions on a hard disk drive. There are many places to access the FDISK utility, but the most common is to use the FDISK utility that is installed with the operating system controlling the hard drive that is to be partitioned. This is the one to use to partition a DOS drive so that both Windows and Linux can share the same drive.

FDISK (Linux). A Linux disk managing utility, like the fdisk (DOS) utility, that is used to manage Linux drives. This is the utility to use after the partition of the drive into a DOS partition for Windows and a non-DOS partition for Linux. The Linux FDISK utility will be used to partition the non-DOS part of the drive for the Linux file system.

file. A collection of data, such as a letter created in a word processing program or a scanned image of a photograph, that is stored on a hard drive or other storage medium.

file permissions. A way to protect files from being tampered with by other users on a computer or network. The user who creates the files owns the files and the directories in which the files are contained. The owner can specify which other users may have access to the files and the type of access.

file server. A computer that maintains data files and allows users and other computers in the network to access those files to which they have permission.

file system. The method and data structure that the Linux operating system uses to store files. The file system can be used to organize and manage files.

foreground process. The application in which the user is currently working. A foreground process receives input from the keyboard and the results are seen on the screen.

Free Software Foundation. A grant-sponsored group at MIT that develops and distributes software for UNIX operating systems. The Free Software Foundation has developed such products as X Windows, emacs, a C++ compiler, and the glib++ library. They are well known for all of their GNU software.

FTP (File Transfer Protocol). A method of sending and receiving files across a computer network or the Internet.

G

Gnome (GNU Network Object Model Environment). A graphical user interface that makes it easier to work with the Linux operating system. Gnome makes it easy to run programs, access frequently used files, and find utilities that are included in the operating system.

GNU project. A project sponsored by the Free Software Foundation to provide a freely distributable replacement for UNIX. Some of the more popular tools are the GNU C and C++ compilers and the GNU EMACS editor.

GUI (Graphical User Interface). A shell that runs over the Linux operating system. This shell allows a user to visually see the operating system in action rather than by using commands. The shell uses windows, dialog boxes, icons, and other graphics to create an environment which is easier to work in. A GUI also supports the use of the mouse to make tasks easier.

H

home directory. The place within the Linux file system where the user stores or saves all the files and directories (or folders) that the user creates.

I

icon. A small picture that represents an application, peripheral, file, or directories.

K

KDE (K Desktop Environment). A graphical user interface used with the Linux operating system. KDE has more Windows-like features and powerful file management utilities.

kernel. The center of the Linux operating system. This piece of software is responsible for the Linux file system and the timing activities of the operating system. Operating system utilities use kernel functions to perform work. The kernel is recompiled occasionally when system changes require it.

kernel patch. To create a new binary file for the core Linux operating system.

L

Launcher. A shortcut icon in the Gnome interface.

LILO (Linux Loader). A program that resides in the boot sector of the hard disk. LILO executes when the computer system is turned on and automatically boots up the Linux operating system from a kernel image stored on the hard drive.

linking loader. A single program that loads, relocates, and links compiled and assembled programs, routines, and subroutines to create an executable file. Also known as link loader and linker loader.

log on/log off. To connect to or disconnect from a network such as the Internet or a corporate intranet. Also, to access a specified user account in the Linux system. Logging on requires a user name and a password.

M

Main Menu button. The button located on the Gnome Panel that looks like a foot. This button displays a menu containing applications, utilities, the File Manager, help, and log out options.

Man pages. Information pages contained in Linux that contain documentation for the system commands, resources, configuration files, and other utilities.

Master Boot Record. The file used to boot the computer's operating system and configure it for all the peripherals and utilities.

minimize. To clear a window from the desktop and cause it to become an icon on the Gnome Pager. To display the window, click on its icon on the Gnome Pager.

mount. A task that is performed before a device; for example, a floppy disk drive or CD-ROM drive can be accessed by the Linux file system.

N

Nickname. A shortcut icon in the KDE interface.

O

operating system. Software that shares a computer system's resources such as the processor, memory, and disk space between users and the application programs that run.

P

panel applet. An icon on the Gnome Panel that launches a program or opens a file.

partition. A physical portion of a disk. Disks are divided into partitions that are assigned to hold various file systems. The root file system is usually on the first partition and the user file system is on a different partition. The use of partitions provides flexibility and control of disk usage, but is restricting in that it denies unlimited use of all available space on a given disk for a given file.

password. A personal code, word, on series of numbers (or a combination of each) used to log onto the Internet, access a network account, or work with files that are protected from general view.

path. A file name given as a sequence of directories that leads to a particular file.

R

root account. See *superuser*.

root directory. The base directory from which all other subdirectories stem.

S

static IP address. An unchanging IP address, usually for those that are permanently connected to the Internet.

superuser. The root or administrator account who has the ability to access the entire Linux system and any user accounts that have been set up. The superuser account is used by the Linux system manager to install software, fix problems, and perform backup routines.

swap space. A place on the computer hard disk drive that is set aside so that it can be used as virtual memory (extra RAM). Linux uses this swap space to store programs that may be running. This swap space is dedicated to virtual memory and cannot be accessed to store files for directories.

U

unmount. To remove a file system that has been previously mounted. Only the user or superuser who mounted the file system can unmount it.

user. A person who uses the Linux system and has been assigned a user account.

V

virtual desktop. The ability to "expand" a workspace to beyond the area of a monitor screen. In Gnome, virtual desktops are contained within workspaces.

virtual memory. To use part of the hard disk to extend the amount of RAM the computer can use. When the computer has used the available RAM, it takes the contents of memory that are not needed to process current tasks and places that information on the hard drive.

W

window. A rectangular area displayed when an application runs on the screen. There can be many windows displayed on the screen at any time. Windows can be moved, resized, closed, minimized, and opened with the click of the mouse.

window manager. The software that controls the way windows look, their functionality, and where they are placed in a desktop environment interface. The Gnome interface with Red Hat Linux 7 works with the Sawmill Window Manager, while KDE uses kwm.

X

X Window. The graphical system that is used by most Linux and UNIX operating systems. This graphical system provides an interface to video hardware, which window managers and desktop environments utilize to create their interfaces.

Index

A

accessing dialog boxes, 14
adapters
    display, 290
    network, 290
Add a Printer Entry dialog box, 219
Add button, 208
Add New Internet Connection dialog box, 256, 259
Add User screen, 296
address book, 207
    adding column headings to contact list, 213-215
    adding new names, 208-211
    opening, 207
    sorting addresses, 212-213
    updating information, 211-212
animation, windows, 30-31
applets, 10
    Gnome Pager
        creating workspaces on Desktop, 46-49
        finding applications, 51-52
    Gnome Panel, 76
        CD Player. *See* CD Player
        games, 76-77
        moving, 79
        removing, 80
Application Starter button, 16
    starting applications, 17-18

applications
    finding, 51-52
    help files, 23-24
    launchers, 9, 80
        adding, 80-82
        changing Launcher icon, 82-83
        deleting, 84
    opening, 42-44
    starting
        from Application Starter button, 17-18
        from Main Menu button, 11
    verifying with GnoRPM, 247-249
    Xconfigurator, 69
appointments
    adding to Calendar, 202-205
    deleting, 205
    editing, 205-206
assigning users to groups, 144-146
Autoconfiguration failed screen, 228
Automatic Partitioning screen, 294

B

backgrounds
    Desktop, 54
        gradients, 57-60
        solid colors, 54-56
        wallpaper, 60, 62-64
    icons, 90-91
bin directory, 98
BMarks button, 22

Book Properties dialog box, 269
bookmarks, 268-271
    setting, 21-22
boot disk, preparing, 165-166
Bootdisk screen, 298
Brief view, 102
Browse button, 234
Browse dialog box, 90
browser, Netscape Navigator, 264
    accessing Web pages, 264-266
    changing home pages, 267-268
    managing email, 276
    receiving email, 276-277
    sending email, 278
    setting up email, 272-274
browsing
    file system, 100-103
    floppy disk drives, 164
buttons, 11-15
    Add, 208
    Application Starter, 16
        starting applications from, 17-18
    BMarks, 22
    Browse, 234
    Close, 12
    Copy Text, 175
    Detailed Information, 151
    Eject, 237
    Emulate, 295
    Exit Time Machine, 168
    Gnome terminal emulator, 196
    KDE Desktop, 17
    Kill, 15
    Local Printer option, 219
    Main Menu, 10, 42, 96, 218, 223
        starting applications from, 11
    Maximiz, sizing windows, 32-33
    Minutes list box, 204
    Modify, 212
    Monday option, 201
    New File, 175
    Normal Tile, 91
    Open Track Editor, 240
    Option, 14
    Paste Text, 178
    Pause, 238
    Play, 237, 239
    Play/Pause, 78
    Revert, 56
    Save File, 179
    Secondary Color, 59
    Skip Backwards, 238
    Skip Forwards, 238
    Stop, 239
    Take from Name, 208
    Task List, 52
    Track Selection, 239
    Try, 56
    Undo, 178
    Use Current Page, 267

C

Calculator, 196
    math equations, 197-199
    starting, 196-197
Calendar
    appointments
        adding, 202-205
        deleting, 205
        editing, 205-206
    changing time view, 201-202
    starting, 200
Calendar Tool, 43
Card Settings screen, 229
Card Type screen, 229
CD Player, 44, 236
    CDDB database, 239-240
    playing, 77-78, 237-239
    starting, 236-237
CD-ROM drives, 290
CDDB database, 239-240
CDs
    CDDB database, 239-240
    playing, 77-78, 237-239
    PowerToo, installing packages from, 250-251
Centered option (wallpaper), 61
Changing Password dialog box, 131
Choose an Icon dialog box, 83
Choose dialog box, 260
clock, resetting, 167-168
Clockchip Configuration screen, 72-73
Close button, 12
Close command (File menu), 181

INDEX

closing
    files, 181
    windows, 39
colors
    Desktop, solid colors, 54-56
    gradient, 58
column headings, adding to contacts list in address book, 213-215
commands, 12
    Commands menu, Find File, 126
    File menu
        Close, 181
        Save As, 177
    Man Pages, 19
Commands menu commands, Find File, 126
Communicator Bookmarks dialog box, 270
Configure Filter dialog box, 220
configuring
    printers, local, 218-220
    sound cards, 226, 228-231
confirmation dialog boxes, 123-124
connections, Internet
    creating, 256
    ISPs, 260-262
    PPP, 256-259
Console, 184
contacts
    adding column headings to list, 213-215
    adding to address book, 207-211
    sorting, 212-213
control menus, copying/moving files, 118-121
controllers
    game, 290
    SCSI, 290
    sound, 290
    video, 290
Copy dialog box, 119
Copy Text button, 177
copying
    files, 116, 190-191
        control menus, 118-121
        drag and drop, 116-118
    text, 177-178
Create a New Directory dialog box, 114
Create New Appointment dialog box, 202

Create the Account dialog box, 258
Custom option, 286

D

databases, CDDB, 239-240
deleting
    application launchers, 84
    appointments, 205
    directories, 189-190
    drawer items, 89
    files, 123, 193-194
    text, 177-178
    user accounts, 139-140
Deleting Account dialog box, 139
Desk Guide, 10, 47
Desktop, 9
    backgrounds, 54
        gradients, 57-60
        solid colors, 54-56
        wallpaper, 60, 62-64
    creating workspaces, 46-49
    Gnome, 9-10
    KDE, 15-17
    moving files to, 126-127
    moving icons, 128
    screen resolution, 68-74
    screen savers, 64-66
    shading windows on, 44-46
    themes, 66-68
Destroy option, 15
Detail System Information dialog box, 151
Detailed Information button, 151
Detailed view, 103
dev directory, 98
dialog boxes, 11-15
    accessing, 14
    Add a Printer, 219
    Add New Internet Connection, 256, 259
    Bookmark Properties, 269
    Browse, 90
    Changing Password, 131
    Choose, 260
    Choose an Icon, 83
    Communicator Bookmarks, 270
    Configure Filter, 220

INDEX

confirmation, 123-124
Copy, 119
Create a New Directory, 114
Create New Appointment, 202
Create the Account, 258
Deleting Account, 139
Detail System Information, 151
Download Packages, 252
Drive Mount Settings, 164
Edit Local Printer Entry, 220-221
Error, 219
Find Destination Folder, 120
Find File, 125-126
gmc, 128
Gnome Help History, 23
Gnomecard, 208
Info, 222
Input, 141
Install, 250
Launcher Properties, 82
Mount File System, 155
Netscape, 273, 279
Open File, 182
Other Options, 258
Package Info, 248
Password, 276
Phone Number and Name, 257
Pick a Color, 55
Preferences, 124, 201, 267
Properties, 122, 289
Really Log Out, 8
RPM Find, 251, 253
Save As, 179
Sawfish configurator, 48-49
Select File, 106
Set Filter, 109
Status of the System, 145
System Properties, 289
Track Editor, 240
User Name and Password, 257
Verifying Packages, 248
Wallpaper Selection, 61
Dialup Configuration Tool, 256
directories, 185
   bin, 98
   changing, 185-188
   creating, 114-116, 189
   dev, 98
   etc, 98
   home, 99
      finding files in, 125-126
   lib, 99
   lost+found, 99
   names, 186
   removing, 189-190
   root, 98
   sbin, 99
   tmp, 99
   usr, 99-103
directory view, 97
disabling user accounts, 137-138
disk drives, floppy, 153
   browsing, 164
   creating, 153-157
   DOS, 157-162
   mounting, 162-164
DiskFree, 166
display adapters, 290
displaying windows, 28-29
DOS floppy drives, creating, 157-162
Download Packages dialog box, 252
drag and drop feature, copying/moving files, 116-118
drawers, 85
   creating, 85-87, 89
   deleting items from, 89
   filling, 87-88
Drive Mount Settings dialog box, 164
drop-down lists, opening, 13
duration slider, 231

E

Edit Local Printer Entry dialog box, 220-221
editing
   appointments, 205-206
   user accounts, 133-134
Eject button, 237
email
   managing, 276
   receiving, 276-277
   sending, 278
   setting up accounts, 272-275
Embossed logo option (wallpaper), 61
Emulate buttons, 295
Error dialog boxes, 219

INDEX 313

etc directory, 98
events, sound, 233-235
Exit Time Machine button, 168
exiting
    files, 181
    Linux, 24-25

F

File Manager. *See* **Gnome File Manager**
File menu commands
    Close, 181
    Save As, 179
file system, 95, 98. *See also* **files**
    bin directory, 98
    browsing, 100-103
    copying files, 116
        control menus, 118-121
        drag and drop, 116-118
    creating directories, 114-116
    deleting files, 123
    dev directory, 98
    etc directory, 98
    filtering files, 109-111
    finding files, 125-126
    Gnome File Manager. *See* Gnome File Manager
    home directory, 99
    lib directory, 99
    lost+found directory, 99
    moving files, 116
        control menus, 118-121
        drag and drop, 116-118
    naming files, 122
    opening, 96
    root directory, 98
    sbin directory, 99
    sorting files, 107, 109
    tmp directory, 99
    usr directory, 99-103
files. *See also* **file system**
    closing, 181
    copying, 190-191
    creating, 174-175
    deleting, 193-194
    groups, 142-143, 146

        assigning users to, 144-146
        creating, 143
        file permissions, 146-148
    moving, 126-127, 192
    names, 191
    opening, 127-128, 182
    printing, 217, 223-224
    saving, 179-180
    selecting, 103
        mouse, 104-105
        selection criteria, 106-107
filtering files, 109-111
Find Destination Folder dialog box, 120
Find File command (Commands menu), 126
Find File dialog box, 125-126
finding
    applications, 51-52
    files, 125-126
    help files, 22-24
    system information, 150-153
floppy disk drives, 153
    browsing, 164
    creating, 153-162
    mounting, 162-164

G

games
    controllers, 290
    Gnome Panel applets, 76-77
Games menu, 18
gmc dialog box, 128
Gnome Configuration Tool icon, 30
Gnome Control Center, 30
Gnome Desktop, 9-10
Gnome DiskFree, 166
Gnome File Manager, 95-97
    menus, 97
    opening file system, 96
    toolbar, 97
Gnome Help Browser, 18-21
Gnome Help History dialog box, 23
Gnome Pager
    creating workspaces on Desktop, 46-49
    finding applications, 51-52

314 INDEX

Gnome Panel
    applets, 76
        CD Player. *See* CD Player
        games, 76-77
        moving, 79
        removing, 80
    application launchers, 80
        adding, 80-82
        changing Launcher icon, 82-83
        deleting, 84
    drawers, 85
        creating, 85-87, 89
        deleting items from, 89
        filling, 87-88
    icons, backgrounds, 90-91
Gnome Terminal Emulator button, 196
Gnomecard dialog box, 208
GnoRPM
    starting, 246-247
    verifying packages, 247-249
gnotepad+
    closing files, 181
    creating files, 174-175
    text, 176
        copying, 177-178
        deleting, 177-178
        selecting, 176-177
gradients, Desktop, 57-60
groups, 142-143, 146
    assigning users to, 144-146
    creating, 143
    file permissions, 146-148

H

hard drives, 290
help, 18
    bookmarks, 21-22
    finding files, 22-24
    Gnome Help Browser, 18-21
hiding files, 109-111
home directory, 99
    finding files in, 125-126
home pages, changing, 267-268
HP printers, 220

I

icon bar, 17
iconifying windows, 35-37
icons, 16
    Gnome Configuration Tool, 30
    Gnome Panel backgrounds, 90-91
    moving, 128
    Panel launcher, 82-83
Icons view, 102
Info dialog box, 222
Input dialog box, 141
Install dialog box, 250
Installation screen, 297
Installation Type screen, 293
installing
    Linux, 285, 291-292, 295, 297-299
        options, 286-287
        preparation, 287
        system devices, 288-291
    packages
        from PowerTools CD, 250-251
        from third-party RPMs, 251-253
interfaces, themes, 68
Internet. *See also* **WWW**
    connections
        creating, 256
        ISPs, 260-262
        PPP, 256-259
    email
        managing, 276
        receiving, 276-277
        sending, 278
        setting up, 272-275
Internet Service Providers. *See* **ISP**
Introduction screen, 226
ISPs (Internet Service Providers), 260-262

K

KDE (K Desktop Environment), 15
    Desktop, 15-17
keyboard
    bell, 231-233
    numeric keypad, 199
Keyboard Selection screen, 292
Kill button, 15
Kpanel, 16

INDEX

L

Launcher Properties dialog box, 82
launchers, 9, 80
    adding, 80-82
    changing Launcher icon, 82-83
    deleting, 84
lib directory, 99
LILO, 285
Linux
    exiting, 24-25
    installing, 285, 291-292, 295, 297-299
        options, 286-287
        preparation, 287
        system devices, 288-291
Local Printer option button, 219
local printers, configuring, 218-220
localhost login, 4
logging out of Linux, 24-25
login, localhost, 4
lost+found directory, 99

M

Main Menu button, 10, 42, 96, 218, 223
    starting programs, 11
Man Pages, 19
math equations, Calculator, 197-199
Maximize button, sizing windows, 32-33
menus, 11-15
    Games, 18
    Gnome File Manager, 97
    moving files, 118-121
Minutes list box button, 204
mistakes, Undo button, 178
modems, 290
Modify button, 212
Monday option button, 201
Monitor Setup screen, 70
monitors, 290
Mount File System dialog box, 155
mounting floppy disk drives, 162-164
mouse, 290
    selecting files, 104-105
    sizing windows, 33-35
Mouse Selection screen, 294

moving
    applets around Gnome Panel, 79
    between workspaces, 51-52
    files, 116, 192
        control menus, 118-121
        drag and drop, 116-118
        to Desktop, 126-127
    icons, 128
    windows, 29, 38
multiple files
    moving, 117
    selecting, 104
multiple windows, 42
    opening, 42-44
    shading, 44-46
multitasking, 42-44
music
    CD player, 44
    CDDB database, 239-240
    playing CD Player, 77-78, 237-239

N

names
    adding to address book, 208-211
    directories, 186
    files, 122, 193
Netscape dialog box, 273, 279
Netscape Navigator, 264
    accessing Web pages, 264-266
    changing home pages, 267-268
    managing email, 276
    receiving email, 276-277
    sending email, 278
    setting up email, 272-275
network adapters, 290
New File button, 175
newsgroups
    reading messages, 280-281
    subscribing, 279-280
Normal Tile button, 91
notification option, Calendar, 204
numbers, adjusting, 14
numeric keypad, 199

O

Open File dialog box, 182
Open Track Editor button, 240
opening
    address book, 207
    applications, multiple, 42-44
    drop-down lists, 13
    file system, 96
    files, 127-128, 182
    windows, 28, 42-44
operating systems, running multiple systems, 287
Option button, 14
ordering. *See* **sorting**
Other Options dialog box, 260

P

Package Group Selection screen, 296
Package Info dialog box, 248
packages
    installing
        from PowerTools CD, 250-251
        from third-party RPMs, 250-251
    source code, 250
    verifying, 247-249
Pager, 10
Pager view, 47
Panel applets. *See* **applets**
Panel Launcher icon, 82-83
paper size, 221
parallel ports, numering scheme, 220
partitions, 287
Password dialog box, 276
passwords, changing, 135-137, 140, 142
Paste Text button, 178
Pause button, 238
PCI Probe Results screen, 227
permissions, setting, 146-148
Phone Number and Name dialog box, 257
Pick a Color dialog box, 55
pixmap arrows, 10
Play button, 237, 239
Play/Pauese button, 78
playing CDs, 237-239
ports (parallel), numbering scheme, 220
PowerTools CD, installing packages from, 250-251
PPP connections, 256-259
PPP Dialer utitlity, 260
Preferences dialog box, 124, 201, 267
previewing screen savers, 65
Prima Tech home page, 264
Printer Tool, 218-220
printers
    configuring local printers, 218-220
    HP, 220
    resolution, 221
    selecting, 221
    testing, 222
printing files, 217, 223-224
program windows. *See* **windows**
Properties dialog box, 122, 289
pushing windows off desktop, 49-51

Q-R

quiting Linux, 24-25

reading newsgroup messages, 280-281
Really Log Out dialog box, 8
Red Hat Linux Hardware Compatibility List, 291
Red Hat Web site, 287
Red Hat Welcome screen, 293
removing
    applets around Gnome Panel, 80
    directories, 189-190
    files, 123
renaming. *See* **names**
resetting clock, 167-168
resolution, print, 221
Reversi window, 18
Revert button, 56
root directory, 98
Root Password screen, 295
RPM Find dialog box, 251, 253
RPMs, installing packages from, 251, 253

S

Save As command (File menu), 179
Save As dialog box, 179
Save File button, 179
saving files, 179-180
Sawfish Configuration Tool, 66
Sawfish configurator dialog box, 48-49
sbin directory, 99

INDEX

Scaled (keep aspect) option (wallpaper), 61
Scaled option (wallpaper), 61
screen resolution, 68-74
screen savers, 64-66
SCSI controllers, 290
searching. *See* finding
Secondary Color button, 59
security permissions, 146-148
Select File dialog box, 106
Select Modes screen, 74
Select Video Modes screen, 73
selecting
    files, 103
        mouse, 104-105
        selection criteria, 106-107
    printers, 221
    text, 176-177
    themes, 66-67
Server option, 286
Set Filter dialog box, 109
setting clock, 167-168
shading windows, 35-37, 44-46
sharing files, groups, 142-143, 146-148
sizes
    directory view, 97
    paper, 219
    tree view, 97
    windows, 29, 31-32
        Maximize button, 32-33
        mouse, 33-35
Skip backwards button, 238
Skip forwards button, 238
sndconfig, 226, 228
solid colors, Desktop, 54-56
sorting
    addresses, 212-213
    files, 107, 109
Sound Card Test screen, 227, 230
sounds
    cards, configuring, 226, 228-231
    controllers, 290
    settings, 231
        keyboard bell, 231-233
        sound events, 233-235
source code RPMs, 250

starting
    applications
        from Application Starter button, 17-18
        from Main Menu button, 11
    Calculator, 196-197
    Calendar, 200
    CD Player, 236-237
    features, 14
    GnoRPM, 246-247
    X Window, 4-6
Status of the System dialog box, 145
Stop button, 239
subscribing to newsgroups, 279-280
system devices, 288-291
system information, finding, 150-151, 153
System Properties dialog box, 289
system sounds, settings, 231
    keyboard bell, 231-233
    sound events, 233-235

T

Take from Name button, 208
Task List, 47, 52
Taskbar, 17
testing printers, 222
text, 176
    copying, 177-178
    deleting, 177-178
    selecting, 176-177
themes, 66-68
Tiled option (wallpaper), 61
Time Tracking Tool, 43
time view, Calendar, 200-202
Time Zone Selection screen, 295
tmp directory, 99
toolbars, Gnome File Manager, 97
tools
    Calendar, 43
    Dialup Configuration, 256
    Printer, 218
    Sawfish Configuration, 66
    Time Tracking, 43
Track Editor dialog box, 240
Track Selection button, 239
tree view, 97

INDEX

Try button, 56
turning on/off. *See* **starting**
    closing, 196

U

Undo button, 178
Uniform Resource Locators. *See* **URLs**
updating address book information, 211-212
URLs (Uniform Resource Locators), 264
Use Current Page button, 267
user accounts, 130
    changing passwords, 135-137, 142
    changing passwords, 140
    changing user information, 134-135
    creating, 130-133
    deleting, 139-140
    disabling, 137-138
    editing, 133-134
    mounting floppy disk drives, 162-164
User Name and Password dialog box, 257
users, creating, 6-8
usr directory, 99-103

V

Verifying Packages dialog box, 248
Video Card Selection screen, 297
video controllers, 290
Video Memory screen, 70, 72
views
    Brief, 102
    Desk Guide, 47
    Detailed, 103
    directory, 97
    Icons, 102
    Pager, 47
    tree, 97
virtual desktops
    creating, 48-49
    moving between, 51-52
    pushing windows off desktop, 49-51

W

wallpaper, 60, 62-64
Wallpaper Selection dialog box, 61
Web browsers. *See* **browsers**
Web pages
    accessing, Netscape Communicator, 264-266
    bookmarks, 21-22, 268-271
    changing home pages, 267-268
Web sites
    bookmarks, 268-271
    bookmarks , 21-22
    Red hat, 287
windows, 16, 27
    animation, 30-31
    closing, 39
    displaying, 28-29
    iconifying, 35-37
    moving, 29, 38
    multiple, 42
    opening, 28, 42-44
    pushing off desktop, 49-51
    Reversi, 18
    shading, 35-37, 44-46
    size, 31-32
        Maximize button, 32-33
        mouse, 33-35
    sizes, 29
workspaces
    creating on Desktop, 46-49
    moving between, 51-52
    pushing windows off desktop, 49-51
Workstation option, 286
WWW (World Wide Web). *See also* **Internet**
    addresses, 264
    browsers. *See* browsers

X-Z

X Window, starting, 4-6
Xconfigurator, 69